Formations of Ritual

Formations of Ritual

Colonial and Anthropological Discourses on the Sinhala *Yaktovil*

David Scott

MINNESOTA

University of Minnesota Press
Minneapolis
London

Portions of this book previously appeared in the following publications: "The Cultural Poetics of Eyesight in Sri Lanka: Composure, Vulnerability, and the Sinhala Concept of Distiya," *Dialectical Anthropology* 16, no. 1 (1991), reprinted by permission of Kluwer Academic Publishers; "Anthropology and Colonial Discourse: Aspects of the Demonological Construction of Sinhala Cultural Practice," *Cultural Anthropology* 7, no. 3 (1992), reprinted by permission of the American Anthropological Association; "Conversion and Demonism: Colonial Christian Discourse and Religion in Sri Lanka," *Comparative Studies in Society and History* 34, no. 2 (1992), reprinted by permission of Cambridge University Press; "Criticism and Culture: Theory and Postcolonial Claims on Anthropological Disciplinarity," *Critique of Anthropology* 12, no. 4 (1992), reprinted by permission of Sage Publications Ltd.

Published by the University of Minnesota Press
2037 University Avenue Southeast, Minneapolis, MN 55455-3092
Printed in the United States of America on acid-free paper

Library of Congress Cataloging-in-Publication Data

Scott, David, 1958-.
Formations of ritual : colonial and anthropological discourses on the Sinhala yaktovil / David Scott.
p. cm.
Includes bibliographical references and index.
ISBN 0-8166-2255-8
ISBN 0-8166-2256-6 (pbk.)
1. Sinhalese (Sri Lankan people)—Rites and ceremonies.
2. Sinhalese (Sri Lankan people)—Religion. 3. Medicine, Ayurvedic—Sri Lanka—Devinuvara—Religious aspects. 4. Exorcism—Sri Lanka—Devinuvara. 5. Devinuvara (Sri Lanka)—Religious life and customs.
I. Title.
DS489.25.S5S38 1994
306.6′943438′095493—dc20 93-5648
CIP

The University of Minnesota is an
equal-opportunity educator and employer.

For my mother's memory
and for my father

"He reviled me! He struck me!
He defeated me! He robbed me!"
They who gird themselves up with this,
For them enmity is not quelled.

"He reviled me! He struck me!
He defeated me! He robbed me!"
They who do not gird themselves up with this,
For them is enmity quelled.

Not by enmity are enmities quelled,
Whatever the occasion here,
By the absence of enmity are they quelled.
This is an ancient truth.

Dhammapada (I:3–5)

As a bush fire burning out of control stops only when it reaches a vast body of water, so the rage of one who vows vengeance cannot be quelled except by the waters of compassion that fill the Ocean of Omniscience.

"The Demoness Kālī," Dharmasēna Thera, *Saddharmaratnāvaliya*.

Contents

Acknowledgments

This book owes much to many people. To begin with I would like to record my deep appreciation to the late Stanley Diamond, chair of the committee that supervised the doctoral thesis on which this book is based. The intellectual space he made possible for me as a graduate student, his unflagging if unorthodox support at all stages of my research, and his compelling vision of the radical intellectual spirit, leave me ever in his debt. My gratitude to Talal Asad is, quite simply, an incalculable. He has read and reread the entire manuscript, challenged me on each occasion with hard questions, offered counsel, and offered friendship. That his own critical thought has left a deep imprint on mine the most casual reader of this book will only too easily discern. As must be the case with other students of Sri Lankan society and culture, little could have been undertaken much less accomplished without the help, encouragement, and indeed inspiration, of that self-styled anthropological Don Quixote, Gananath Obeyesekere. Not only has he read and commented on an earlier version of this book, but his work too has had a profound impact on my thinking; it is the kind of work from which one never ceases to learn. I am grateful too to Leslie Gunawardana, Charles Hallisey, and Steven Kemper, who read earlier versions of the manuscript, and whose suggestions for improving it I have tried to incorporate. Elizabeth Eames not only read critically one of the chapters in an earlier draft, and argued with me on much more, but, as the last revisions got going, gave me a son, Nimal—no spoken gratitude would ever suffice. I would also like to thank my editor, Janaki Bakhle, for keeping faith when I most needed faith kept. That this book is no worse than it is I owe to these caring and careful minds; that it is no better, needless to say, only I am responsible.

Of the many people in Sri Lanka, I would like first of all to extend my gratitude to D. A. Ariyadasa, Samarapala Liyanage, Äddin Lokuvela,

Saraneris Appu, and, most especially, S. A. Piyasena, who opened to me both their knowledge and their friendship. What this book owes to the patience and humor with which they indulged my persistent curiosity is such as cannot be put into words. For their welcoming hospitality and generous friendship I thank Derrick, Manel, Mahen, Rowan, and Manoji Fernando. To Mahinda, Sirima, Shiromi, Samanthi, Gayan, and Lakmal Nanayakkara, I extend my deepest appreciation for taking me into their family. One day around 1912 my maternal grandfather T. H. Samil left Lankā. He found himself in Jamaica and was never to return home. I never knew him, but living with the Nanayakkara family always made me wonder what he and his family might have been like.

In Sri Lanka, too, Michael Roberts offered both friendship and encouragement. Tissa Jayawardene of the Department of Sinhala, University of Colombo, was most helpful in guiding my steps through Sinhala. I should be remiss if I did not also record my indebtedness to the late Newton Gunasinghe of the Department of Sociology, University of Colombo. The respective staffs of the Ceylon Room of the library at the University of Colombo, at the Colombo Museum Library, and at the Sinhala Dictionary Department, Colombo, were very helpful. And last, but by no means least, I thank Mr. A. H. M. Harischandra, my field assistant, for his interest and good work.

The research upon which this book is based was made possible by generous grants from the Wenner Gren Foundation for Anthropological Research and the Institute for Critical Anthropology. To both institutions I offer my thanks.

On Transliteration and Usage

In this book I have for the most part followed the established conventions for the transliteration of Sinhala words. Plurals are typically formed by adding an *s* to the Sinhala singular (e.g., the plural of *ädurā* is *ädurās*). There are a few exceptions, in particular, *yakā*, where I alternately use the Sinhala plurals, *yaksayō* or, more usually, *yakku*. The vowels *a, ā, ä, ǟ, e, ē, i, ī,* are pronounced like the first vowels in *sun, salt, may, bad, end, made, in,* and *feel,* respectively. Among the consonants, *c* is pronounced *ch;* the *ṣ* gives a *sh* sound; *ṭ* and *ḍ* are palatals pronounced with the tongue far back; and *g* is always hard. All Sinhala words—except for names of people, places, and sections of *yaktovil*—are italicized.

A number of abbreviations are employed throughout this text: p. for Pāli; sk. for Sanskrit; s. for Sinhala; sing. for singular; pl. for plural; masc. for masculine; and fem. for feminine.

Finally, a note on the name of the country. It is, of course, a long time now (over two decades—22 May 1972) since the colonial name *Ceylon* was replaced by *Sri Lanka*. In ancient texts as well as in many contemporary popular stories, the name *Lankā* is used, and when referring to these texts or their images I have retained this usage. When referring specifically to British colonial representations of the island, I have used *British Ceylon*, or simply, *Ceylon*. And on those occasions when I refer to contemporary images and representations, I use either *Sri Lanka* or *Lankā*.

tions or arguments that establish themselves within the general discussion about ethnographic "representation."

I will roughly, and I should say, provisionally, designate these positions/arguments "postmodernist" and "postcolonialist." They are, of course, not mutually exclusive. Indeed, how could they be? After all, they draw in many respects on a similar canon of contemporary transgressive theoretical strategies—Foucauldian genealogy, Gramscian interrogations of hegemony, Derridean deconstruction, Jamesonian Marxism, feminist problematizations of subject positions, and so on. But they are nevertheless, I would suggest, distinct, inasmuch as while both are equally concerned with the "problem of representation," one takes as its point of departure a number of themes associated with postmodernist literary criticism (heterogeneity, antitotalizing discourses, decentered subjects, defamiliarizing experimentation, etc.), and the other is principally concerned about the implications of representing the former colonized (ethnic and racial stereotyping, assimilation, reductionism, ventriloquism, etc.). And indeed, perhaps as a consequence of this difference in focus and emphasis, one position—the "postmodernist"—is altogether more optimistic than the other—the "postcolonialist"—as regards the future of anthropology. But in any case, both have had their spheres of influence and both have offered valuable criticisms of contemporary anthropology. My principal concern in examining them, it is to be understood, is not to criticize either postmodernist or postcolonialist arguments as such, but rather to raise some questions about the kind of anthropological object they often seem to establish in their own texts in the course of their critical agendas. I therefore do not aim at an exhaustive interrogation of either position, but rather to try to clarify some aspects of the question of the prospects for, or idea of, an adequate anthropological criticism—and this too, mind you, as a sort of starting point for my own inquiry into aspects of Sinhala discourse and practice.

Perhaps one of the central tenets of the recent "postmodernist" critique of anthropology is that "cultures" are mobile, unbounded, conjunctural, and open-ended.[5] On this view one should now speak of the "betweenness" of cultures, the displacement, the overlapping, the hybridity, of cultural experience. It is argued that in an older genre of anthropological text (that produced by the school of British structural functionalism in particular, but also that produced by post-World War II American cultural materialism), cultures were represented as though they were timeless, historyless, spatially immobile, unmixed. Against such a view, Clifford has quite rightly maintained that " 'cultures' do not hold still for their portraits. Attempts to make them do so always involve simplification and exclusion, selection of a temporal focus, the construction of a particular self-other relationship, and the imposition and negotiation of a power relation."[6]

Now I do not entirely disagree with this view. By this I mean that I can readily agree that in yesterday's "traditional realist" ethnographies there was often an unproblematized representation of culture as static, and the rest. And yet I think that this recognizably "antiessentialist" characterization of culture as mobile, as unbounded, as hybrid, and so on, is itself open to the question: For *whom* is "culture" unbounded? For the anthropologist or the native? That is, for (Western) theory, or for the (local) discourse which theory is endeavoring to engage, inquire upon? And note that my questions here are not the more familiar ones about the supposed objectivity (or lack of it) of the anthropologist's point of view as against that of the native (the old debate about rationality and relativism). Rather, what I am trying to suggest is that the "boundedness" or otherwise of "culture" is something that gets *established* in kinds of discourse, more precisely, in kinds of authoritative discourse—of which Western theory is one, and the native's discourse another. Obviously, neither "boundedness" nor its absence are given in the world. To say a priori that "cultures" are *not* bounded therefore is misleading since local discourses do in fact "establish" authoritative "traditions," discrete temporal and spatial parameters in which it is made singularly clear to cultural subjects *and their others* what is (and who are) to belong within it and what (and who) do not. Surely part of the profoundly unhappy dispute between Sinhalas and Tamils in contemporary Sri Lanka, for example, has to do precisely with the question of *how* the "boundary" of Sinhala culture and the "boundary" of Tamil culture are authoritatively established and maintained. In short, the important issue here is not the ontological one of whether the being of culture is "bounded" or not, and the epistemological question of how we know that this is the case, but the political one of how and in what kinds of material circumstances, through what kinds of discursive and nondiscursive relations, claims about the presence or absence of boundaries are *made*, fought out, yielded, negotiated. I want to suggest, in other words, that the idea that cultures are not bounded can itself seem to presuppose an unquestioned position (i.e., that of

Western theory) from which one could, as it were, point to authentic, seamless "cultures" out there in the real world, moving in and out and in between other equally authentic, seamless cultures. And so doing, such conceptions merely displace one kind of essentialism (culture as essentially static) with another more disguised version (culture as essentially mobile, changing). The dilemma derives, of course, from the attempt to formulate a priori conceptions of what "culture" is or is not. And to that extent at least they are unsatisfactory.[7]

The work of Edward Said, particularly *Orientalism*, has been central to the recent renewal of the postcolonial critique of anthropology.[8] Certainly no work of the last twenty years has contributed more to unmasking the persisting economy of colonial discourse, to marking out its distinctive features, to calling our attention to its strategies and its ruses. If in that work anthropology was implicitly rather than explicitly criticized, in a more recent essay, "Representing the Colonized: Anthropology's Interlocutors,"[9] Said has been unsparing in his direct criticism of anthropology's relationship with imperialism, even going so far as to doubt the future value of the discipline as a whole. In closing this essay he wrote, in part:

> I cannot say whether it is now possible for anthropology as anthropology to be different, that is, to forget itself and to become something else as a way of responding to the gauntlet thrown down by imperialism and its antagonists. Perhaps anthropology as we have known it can only continue on one side of the imperial divide, there to remain as a partner in domination and hegemony. (p. 225)

These are strong words of condemnation. But what worries me about this passage is not so much its dire image of a beleaguered anthropology slowly taking up the gauntlet, as the allusive ambiguity of such conceptions as the need for anthropology "as anthropology" to "forget itself" as a way of becoming "something else."

If the implication of Said's remarks is that there is really *no* possibility for an internal revision of the strategies through which anthropology goes about the task of describing and analyzing the practices and discourses of the former colonized, and this because ethnographic representations are *necessarily* imperialist accomplices ("a partner in domination," as he says), then it seems to me that, without a careful argument showing how, *conceptually*, this is so, it remains an understandably indignant but otherwise unpersuasive assertion. But if, on the other hand, the implication of Said's argument is the political and ideological one that for historical and conceptual reasons anthropology has arrogated to itself the unquestioned space from which to represent the "essence" of non-Western cultures to Western (or, of course, Westernized) audiences, the space from which to identify and disconceal a "truth" about native lives hidden from the mystified natives themselves; and if the further implication is that as a consequence anthropology needs to reconstitute its *object* (and, so doing, its problematic—that is, the kinds of questions it asks, and the conceptual framework in which these questions are posed) in order to transform its *project*, I would endorse this and propose that we set about this task in concrete, historically specific studies.

If indeed this is the implication, then this book proposes to be a small contribution in that direction; and it takes as its conceptual point of departure the reformulation of an anthropological criticism suggested some years ago by Talal Asad in his essay "Anthropology and the Analysis of Ideology."[10] This was, of course, originally Asad's Malinowski Lecture of March 1979, and while he has written much since this essay that elaborates the general thematic of the relation between anthropology and the discourses of Western modernity,[11] this essay constitutes, in my estimation, a most instructive intervention on the theme of anthropological representation. Let me extract, therefore, what seems to me to be the central thrust of its argument, and draw out what I take to be some of its theoretical implications, as a way of trying to repose the question of culture, colonialism, and an adequately critical anthropology.

Asad in fact stages the argument of this essay around what he takes to be a telling omission in the early debate about the relation between anthropology and colonialism. In the criticism and countercriticism of the 1970s, what was forgotten, he suggests, was that "the really interesting questions concerned the ideological conditions of anthropology, and the implications of these conditions for its discourse" (p. 607), not the moral issue of the personal motives or politics of its producers. But rather than tackle this question directly, Asad wishes to link this to a more "general puzzle," which he outlines in the following way:

> The modesty of anthropologists regarding the ideological role of their discourses in the determination of colonial structures does not seem to be matched by a corresponding skepticism regarding the role of ideology generally in the determination of social structures which are the objects of their discourse. Their science as discourse, so it is said, is not

> determined by social reality. And yet the social reality of which that science speaks is typically nothing but discourse. (pp. 607–608)

This apparent paradox is then explored in relation to some of the writings of, among others, Maurice Bloch, Edmund Leach, and Mary Douglas.

As I understand him, Asad's central argument is that the anthropological analysis of ideology has largely foundered on the ideological constitution of the anthropological object itself. This object—broadly, "culture," "society," "social structure," or more narrowly, "religion," "ritual"—is typically produced and presented in anthropological texts through a continual slippage toward a preoccupation with "a priori systems of essential meaning"—those meanings which are argued to give definitive integrity to specific social orders. This slippage, Asad suggests, often emerges through a conflation of conceptual registers that are, in fact, distinct: on the one hand, the discourse of the anthropologist (a systematic and interpretive discourse in which objects are analytically constructed); and on the other, the discourse of the society (those local knowledges through which people's lives are *lived*). As he puts it: "The ambiguity . . . is between what is supposed to be the way the anthropologist actually thinks and speaks *about* social life and the way the people the anthropologist is studying are supposed actually to think and speak *in* their social life" (p. 613). This preoccupation with the representation of the "authentic system" of native practice in the systematic discourse of the anthropologist clearly leaves unposed at least two distinct kinds of question, both of which turn on the ideological constitution of the anthropological object. The first is the question of the genealogical determination of the particular objects of specific anthropological concerns; and the second is the question of how historically specific local discourses come to be produced and maintained as authoritative.

In his effort to rethink the anthropological problem of critical cultural inquiry, Asad introduces the useful concept of "authoritative discourse." Authoritative discourse, he maintains, is to be understood as

> materially founded discourse which seeks continually to preempt the space of radically opposed utterances and so prevent them from being uttered. For authoritative discourse, we should be careful to note, authorises neither "Reality" nor "Experience" but other discourse—texts, speech, visual images, etc., which are structured in terms of given (imposed) concepts, and reproduced in terms of essential meanings. Even when action is authorised, it is as discourse that such action establishes

> its authority. The action is read as being authorised, but the reading and the action are not identical—that is why it is always logically possible to have an alternative reading. (p. 621)

In my view, this concept of authoritative discourse enables us to clear a conceptual space in which to think historically produced configurations of knowledge and power, whether in theoretical practices such as anthropology or local practices such as the Sinhala *yaktovil*.

In the kinds of terms Asad is suggesting to us, therefore, the very issue whether "culture" is "bounded" or "unbounded" is displaced by a different sort of history-in-anthropology problematic altogether, one that seeks to think together the *internal* historicity *both* of the theoretical discourses we employ *and* the social and cultural discourses we use these theoretical discourses to study. This kind of historical problematic may usefully be thought of as turning around the relation between theory and tradition. A double strategy is entailed in this view. On the one hand, the (anthropological) theory that so confidently takes itself to be inquiring into the "traditions" of others, the Buddhist tradition of the Sinhalas, say, has to recognize that the very practice of asking the questions it does about the discourses and practices of others itself requires what Alasdair MacIntyre calls the "context of a tradition"—*its own*.[12] For, after all, anthropology too is a kind of local knowledge. And note that this claim is not the same as the more familiar one that theory (or anthropology in this case) endeavoring to understand non-Western practices should not employ Western concepts. Rather this is the claim that *these concepts have histories*. And in order to gauge what kind of object these concepts are producing, something of these histories has to be appreciated—all the more so when these histories intersect the traditions of others in ways that transform the social and discursive terrain of those traditions. On the other hand, the anthropologically constituted object—"typically nothing but discourse," as Asad says—has also to be situated within the discursive terrain of the local tradition it participates in. And on this view, the business of anthropology is not to seek to discover the authentic meaning of symbolic practice, but to grasp its *position* in that discursive tradition, and the social projects within which it is employed. I can derive two levels of anthropological question from this strategy: First, how, and *through* what kinds of relations of power, and *in* what kinds of discourses, has the West inaugurated the local practices as objects of Western knowledge? And second, through what kinds of social practices authorized through what kinds of social discourses is a distinctive tradition *established* among the people being studied, and how within it do they learn to recognize themselves as distinctive subjects?

Aims and Arguments

This book aims to be a critical historical ethnography. It inhabits the theoretical field mapped by the two levels of question I derive from Asad's intervention, and it seeks to elaborate them in relation to a particular ethnographic topography—that of the Sinhala discourse of *yakku*—and a particular set of arguments—colonial and anthropological—regarding Sinhala ritual (one especially, namely, *yaktovil*) and religion. It is left, then, only to specify the project I undertake in these pages and how it relates to these levels of theoretical inquiry. This kind of specification is all too necessary these days, when theoretical discourse is marked as much by a range of productive insights as by a curious confusion of registers, and a curious medley of overarching dismissals and valorizations. Therefore it may be as well, in seeking to mark out the conceptual space I envisage for this book, to say what this project entails and what it does not. And this is not the least because I take this book itself to inhabit a relation of tension (I hope, a productive one) between the tradition of anthropological and ethnographic discourse that forms the background of its arguments and the theoretical intervention that seeks a new horizon of inquiry into social discourses and practices that themselves belong to other traditions of life and of argument.

To begin with, this book is not the study of a village. Nor will the reader find in my discussion of *yakku* (a class of malign supernatural beings) and *yaktovil* (a healing ritual) much in the way of the kind of positive sociological data (demographic statistics, class and caste backgrounds, household schedules, biographical profiles, and, even less, kinship charts) that distinguishes the classical—the so-called realist or modernist—ethnography. However, it needs to be understood (especially in the light of recent talk of "experimental" ethnographies) that the positive absence of this kind of data is not because I think that they are irrelevant to contemporary ethnography as such, since, in effect, I do not think any such thing—"ethnography as such"—exists. Rather, my claim is a more modest one, namely that ethnographic topographies should depend on the kind of anthropological—that is, theoretical—*project* at hand, and whereas such data may well be crucial to the point of certain kinds of theoretical project, it is simply not crucial to the one I am undertaking here.

So although I lived in Devinuwara in the Matara district of the Southern Province for the better part of my sixteen months in Sri Lanka, this is not a study of that old and legendary town. I rather studied *in* Devinuwara than studied Devinuwara—to paraphrase one of Geertz's pithy remarks. The British, who were colonial rulers of Lankā between 1796 and 1948, called the town Dondra; locals call it Devundara. It is the southernmost town in Lankā, roughly four or so miles to the southeast of Matara Town, a town of renowned Buddhist learning and the center of the Southern Kingdom of Ruhunu.[13] Devinuwara, which literally means "city of the god," is itself a town of considerable historical importance. It has been a center of pilgrimage to the god Upulvan (or Uppalavanna, the Pāli) since at least the twelfth century C.E.[14] And they were both—Matara and Devinuwara—of great symbolic importance to successive colonial powers: to the Portuguese, who sought to loot and destroy them in the late sixteenth century; and the British, who sought the conversion of their inhabitants in the nineteenth. Thus, for example, wrote Diogo de Couto of the destruction carried out in Matara and Devinuwara in the year 1588:

> The important city of Mature with its wealthy population of merchants was half a league further off [i.e., from Mirissa] and was destined to be given over to the plunder of our troops. We stormed it after some severe fighting and set fire to it in various places, our men plundering whatever they thought best. Among the buildings which were burnt were three pagodas of great beauty, a store full of cinnamon, and a large ship which was in the harbour.
>
> We took one hundred and ten prisoners and then went on board to proceed to the pagoda of Tanaverem [i.e., Devinuwara], half a league further off, the most celebrated temple in the Island, and, next to Adam's Peak, the most frequented by pilgrims. The building was like a handsome city with a circuit of a full league. The temple itself was vast in size, all the roofs being domed and richly carved; round about it were several very handsome chapels and over the principal gateway was a tall tower entirely roofed with copper, gilt in various parts. Within was a large square with verandahs and terraces with a handsome gate on each side, while all around were planted sweet-smelling flowers which were used during the processions. There were several

> handsome streets where lived all the servants attached to the temple, chief among them being the women dedicated to its service.
>
> On approaching it we encountered a fierce storm which the Lascarins declared had been sent by God for the protection of His temple and they whispered that the Portuguese would never get near it. To disabuse their minds the Captain swore that he would destroy the building. The next day he landed his men and after storming the fortifications which they had on the shore we advanced to the temple, only to find that it had been abandoned and that there was no one left to resist our occupation. We burst in the gates and proceeded to destroy the idols of which there were more than a thousand of different figures of clay and wood and copper, mostly gilded. We destroyed the domes and colonnades and sacked the stores where we found a vast accumulation of ivory, fine cloths, coffee, pepper, sandalwood, jewels, precious stones, and all the fittings of the temple, which we plundered as we desired and set the rest on fire. As the greatest affront that could be offered to the place we slaughterd within some cows, this being a stain which could not be purified without the most elaborate ceremonies. We also burnt a magnificent wooden car built like a tower of seven stories and beautifully painted and gilt—a magnificent vehicle in which they were accustomed to convey the chief idol around the city. After this we returned to Beligão [i.e., Weligama] laden with booty and remained there awaiting instructions from the Captain at Columbo.[15]

As I will relate in chapter 2, there is a local story that runs counter to this colonial account; it is the story about the installation in Devinuwara, by a king named Dapulsen, of a red sandalwood image of the god Upulvan (no doubt the god about whom the Lascarins in de Couto's narrative were whispering, and who sent the "fierce storm"), which resists the Portuguese in a most distinctive way—with the beam of its eyesight.

Matara and Devundara were also, as I said, important for the British, though for a different reason. The southwest coast was a focus of British colonial evangelicalism, and many of the best-known missionaries (Rev. John Callaway and Daniel J. Gogerly among them) served in the Matara chapter of the Wesleyan Methodist Mission. But, interestingly enough, it was a town in which the missionaries met with considerable and indeed exasperating intransigence. For instance, in one contribution to the Wesleyan organ, *Friend*, of December 1837, entitled "The Wesleyan Mission Station, Matura," there is reprinted a candid letter (dated 30 October 1837) written by the esteemed missionary, Gogerly. It was addressed to the Wesleyan headquarters in England, and in it Gogerly laments the "moral" state of affairs in Matara generally, and in Devinuwara in particular. He writes, "Generally speaking I think that Matura is one of the least promising of all the fields cultivated by this mission. Budhism has here its full operation."[16] And he continues:

> On the Dondra side of the Station, although we have labored long, in Dondra itself little fruit appears. We have preaching regularly on Sundays and Week-days in two places, and the congregations are sometimes respectable, but this vicinity abounds in vice as well as in superstition. Drunkenness and uncleanness are ruling crimes, and scarcely attempt to hide their heads. (p. 105)

Such, then, is the distinctive honor bestowed upon these ancient towns.

I went to Sri Lanka in early November 1986 to conduct fieldwork on the Sinhala practice known as *yaktovil* (or simply, *tovil*).[17] *Yaktovil* is an elaborate healing practice popular among Buddhists in the Southern and Southwestern Provinces of the island. It may, in fact, well be the most elaborate of that whole group of practices which, together, Sinhalas call *ädurukama* or *gurukama* (literally, "the work of the teacher"). These practices are employed by Sinhala adepts—practitioners known as *äduräs*—to influence, indeed more instrumentally, to manipulate, certain supernatural beings known as *yakku* (sing. *yakā*, or *yaksayā*). (In fact, more formally, these practices would be classified under that section or speciality of Āyurvedic practice known as *bhūta vīdiya*, conventionally glossed as "science of spirits,"[18] but since none of the *äduräs* I knew used this term, I will follow their usages.) As I observed the performance of *yaktovil* ceremonies in and around the Matara area, it occurred to me that there was something very misleading about the way in which the anthropological literature has described and analyzed these practices. They have been described and analyzed as "exorcisms," the malevolent figures, *yakku*, have been described as "demons," and the state of the person afflicted by their malevolence has been described as "possession." This observation led, in turn, to a train of reflections the axial thought of which may be stated in the following way: whether or not there are, in Sri Lanka, "demons" that "possess" Sinhalas, and that are "exorcized" in "demon ceremonies," cannot be taken for granted simply in virtue of existing Western conventions of translation practice. Rather, it seemed to me that this convention of translation practice itself needed to be problematized. And this led to two kinds—or levels—of question: one, an *ideological* question, regarding the way in which the conceptual problematic through which *yaktovil* was inaugurated as a visible area of Western knowledge came into being; and two, an *ethnographic* question, regarding the nature of the influence *yakku* are understood to exercise over Sinhala subjects, and the nature of the vulnerability through which that influence is effected. It is these two levels of question that form the point of departure for the thinking that constitutes this book.

Chapters 1, 2, and 3—the constituents of Part I—map the ethnographic topography within which I situate the arguments I am concerned to construct. Ethnographic detail is foregrounded here, therefore, but, to be sure, what is presented is selected and organized in relation to the project at hand. I shall call this ethnographic topography—an essentially discursive one—the "discourse of *yakku*." By "discourse of *yakku*" I mean to mark out that discursive field of local Sinhala knowledges (statements, narratives, concepts, images, etc.) through which the figure of *yakku* as malevolent, ill-producing beings is constructed, mobilized, and put to use. In chapter 1 I try to indicate something of the way this discourse positions *yakku* in the moral universe of Sinhala Buddhists, and something of the nature of the afflictions they cause. This entails, among other things, a consideration of the concept of the three humors (*tun dos*) that constitute the Sinhala body and regulate its balanced functioning. This notion of an internally balanced body introduces a theme, and indeed points to a cultural ethical *good* (insofar as it indicates a culturally valued way of being), which I take up in chapter 2 in relation to what I understand to be a Sinhala practice of care for the composure of the mind and body. In this chapter, I focus specifically on that concept which, so far as I am able to grasp it, is central to the way *yakku* produce, or rather *transmit*, their malevolence, that is, the concept of *diṣṭiya*. *Diṣṭiya* is, to be sure, a difficult concept, and I try in this chapter to situate it in relation to a broader Sinhala conception of eyesight as an obtrusive energy that can have disturbing—that is, discomposing—effects at the level of both mind and body.

About chapter 3, I need say but little. I have sought there to provide a full description of one of the many *yaktovil* performances I saw. Most of the *tovil* ceremonies I observed in the Matara area of southern Sri Lanka were performed by a single troupe of performers, *tovil kārayas* as they are called, consisting of four *äduräs* (who dance and sing and charm, and generally lead the proceedings), and two drummers (*bera kārayas*) who provide the accompanying drum rhythms.[19] The *tovils* performed by this troupe (whose members, I might add, individually and together, were much in demand up and down the Matara district, and beyond) were distinctive in at least one respect. Their performances often, indeed more often than not, involved sequences in which, a trance having been induced upon the *āturayā,* he or she was deliberately exhausted in repeated rounds of "dancing and singing," and then subjected, after each such round, to questioning by the *ädurā*. In my description of the two *yaktovils* performed for Lila Amma in October 1987, I present these episodes at length. Closing Part I, chapter 3 provides a concrete instance from which to consider the discussions that follow.

Part II opens the kind of critical inquiry that, as I have already indicated, seems to me of fundamental importance for postcolonial anthropology. If critical inquiry often means no more than a few sharp remarks regarding a general theoretical program, I think that it is also important to take specific instances of a theoretical problematic, particularly ones inhabiting commanding positions in a conceptual or disciplinary field, and to subject them to close, critical scrutiny. This is why in the next chapter, chapter 4, I undertake a careful reading of one ethnographic description and analysis of *yaktovil*—Bruce Kapferer's widely regarded *A Celebration of Demons*. Not only is this the only modern ethnographic monograph on *yaktovil* to date, but it is a highly sophisticated one, written from a self-consciously theoretical standpoint, and exhibits an impressive range of sociological data. If, in the end, I find the book's arguments wanting, my concern is less to impugn the author's judgment than to make visible the way in which ideological problematics continue to find their way into anthropological arguments—in this case, a colonial demonology that depends on certain assumptions about authentic experience. It will be evident that my concerns here bear some relation to a body of theoretical inquiry into the relation between anthropology and colonial discourse—one thinks particularly of Talal Asad's early essay, "Two European Images of Non-European Rule," Edward Said's *Orientalism*, and Johannes Fabian's *Time and the Other*.[20] My aim in this chapter is to make the case that anthropological investigation that takes its conceptual objects as self-evident, that tends to see its relation to history narrowly, that is, as merely a matter of an *external*, positive history of the practices it is inquiring upon, rather than an internal genealogical one of the concepts through which these practices have been produced as the objects of

Western discourse, can hardly avoid the reinscription of such colonial problematics.

I turn to such a genealogy in chapter 5. Here I aim at a partial tracing out of nineteenth-century constructions of "Sinhala religion." Again, I should not be taken as saying here that social histories, such as, for instance, Kitsiri Malalgoda's unsurpassed *Buddhism in Sinhalese Society 1750–1900*,[21] are irrelevant to historical concerns within anthropological discourse. Far from it. Nor am I to be taken as suggesting that the theme of "religion and change" that has gained some prominence in recent anthropological research—one thinks of Michael Carrithers's *The Forest Monks of Sri Lanka* and Richard Gombrich and Gananath Obeyesekere's *Buddhism Transformed*—is not a substantial gain. To the contrary; these have, after all, made it clear that Buddhist history in Sri Lanka is not a unified one. I *do* want to suggest, however, that what is important for the kind of critical anthropology which this book advocates is that these social-historical concerns have a *conceptual* yield in terms of making visible the ideological nature of the objects themselves—"religion," "ritual," etc.—that come to inhabit the disciplinary space of modern anthropology. For these are the concepts we *think* with, and that organize the possible field of questions we ask. In this regard it seems to me that anthropologists interested in religion, for instance, have a lot to learn from studies such as David Pailin's *Attitudes to Other Religions* and Peter Harrison's *"Religion" and the religions in the English Enlightenment*.[22] Where "Buddhism" is concerned, Philip Almond's *The British Discovery of Buddhism* is a landmark study, as—for the case of Sri Lanka—is John Carter's important article, "A History of *Early Buddhism*."[23] The general matter of the historicity of our concepts however, is, I believe, of much theoretical significance for what it is that anthropology takes itself to be, and I shall return to it in the conclusion of this study.

Part III opens the kind of reconstructive project I think is important to undertake. The arguments in chapter 6 have their sources in chapter 5's genealogical inquiry—in the tracing of the colonial problematic by means of which "two religious systems" have been identified among Sinhalas—but my objective here is a different one. When, in the 1960s, anthropologists undertook to constitute "Buddhism" as the object of an explicitly social and cultural inquiry, they effectively intervened in an old and venerable field of "Buddhist studies" presided over by the classic indological questions—philological and historical and hermeneutical questions. The intervention was, I think, a momentous one, and in the three decades since there has emerged a substantial body of ethnographic knowledge of a range of cultural practice among village peasants in South and Southeast Asian countries bearing an allegiance to the Theravāda tradition: Burma, Sri Lanka, Thailand, Laos, Cambodia. Much of this anthropology of Buddhism—that, anyway, which has sought explicitly to think about the concepts through which the Buddhism/society nexus is constructed—has turned on a distinctive set of oppositions: the proximity between practice and precept, the authenticity of village as against textual Buddhism, the extent to which real Buddhist conviction adheres to claims made by Buddhists, clerical and lay, the functional relation between two distinctive "religious systems," and so on. There is, it seems to me, a critical historical investigation waiting to be carried out on the ideological history of this tenacious preoccupation. Chapter 7 does not undertake this, however—at least not in any comprehensive way. Rather, by way of a reading of the work of one of the most fruitful thinkers in this tradition, Gananath Obeyesekere, I indicate some of the constituent assumptions of this construction of Buddhism as an anthropological object and suggest that the functionalist problematic that informs it might now usefully be put aside. I suggest in its stead, following once again the instructive work of Talal Asad on Islam, that, as an anthropological object, Buddhism is better understood as a "discursive tradition."[24]

Finally, chapter 7 takes us back to the beginning, that is, to *yaktovil*. In this chapter, I seek to provide an inquiry into *yaktovil* which does not depend on a priori assumptions about the essential character of cultural practices. I offer a reading in terms of a concept of "strategy," and it will not be hard to see in my discussion the influence of such thinkers as Talal Asad, Pierre Bourdieu, and Michel Foucault. It should be clear that I do not think, as many seem to, that in the face of the anticolonial and antiessentialist assault of the last years anthropology need abandon its "traditional" concern with seeking to provide theoretico-descriptive analyses of such social practices as the Sinhala *yaktovil*. The important fact about colonial objects (to repeat a point that bears repeating) is not their moral, but their *conceptual*, status. As such, the point of theoretical discourse is to interrogate, criticize, and displace such objects, not lament them. And this, moreover, not as a way of avoiding earlier kinds of engagements, but as a way of *repositioning* them. Therefore, even as this book participates in, and tries in its way to more carefully delineate, the discursive space of an anthropological criticism, it also seeks to reposition the problem of how we might better understand those social practices that were, in effect, the starting point of our deliberations.

One caveat, and these days a delicate one: in these introductory remarks I have used—and will, throughout the course of this book, use—the term "Sinhala Buddhism" to refer to discourses and practices of people who, in the "ethnographic present," as we say, identify as "Sinhala Buddhist." Now, that what gets identified and counted as "Sinhala," as "Buddhist," and again, as "Sinhala Buddhist," are historical matters, is part of the concern of this book, especially in chapter 6, where I seek to displace a functionalist conception of Buddhist tradition in Lankā. And so, where this term appears I should not be read as projecting present identities onto a past, but rather as marking the contemporary space of ideological identifications.

Part I

Ethnographic Topoi

Chapter 1

Situating *Yakku*

The Story of Ālavaka

There is a story well known to Buddhists of all walks of life in Sri Lanka. It is the story of Ālavaka or Alav *yakkha* (p.; s. *yaksayā, yakā* [pl. *yaksayō, yakku*]; sk. *yakṣa*), a legendary figure in Buddhist literature and folklore. The story of Ālavaka is largely the story of the conversion of the man-eating being of that name to the Buddha's *dhamma* (s. *dharmaya*) or doctrine.[1] It is in fact an old Buddhist story with many versions, canonical and local, and, in some of its forms at least, it is a story of great beauty, wit, and compelling moral complexity. Although not part of the repertoire of narratives operative in the ritual I am concerned with in this book—that is, *yaktovil*—I would nevertheless like to begin by considering one story of Ālavaka in some detail because it offers what seems to me a very useful way of mapping the discursive field in which knowledges about *yakku* are produced. The story vividly illustrates a number of concepts and principles in Sinhala Buddhist thinking about *yakku* and, by extension, the various other beings that populate the moral universe they inhabit. This chapter will seek to lay out some of these concepts and principles—those of *prārthanāva, varama, karma, dōṣa* especially—focusing on the way they serve to position *yakku* as moral agents of a particular kind.[2]

Before I get to the story of Ālavaka itself, though, a word about the *yakkha* figure in Buddhist history may be pertinent. The figure derives from the mythological Vedic *yakṣa*, a sort of morally ambiguous lower deity. Neither completely benevolent nor completely malign, the *yakṣa* is a figure associated with fertility, vegetation, wealth, and water, and with such habitations as trees, rivers, oceans, and rock mounds. At least by the later Upanishads *yakṣas* were represented as objects of a popular cultus, and they were incorporated into the early Buddhist monumental art of Sāñcī and Bhārhut (second century B.C.E.). As Gail Sutherland has recently suggested, *yakṣas* were part of the iconographic strategy employed in a formative period of Buddhist art when the anthropomorphic depiction of the Buddha himself was inadmissible and a number of other figures were used to indicate his presence.[3] This strategy, she argues, "permitted ever-widening circles of conceptual relationship, in which pre-Buddhist mythological figures such as the *yakṣa* became vital elements in the redrawn map of Buddhist mythology and narrative" (p. 14). These early representations depicted relatively benign figures—the *yakṣa* (*yakkha*), for instance, bestowing wealth or offering protection. By the later, literary representations, however (those, for example, in the stories of the former births of the Buddha-to-be or *bōdhisattva*, the *Jātakas*), the motif of the fierce and malevolent *yakkha* becomes the predominant, if still not the only one.[4] In these narrative constructions, the *yakkha* figure is positioned in a more clearly delineated moral hierarchy as a device to exemplify the ethical antithesis of the Buddha (or, in the case of the *Jātakas*, the *bōdhisattva*) and his doctrine—to represent the "apotheosis of carnality, delusion, and ignorance," as Sutherland puts it (p. 135). These attributes of the *yakkha* figure are set off against the clarity of the Truth of the Buddha's *dhamma* and the serene, compassionate ethos of its virtues. In the Buddhist tradition, in short, the *yakkha* became that figure which, more than any other, embodied the Buddha's teaching on the essential unsatisfactoriness of life and its sources in attachment and desire.[5] And, as Sutherland further suggests, what is notable in the Buddhist construction of this malevolent figure is that the *yakkha*/Buddha opposition is always mediated through the conversion of the lower being. Conversion, in other words, is employed in these texts as a narrative mechanism through which the Buddha is able to subordinate these malevolent (or pre-Buddhist) deities and incorporate them within the discursive field of his *dhamma*.

The story of the conversion of Ālavaka is in this tradition of subordination and incorporation. Indeed, it is, the noted Buddhist and Pāli scholar, G. P. Malalasekera, has remarked, "considered one of the chief incidents in the Buddha's life."[6] In the canonical corpus that constitutes the Theravāda tradition, the story of Ālavaka is one of the *Yakkha Suttas* (*Yakkha* Discourses)—the *Ālavaka Sutta* (Discourse on Ālavaka)—of the *Sutta Nipāta*, a section of the Theravāda Canon reputedly containing some of the earliest traditions of Pāli Buddhism.[7] It also appears as one of the *suttas* in the *Samyutta Nikāya*. The *Ālavaka Sutta* takes the form of an encounter between the Buddha and Ālavaka in which the Buddha is first accosted and ordered about by the *yakkha* ("Go out, O Samana!," "Come in, O Samama!"); then threatened by him ("I will put to you a question. If you do not answer it, I shall either confound your mind, or split your heart, or, taking you by your feet, throw you on the other side of the Ganges"); and finally "tested," with questions regarding true happiness, rebirth, correct knowledge, and the living of the virtuous life. Here, for instance, is Ālavaka's first question to the Buddha and the Buddha's response:

> ĀLAVAKA: What is the best wealth to a man in this world? What thing well done produces happiness? Of savoury things, which indeed is the most savoury? The life of one who lives in what manner, do they say, is the best?
>
> THE BUDDHA: Faith is the best wealth to a man here. The observing well the Law produces happiness. Truth is indeed the most savoury of all savoury things. The living endowed with wisdom, they say, is the best of all modes of living.[8]

A tradition among Theravādins has it that Ālavaka had learned the questions he put to the Buddha, Gautama, from his parents, who in turn had them from a former Buddha, Kassapa.[9] At any rate, persuaded by the wisdom and truth of the Buddha's teaching about the good, the *yakkha* then vows henceforth to go "from village to village, from city to city, making obeisance to Buddha and his perfect Law"—in short, he is converted, and becomes a disciple of the Buddha's *dhamma*.

In a note to his nineteenth-century English translation of this *sutta*, Sir Muttu Coomaraswamy observed: "This is a sutta which is very popular amongst the Ceylon Buddhists."[10] If this is still the case today, as I believe it is, this no doubt is not on account of such spare Pāli verses as I have quoted. It is rather because this encounter between the *yakkha* and the Buddha has lent itself to the imaginative life of the Buddhist story-telling tradition.[11] Like the remarkable story of that legendary robber and murderer, Aňgulimāla (the fingers of whose victims garlanded his neck—thus his vivid name—and who met a similar fate, conversion),[12] the story of Ālavaka is popular in the sermons (*bana*) of village monks: typically the narrative story is told in Sinhala and then the questions and responses are chanted in the sacred language, Pāli.

In the local traditions of Sinhala Buddhists the story of Ālavaka is known as the *Ālavaka Däpanaya* ("the magical spell of Ālavaka"), or, perhaps more usually, the *Ālavaka Damanaya* ("the subjugation of Ālavaka"). On Charles Godakumbura's account, this was originally a verse poem containing 447 stanzas written in 1681.[13] The poem, he goes on, was based on the *Ālavaka Sutta* and was composed at the request of a local chieftain known as Davatava Nilame. In Hugh Nevill's collection there are specimens which he reckons to be at least two hundred years old.[14] One long narrative version was told to me by S. A. Piyasena, officiant (*kapuvā* or *kapurāla*) of Basnāhira *deviyō* ("god of the west") in Devundara, himself an erstwhile *ädurā*, and generally, as we shall see throughout this book, a man of incomparable knowledge of local traditions.[15] I tell the story much as it was told to me one afternoon in Devundara in late 1987. It will be noted that although as in the *Ālavaka Sutta* the conversion of the fierce *yakkha* is the ultimate telos of the narrative, it is closer in form to the narrative economy of the *Jātakas* in that it is rebirth and therefore the problem of merit that organizes the moral of the story.

The story, then:

> In the city (*nuvara*) of Alav in the province (*raṭa*) of Alav, there lived a King who ruled over eighteen provinces. This King was very just (*bohoma dähämayi*). He also much enjoyed sport (*vinōdaya*). One day he gathered his ministers of court (*ämati manḍalaya*) and suggested going on a hunt (*daḍayama*). He issued the challenge that should a chance be missed to kill a deer (*muva*) running close by, whether minister or King, the person will be punished. So they set off with their bows and arrows and food and drink, and after some distance in the jungle they became very tired. Just then, however, a deer ran close by the King, but when he dispatched an arrow he missed (*viddha vädun nā*). Ashamed (*lejjāven*), he gave chase for several miles. Eventually, the deer fell into a swamp (*häla*) and the King was able to kill it. He took the deer out of the swamp, bound it on a pole (*kada*), and started to make his way back. He lost his way, however, and seeing a big tree (*rukgasa*) in a good, clean clearing, he decided to take a rest.
>
> No sooner had he put down the deer and begun to rest than a *yaksayā* descended from the tree and made ready to eat him.[16] With a great show of self-importance, the King said to the *yaksayā*: "I am the King of the city of Alav who rules over eighteen provinces. So don't eat me. Allow me to go and eat this deer." Unimpressed [and with a nice touch of irony, I might add], the *yaksayā* replied: "Great King, when I have eaten you where can the deer go? Is that dead deer's little flesh

(*mas ṭika*) going anywhere? It will remain where it is and I can eat it afterwards. First, though, I will eat you."

The King then offered the *yaksayā* the following proposal: "If you eat the deer and myself it will only satisfy you for today. If, however, you allow me to go I will give you a plate of rice (*bat taliyak*) and a human being (*manusyek*) every day. So allow me to go. And if this promise is not kept (*poronduva boru unot*) go ahead and destroy (*vinasa karanavā*) the entire city of Alav." The *yaksayā* liked the offer. He ate the deer and allowed the King to go.

When at last he found his way to the Palace, the weary King reclined and reflected on the seriousness of what he had done. His ministers, when they arrived, found him very sad (*dukin innavā*). "What happened?" they inquired. And the King replied: "Ministers, what was done is far more significant than what happened." And when they asked what he meant, the King told them about his encounter with Ālavaka and what he had promised him. Deeply troubled, he told his ministers that the task of providing the humans was an impossible one. But the ministers consoled him saying that they would release one person per day from the prison (*hiragedara*), giving him a pot of rice and instructing him to take it by the appointed tree. At this the King's mind was put at ease (*hita honda unā*).

So every morning a pot of rice was cooked and taken by the ministers to the prison, where an offer of freedom was made. People wrestled (*pora allanavā*) each other for the boon. And when the poor, unsuspecting person desiring to go home (*gedara yana āsāven*) had taken the pot of rice and gone by the appointed tree, the *yaksayā* seized and ate him.

This went on for ten years until the prison houses were all depleted. The ministers then suggested giving old people (*vayasaka minisu*) to be eaten, but the King, thinking about his own parents and grandparents, refused. In that case, said the ministers, let us give the little children (*kudu lamayi*). To this the King agreed even though he himself had a child of seven months. And each day the King's servants went to a house and snatched (*uduragattā*) a child, who was then placed with a pot of rice at the foot of the tree. This went on until there were neither children nor pregnant women left in all of the city of Alav—except, that is, for the King's own son.

Now, Alav *yaksayā* had sixteen beautiful queens (*bisovaru*) whom he kept captive in a stone cave (*gal guhāva*) the door of which could be opened only by him. These queens had been seized by Alav *yaksayā* from various Kings in the surrounding provinces. After eating each human being, he gave the queens the pot of rice.

At that time, the Buddha was looking to see who he could send off along the right path (*honda magaṭa piṭat karanavā*), and he saw Alav *yak-*

sayā. So in the first watch of evening (*perajāmaya*) the Buddha went to Alav's residence (*vimānaya*)—the stone cave whose door only the *yaksayā* could open. However, with firm resolve the Buddha placed his foot on the door and it opened.[17] He entered and, looking for a place to sit, sat on the *yaksayā*'s gem-chair (*menik putuva*). Then he spread his Buddha-rays (*buduräs*) and began to preach to the queens, some of whom realized who it was and some of whom did not. While the Buddha was preaching to the queens, two *yaksayās*, Satagira and Giro Hemavata, sought to fly to Asamola Rock where the assembly (*samāgama*) of *yakku* were meeting. Unable to go above the Buddha, however, they were forced to come down to the ground and first worship him, and seek his permission (*avasaraya*) to go. Arriving at Asamola Rock, Giro Hemavata said to Ālavaka: "Ālavaka, today your time is over. The Buddha has come to your residence."

Hearing this Ālavaka grew very angry (*hari kenti giyā*). He proclaimed that the Buddha does not know how powerful he is, and he thought to himself that he should go and seize him, make a lump of him (*guli karalā*), and eat him. To his fellow *yaksayās* he demonstrated his power by stabbing at Rock Asamola so that a big hole was bored (*harunā*) in it. Then he left and flew to his residence to confront the Buddha. When he went in, the frightened queens ran away.

Very angrily, Ālavaka approached the Buddha, who, by contrast, remained serene (*nissabdāven innavā*). The *yaksayā* said to the Buddha: "Māhana (monk), it is not right for you to open my door, sit on my gem-chair, and speak to my queens while I am not here. Why did you do such a thing?" The Buddha replied: "It is in order to be of assistance to you that I came" (*umbaṭa pihitak vennayi mama āve*)." At this the *yaksayā* thought to himself, "I don't need your help." And he thought of making a wind blow so hard as to blow away the Buddha and kill him. But the Buddha already knew his intentions and when the wind blew, not even a fold in his robe was shaken (*sivru patakvat hälune nä*). Ālavaka was astonished at this. Then he made it rain cedar charcoal (*kihiri anguru varusāva*), but it did not fall where the Buddha was standing. By this time it was late at night and Ālavaka was getting more and more angry. In his possession was a powerful curved club (*pārāvalalla*). If the sky was hit with it the stars would fall; and if the earth was hit with it it would become white as when sand without water goes dry; and if the sea was hit with it it would be as if the waves broke into pieces. The *pārāvalalla* was as powerful as that. As Ālavaka started to spin the club on his finger, the sky thundered (*ahasa goravanavā*) and the earth exploded (*pupuranavā*). But the Buddha remained still (*nisolmane*). And when the *yaksayā* threw the *pārāvalalla* it became a mat at the feet of the Buddha. Ālavaka is speechless (literally, can do or say nothing: *Ālavakaṭa kara kiya ganna deyak nä*).

By now it was dawn (*elivenna jāmaya velā*), and even though his power was considerably diminished, and things were not going well, Ālavaka was planning something else. He thought of making the Buddha walk, at which point he would make his legs lifeless so that he could seize him, throw him on a stone, and kill him. So he said to the Buddha: "Ah, Māhana, since evening many things have been performed. You are a good *mantrakāraya* (charm-worker). Now get up and leave this place immediately (*vahāma metanin nägitilā yanna*)." The Buddha got up and walked away. Then Ālavaka called him back and told him to sit. And again he sent him away and called him back. On the third occasion, however, when he ordered the Buddha to get up the Buddha said: "Ālavaka, since early evening you have sent a cloud of wind (*mēga hulangak*); you have caused cedar charcoal to rain; you threw the *pārāvalalla*. But you could not defeat me with any of these things. Now you think that you can make my legs lifeless and then seize and throw me down on a stone. But that won't work either. If I get up for a third time your head will burst into seven pieces (*hisa hat kadakaṭa pupuranavā*). So I won't get up." And when the Buddha said this Ālavaka fell and worshiped him. He realized that the Buddha knew his every thought. He was then made to sit up, and the Buddha began to preach to him.

In the meanwhile, there was now no one left to be given for the sacrifice—no one but the King's seven-month-old prince. And though the Queen tried to save him the King's servants snatched him away, and with a pot of rice took him to the tree. Unlike other days when they approached Ālavaka's tree, however, the servants realized that they felt no fear. And when they called Ālavaka, he came shamefully (*lejjāven āva*). He took the prince and gave him to the Buddha. But because he was not old enough to join the Order of Monks (*sangha*), the Buddha entrusted him to the King's servants, giving them instructions to accompany him, at the age of seven years, to Jetavanārāmaya, where he would be made a monk (*māhana karanavā*).

With the Buddha's sermon (*bana*), all became clear (*sampurna pähädilla*) to Ālavaka. And what the Buddha said in his sermon was that he had been born a *yaksayā* who ate people. This is what he told him: Once long ago there was a poor peasant of low caste living in the city of Alav. One day while this peasant was digging in his paddy field, a water snake (*diya bariyek*) was cut by his mammoty. The two pieces of its body remained joined by a very small piece of skin. The peasant held the snake—which had not yet died—by the tail and threw it onto the ground. The water snake fell on a thicket (*rähäniyaka*) where there was a nest of red ants (*dimigottak*). The ants immediately set upon the water snake, which, lying still, had not yet died. In pain the water snake wished, "I will eat you, I will eat you, I will eat you (*Vēdanāven prārthanā karā, topi kanavā, topi kanavā, topi kanavā*)." When its flesh was finished and there were only bones left, a little baby red ant, too young even to know how to eat, followed the others along the bone of the water snake.

It is that peasant, said the Buddha [in that strategy of making known what was concealed by rebirth], who, having been born in another lifetime (*ātmaya*), became King in the city of Alav. It is that water snake who became Alav *yaksayā*; it is he whose dying wish was to eat the ants. He had gotten a warrant (*varama*) from King Yāma [the great King of the underworlds] to take revenge (*paligannavā*) for what was done in a previous *ātmaya*. The red ants, having been born as human beings in this lifetime, are all those who were eaten by Alav *yaksayā* as a result of the promise made by the King. And the little baby red ant who followed the others along the bone of the water snake but did not eat was born in this lifetime as the prince of the King of Alav.

Having listened to the Buddha's sermon, the *yaksayā* attained a good state (*honda tatvaya uda unā*), and became a Stream-Enterer (*sōvan unā*).[18] He then asked the Buddha for permission (*avasaraya*) to accompany him on his journeys. But the Buddha said to him, "Ālavaka, you are a *yaksayā* who has eaten human beings for a long time. If you go to a village, people there will be frightened and run away. Even though you are on the right Path people are still afraid. Therefore you can't come on my journeys. After this, though, having lived without doing wrong (*väradi nokarē*), you will go to a good place (*honda tänak*)." And from that time on Ālavaka never ate flesh, but only the leaves (*kola*), nuts (*gedi*), flowers (*mal*), and leaf shoots (*dalu*) that he found in the jungle. And while living in this exemplary way, he was injured by a splinter (*ulak*) and died, whereafter he was reborn in the divine world (*divya lōkaya*).

As I said at the outset, this is an exemplary Sinhala Buddhist story. It embodies the fundamental teaching of the Buddha concerning the disastrous consequences of enmity and vengeance and the importance of forgiveness. In this it bears much in common with the story of the *yakini* (female *yaksayā*) Kālī discussed recently by Ranjini and Gananath Obeyesekere, and in my reading of it I am indebted to their illuminating essay.[19] In attempting to understand the way the *Ālavaka Damanaya* positions *yakku*, I think that it is important to see not only that the *yaksayā* and the Buddha are counterposed in the narrative, and that one is in the end subjugated by the other; that much, surely, is obvious. The really interesting issue is how—that is, by means of what distinctive Sinhala Buddhist concepts—this counterpositioning works, is effected, and what it illustrates about the character of the respective figures in the narrative drama. The concept that I will focus on is that of *prārthanāva*.

Ālavaka's—that is, more properly, the water snake's—rebirth as a *yaksayā*, a vengeful, man-eating being, is the result of an unmeritorious but nevertheless fervent desire or wish or aspiration, namely, to eat the ants who are eating him. The common Sinhala word that expresses this kind of wish is the noun *prārthanāva*, or the verb *prārthanā karanavā*—as in Piyasena's colorful phrase: "Vēdanāven prārthanā karā, topi kanavā, topi kanavā, topi kanavā, kiyalā." ("In pain [the water snake] wished: 'I shall eat you, I shall eat you, I shall eat you").[20] Richard Gombrich, whose *Precept and Practice* provides a very useful discussion of *prārthanāva*, glosses it as "religious wish" or "earnest wish," and suggests that its nearest Christian analogy is prayer (p. 217). In this it is notably different from an *āsāva*, which is a rather mundane sort of desire, which, even though it may be earnest indeed (like the wish, for instance, of the prisoners in the story to go home), lacks the profound moral connotations of the aspiration involved in a *prārthanāva*. In *The Cult of the Goddess Pattini*, Gananath Obeyesekere suggests the meaning: "a wish associated with an act of merit," or a "will to achieve a Buddhist goal" (p. 80); and in her *Jewels of the Doctrine*, Ranjini Obeyesekere suggests "Fervent Rebirth-Wish" (p. 79 n). The notion of a "will to achieve" a desired goal captures nicely the sense that the water snake's earnest resolution is not dependent on an external agent—a god, say, as in prayer—to be fulfilled, but rather is a matter of pure, self-willed intention (though, of course, in this case the content of the wish or intention is far from being a Buddhist one). It therefore also links *prārthanāva* to, and serves to underline, the pervasive Sinhala Buddhist idea of the mind's power to produce desired (if even inadvertently desired) effects, both mental and material. This idea is a *very* important one. We meet it again and again both in everyday life and in ritual practice through a family of Sinhala Buddhist concepts. One significant instance of this notion in our story is found in the notion of *adhiṣṭhānaya—buduhāmuduruvō adhiṣṭhāna karalā*. This is the idea of an unshakable fixity of purpose, a concentrated intentness, and a general intensity of mind that produces otherwise unattainable effects. This sense of the mind's ability to produce moral and material effects will be especially crucial in my discussion in the next chapter of the concepts *diṣṭiya* and *tanikama*, and in chapter 7 of the strategy of *yaktovil*, because I will want to suggest that for Sinhalas "troubles" (*dōṣas*) and their eradication can in a literal way be matters of the mind (*hita*), or of thought (*adahasa* [will], *kalpanāva* [thought, consideration]—each of which has slightly different, but equally significant, connotations). But to return to *prārthanāva*, bearing these connections in mind. As Gombrich suggests, there are *prārthanā* made for others (that they may achieve a desired goal) and *prārthanā* made for oneself (that I may achieve a desired goal).[21] Both of these uses in turn are embedded in the conceptual field of *karma* and merit-making (*pinkama*), about which an initial word or two is necessary.

Karma is an overarching and inexorable moral law of causation.[22] Working like a self-regulating machine, it structures a moral universe in which all living beings are placed in a hierarchical order: gods occupying the topmost plane, human beings the middle plane, and animals, mean spirits, and malevolent beings the bottom planes. One's place in this cosmological hierarchy is determined by one's *karma* (literally, "actions"), and more specifically, by the balance of one's good and bad actions in previous lifetimes or births: a balance of good actions (*pin*) secures a better place, while a balance of bad actions (*pav*) leads to lower planes. The further up the hierarchy one is the greater is one's moral and material power, social prestige, well-being and longevity, and ability to help others; and the better are one's chances of attaining that state of moral perfection—at once enlightenment and release—known in Sinhala as *nivan* (sk. *nirvāna*; p. *nibbāna*). To have attained it, is to have placed oneself beyond the effects of *karma*. The point to be noted here is that in principle *karma* is uninfluenceable. As long as one remains part of the long run of life-death-rebirth—or, to use a more Buddhist simile, so long as one is still crossing over the vast ocean of *samsāra*—one is subject to *karma* effects. And thus, as a good Buddhist it is one's duty to strive in this lifetime to such actions—those that embrace the supreme virtue of generosity (*dāne*) especially—as will ensure one a better rebirth.

However, whereas the general moral status of all living beings is always, so to speak, overdetermined in this way, Sinhala Buddhists seek in one way or another to mitigate the effects of *karma*. One of the most common of these is the practice of transferring merit (*pin dīma*).[23] The concept of merit is central to the everyday life of Sinhala Buddhists' moral behavior. *Pin*, notably, is both quantifiable and transferable. It is quantifiable insofar as each good deed (like the potter in the story of "The Monk Tissa, The Fat," giving space in his shed to one, and then a second, ascetic)[24] is separately accounted, and the amount of merit gained depends on the nature of the deed, and of the recipient of the good work; similarly, the amount of *pav* or demerit depends on the enormity of the bad deed and the intention with which it is committed; and it is transferable in the sense that a quantity of merit can be passed on to a god, the dead, or one can oneself acquire some vicariously through sympathizing in someone else's good work.[25] So that, in general, while one earns merit (*pin*) for oneself by doing good deeds in one's lifetime (as Ālavaka did between his conversion and his death), one may also gain merit by participating in merit-making occasions: for instance, one may rejoice in a god's good deeds (thus both earning merit oneself and helping the god earn merit); or one may listen to a monk preaching a sermon (*bana*). These occasions of merit-making are also, as Gombrich indicates, formally occasions of *prārthanāva*. One expresses the wish that the god may achieve buddhahood; or the monk expresses the wish that all may attain *nirvāna*.

However—and this is the crucial point for grasping the Ālavaka story—one may also seek to influence one's own future, one's *karma*; in other words, one may will to achieve (*prārthanā karanavā*) a certain future status for oneself. This practice of making *prārthanā* for oneself is associated with the notion that one's very last, that is, deathbed desire is *the* decisive one for the status of one's rebirth. Describing a class of *yakku*, Mala Yakku (literally, "death *yakku*"), the nineteenth-century writer Dandris de Silva Gooneratne writes: "If a man, who lives at enmity with another, remember, on his deathbed, just before he dies, and at the very moment of his expiring, anything relating to that enmity, and if, instead of a feeling of forgiveness, resentment and hatred take possession of his mind, he is supposed to become, after death, a demon of this kind."[26] Gooneratne does not say explicitly that this is a case of *prārthanāva* (indeed, curiously for so meticulous and exhaustive an observer of local village discourse as Gooneratne was, he does not mention this notion at all); nor indeed does Gombrich, who uses this passage, do so directly in the context of *prārthanāva*,[27] but this is what I take Gooneratne to be describing in his characteristically vivid way. In itself this view is not necessarily inconsistent with the theory of *karma* since it is understood that a person's dying thoughts will be broadly conditioned by the life he has lived—the merits and demerits he has accumulated—but it is clearly a view that suggests that one can act more immediately to secure a desired objective.[28] This no doubt must turn on the quality of the wish, by which I mean not its moral content, but rather the authenticity itself of the aspiration it embodies, whether for ill or good. A *prārthanā* for oneself, therefore, often has a sense of being impulsive and spontaneous—a fervent mental impulse to achieve a goal—and this in turn heightens its sense of resolve. But whether or not this is the case (the novice in the story of "The Senior Monk Nāgasēna," for example, makes a fairly calculated rebirth wish), it has nevertheless to be deeply—resolutely—felt.[29]

The water snake, a being already fairly low on the scale of living beings, has a malicious but earnest resolve (or in Obeyesekere's felicitous phrase "will to achieve")—"I shall eat you, I shall eat you, I shall eat you." And the more or less immediate consequence is that he is reborn in precisely that status whose essential nature that wish befits—i.e., a *yaksayā*, a vengeful, man-eating being. Now notice further that in the story this *prārthanāva* is represented, in perfectly ordinary circumstances (a peasant in his paddy field, a water snake, a nest of ants), as a perfectly intelligible response to any creature's suffering so unjust a death as being eaten alive. The narrative strategy is not, therefore, to comment on the water snake's personal character (which is neither here nor there), but to indicate the internal dynamic of a general moral principle: that consequences follow ineluctably upon actions and thoughts, and actions and thoughts such as violence, heartlessness, and malevolence, which are contrary to Buddhist virtues (of nonviolence [*ahimsa*], pity [*anukampāva*], compassion [*karunāva*]), have inevitably regrettable consequences where one's next birth status is concerned. The Buddhist lesson of the story is that one has to learn to be like the baby ant, who in its innocent "not knowing" was beyond the worldly justifications of either the hunger of its elders or the wrath of the water snake. It is the same point made by Dharmasēna Thera in the story of Kālī. In an extraordinary passage in this tale, after a long succession of births and rebirths in which the vengeful human-eater and the victim exchange places (and precisely on the strength of their *prārthanāvas*) so often that it is no longer clear who was the original perpetrator of the malicious wrong, Dharmasēna has the Buddha say to the *yakini* Kālī:

> As spit, snot, and such like are washed off with clean water, and that water, because it is pure, can cleanse a filthy body, so hatred that burns on the fuel of justifications must be quenched with the water of compassion, not fed with the firewood of reasons and causes. Compassion is fundamentally right, free of Malice, and is the source of all good. Good, founded on compassion, destroys evil and puts out the fire of

> enmity. When that fire, which is most difficult to extinguish, is put out, then the ten other fires kindled by the various types of passions such as the desire for wealth, will also die. When there is no more wood, even fires that have been burning for long years die down. Once all eleven fires are extinguished, just as rice plants thrive in flooded fields, so in the rice field of the mind softened with the waters of Compassion, seeds of Moral Conduct and Contemplation will sprout, and a rich harvest of worldly blessings and of Spiritual Attainments can be had.[30]

And as he did with Ālavaka, the Buddha gave Kālī a "handful of Stream-Enterer rice" to start her along the Path.

I think that this concept—*prārthanāva*—has very important implications for the way in which *yakku* are positioned in the moral universe of Sinhala Buddhists. *Yakku* are malicious, it is true—frightfully so, in fact—as the stories of Ālavaka and Kālī amply illustrate, and this maliciousness belongs in some sense to the nature of their being. But this "being," one has to understand, is really a *status*, not a personification. *Karma* structures an impersonal hierarchy of moral statuses whose natures are always already given. A *yaksayā* is a being whose *samsāri*c vocation (so to put it awkwardly) is to vengefully consume flesh (see my discussion later in this chapter of the *yaksayā* Maha Kōla Sanniya, whose birth story vividly positions these figures in relation to the consumption of flesh). Removed from this status is to be removed from this nature. "Evil" (insomuch as one can call it that),[31] therefore, is here inscribed in a status, not in an individual Soul, and one can—anyone can—on the earnestness of a mere malicious last wish sink to the status of a *yaksayā*. By the same token, anyone can, with sufficient good actions (*pin*), subsequently leave this status—as, of course, both Ālavaka and Kālī did. But again, since one has always to "live out" the consequences of one's actions, it is only death and rebirth that can accomplish this change. So it is interesting and significant that although Ālavaka is formally converted and becomes a disciple of the Buddha's *dhamma*, his *yakkha* nature, so to speak, leads the Buddha to forbid him to accompany him on his tours. He must live by the *dhamma*, die, and be reborn in a more pleasant status. Thus the narrative stages an innocuous death—by a splinter (*ulak*)—to quickly dispatch him on his *samsāri*c journey.

So much, then, for the concept of *prārthanāva*. There are two other points about the story that are useful to note briefly, and which will take us into the following section's discussion of authority in the moral universe of Sinhala Buddhists. The first has to do with the representation of the relation of power between Ālavaka and the Buddha. Canonically, the Buddha's power is a strictly moral one: the power of the Truth, and how, with what kind of virtuous life, to attain it. This is what the Four Noble Truths embody, and what the questions and answers that compose the *Ālavaka Sutta* are about. In the *Ālavaka damanaya*, however, although this remains the case, things are much more as they are in the *Jātakas* (as they are, for example, in the *Gagga Jātaka* [no. 155] or the *Devadhamma Jātaka* [no. 6]), where the *bōdhisattva* is represented as being not only morally superior but more clever and artful than the *yaksayā*, and able to outwit him. Thus Ālavaka can say to the Buddha with genuine admiration that he is a good *mantrakārayā* (literally, a "charm worker"). The second point has to do with the outcome of this moral encounter. It ends with conversion, true enough, but it may be more accurate to say with Lowell Bloss[32] that it ends with the establishment of a sort of "contract" between the Buddha and the *yaksayā* by means of which the former designates a certain field for the efficacy of the latter's power. In Sinhala Buddhist vocabulary this "contract" is expressed in the important concept of *varama* ("warrant"), which I will turn to in the following section.

Yakku, Varama, and Sinhala Buddhist Cosmology

As I said earlier, the story of Ālavaka does not feature in the large repertoire of narratives operative in those contemporary *gurukama* practices that are the main subject of this book—those practices involved in influencing *yakku* and of which *yaktovil* is but the most complex and dramatic instance. It is employed rather, I suggested, by village monks and by lay Buddhist schoolteachers to illustrate the virtues of the *dhamma*: the possibilities of ultimate salvation, but especially the practical value of "making merit." For as Ranjini and Gananath Obeyesekere observe, " 'merit-making' constitutes the basis of Buddhist ethics in peasant society."[33] And the whole point of the story, of course, is that Ālavaka, on the basis of his merit, is no longer a *yaksayā* (*yakkha*). He is, for all we know, well on his way to *nirvāna—sampūrna sōvahan unā*. By contrast, the *yakku* who populate the repertoire of local narratives known to Sinhala *yakädurās* have not yet been saved (*mudavanavā*) by the Buddha and thus have not been "sent off" along the right Path. These *yakku* are situated not within a soteriological narrative map, however vivid and pointed, but rather within stories about sorcery, misfortunes or troubles (*dōṣa*), and healing. Still, as we will see, the moral principles situating them—in relation to vengeance, wrathfulness, and thus *prārthanāva*—are the same.

According to a familiar Sinhala story, *yakku* were the original inhabitants of Lankā. They were a cannibalistic species, given up to lives of lawless extravagance, to song and dance and food. Merriment and devastation were their chief pastimes until the Buddha (*buduhāmuduruvō*), grieved by what he saw and appealed to by the gods, intervened and *yakku* were exiled to the fabled island of Yak Giri (*Yak Giri diva*).[34] The Buddha, however—at least in a version told in Matara—in so ridding Lankā at last of these dreadful creatures, worked a curious but significant compromise. For as part of the *varama*, or "warrant," by which these *yakku* were "bound" (*bandinavā*) he, so to put it, gave them leave to make people ill on the sole condition that having done so they then accepted the offerings made to them in his name by the authorized persons, *yakädurās*, and removed their malign influence. This, so to speak, was their dispensation. *Yakku* were allowed a curtailed, controlled, and much-restricted margin for their malevolence. In Chapter 6 I consider the narrative of the "establishment" of Buddhism in Lankā; and in chapter 7 I will discuss the importance of the concept of "binding" (*bandinavā*) for the practice of *yaktovil*. Here, however, I want to focus on the concept of *varama* (pl. *varam*).

All beings are, in authority, power, knowledge, and virtue (an intertwined set for Buddhists), subordinate to the Buddha, and dependent upon him for what power they possess. In order to understand this, and particularly how *yakku* are situated in relation to this concept of power, we need a more detailed consideration of the order of the moral universe of Sinhala Buddhists. I have already said that this moral universe is a hierarchical one. The highest position in the hierarchy belongs to the Buddha. He occupies, in Obeyesekere's now well-known phrase, the "presidential" position, regulating but standing above the "pantheon" proper.[35] The Buddha, the Blessed One, is the All Perfect. He is completely without trace of moral (or indeed, physical) blemish. Five hundred and fifty births since the time when as Sumedha in the *sāsana* (Teaching) of Dīpamkara the first Buddha, he made his vow to become a Buddha himself and found a *sāsana* of his own, he finally attained *nirvāna*, in the lifetime of Gautama. He lived. He subsequently died (or more correctly, entered *parinirvāna*). But during that life of eighty years (he actually lived forty-five years after enlightenment) he (re)discovered the Truth taught by Buddhas before him that life in its essence is "unsatisfactory," "suffering" (*dukkha*); that this condition is a consequence of "craving" (*tanhā*) or attachment; that the end of suffering requires the "cessation" (*nirodha*) or "blowing out" (*nibbāna*) of craving; and that there is a Path (p. *magga*; s. *mārga*) by means of which this could be accomplished (i.e., the Four Noble Truths).[36] It is this Path, he taught, not the gods, that constitutes the way to *nirvāna*. Doctrinally speaking, therefore, the Buddha is not a deity, and the orthodox attitude toward him is one of commemoration, not propitiation. But Sinhala Buddhists treat (perhaps have always treated) him as a living presence, alive in images (*pilimaya*) of him and in his relics (*dhātu*), and attribute to him such supernatural powers as we observed him to have in the story of Ālavaka: instant locomotion, superhuman strength, and the ability to see everything at once.[37]

Below the Buddha are the deities proper, the gods (*dēvas*), highest among beings still subject to the law of *karma*, to death and rebirth. And first among Sinhala Buddhist gods is the beloved Sakra (p. Sakka), King of the gods, and often the first of the gods to be mentioned in narratives about the Buddha, the gods, and *yakku* (see chapter 6). He plays no significant part in the round of Sinhala Buddhist pilgrimages and propitiation, but he is beloved because it is of course to him that the Buddha entrusted the protection of the Buddhist tradition (the *sāsana*) in Sri Lanka. And Sakra in turn gave over this trust to Viṣṇu, one of the *hatara varam deviyō* or Four Warrant Gods who are at the next grade in the hierarchy. In the Matara area these are, besides Viṣṇu (or—and in Devundara particularly—Upulvan [Upuluvanna], meaning "blue"), Nātha, Kataragama, and Saman. The concept of the *hatara varam deviyō* is an interesting and, in ritual practice, a formally important one. They are, for instance, the first figures invoked in a short solemn rite in the opening moments of *yaktovil* ceremonies I saw in the Matara area: a small coconut-oil lamp (*pol tel pahana*) is held by the afflicted person, and she or he is instructed by the *ädurā* to think about these gods and about the Buddha. It is understood that by inhaling the aroma (*suvanda irīmen*) of the lamp a lot of "troubles" generated in the mind (*hitē ätivenne dōṣa*) are destroyed (see chapter 3). That the lamp is said to be for the Buddha as well as the gods underscores the relationship between these gods and the authority of the *dhamma*. Obeyesekere has referred to them as principal "defenders of the faith" in

Sri Lanka.[38] The concept he suggests derives from the classical Buddhist concept of the guardian gods of the Four Quarters: Dhrtarāṣṭra, guardian of the East and chief of the Gāndharvas; Virudha, guardian of the South and chief of the Kumbhāṇḍas; Virupakṣa, guardian of the West and chief of the Nāgas; and Vaisravana, guardian of the North and chief of the Yakkhas.[39] Of these, only the last, Vaisravana (s. Vessamuni) is important as the lord of the *yakku*. I return to him later. Gombrich and Obeyesekere point out elsewhere that while the number of the Warrant Gods is always four, the occupants are not always the same four.[40] In some traditions, Vibhīsana, brother of the *Ramayana*'s Rāvana, whose main shrine is at Kälaniya (in Sinhala Buddhist tradition, the last place in Lankā visited by the Buddha) in the Western Province, is one of the *hatara varam deviyō*; so too is Pattini, whose main shrine is at Navagamuva, also in the Western Province.

Below the Four Warrant Gods are a number of more minor, less powerful gods, among them Ganēṣa or Gana deviyō (Kataragama's brother), Vallī Ammā (mistress of Kataragama—whose wife, Tēvānī Ammā, interestingly enough is not a god),[41] Basnāhira (the god of the west, and whose *dēvālē* or shrine-house in Devundara was presided over by S. A. Piyasena). Within the large Viṣṇu *dēvālē* in Devundara, there were images of two other deities on either side of the enclosure of the Viṣṇu image (kept behind a curtain except when *pūjā* was being offered). On its right was a small glass-encased image of Däḍimunda (Alutnuvara *deviyō*), and on its left, an image (also glass-encased) of Sūniyam *dēvatāva*. The *kapurāla* explained that Sūniyam is Däḍimunda's minister.[42] The Sūniyam image was becoming very popular while I was in Devundara.

Gods are gods because of their good *karma*, their accumulation of merit (*pin*). They live in a heavenly abode known as *divya lōkaya*, and they have the power to grant favors. They are understood to be closer than mere mortals to salvation (enlightenment), though they have to be reborn as human beings in order to attain it. Salvation is (and this in a gendered sense, too) the task and privilege of "man." Indeed, the gods are thought to be *bōsats* (s.; sk. *bōdhisattva*; p. *bōdhisatta*), that is, future Buddhas. The closest to this ultimate goal is Nātha, who is viewed as the very next Buddha, Maitreya.[43] Generally, the gods are worshiped at their respective *dēvālēs* or shrine-houses—generally because many individuals also have small shrines in their homes to certain deities like Kataragama and, increasingly, Sūniyam. These *dēvālēs* are presided over by officiants known as *kapuvās* or *kapurālas* (we have already met the estimable Piyasena), who are servants of the gods (*dēva gäti*); or again, intermediaries between the gods and their petitioners, and as such they were often described by analogy with proctors (*perakadōru*). Unlike the Buddha, who is the embodiment of perfect benevolence and therefore does not punish, the gods are *both* benevolent and punitive. This punitiveness is, however, as Obeyesekere puts it, a "rational" punitiveness, meaning to say the gods are just:[44] their punishment follows transgressions according to culturally understood rules governing behavior toward gods. Some gods are more punitive than others. Kataragama is perhaps the most exacting and severe (*tada*) of the major gods.

Then there are humans (*manusya*). In the moral universe of Sinhala Buddhists, human beings occupy the central position: neither overburdened by bad *karma* as are the malign beings, nor overprivileged with the fruits of good *karma* as are the gods in their heavenly abodes, to them falls the real task of attaining *nirvāna*. It is only humans, I was told by one *ädurā*, who become Buddhas; only humans who become gods; it was a human who became Lord Jesus (*Jīsas vahanse*). All the authors of religions (*āgam katuvaraya*) are humans. Without being born as a human one cannot attain to any great thing. In which case, he concluded, the basic place (*mulika stānaya*) or principal position (*pradhāna täna*) belongs to humans. Among humans, there are those who have renounced the world and committed themselves to the task of advancement toward *nirvāna*: monks. And there are those who have not renounced the world: laymen or householders (masc., *upāsaka*; fem., *upāsikā*). The only "religious" obligation of lay Buddhists is to take the Three Refuges (*tisarana*) and observe the moral code of the Five Precepts (*pan sil*).[45] Monks have taken the Ten Precepts (*dasa sil*) and submitted to the rules of monastic life (*vinaya*).[46] The main "religious" concern of laymen is for rebirth in a more "pleasant" station, and therefore with the merit-making that will earn them that reward. Ultimate salvation, *nirvāna*, is thought of (insofar as it is thought of at all) as a dim prospect, and it has been widely felt that the immediate aim should be to hope for as good a rebirth as possible in the time of the next Buddha, Maitreya, when attaining *nirvāna* will be easier. This, however, is precisely where there is much contemporary dispute within the Buddhist tradition in Lankā.[47]

Below the plane of humanity there are the mean and malevolent beings. First of these are *yakku* about whom, of course, I will have much to say in the following section. Suffice it to say here that, as we have seen with Ālavaka, *yakku* are *yakku* not because of some inherent "evil," but because of their bad *karma*. It is in their nature as *yakku* to harm without cause, and at their malevolent whim, they continue to accumulate bad *karma*. As Obeyesekere has suggested, "They are thus caught in a vicious circle: by nature they must perforce do evil but by continuing to do evil they increase their load of 'sin', thus denying themselves the chance of improving their present degraded status. Though salvation is not completely denied to them, they come close to a Buddhist analogue of eternal damnation."[48] Unless, of course, they have the good fortune to meet the next Buddha, Maitreya, and like Ālavaka, who encountered Gautama, be saved and sent off along the Path to *nirvāna*. Being malevolent, *yakku* are not propitiated with the same kinds of offerings given to the Buddha and the gods—vegetarian foods, auspicious flowers, and incense. They are invoked with burnt meat (*pulutu*), inauspicious flowers, and resin (*dummala*, a rough, acrid incense). Indeed, the very word for offering in each case is different: the Buddha and the gods get *pūjāvas*, *yakku* get *dola* (the latter, as Obeyesekere suggests, has a connotation of one of those most un-Buddhist of qualities, "craving").[49]

Below *yakku* are the *prētayō*, the discontented spirits of dead kinsmen who return to harass and generally create all manner of trouble and misfortune (*dōṣa*) for their living relatives. Not all the dead become *prētayō*, however. Whether one does or not depends on the character of one's life, but especially on the contentedness with which one dies. Again we find the notion that one's thoughts as one passes from this life are crucial for the determination of one's next status. If a person, in the last moments before death, has a frustrated desire for food or cigarettes or some such thing—in effect, an attachment for worldly things—it is likely that he or she will become a *prētayā*. The *prētayō* are said to form groups which are 108—a constantly recurring number in Sinhala ritual practice. No *ädurā* ever named more than eight or nine, however. Some of those mentioned to me are the following: Ganda Prētayō—these have ugly faces and an injury (*tuvāle*) the size of a coconut and germs all over their bodies. When they open their mouths a very bad smell emanates (hence the name). Diga Lōma Pretayō—they have long, knotted hair (*diga lōma*) coiled around their body, red eyes, and an ugly face. They are always hungry. Gal Prētayō—these are said to be nothing but a body trunk, having neither a head nor limbs. The reason for this condition is that they were persons who were excessively miserly and greedy in life, and as a result they are the only group of *prētayō* who are unable to accept offerings (*pidēni*). Kāku Prētayō—they are, like vultures (*kāka*), after whom they are named, greedy for food, but for other material things as well. There are two groups of *prētayō* who are less mean than the others: Ñāti Prētayō, who were persons so attached to their relatives (*ñāti*) that they were on their minds at the moment of their death. These *prētayō* are sometimes said to be beneficial (they are similar to Mala Prētayō); and Gevala Prētayō (house-dwelling *prētayō*), who were similarly inordinately attached to their relatives and the place where they lived. These, however, are exceptional in that they can earn enough merit (when the *ädurā* instructs the afflicted person to transfer merit to the *prētayā* during an offering ceremony for *prētayō*, *Prēta Pidēniya*) to be released from this condition.[50] *Prētayō* are said to live in and around the habitats of humans but in rather unwholesome places such as near garbage, at the back of houses where animals are kept, and in latrines. They are also said to linger around cemeteries and along streams. A person who has been afflicted by *prētayō* is said typically to suffer from poor appetite, to wear dirty clothes, and to constantly dribble spittle. It is also commonly said that when rice from the day before gets lumpy, this is the work of *prētayō*. Lowest of the low, they are propitiated with such degraded objects as spittle (*kela*), blood (*lē*), arrack (*arakku*), marijuana (*gañja*), and opium (*abin*), along with other things—curries (*mālu*), sweets (*kävili*), yams (*ala*), fruit (*palaturu*)—that may be given in offerings to *yakku*.[51]

Another group often said to be associated with *prētayō* are the *bahīravayō* (sing., *bahīravayā*). At least one *ädurā* described them as being of the same group; at any rate, they are both said to be "low" or "contemptible" (*nīca*). They are said to be short and small like a sort of human being (*minis varigayak vagē*). When a house is afflicted by these *bahīravayō*, goods unaccountably disappear (*baḍumūṭṭu ibēma nätivenavā*). Money (*salli*) disappears in the same way. When this happens, people say that the *bahīravayō* are "fetching" (*bahīravayō adinavā*). Offerings are especially made to this group when gem mines are being dug; it is obvious why.

I have left out one plane about which something needs to be said since it also has a bearing on *yaktovil* practice, that of the *dēvatāva*. In Sinhala Buddhism, as Obeyesekere has said, the term *dēvatā* (more typically *dēvatāva* in Matara) is used in a variety of ways. Primarily, he says, it refers to tree deities (as indeed is often the case in the doctrinal texts). The term is also used as an honorific when addressing certain *yakku*, particularly when an *ädurā* wishes to flatter them to make them more obedient–I frequently heard Mahasōna, for instance, referred to as Mahasōn *dēvatāva* (and indeed sometimes even as Mahasōn *dēvatāvun vahanse*, which may be rendered something like the Venerable Godling Mahasōna). However, the most important use of the term is to refer to an ambiguous class of deities, neither completely *yaksayā* nor *dēva*, or some composite of both. From the point of view of the practice of *yaktovil*, the most interesting instance of this kind of figure is Sūniyam. Sūniyam or hūniyam is the word for sorcery and the name of the deity who is typically involved in these practices. Sūniyam is *both* a *dēvatāva* and a *yaksayā*. The way *ädurās* explained this was that when the moon is waxing (*pura*) he is a *dēvatāva*, and when it is waning (*ava*) he is a *yaksayā*.[52]

Sūniyam was an important figure in those *yaktovil* ceremonies I witnessed in the Matara area. There were typically separate sequences in which Sūniyam as *dēvatāva* and Sūniyam as *yaksayā* were addressed. At the beginning of each *yaktovil* ceremony there is a sequence known as the Consecration of the Sūniyam Stand (*Sūniyam Vīdiya Käpakirīma*). One element of this crucial sequence involves the *ädurā* addressing himself to Sūniyam *dēvatāva*, asking for his protection during the course of the dangerous and exacting ceremony. Here Sūniyam is an *iṣṭa dēvatāva*, a personal guardian for the *ädurās*.[53] Later in the *tovil* there is an offering, a *pidēnna* (part of the sequence known as *Kattrīka Hatara Käpakirīma*), this time for Sūniyam *yaksayā* when he is invited to cast his look (*bälma*) on the offerings (*dola pidēni*) being made to him to induce him to remove his malign influence from the afflicted person.

If this structure is a moral one, it is one with an unambiguous source of moral authority: the Buddha. All beings are integrated in the structure through their relation to the authority of the Buddha, and the concept of *varama* organizes the dispersal or delegation or distribution of that authority. The central concept in the Sinhala story about the relation between *yakku* and the Buddha is *varama*. A *varama* is a "warrant," a kind of authorization, a grant of restricted power or influence. Sometimes *ädurās* speak of *aṇavaram* or "commanding warrants." The Buddha gave *yakku* warrants: *buduhāmuduruvō yakkunṭa varam dunnā*. Or, *yakku* obtained warrants from the Buddha: *buduhāmuduruvangen varam labāgattā*. But an authorization to do what? What is this warrant for? It is important to notice that the Buddha is not, in virtue of this *varama* given to *yakku*, positively sanctioning, in the sense of approving, their malicious (*viraya*) and wrathful (*krōdaya*) ways. Remember that it is in the nature of that class of beings to be malevolent and man-eating. The *varama* therefore is not to make people ill as such but rather a restriction on the kind of malevolence and a permit to take the offerings (*dola pideni*) made to them. The *varama* is so much as to say: First of all, you can't do the kinds of things you used to do, namely eat people. Now you can only make them ill; but second, it has to be agreed that having so done you will accept the offerings made to you by the authorized persons, namely *ädurās*, and remove the illnesses. There is in this an interesting mutual recognition of power. *Yakku* acknowledge and of course submit to the greater power of the Buddha, but the Buddha in turn acknowledges that the ways of *yakku* have to be at least partially accommodated. As we will see in chapter 3, this accommodation has important consequences for the practice of *yaktovil* because it opens up the space for a more or less protracted engagement in which the commands (*aṇa*) of the Buddha have to be met, but at a cost of more or less substantial compromises.

The concept of *varama* thus embodies the idea of a power that is granted or allowed by a higher authority for the purpose of carrying out certain activities or exercising a certain influence. It situates power and authority in relation to its sources and parameters in the Sinhala Buddhist universe. In this universe, the Buddha is the ultimate repository of all power. The power exercised by all beings is in some way derived from or authorized by the Buddha. Usually power is understood to be delegated to a god to exercise on behalf of the Buddha. As we have seen, the Buddha authorized Sakra, king of the gods, to look after Sri Lanka, and Sakra in turn gave over the charge to Viṣṇu. Similarly, as I will enlarge upon shortly, the Buddha gave charge of *yakku* to the god Vessamuni. According to Obeyesekere, the notion is derived from the ideology of kingship:

> The king as the supreme lord of the soil (*bhupati*) delegates his authority to others. Subkings and governors of provinces have a warrant or *varan*; they in turn delegate their authority to lesser officials, and so down the line to village headmen. The warrant to exercise authority, or *varan*, is often enshrined in a letter of authority, or *sannasa*. These ideas are transferred to the organization of the pantheon, so that in some ritual

> dramas the deity may actually read out the letter of authority he received from the Buddha.[54]

Indeed, one *ädurā* with whom I talked about *varama,* Äddin Lokuvela, suggested the analogy of village that one has been assigned to look after (*balāgannavā*). In fact, the entire scale of positions of authority as determined by this field of knowledge is mediated by this concept of *varama.* So that *äduräs* are themselves recipients of a sort of *varama.* The *ädurā* takes *varama* from his teacher (*guruvaraya*), who in turn obtained it from his teacher: there are teachers of teachers (*guruvarayinget guruvarayō innavā*). Nevertheless, here too supreme precedence is accorded to the Buddha—*äduräs* will say that they salute (*namaskāra karanavā*)[55] first the Buddha with the clasped hands above the head, and only then their teachers with the hands at face level—because it is ultimately from him that their knowledge and influence derive.

This concept of *varama* is invariably connected with another, that is, *aṇaguṇa,* principally the *aṇaguṇa* of the Buddha (but it may also be the *aṇaguṇa* of a *dēva*). The word *aṇa* means "commands" or "authority"; and *gunaya* means "virtue" or "excellence" or "goodness." I will therefore translate *aṇaguṇa* as "virtuous commands," though it should be understood that it has the direct connotation too of being *commanding*—in the sense of authoritative—virtues. *Aṇaguṇa* conveys in fact the very *force* of the Buddha's moral authority. When the Buddha gives a warrant to exercise a restricted influence (a *varama* in other words), it is presupposed that the recipient (the person who has sought and obtained it) is bound or obliged to observe (*pilipadinavā*) the most excellent commands (*aṇaguṇa*) of the Buddha. There is no *varama* without the implication of *aṇaguṇa.* They participate in one and the same semantic field. One *ädurā* explained these related concepts in the following straightforward way: "*Varama* means obtaining (*labāgannavā*) from you something I do not have; *aṇaguṇa* means the listening (*ahagenīma*) to what is said, and the observation (*pilipadīma*) of what one is told to do." Often in *yaktovil* ceremonies the *ädurā* will ask some such question as: If the Buddha's virtuous commands are valid, what *yaksayā* and what *prētayā* are in this body (*Buduhāmuduruvangē aṇaguṇa valangu nam, mona yaksayek da, mona prētayek da, mē sarīra abhyantarē vāsaya karanne*)? Thus *varama* and *aṇaguṇa* are central to the construction of authority in the discourse of *yakku.*

Yakṣa Samūhaya (The Hosts of *Yakku*)

In a long passage worth quoting, Dandris de Silva Gooneratne introduces the host of *yakku* and their organization:

> The demons or Yakseyo are a class of beings forming a large community, under a government conducted by a King, and subject to laws enacted by him for their control, any infringement of which is followed by severe punishment. Wessamonny, this dreaded king, whose subjects throng every part of the sky, carries in his hand a sword of gold, of such wondrous power, that, when he is displeased with any of his subjects, it flies out of his hand of its own accord, and, after cutting off the heads of a thousand offenders with the rapidity of lightning, returns to his hand again. His laws are such as become the character of his subjects,—cruel, severe, and merciless, death being the rule, and any lighter penalty the exception in the punishment of any crime—burning, boiling, roasting, broiling, impaling, flaying alive, pouring metal down the throat, driving sharp nails into the crown of the head, and a variety of other punishments numbering 32 in all, distinguish his penal code. He has viceroys, ministers, and other officers necessary for the proper administration of his government. Between His Majesty and the mass of his subjects, there is a series of chiefs in regular gradation to each other, each of whom within his own allotted sphere of action exercises almost an unlimited amount of power. He exacts from all his subjects a degree of servile obedience to his will, which not the most despotic of earthly sovereigns ever pretended to claim; and the mere mention of his name is sufficient to make any of his subjects tremble with fear.[56] His subjects spend their time almost always in amusing diversions of various kinds. Many of them at one time were so little under his rule that they openly attacked men, and either devoured them alive bones and all, or sucked their blood. Every Saturday and Wednesday, all the respectable demons attend a sort of pandemonium called a *Yaksa Sabawa*, where each chieftain gives an account of the conduct of those under him to the principal chiefs; after which, they all engage in dancing, singing, playing on musical instruments, and in the display of exploits of skill and dexterity.[57]

(Recall that it was at just such a meeting that Ālavaka was when he received the fateful news from Satagira and Giro Hemavata that the Buddha had gone to his residence to see him.)

Whereas *yakku* as a whole, that is, as a class of beings, obtained *varama* (warrant) from the Buddha in that inaugural event in which they were subjugated, actual control of *yakku* is in the hands of King Vessamuni (Vessamuni *rajjuruvō*) whom I have already mentioned as being Lord of the Northern Quarter and one of the four deities guarding the four corners of Rock Maha Meru. As it was explained to me, in his human lifetimes or *ātmayas*—of which there were a mere nine!—Vessamuni was a man with excellent qualities: he was fearless (*nirbītava*); he had compassion (*karunāva*); he lived without misdeeds (*pav*). In a subsequent rebirth he ascended to the plane of the gods, *divya lōkaya*, and there assumed the task of protecting (*ārakṣākaranavā*) Rock Maha Meru. During that time the Buddha named Pussa was looking for someone to entrust (*bāradenavā*) the host of *yakku* (*yakṣa samūhaya*) whom he had subjugated. Vessamuni appeared a most suitable candidate, and the Buddha gave them over to his superintendence (*pālanaya karanavā*). It was, as one *ädurā* put it, the Buddha's assignment (*pävarīma*) to him. Vessamuni marked off an area of jungle called Visāla Maha Nuvara (the Great City of Visāla) within the boundaries (*sīmava*) of which *yakku* were restricted. Henceforth, *yakku* would be unable to take offerings (*pidēnna*) or sacrifices (*billa*) without first having sought and obtained a *varama* (warrant) to do so from King Vessamuni. Vessamuni, then, has immediate charge of *yakku*, but it is the Buddha's *aṇaguṇa* ("virtuous command") that is the original (*mulva*) and principal (*pradhāna*) command, that is, in other words, the overarching suzerainty under which *yakku*—as indeed all beings—live.

On the accounts of *ädurās* there are an uncountable number of *yakku*. However, there are only a handful of them who are mentioned in the practices—in the songs (*kavi*) and charms (*mantraya*)—employed to influence and control them.[58] Among these, the most frequently mentioned are: Kalu Kumāraya (the Black Prince), who usually appears with his consorts the Rid yaksanin or Riddi Bisavun; Mahasōn *yaksayā* (Mahasōna or Mahasohona, the Great Yaksayā of the Cemeteries); Sūniyam *yaksayā* (the sorcery *yaksayā*); the host of eighteen Sanni *yakku* led by Maha Kōla Sanniyā;[59] and the host of nine Riri *yakku* (the blood *yakku*). Most *yakku*, like Mahasōna, are understood to have obtained *varam* (warrants) from King Vessamuni. But some, for example, Iramudun Riri *yaksayā* (the blood *yaksayā* of the noontime) and Sūniyam *yaksayā*, have birth stories linking them with greater, more powerful beings like Sūriya *divyarāja* (the Divine King Sūriya). Nor do all *yakku* have equal *varam* (warrants). For instance, Mahasōna, Maha Kōla Sanniyā, and the Iramudun Rīri *yaksayā* are often thought of as leaders (*nāyaka*) among *yakku* and to have a greater *varama* than other lesser associates like Aiymāna *yaksayā*, Bille *yaksayā*, or Tota *yaksayā*.

As will have been clear from my discussion of Ālavaka and of *karma*, the moral generative law of the Sinhala Buddhist universe, one cannot speak of the origins or birth of a group of beings called *yakku*. This was reiterated to me again and again: a separate group were not born as *yakku* (*yakuma kiyalā kotasak venama upanne nä*). Indeed, the whole matter of "beginnings" and "endings"—in their cosmological sense—is hardly relevant to Sinhala Buddhists, for whom the universe has a cyclical dimension. *Yakku*, then, are persons (or of course, in principle, other beings, as the Ālavaka story indicates, but humans by and large, as far as I can gather from more expository discussions) who as a result of a wrathful or vengeful *prārthanāva*, their will to vengence for the wrong done to them, are reborn as *yakku*. As it was explained to me on one occasion, "*yaksayā*" is a name customarily given for the harsh work (*tada väḍa*) that is done by them. So that even humans who do dreadful things are sometimes called "*yakṣa*-like" (*yakṣayak vagē*)—a person, for instance, who is given to boisterous behavior such as shouting (*kägahanavā*) and to heedlessly destroying or crushing (*poḍi karanavā*) things, and so on, may well be called *yakṣa*-like. Indeed, any *krōdakārayā* (or "wrath-monger") may be described as evincing the qualities of a *yaksayā*.

Of the many stories of *yakku* I heard in the Matara area, none so vividly conveys Sinhala Buddhist ideas about these malevolent figures as does the story of Maha Kōla Sanniyā, the leader of the eighteen Sanni *yakku*. It is, in a certain sense, the *locus classicus* of the popular *yakṣa* stories. The major ritual to propitiate him and his associates, the Sanni Yäkuma, was rare in Matara, but his story is exemplary. Although versions of the Sanni story have been given by others,[60] I should like to relate one I was told since there are elements—that of *prārthanāva* in particular—in it that are not found in the others, and these elements are precisely those, I judge, that illustrate the distinctive characteristics of this class of beings.

> There was once a king named Sankapāla who ruled the kingdom of Visālā Maha Nuvara. It was a splendid kingdom with metal parapets, stone parapets, walls, dry ditches, and beautiful ditches. There were people from various castes (*jāti*), Brahmanas (*bamunu*), traders (*velaňdā*), farmers (*govi*). It was, it appeared, a kingdom that wanted for nothing (*bohōma kisi deyakin aḍu näti rājyek*). King Sankapāla had five hundred wives (*pan siya bisōvaru*), but none of these queens had conceived a child (*daru gäbak*). As a result, the king was very sad, for there were neither babies to fondle nor a son to inherit the kingdom. He made this known to his ministers, and after the Brahmans who know the auspi-

cious times (*näkat*) were consulted, a woman able to conceive was made the five hundred and first queen. Her name was Princess Asupāla and she was very beautiful. She became the principal queen (*aga bisavun*), and in the following three months because of her merit (*pin*) a baby was conceived.

The other five hundred queens in the meantime were very angry (*hari krōdayi*) with Asupāla. They were no longer well regarded by the king, they were called women of ill omen (*mūsaliyo*), and they even feared for their lives. So they were frightened (*bayayi*) and angry (*viruddayi*). They said nothing to anyone, however, but they plotted among themselves and devised a scheme (*upakramaya*) to have the queen killed. As the baby grew from day to day and month to month, the five hundred queens thought to themselves, "we will eat you (*tō kanavā*)."

There was at the time a flower mother (*mal ammā*) who gave flowers every day to the king. She was an old woman (*mähäli katak*) who had never herself given birth to a child. The queens entertained (*sangraha karanavā*) her and told her a story they had concocted in order bring down Princess Asupāla.

One morning as the king was about to climb on his elephant to go on a tour, the five hundred queens rushed up to him and pleaded with him not to go anywhere. "Great King," they said, "don't leave the palace for seven days. We've had a dreadful dream (*maha darunu hīnaya*) last night." This, of course, is the stratagem the queens had hatched. The unsuspecting king was frightened and asked: "Is this a calamity which has befallen the province? To whom? What is it!? (*raṭaṭa van vipatat da? Kātada? Mokada!?*)." "No, no," said the queens, "it is a danger that is about to befall you." As a result the king decided not to go anywhere. Later, the flower mother came to the palace as usual to deliver flowers. As on other days, she paid obeisance (*namaskāra karanavā*) to the king. But this time, as she was told to do by the queens, she said to him: "Lord Svāmīnī, last night I had a fearful dream." The king, feeling that since he had now been told on separate occasions of an inauspicious dream that there must be truth to it, asked, "What is the dream?" And this is what he was told: "Four mountains of fire (*gini kandu hatara*) are raising the four corners of Visālā Maha Nuvara. Visālā Maha Nuvara is blazing (*piccenavā*)! A big seven-hooded cobra (*maha penagoba hatak äti nāgaya*) is at the head of your bed and biting your head (*sirasaṭa dashṭakaranavā*). Such a fire is blazing that the entire army is lost (*sērama sēnāva nätivenavā*)."

"*Ammaṭa uḍu!*" the frightened king exclaimed. Not knowing that the Brahmans had also been bribed (*allas dīla*) and told what to say by the five hundred queens, he summoned them to interpret the dream. "Great King," they said, "the mountains of fire raising the four corners of Visālā Maha Nuvara are an indication that this city will be destroyed in three months; the seven-hooded cobra, Lord, is the Prince who has been conceived in the womb of your chief queen. Within seven days of his birth, having assumed the form of a *yaksayā*, he will kill you and eat the whole army. This, Lord, is the meaning of the dream."

Immediately, misled by this lie (*boruva*), the king summoned the executioner (*vadakayā*). There was to be no further inquiry into the matter (*vaga vibhāgayak nā*). The executioner was instructed to take Princess Asupāla to the cemetery (*amu sohona*), place her under the Nuga tree, cut her in half, and hang the two pieces on branches facing north and west. So the princess was dragged (*adala gattā*) away from the palace, but as she passed the king she said to him: "Svāmīnī, if without having erred I am killed (*noväräddе märuvot*), the prince who has been conceived in my womb and who has merit (*pin*), will destroy the whole city." The king, however, did not listen. As she was split in two, the unborn prince moved to one side. The pieces were hung as specified, one facing north and the other west. However, within minutes of the executioner's leaving, the pieces fell from the branches, and falling, were reunited (*hā-unā*). The prince remained in this death womb (*mala gäba*) for another twenty-one days, during which the body of his dead mother did not rot (*kunu nove*). At dawn on the morning of the last day of the tenth [i.e., lunar] month the prince was born. When he was born, having nothing else to feed on, he licked the fluids and pus (*ōjas särava leva kanavā*) of the now rotting dead body.

For several years, the prince lived by consuming the fluids of the dead bodies brought to the cemetery. At the age of seven he thought to himself: "I have no one. Neither mother nor father. Why am I like this (*Maṭa kenek ättet nä̆. Maṭa demav piyan ättet nä̆. Moka da man mē*)?" Shortly afterwards, he met the caretaker of the cemetery. The prince seized him and asked him who he was. "I am a servant of King Sankapāla, who rules this country," he said. "It is I who am in charge of this cemetery." "And do you know who my parents are?" asked the prince. The caretaker then remembered Princess Asupāla and thought that this must be her son. He said to the prince: "Look here, Lord, you were fathered by King Sankapāla. Your mother's name is Princess Asupāla. Even though she had done nothing wrong she was killed. You, it appears, are her son." "But why," asked the prince, "was she killed if she had done nothing wrong?" And the caretaker then told him the whole story. At hearing this, the prince thought to himself: I want to go and seize my father and avenge my wrath at my mother's having been killed even though she had done no wrong.

Having no clothes, the prince adorned himself in 108 kinds of branches. Branches of the ironwood tree (*nā atu*), the *bō* tree (*bō atu*), the *käballa* tree (*käballa atu*), the *burula* tree (*burula atu*), the *ruk* tree (*ruk atu*), the margosa tree (*kohomba atu*), and the woodapple tree (*divul atu*), were

> broken and their leaves (*kola*) used for clothes. He then took two dead bodies in his hands, a sword, and jumped onto the flower couch (*mal yahana*) where King Sankapāla was resting. But just as he was about to cut off his father's neck, the Buddha, seeing what was about to happen and determined to do something (*adhisṭhāna karagena*), came there and preached a sermon (*bana*) to the prince (i.e., the *yaksayā*). Then the Buddha said to him: "If you are still doing wrong deeds, do them no more (*Tavat pav karanavā nam, tavat pav karanna epā*)." He then asked him if he knew the reason he had become a *yaksayā*. Not knowing, the Buddha told him that in previous lifetimes (*ātmayas*) he had done good deeds and offered cloth for robes (*kaṭine*) for several Buddhas. But because of the aspiration (*prārthanāva*) to eat dead bodies in order to avenge the wrong done to his mother, he had now been born as a *yaksayā*.

This story clearly has many features in common with the story of Ālavaka. Principally, they both turn on the fundamental notion of *prāthanāva* ("will to be"), in each case a vengeful will to be that follows being the victim of injustice. But the story of Maha Kōla Sanniyā is interesting because it were as though the unborn child comes to embody *his mother's* aspiration for him. A terrible wrong is done to Princess Asupāla, a woman of much virtue. And as she is being taken away to be killed, she says—one should perhaps say she *vows* (though the storyteller does not use the word)—to the King that for this injustice her (and his) son will seek revenge. This vow too is a *prārthanāva,* a profoundly felt aspiration: the Queen *wills* her son to be born as that kind of being whose vocation it is to destroy vengefully, that is, a *yaksayā*. Notably, too, the narrative marks the fact that Queen Asupāla was very virtuous; and it is perhaps significant that it makes her pregnancy a product of her accumulated merit (*pin*), not only suggesting that the barrenness of the other five hundred queens is a consequence of their bad *karma,* but preparing us for the enormity of the wrong that is about to be done to her and the profundity of her desire for vengeance. As in the Ālavaka story, we are to understand that vengeance is a perfectly intelligible response to injustice, but one nevertheless that can (or rather will) have dire consequences. The *yaksayā,* the literal embodiment of this wrathful *prārthanāva,* must live out these consequences, consuming the gory stuff of vengeance: flesh, blood, *ōjas,* etc. Like the Ālavaka and Kālī stories, this too is a compelling Buddhist fable about the nature of wrongs—wrongs begetting wrongs begetting yet more wrongs. And the moral is the same: it is not "justifications" that derive from reasons and causes but the "waters of compassion" that will right wrongs and put an end to vengeance.

Yakku and *Doṣa* (Troubles)

The Buddha's injunction stipulated that the power of *yakku* was to be reduced to making people ill. More precisely, what *yakku* have henceforth done to people is make *dōṣas* (literally, "troubles"). The concept of *dōṣa* is another of those concepts, neither strictly Sinhala nor strictly Buddhist in origin, without which it is impossible to adequately understand the Sinhala discourse of *yakku* and practice of *gurukama*. (We will have to consider this concept further in connection with *diṣṭiya* in the next chapter.)

As Obeyesekere has shown in some detail, the Sinhala Buddhist conception of illness (*rōga, leda*) is based on the classical *tridoṣa* theory of Āyurveda systematized by such eminent sages as Suśruta and Caraka.[61] In this conception the body is constituted of seven *dhātus* or elements: food nutrients, blood, flesh, fat, bone, marrow, and semen. These *dhātus*, constitutive of the entire structure of the body, are themselves modified forms of the five basic entities or elements or *pañcabhūtas*—Ether or Space, Air, Fire, Water, and Earth—of which the universe itself is constituted, and which therefore are contained, in some combination, in all life.[62] These five *bhūtas* appear in the body in the three humors (s. *tun dos*; sk. *tridoṣa*) that do the actual work of regulating its constitution. These humors are: *vāta* (sk. *vāyu* or *vāta*) or "wind," a manifestation of the element of Air; *pitta* (the same in Sanskrit) or "bile," a manifestation of the universal element of Fire; and *sema* (sk. *śleṣma* or *kapha*) or "phlegm," a manifestation of the element of Water. These three *dōṣas* are understood to have distinctive attributes, to reside or originate in particular places in the body, and to have biological, physiological, and psychological effects. *Vāta* (wind), for instance—the seats of which are the large intestine, the pelvic cavity, the bones, the skin, and the thighs—is dry, light, and cool in substance, and perhaps most important is possessed of movement. Principally *vāta* is an energy propelling the body and enabling a variety of vital actions and functions such as the inhalation and exhalation of breath (*prāna*), blinking, the swallowing of food, speaking, heart pulsations, and the proper discharge of excreta. *Vāta* also governs such feelings and emotions as nervousness, fear, anxiety, tremors, and spasms.

The seats of *pitta* (bile) are the stomach, the small intestine, blood, and the eyes. It is wet and fetid. Its distinctive characteristic is heat, so one of its main functions is to irradiate the body with warmth. It governs metabolism, but also intelligence, and is the main humor involved in anger, hate, and jealousy. *Sema* (phlegm) has its seats in the spaces in the body: the stomach, chest, throat, head, and so on. It is mild, cool, heavy, and sticky, and its principal function is to cement the elements of the body, impart moisture to it, and lubricate its joints. *Sema* is the humor involved in attachment, greed, and envy, but it is also expressed in attitudes of calmness, tenderness, forgiveness, and love.

The three humors (*tun dos*)—*vāta* (wind), *pitta* (bile), and *sema* (phlegm)—ensure the physical functioning of the body. What is important to grasp is that these life-supporting forces and faculties in the body's organism are understood to be microcosmic counterparts of those larger, all-pervasive forces in the universe which maintain it through various antagonistic and cooperative activities.[63] A basic principle of health according to Āyurveda follows from this, namely that it is possible to create (or re-create, as the case may be) a balance between the internal energies and forces working in the individual and the larger macrocosmic forces by altering diet and other life habits as the need arises. Ideally, for the body's physical and mental health, these humors should be in a state of equilibrium or balance. And in the general, everyday course of things, one seeks to maintain this homeostasis in a variety of ways, the most important of which is by eating a balance of foods that are "heating"—e.g., meat (*mas*), prawns (*issō*), breadfruit (*del*), mango (*amba*), papaya (*päpol*), and such spices as mustard (*aba*)—and foods that are "cooling"—e.g., milk (*kiri*), milk rice (*kiri bat*), curd (*dīkiri*), ash pumpkin (*alu puhul*), oranges (*doḍan*), king coconut (*tämbili*), and jackfruit (*kos*). But there are other measures as well that are important for the healthy everyday life of the humors: for example, taking adequate precaution during inclement weather (covering the head in rain [*vässa*], for instance, or shading it from the sun's heat [*avva*]), expectorating the excess phlegm that has built up during the night's sleep, and (most important for our purposes) avoiding circumstances known to be detrimental to the organism's balance—in particular, circumstances that may lead to fright (*baya*) and the raising of the temperature of the body.

Illnesses occur, however, when there is an agitation of any or all of these three humors. When this occurs they become *dōṣas* (literally, "troubles"): *vā, pit, sem, tun dos kipilā* (the three humors, wind, bile, and phlegm have become angry or agitated), as Sinhalas are wont to say on such occasions. If the humor of wind (*vāta*) is upset, it may result in a tendency to fall, cheerlessness, and a general loss of activity, thirst, tremors, piercing pains; if the humor of bile (*pitta*) is upset, it can cause burning sensations in heart, throat, and stomach; and if the humor of phlegm (*sema*) is upset, the symptoms are likely to include indigestion, loss of appetite, aches in the joints. Treatment interventions aim at restoring humoral balance by calming the humor that is "irritated" or "agitated." In Āyurvedic practice this is typically done by prescribing foods or decoctions that have a countervailing effect on the agitated humor. So, for instance, the "cooling" decoction *kasāya* may be prescribed where the humor of bile is upset. This figure of the composed body, as we shall see with the following chapter's discussion of the role of eyesight and *diṣṭiya* in the making of *dōṣas*, has its counterpart in the figure of the composed mind (*hita*), and both are crucial to understanding what *gurukama* (and particularly, *yaktovil*) seeks to accomplish.

The concept of *dōṣa*, Obeyesekere points out, provides a link between the medical tradition of Āyurveda and the religious and ritual tradition of Sinhala Buddhists. Sinhala Buddhists use the term to refer to illnesses proper, but also to a wider range of "troubles" and "misfortunes." *Dōṣas* can have either natural or supernatural causes. According to Obeyesekere, some specialists explicitly make a distinction between *amanuṣya dōṣa* (*dōṣas* caused by nonhumans) and *svābhāvika dōṣa* (*dōṣas* with natural causes), or *ätul pantiyē dōṣa* (the internal class of *dōṣas*) and *piṭa pantiyē dōṣa* (the external class of *dōṣas*).[64] *Dōṣas* with natural causes are attended to by the Āyurvedic physician (*vedarāla, vedamahattaya*). Those caused by supernatural agents—*dēvas, yakku, prētayās*—are attended to by the respective ritual specialists. What is important to note, though, is that whether the cause is natural or supernatural the result invariably is a condition in which the three humors are out of equilibrium.

All deities in the Sinhala Buddhist pantheon, malevolent and benevolent alike, can cause misfortunes, *dōṣas* which may afflict an individual, a household, or even a whole village. Those caused by the anger of a *dēva* or god are known as *dēva dōṣa* (or *deviyannē dōṣa*). An individual who has failed to make good a vow (*bāra*) may be struck with illness, or a village that has not held an annual rite may be struck with plague or drought. In either case a *kapurāla* will have to perform certain rituals—in the case of the individual to renew the contract with the god, in the latter perhaps a *gammaḍuva* to rid the community of the affliction. Obeyesekere has discussed the way in which rituals in the *gammaḍuva* like water cutting (*diya käpīma*) and fire walking (*gini pāgima*) are explicitly about controlling the elements in the universe that are upset, namely, water and fire, respectively.[65]

The *dōṣas* caused by *yakku* (typically, various illnesses depending on the *yaksayā* involved) are known as *yakṣa dōṣas*. Once it is diagnosed that the *dōṣa* is in fact caused by a *yaksayā*, an *ädurā* will have to perform some kind of *gurukama* (or ritual for controlling the effects of *yakku*) the essential task of which is to restore the humoral balance of the afflicted person (*āturayā*). Each *gurukama* practice (I should say, for reasons I give in chapter 2, each therapeutic *gurukama* practice) is concerned precisely with the restoration of humoral balance. I will take this up in detail in chapter 7, but consider the following example. A person has been struck by the malign influence of the Mahasōna and is in a state of agitation, fright, and suffering from fever (*una*). One of the preliminary things an *ädurā* may do is to mix some turmeric (*kaha*) in coconut water and, after uttering the appropriate *mantrayas* (charms), give it to the person to drink. Turmeric water (*kaha diyara*) is a well-known "cooling" decoction. Perhaps more important where the restoration of humoral balance is concerned are the head-to-feet verses called *sirasapādaya* sung in every *yaktovil* ceremony for making the *dōṣa* descend from the head to the feet (I describe this in chapter 7).

The mean spirits of the dead, *prētayās*, also cause misfortunes known as *prēta dōṣa*. These may be illnesses, but are very often troubles that afflict whole households, like domestic quarrels or financial woes. This will require an *ädurā* to perform a *prēta pidēnna* or offering to *prētas* to rid the person or household of these misfortunes. Other categories of *dōṣa* include: *graha dōṣa*, troubles arising from inauspicious planetary influence and requiring a ceremony called *bali tovil*; *sūniyam dōṣa*, illnesses and other misfortunes resulting from sorcery and which may require a ceremony called a *sūniyam sāntiya* to remove the influence; *äsvaha*, *kaṭavaha*, and *hōvaha dōṣas*, illnesses arising from bad eye, bad mouth, and bad thoughts, respectively; and, importantly, *karma dōṣa*, misfortunes arising from bad *karma*. As Obeyesekere notes, these several categories are not mutually contradictory. "Thus, my illness may be due to *preta doṣa* (i.e., intrusion of a mean spirit). However, the *preta* may have been put into my body by the action of a sorcerer, *hūniyan doṣa*. This in turn had a particularly strong effect because of my astrologically bad times, *graha doṣa*, and this is surely due to my bad *karma* from a previous birth, *karma doṣa*."[66]

This concept of troubles and illness raises the interesting question: in what sense (if at all) are Sinhala Buddhists culpable in their becoming victims of the malign influence of *yakku*? As Sinhalas have it, a god, Kataragama for instance, may be angry because an individual has not kept a vow (*bāra*) after securing for him his request, and he may afflict the person with an illness; or Pattinī may be angry because a village has not performed an annual rite and she may afflict the community with drought. These afflictions, it is important to notice, are punitive in the sense that they are, straightforwardly, punishments for transgressions of what may be called a compact between the just god and the petitioner. With *dōṣas* caused by *dēvas*, therefore, it is legitimate to say that the afflicted person is culpable in a moral (blameworthy) sense. He or she has offended the god. This is not the case with the *dōṣas* caused by the malevolent supernatural agents, that is, by *yakku* and *prētas*. The *dōṣa* caused by *yakku*—*yakṣa dōṣa*—are not punishments in the sense that they are not penalties for some offense or transgression or fault. *Yakku* merely take advantage of anyone, *whenever* they can, during those abbreviated periods in which the Buddha has allowed their malign power efficacy (I discuss this notion in the next chapter). If you happen to be passing a graveyard alone late at night, the Mahasōna may well use this opportunity to "jump" (*paninavā*) at you, as people say, but this is not on account of, or as punishment for, your moral behavior. True, it is in the *final* instance the result of bad *karma*, which is itself a product of prior misdeeds. It is only in this sense—the permanent sense in which a Buddhist is *always* responsible for what befalls him or her—that one is responsible for becoming the victim of a *yaksayā*'s malevolence.

This survey should, I hope, be sufficient to indicate something of the place of such concepts as *prārthanāva*, *karma*, *varama*, *aṇaguṇa*, and *dōṣa* in the discursive field in which knowledges about *yakku* are constituted. As a preliminary to the next chapter's concerns, though, I would like to reiterate that the concepts of *dōṣas* and the three humors (*tun dos*) construct a distinctive notion of the Sinhala body and what it is that *yakku* (and other beings) potentially do to it. I will return to this in relation to the concept of *diṣṭiya* in the following chapter, but it needs to be emphasized that central to this conception is a body ideally balanced and regulated, a body whose processes and forces are in homeostasis. *Yakku* make illnesses. And they do so because their actions have the indirect effect of upsetting one or other of the three humors (*tun dos*) and disrupting the body's equilibrium. For well-being to be restored, these humors have to be returned to homeostasis. This, we shall see, is the task of *yaktovil*.

Chapter 2

Malign Glances: *Diṣṭiya* and the Ethics of Composure

By the Buddha's intervention—according to the local tradition in which I worked—*yakku* were allowed but a curtailed and much-restricted margin within which to pursue their malevolent ends in Lankā: they could make people ill so long as they then accepted the offerings made to them and removed the affliction. The marking out of such a space of delimited efficacy, I have noted earlier in connection with Ālavaka, is in fact characteristic of the way in which the *yakā-* (*yakkha-*) figure is positioned in Theravāda narratives. Among Sinhala Buddhists, however, not only was a restriction imposed, but most important perhaps, by the Buddha's intervention the *mode* of malevolent action of these *yakku* was also circumscribed; indeed, it was radically transformed. In their long, immemorial reign in Lankā—so this tradition has it—*yakku* had been accustomed to sating their craving for flesh and blood by seizing and eating human beings with impunity. The Buddha put an end to this lawless liberty by expelling *yakku* from Lankā and drawing an impenetrable *sīmāva*, or boundary, around it, preventing them thereby from *physically* reentering the now favored island, *dhamma dīpa*, the island of his Doctrine. But in order, as it were, to partially accommodate these malevolent beings, or at least to contain these designs in a diminished form and within a designated field of efficacy, the ever generous and compassionate Buddha permitted them a distinctive modus operandi. Henceforth, *yakku* were allowed only to cast their glances or "look" (*bälma*) upon Lankā and its inhabitants—to look at (or upon) them, as one *ädurā* significantly put it, as "through the eye of needles (*idikatu siddrāven*)." And it is this "looking" which, from that inaugural day to this, has constituted the register of the malign power of *yakku* in Lankā.

On the Buddha's authority, moreover, this "looking" was itself confined to short and specific periods during four "watches" (*jāmaya* or *yāmaya*) of the Sinhala day—at 6:00 during the first watch of the night (*pera jāmaya*), at 12:00 during the midnight watch (*mäda jāmaya*), at 6:00 during the dawn watch (*alu jāmaya*), and at 12:00 during the midday watch (*daval jāmaya*).[1] At these times the malevolent presence of the "look" of *yakku* is especially likely to be around, particularly in those places they are known to favor—cemeteries especially, rivers or ponds, and crossroads—and Sinhalas are apt to be weary of traveling alone during these hours. As that incomparable nineteenth-century observer of Sinhala cultural practice, Dandris de Silva Gooneratne, noted: "A Singhalese never travels during these Yamas, if he can help it; but if not, he takes care not to go alone (unless it be the midday Yama), unless the country is very thickly inhabited, for solitary travellers are most exposed to the attacks of the demons."[2] Also, since the "look" of *yakku* has malevolent efficacy at specific periods more so than at others, these four *jāmayas* are especially favorable for those practices (*gurukama, ädurukama*) that seek to influence *yakku*. These are referred to as the "*samayama* times" (*samayan velā*): *händä samayama* or evening ceremony time, when most of the large-scale *yaktovil* ceremonies begin; *maha (rä) samayama* or midnight ceremony time, when major offerings are made and dances are performed for the main *yaksayā* being propitiated (e.g., Maha Kalu Kumāraya in the Maha Kalu Kumāra Samayama, the Mahasōna in the Mahasōn Samayama, and the several Sanni Yakku in the Sanni Yäkuma); and the *iramudun samayama* or midday ceremony time, the time to make offerings to that most feared of *yakku*, the Iramudun Rīri Yaksayā.

The "look," then, is the medium of the malevolence of *yakku*. When talking about the "look" of the *yaksayā*, Sinhalas most often use the term *diṣṭiya*, a complex concept indeed, but which may be glossed as the "essence" and "energy" of the "look" of the *yaksayā*. In this chapter, my central concern is to describe this concept, *diṣṭiya*, in relation to what I shall call an ethics of composure among Sinhala Buddhists—that is, and with an obvious indebtedness to Foucault's later work,[3] what I understand to be a Sinhala Buddhist practice of care for the composure of the body (*äṅga*) and the mind (*hita*). In Buddhist culture composure is a good, its cultivation a virtue. For monks, of course, those committed to the Noble Eightfold Path (that is, the Path from suffering to *nirvāna*), Right Effort (*sammā vāyāma*), Right Mindfulness (*sammā sati*), and Right Concentration (*sammā samādhi*)—the constituents of the practice of meditation—comprise this ethic in a systematic and elaborated way. But in the everyday life of ordinary Buddhists this ethic forms part of the most routine of habits—keeping a dietary balance of "heating" and "cooling" foods, for example, is one such elementary practice, as is the practice (which I will discuss later) of keeping the mind protected against the possibility of fright. The thing to bear in mind is that, as I discussed in chapter 1 in relation to Āyurvedic theory, for Sinhalas, the mental and the bodily are interwoven, distinguishable to be sure, but in terms of the registration of effects, inseparable.

If in the previous chapter I was interested in the way *yakku* are positioned in a structure of knowledges about what kinds of beings inhabit the universe, in this chapter I am more interested in the moral economy of their malevolent effects on those afflicted by them—malevolent effects transmitted, as I have said, in the medium of the "look," of eyesight. For Sinhalas there is a relation between composure and physical and mental well-being, and, conversely, between the disruption of this composure and "troubles," "misfortunes," "illnesses"—that is, the range of conditions covered by the concept *dōṣa*. What interests me particularly in this chapter is the way the malevolent effects of the "look" of *yakku* are understood to disturb the composure or balance of the body and the mind. First, then, I will discuss *diṣṭiya* in relation to Sinhala conceptions of the body, especially as it relates to the concept of the three humors (*tun dos*) and "troubles" (*dōṣa*) explored in chapter 1. And second, I will discuss *diṣṭiya* in relation to certain Sinhala conceptions of subjectivity, particularly those that intersect the difficult but indispensable concept of *tanikama* (roughly, "aloneness"). Again, I should say that no claim is made here to an exhaustive description of *diṣṭiya*'s semantic range. My aim is primarily to indicate the importance of a distinctive notion of eyesight among Sinhalas—eyesight as an obtrusive flow, eyesight as a ray of energy or a force, eyesight as potentially disturbing in a way simultaneously moral and physical—and something of the place of this conception in a Sinhala ethics of composure. So before focusing my attention on *diṣṭiya*, it will be useful to consider some aspects of the broader place of the figure of eyesight in Sinhala cultural discourse; for it seems to me that the concept of *diṣṭiya* participates in a larger and constitutive cultural discourse about eyesight among Sinhala Buddhists.

Eyesight in Sinhala Cultural Discourse

The figure of eyesight is a powerful register for Sinhalas, as indeed it is for other South Asians.[4] Something of the nature of this power can be illustrated, I think, in an interesting story I would like to relate. It is not about *yakku*, however, but about a *dēva* (god), Uppalavanna (Upulvan) or Viṣṇu, whose eyesight is legendary to people of Devinuvara—literally, remember, "city of the *dēva*"—on account of its heroic resistance to the Portuguese colonizers in the late sixteenth century. The story was told to me on more than one occasion by some of the more elderly residents of this ancient town. It seems to me to demonstrate a distinctive discursive practice through which Sinhalas construct and narrativize particular aspects of their cultural life—in the case at hand, through which they fashion a distinctive historical memory. What I want to suggest is that if cultural discourses and practices are marked by the idiom in which they are lived and articulated, certain local discourses and practices of the Sinhalas are constituted through a troping of eyesight. Here is the story:

> In Devinuwara, the King of the Southern Kingdom of Ruhunu, Dapulusen, once offered a reward to any man who could carve, out of the red sandalwood he would make specially available for the purpose, an image of the deity of the town, Uppalavanna. Many tried, and as many failed. In time, however, there appeared a man of humble bearing who made known his desire to try as others had. He shut himself in the room with the sandalwood and there remained for days on end. At length the King himself, growing curious and impatient, went to inquire as to the progress. He opened the door, and there before him stood a nine-foot sandalwood image of Uppalavanna. The man, however, was nowhere to be seen. Nor was there any evidence, in the way of wood shavings, say, of the sandalwood having actually been worked. All who saw were astonished. The image was then taken to the top of a small hill [the site, it is said, of the original *dēvālē* or shrine-house of this deity],[5] and there installed such that it *looked* directly over the southernmost tip of the island. In time the Portuguese came and conquered the maritime areas of Lankā. They came to Devinuwara. But try as they might they could not sail across the line of the deity's eyesight. Enraged, they committed an atrocity upon the image, cutting the legs so that the sight of the deity now fell upon the ground. The deity was thus rendered powerless to stop their rampage. Or so the Portuguese thought. Eventually, in retreat from their colonial successors, the Dutch, the Portuguese ransacked the ancient town of Devinuwara. They loaded their ships with the loot. And, of course, they loaded the red sandalwood image of Uppalavanna whose eyesight had so impeded their marauding designs. But taking flight, their ships sank. And the sandalwood image of Uppalavanna floated around the western coast of Lankā, beaching itself at the town of Chilaw. From there it was taken to the

great Rock Temple at Dambulla in the central highlands. And even today it can still be seen there.[6]

The eyesight of Sinhala Buddhist deities, therefore, is invested with an energy, an uncanny force—in the case of the deity of this suggestively anticolonial narrative, Uppalavanna, a protective energy. Uppalavanna's unblinking sight, stretching out over the ocean, formed a steadfast, transparent wall, a sort of beam of eye energy, preventing the trespass of the colonial invaders. Now one of the things that is particularly interesting about the economy of this narrative is the way in which it locates knowledge of the *source* of the obstructing force. The narrative, we notice, attributes to the Portuguese themselves the knowledge that the source of their obstruction is to be found in the eyesight of the image of the deity. It is, for instance, not a native Sinhala who is made to divulge to them this critical piece of local knowledge. Rather, that it is *eyesight* that constitutes the source of the obstruction is something treated as *self-evident*; so that it functions narratalogically as an ingenious self-confirmation to Sinhalas of the potency of eyesight, of the fact that eyesight constitutes a zone of energy and force. But notice too something else: the distinctive *modality* of this obstacle of eyesight. It is not that the Portuguese are, let us say, *seen* by Uppalavanna while trying to secret their way into Devinuwara, and that their *presence* is then made known by the pool of divine light suddenly surrounding them. The Portuguese are not *revealed* to Sinhala Buddhists in their wicked presence. For although, as we shall see in a moment, the figure of sight in the cultural conception of Sinhala Buddhists is indeed linked to a dialectic of moral darkness and moral light (through the Buddhist concept of *diṭṭhi* [p.] or *driṣṭi* [s.]), the level of moral eye-effects produced by this narrative is not one of revelation so much as one of *impedance*. The eyesight of the deity, Uppalavanna, has the consistency of a beam and the intensity of a powerful energy that forms a *physically* impassable barrier. The Portuguese in the narrative are not detected; they are, quite literally, *blocked* by divine eyesight.

In an interesting article on visual interaction in Hindu practices in India, Lawrence Babb discusses just this kind of cultural troping of the register of eyesight, the construction of eyesight as a beamlike energy that contains the essence or power of the deity.[7] Hindu devotees, Babb suggests, want both *to see* their deities and *to be seen* by them. The eyes of deities in Hindu religious practice are central to the interaction between worshiper and deity; and this is so because the eyes are associated with the very "life" of the deity. This association between the eyes and the "life" of the deity is suggestively conveyed by Diana Eck in a passage relevant particularly to the Sinhala Buddhist case of images of the Buddha (discussed below):

> In the later Hindu tradition when divine images began to be made, the eyes were the final part of the anthropomorphic image to be carved or set in place. Even after the breath of life (prana) was established in the image there was the ceremony in which the eyes were ritually opened with a golden needle or with the final stroke of a paintbrush. This is still common practice in the consecration of images, and today shiny oversized enamel eyes may be set in the eye-sockets of the image during this rite. The gaze which falls from the newly opened eyes of the deity is said to be so powerful that it must first fall upon some pleasing offering, such as sweets, or upon a mirror where it may see its own reflection. More than once has the tale been told of that powerful gaze falling upon some unwitting bystander, who died instantly of its force.[8]

So the presence of the Hindu deity (or of its image) is virtually synonymous with its facility and power of sight; and, moreover, if sight is associated with the "life" of the deity, the eye itself is also understood to be *alive*. What is especially interesting for us is the way in which the deity is understood to be able to *transmit* its effects. Underlying the belief in the efficacy of eyesight, Babb suggests, is a particular conception of "seeing," which he describes as an "extrusive flow-of-seeing that brings seer and seen into actual contact."[9] Eck makes a similar observation when she says that, in the Hindu context, "seeing is a kind of touching,"[10] and she quotes a significant passage from the work of art historian Stella Kramrisch to the same effect: "Seeing, according to Indian notions, is a going forth of the sight towards the object. Sight touches it and acquires its form. . . . While the eye touches the object, the vitality that pulsates in it is communicated" (p. 9). This idea of the "communication" of the "pulsating vitality" of the eye to what the glance is cast upon, is, as we shall see, very important for the Sinhala Buddhist understanding of the "look" of their own deities, both benevolent and malevolent.

On this view, then, seeing effects a form of contact, at once moral and physical. For, of course, being the "life" of a moral agent, the sight of the eyes of the deity is alive with *moral*—good or bad—effects. The deity's sight can have benevolent or malevolent effects on what is seen, and this depends, of course, on whether the glance is one of compassion or one of anger. As Babb puts it later in the same article quoted earlier: "The point is that in the Hindu world, 'seeing' seems to be an outward-reaching process that in some sense actually engages (in a flow-like way . . .) the objects seen. Therefore glances can affect the objects at which they are directed, and bad glances can have harmful effects" (p. 393). More generally, what the moral character of this vitality makes clear is the relation between the eyes and the mind, or rather between sight and *intention*. Underlying these eye-effects, as Jan Gonda argues, is the *mind* and especially the quality and force of its intentions.[11] The eye and the mind therefore have a profoundly integral relation. A bad or poisonous intention (envy, hatred, revenge) or a benevolent one (compassion, care, love), these are transmitted in the medium of eyesight. This notion is important for understanding the positioning of *yakku* and the malevolence of their eyesight.

It is also important to mention another aspect of the relation between sight or seeing and the mind; this is the pleasure the mind derives when the eyes alight upon or contemplate pleasant sights—because this is important too for understanding certain sequences in *yaktovil* performance. Eck has instructively discussed the central place of images in Hindu religious practice and the joy involved in looking at them. For Sinhala Buddhists also, the very contemplation of certain iconic images, particularly those of the Buddha or gods, or of aniconic images of the Buddha such as a *bō* tree or *stūpa,* gives the mind joy or gladness or happiness, that is, *prītiya*.[12] More generally, though, what is presented to the eyes is understood to have mind-effects, and because of the integral relation between the mind (*hita*) and the physical body (*äňga*), *dōṣa*-effects too. An agitated mind should look upon pleasant images—preferably images of the Buddha or of gods, but not necessarily, other, more "secular" objects like movies will do—because these can have the effect of stirring pleasant thoughts and thus restoring calm and composure, both to the troubled mind and to the agitated humors. I will return to this relation later on in this chapter, and its importance will become clearer in chapter 7.

As the story of Uppalavanna suggests, among Sinhala Buddhists in Sri Lanka one finds a similarly distinctive conception of the power of eyesight. Robert Knox, that indefatigable seventeenth-century English sailor who was held captive in the Kandyan provinces for nearly twenty years, was perhaps one of the first Europeans to make some mention of its importance—as indeed of the importance of much else—for Sinhala religious practice. In his account of the practices he observed among the Sinhalas, *An Historical Relation of Ceylon*, published in London in 1681,[13] Knox noted the preoccupation with the eyes in the fashioning of images of Sinhala Buddhist deities. "Before the Eyes are made," he wrote in a well-known passage, "it is not accounted a God, but a lump of ordinary Metal, and thrown about the Shop with no more regard than anything else. But when the Eyes are to be made, the Artificer is to have a good gratification, besides the first agreed upon reward. The Eyes being formed, it is thenceforward a God" (p. 155).[14] In fact, however, not only deities but *all* figures in Sinhala Buddhist cosmology are attributed at least a potential power or force in the register of eyesight. Images of the Buddha (*budupilimaya*) too, for instance, are understood to have a power at the level of eyesight. As Richard Gombrich's description of a *nētra pinkama* ("eye-laying ceremony") suggests, the eyes of Sinhala images of the Buddha—as with those of Hindu images of their gods described by Eck—are invested with a considerable and potentially harmful force.[15] Performing the rites of the eye-laying ceremony (the last and consecrating act in the fashioning of a Buddha statue in which the "eyes" are painted on), much care has to be taken not to neglect the various precautionary procedures (e.g., the use of a mirror to deflect the direct glance of the image) in order to avoid the effects of *vas dos* (literally, "poisonous troubles").[16]

This cultural conception of eyesight, however, extends to the "look" of human beings (*manusya*) as well, and here the relation between eye and mind is particularly clear. The "look" of humans is at least potentially imbued with a malign energy. In certain situations, this malign energy emanates from the eyes of people and, "touching" (*vadinavā*) another person or thing, causes "troubles," *dōṣas*. As we saw in chapter 1, this malign energy is called *äsvaha* (literally, "eye poison"), and the effected condition is known as *äsvaha dōṣa* (literally, "eye poison troubles").[17] One generally cannot determine in advance the persons having this facility, although certainly they are typically thought to be women. On one occasion though, I was told that these malevolent people are recognizable, at least in part, by the special quality of their spittle (*kela*). It tends to be sticky, the *ädurā* said, adhering to the lips while the person speaks: *tolen toleṭa kela nūl ädena vagē venavā katakaranakoṭa* (when speaking the spittle is pulled from lip to lip like thread). The victims, at any rate, are usually little children, women, and shopkeepers (*mudalālis*)—basically in that order. *Äsvaha* is linked to envy and the malevolent intentions it inspires. Commonly, it is said to be the result of desire (*āsāva*) for something *seen* but not possessed. The case of a woman's unfulfilled desire to have a baby is often illustratively used—in fact almost invariably so. The scenario might be as follows. A woman who does not have a baby visits a household in which there is a delightful little baby. She looks and thinks desirously (*āsāven*): "this baby is so very beautiful; it has no illnesses (*mē babā harima lassanayi. Kisima rōgayak nā*)." She then compliments the parents accordingly and departs. But no sooner has she left than little bumps (*bibili*) appear on the baby's face and body. The parents of this baby will be in no doubt that they have been the victim of envious "looks."[18]

There is another, perhaps more important, facet of *äsvaha*, however, which emphasizes in an interesting and very illuminating way a relation between desire (*āsāva*) and anger (*krōdaya*), and between these two and the *transmission of an effect* in the medium of the energy of eyesight. This is particularly well illustrated in the following passage, again quoting from a conversation with S. A. Piyasena:

> Now when I see a beautiful thing (*lassana deyak*) a desire for it occurs to me (*maṭa ēkaṭa āsāvak hitenavā*). The desire having been formed, I think, "I don't have a beautiful thing like that (*ē vagē lassana deyak maṭa nā*)." Because of that I become angry (*krōdayak hitaṭa haṭagannavā*). Because of my bad intention (*tamangē naraka cētanāva*) and bad thoughts (*naraka hitīma*), that anger causes a humor to become upset (*dōṣayak mēvavenava*).[19] The person seen is touched by an ill effect (*dōṣayak vadinavā*). By thinking about that [i.e., the beautiful thing] a power touches the thing that is seen (*ē gäna hitīmen pavar ekak vadinavā ara däkkapu deyaṭa*). Then the thing becomes spoiled (*narak venavā*). It becomes unsightly (*avalakṣana gahanavā*).

This passage provides a very clear sense of the action of (the energy of) eyesight. Anger, an unwholesome mental state, arising (in this case) as a result of desire, causes one of the humors (*dōṣas*) of which the body is composed to become agitated. The ill effects of this agitation (also, remember, referred to as *dōṣas*) are *transmitted* by the act (and in the medium) of "seeing" the object or person. So transmitted, this energic ill effect adversely affects what is seen. This, of course, recalls Kramrisch's remarks quoted earlier that the "vitality" of the eyesight is what is communicated when the eyes are cast upon an object.

In the Sinhala sense, therefore, "sight" is not a mere passive registration of external objects in the physical or reflecting eye of the inert seer—as if the "eye" were simply an organ receptacle catching the refracted light off the objects passing within its field. Nor, on the other hand, is sight the simple inverse of this in which the "inner" or "psychological" eye constructively perceives and thereby establishes its field of vision. One might say that for Sinhalas the visual metaphor is not caught up in a problematic of "representation" where what is at stake is the "registration" or "reflection" of an image.[20] These latter metaphors belong perhaps to another cultural discourse elsewhere, and organize a different relation between sight, knowledge, and physical and mental dispositions. But they are far removed from a Sinhala conception. As with the Hindu practices Babb and Eck describe, the image of "sight" and "seeing" in Sinhala cultural conception is rather that of an internally generated activity, a mobile *energy*, a continuous flow, precipitated *outward*, as it were, from the seer *to* objects. And these objects, it should be understood, are not merely brought within the field of the seer's gaze, illuminated (in either the active or contemplative sense) as though to be read, but *brought into contact with the force of its energy*. Among Sinhalas (as will become clear with my discussion of *diṣṭiya*), sight is something that can actually, deliberately, be "put" (*lanavā*) on, or, more vividly, "cast" (*halanavā*) upon, an object by the seer so as to be able to "touch" (*vadinavā*) it. Sight can be deliberately placed and displaced, but this *place*-ment does not imply thereby a detachment or interruption of its flow of energy. This is important to bear in mind. You will recall that Uppalavanna's eyesight was not cut off (he was not, for example, blinded) but rather "deflected," *maga harinavā*—a concept of vital importance for understanding the practice of *yaktovil*.

Yakṣa Diṣṭiya

The malign eyesight of *yakku* is only a special class of this wider Sinhala conception of eyesight, and we can now turn to a more focused discussion of it. In talking about *yakku* and the feared malevolence of their eyesight, I have suggested, people most often use the term *diṣṭiya* or *diṣṭi*. Indeed, it seems to me that *diṣṭiya* is the most vital concept involved in the whole Sinhala Buddhist discourse of *yakku* and practice of *yaktovil*. Seeking to understand it, therefore, is to my mind of the first importance. This, however, is less easy than it may immediately appear, for *diṣṭiya* is one of those cultural concepts that are not readily narrativizable.[21] If you ask an ordinary villager, or indeed, for that matter, a practiced *ädurā*, what *diṣṭiya* is (*diṣṭiya kiyanne mokkadda*?), the response is most likely to be something like: "*diṣṭiya kiyanne bälma*," that is, "*diṣṭiya* means the look." This is certainly the case—*diṣṭiya* does indeed refer to the "look." But this popular formulation, I think, is rather a shorthand way of giving expression to what Sinhala Buddhists have no need to articulate explicitly. If, however, we examine closely the semantic field in which this concept operates discursively in relation to the nature of the effects *yakku* are understood to have, I think that we may be able to discern some of the ways in which it is understood to work. This will be the task of the following sections of this chapter. *Diṣṭiya*, I shall suggest, is most usefully understood as the malign *energy* or essence of the eyesight of *yakku*. (In point of fact, *diṣṭiya* is not always malign, nor is it always associated with *yakku*. One can, for instance, speak of *dēva diṣṭiya*, meaning the beneficent essence or energy of the eyesight of a *dēva* [god]). And, as we will see, it is possible to say that *diṣṭiya*, this malign energy of eyesight, is virtually synonymous with the very *presence* of *yakku* themselves.

It may be useful to begin, however, by looking at the field of associations attached to the word *diṣṭiya* and words related to it. The primary meaning given by Wijayatunga's *Practical Sinhala Dictionary* (*Prāyōgika Sinhala Ṣabdakōṣaya*)[22] is "*penīma*," the verbal noun of "appear"; and the secondary meanings given are *bhūtāvēśaya* (from the two words, *bhūta*, the general name for all malign supernatural beings, and *āvēśaya*, which may be glossed as "trance" until I take it up later in this chapter), and *driṣṭiya*, the more nearly Sanskrit form of the word which I turn to below.[23]

The Pāli and Sanskrit sources of the word *diṣṭiya* are more suggestive still, setting before us an almost endless list of senses, relations, and associations, from which we can nonetheless distill—at least for our purposes—a few central themes. The Pāli word is *diṭṭhi*. Under this entry in their Pāli-English dictionary, T. W. Rhys Davids and William Stede give us the following: "view, belief, dogma, theory, speculation, esp[ecially] false theory, groundless or unfounded opinion."[24] For canonical Buddhism, however, the word takes on an added complexity.

While all "views" are ultimately disvalued, a distinction is drawn between two kinds of "views": *sammā diṭṭhi* and *micchā diṭṭhi*. Continuing, Rhys Davids and Stede state that "the right, the true, the best doctrine is as *sammā d[iṭṭhi]* the first condition to be complied with by anyone entering the Path. As such *sammā d[iṭṭhi]* is opposed to *micchā d[iṭṭhi]* wrong views or heresy" (p. 156). In Buddhist conception, then, there is an explicit relation between "seeing" or "view" and knowledge or cognition. As Rhys Davids and Stede put it, "Since sight is the principal sense of perception as well as apperception . . . that which is seen is the chief representation of any sense-impression" (p. 155). Therefore, "knowing" or "cognition" is not only linked to a visual metaphor, but this latter representation is always, in a Buddhist context, part of a network of normative and ethical practices. This is worth bearing in mind.

The Sanskrit form of the word is *dṛiṣṭi*. Sir Monier Monier-Williams's invaluable Sanskrit-English dictionary[25] gives us the following: "seeing, viewing, beholding, (also with the mental eye)"; "sight, the faculty of seeing"; "the mind's eye, wisdom, intelligence"; "regard, consideration"; "view, notion"; "(with the Buddhists) a wrong view; theory, doctrine, system . . . eye, look, glance" (p. 492). Then there are such compound forms as the following: *dṛiṣṭi-dōṣa* is given as "the evil influence of the human eye"; *dṛiṣṭi-nipāta*, as " 'the falling of the sight', look, glance"; *dṛiṣṭi-pa*, as "drinking with the eyes"; *dṛiṣṭi-bāna*, as " 'eye-arrow', a glance, a leer"; *dṛiṣṭi-viṣa* as " 'having poison in the eyes', poisoning by means of the mere look" (p. 492). These compound expressions are particularly interesting because, as we shall see, similar ones form part of the Sinhala conception of the malign action of *diṣṭiya*.

In the scholarly literature on Sinhala religion and ritual, there are a number of references to *diṣṭiya*. Curiously, not as many, nor as substantial a discussion, as one might have thought would be the case for so central a concept.[26] Still, the references are very useful, and it is worth reviewing them briefly. In the earliest that I know of, Dandris de Silva Gooneratne makes the following keen observation:

> Although demons are said to shew themselves in these ways to men [i.e., in various apparitions], yet the opinion of those, who may be called the more orthodox of the demon-worshippers, is that these apparitions are not the demons themselves, but certain puppet-like spectres, which they create and present to the eyes of men, in order to frighten them; that the demons themselves are millions of miles distant from the

> earth; and that on these occasions of sending forth these spectres, and on every other occasion, whether during demon ceremonies, or at any other time when they are supposed to be present, they do not come themselves, but send their *dristia*, with or without the spectres, according to the circumstances of each case, or merely according to their own whim. By *dristia*, which means literally "sight," or "look," is meant that, although they are not personally present, yet they have the power of "looking" at what is going on below, and of doing and attending to every thing required of them, as if they were actually present. This opinion however is one, which is confined to the more learned of the demon worshippers; the more ignorant believe that the demons themselves are bodily present at these scenes, although they assume some sort of disguise, whenever they choose to make themselves visible to men.[27]

This penetrating passage contains a number of insights. First of all, as Gooneratne suggests, *yakku* cannot themselves be bodily present in Lankā (which we understand from our previous discussion of the nature of the Buddha's intervention and his *varam*) and so present themselves, so to speak, by "send[ing] their *dristia*." Moreover, though unable to present themselves bodily, they are able to make use of various apparitions and "spectres." For instance, the *yaksayā* known as Mahasōna makes use of dogs (*balla*) and monitor lizards (*talagoya*), and the Riri Yaksayā makes use of monkeys (*vaňdurā*). Finally, as Gooneratne indicates, these notions form part of an esoteric local knowledge. Whereas as most people I broached the subject with in the Devinuwara-Matara area knew that *diṣṭiya* meant "the look," only *äduräs* elaborated the fine distinctions—and even here there were substantial differences in extent of knowledge.

Perhaps the first modern anthropological reference occurs in Gananath Obeyesekere's important essay, "The Ritual Drama of the *Sanni* Demons," where he writes:

> Yaksha misfortunes arise when demons cast their eyes (*bälma*) on a patient. This can happen in various ways. For example the demon may himself cast his eyes on a person and thereby make him ill. Alternatively, a demon may be made to do so by another person, a sorcerer; for according to Sinhalese magic, ingredients used in sorcery contain the essence of the deity. When a demon's look falls on a person or object, the latter is infused with the spirit or essence of the deity known as *dishti*. The idea that the eyes, or the look, contain the essence of the deity is very important in Sinhalese belief.[28]

This characterization of *diṣṭiya* as the "essence" of the *yaksayā* is, I think, absolutely correct. The efficacy of the *yaksayā* is understood to reside in the "look" or eyes. It seems to me necessary to add, however, that *diṣṭiya* can also be said to be the *energy* (*vēgaya*) of the eyesight of *yakku*, or again their malevolent *propensity*.

Later, in *The Cult of the Goddess Pattini*, Obeyesekere discusses the relationship between *diṣṭiya* and the presence of gods or *dēvas* in the village ritual *gammaduva* in the following instructive way:

> The gods are present on earth in the hall, but in what form? Obviously they are invisible, yet they are present in an almost physical sense. Not only are they present in a particular community, but they may be present if invoked in other communities and shrines at the same time. They must be in this place and that, in the then and the now. They therefore obviously cannot be present in person; rather they are there in essence. How can the gods' essence be manifest in a variety of places at one time? The Indian theory, on which the Sinhala concept is based, tells us that the essence of the supernatural being is manifest in his sight (*diṣṭi*, from the Sanskrit *driṣṭi*), or look (*bälma*). The gods are present in their looks; when the gods look upon the altars constructed for them, they are also present in essence in those altars. Thus *bälma* or *diṣṭi* can be glossed as "look cum essence." This meaning is even more clear in the cultural theory of divine or demonic possession and mediumship: it is the essence of the deity, representing the deity himself, that is present within the possessed individual, or medium. (pp. 51–52)

Again, Obeyesekere's observations are helpful. Although bodily absent, the gods are very much there in an almost physical sense. And it is in the nature of this presence that it can be manifest in many places at the same time. Moreover, the quality of *diṣṭiya* is such that whatever it touches becomes infused with it. These are most important. As we shall see in a moment, this is as pertinent to the *diṣṭiya* of *yakku* as of *dēvas*.[29] I would only add that because *yakku* are angry and vengeful beings, *krōdakārayās*, their *diṣṭiya* is characterized by a harsh rather than a benign intensity—their "look" is invariably said to be *tadayi*, severe, and therefore has a disturbing effect.

Diṣṭiya and the Balance of the Body

I would like to turn now to some of the ways in which Sinhala Buddhists talk about the malign action of *diṣṭiya*. In this section I will seek to describe aspects of the relation between *diṣṭiya* and the Sinhala body. This will entail an exploration also of the relation between the action of *diṣṭiya* and the regulation—and disruption—of the *dōṣas* or humors. First, though, in considering this relation between *diṣṭiya* and body, it is necessary to raise some questions about the use of the metaphor of "possession" (insofar, that is, as this is an expressly *body* metaphor) employed by anthropologists of ritual practice in Sri Lanka. For conceptual reasons the matter is, I judge, an important one, and therefore bears an initial reflection and clarification.

Anthropological discussions of *yakku* and *yaktovil* have, by and large, been inscribed within the larger and well-established conceptual framework of the anthropology of possession and exorcism.[30] On this view, Sinhalas are "possessed" by *yakku*, that is, "demons," which are then "exorcised" in certain demon ceremonies called *yaktovil*. This being taken as the self-evident ethnographic case, the explicit anthropological problem has then generally been formulated in terms of explaining the social and/or psychological "function" of this "demonic possession," that is, with determining the latent social or personal (or again, interpersonal) conflicts it serves—in its culturally appropriate idiom—to publicly express.[31] It is easy to see that on this kind of account the nature of the relationship between the external force or being and the body of the afflicted person or victim—that in fact the conceptual metaphor "possession" is supposed implicitly to organize—will generally be taken as unproblematic and therefore will go unexamined. Or, where the body serves as a point of focus, the account will assume the nature/culture paradigm in which view the body is taken as a "real" and unchanging material substrate, a repertoire of latent biophysical capacities, grounding or substantializing varied cultural representations.[32] So understood, the kind of question to be put to ethnographic data on Sinhala "possession" will be familiar enough: *given* the human body, how do Sinhalas imagine or represent (or indeed "experience") the action and effects of the malign eyesight of *yakku*? This is a question that, in effect, repeats the whole archive of the science/ideology (and biology/culture) problematic in which an allegedly universal body enveloped in ideological or cultural representations is supposed nevertheless to be accessible to science for confirmation or correction. The social function model and the sociobiological model are, in my view, sides of a coin: they both work on the metaphor of a relationship between a "real" (whether described in terms of latent physical capacities or latent social conflicts) and its "representations," and they both see the anthropological task as a matter of reading off the former from the latter.

My own inclination is to come at the matter from a different set of assumptions and questions—assumptions and questions that I believe avoid this kind of conceptual dilemma. I take as my point of departure the view first sketched by Mauss in his 1934 lecture "Techniques of the Body," and subsequently elaborated and developed by Michel Foucault and such feminists as Susan Bordo.[33] On this account, there is no universally invariable body but rather several historically and culturally specific bodies. The pre-Socratic body for which divinity and corporeality were not radically dissociated, for instance, was not the same as the body of the Gnostics of late Antiquity for whom it was a "prison" in which the divine principle or Soul was kept captive. Or again, the Daoist body, which in its organization replicates the Universe, is not the body of the modern American physician with its internal physical geography of pulsating organs. Bodies, that is to say, are given to modalities, gestures, aptitudes that are subject to the variable strategies and structures of their forms of life. And these strategies and structures have to do with the several locally concrete and pragmatic ways in which bodies are disciplined, exercised, and employed, and in which bodies, consequently, come to be *taken* as what they are and *lived* through their attributed or imposed capacities, potentialities, and vulnerabilities. The point here is that these capacities and vulnerabilities themselves constitute a density and not a mere symbolic transparency. So that, in short, bodies may be said to be subject to a variation which is not that of their ideologies or symbolizations, but that of their variable living and use.

In a conception of the body so recast, it becomes possible to ask a different sort of question about bodies in Sinhala cultural practice constituted by the discourse of *yakku*. And this question may be posed as follows: In light of the characteristic power attributed to the malign nature of the eyesight of certain supernatural figures, what kind of body must the Sinhalas endow themselves with, what kind of body must they acquire in their cultural practices relating to these figures? For again, bodies in this turn of conception are the *effect* of the cultural practices that produce them, not their immutable and enduring substrate.

In colloquial Sinhala there are a variety of ways of referring to the malign disposition of *diṣṭiya* in relation to the body of the afflicted person. In the first place, the action that constitutes an attack by *yakku* who have "cast down" their "look" (*bälma helanavā*), as people say, upon Lankā, is one of *diṣṭiya* "falling on the body," and of *diṣṭiya* "covering the body." *Diṣṭiya* "falls" and *diṣṭiya* "covers" the body: these are vivid and significant metaphors. Often, in response to an inquiry after someone, for instance, one might be told that, "a *diṣṭiya* has fallen on that person's body" (*eyāṭa äṅgaṭa diṣṭiyak väṭilā tiyenavā*), or else, "a *diṣṭiya* has covered that person's body" (*eyāṭa äṅgaṭa diṣṭiyak vähilā tiyenavā*). These are, perhaps, the two most common ways of expressing the fact that a person has been the victim of "the look" of a *yaksayā*. The negligible difference between them is a slight temporal one. *Yakku*, recall, are far away, and, on the Buddha's sanction, are no longer able bodily to reenter Lankā. At the times appointed them, they "cast" or "put" their "look." It—or rather, its essence, energy, *diṣṭiya*—"falls" on a person's body. This is, as it were, the moment of the encounter with—and given the Sinhala conception of the character of eyesight as an obtrusive, beamlike flow, one might even say *impact* of—the *yaksayā*. Indeed (as I discuss in the following section), it will typically be accompanied by an experience of fright. Having fallen, however, that *diṣṭiya* works its malevolence by "covering" the body, that is, in its entirety, from head to feet. To understand this it has to be recalled that the Sinhala body is constituted of humors (*dōṣas*), and I will return to this.

However, *diṣṭiya* "falling" and "covering" are not the only ways in which its action or disposition in relation to the body is talked about. After the lapse of a day or more, a person "covered" by *diṣṭiya* will also be spoken of as "having" a *diṣṭiya* (*diṣṭiyak tiyenavā*), meaning that his or her body "has" in some sense the malevolent, disturbing energy or essence of "the look" of a *yaksayā*. Or again, a person's body may be said not merely to "have" a *diṣṭiya* but more specifically to have a *diṣṭiya* "in," or "on" it—*eyāgē äṅgē diṣṭiyak tiyenavā* (that person's body has a *diṣṭiya* in/on it). Here it is the locative form of the noun *äṅga* (body) that expresses this more precise disposition of *diṣṭiya*. And this more precise location of *diṣṭiya* can be even further emphasized in those not unusual instances in which the adjective "*ätulē*" is used to give a positive sense of *diṣṭiya* actually being "inside" or "within" the body of the afflicted person (*äṅga ätulē diṣṭiyak tiyenavā*). As we will see in the description of the *yaktovil* ceremony in the following chapter, there are several moments when, interrogating the *āturayā*, the *ädurā* refers to this disposition of *diṣṭiya* in relation to the body. So, for example, the *ädurā* might ask whether the virtuous commands of the Buddha are valid for the *yaksayā* that is within this body (*mē sarīra abhyantarē vāsaya karanavā*). A number of things about this formulation are notable. First, it is phrased so as to give a positive sense that the *diṣṭiya* is "within" the body of the afflicted person. Second, there is an equation of *yakku* with their *diṣṭiya*. If you ask an *ädurā* whether the *yaksayā* is really there, bodily, in the body, he will probably say no, how could it be, but the *diṣṭiya* is there, so the difference is of no consequence. For *diṣṭiya* is, as Obeyesekere suggests, the "essence" of the deity.

The difference may be of no consequence to *yaktovil* practice, but I think that it bears on our (i.e., anthropological) understanding. In Sinhala discourse about *yakku*, the body is organized as a potential object for the "falling" and "covering" of the malign energy of their eyesight. Then one's body can be spoken of as "having" a *diṣṭiya*, or else having a *diṣṭiya* "in," "on," or even "inside" it. There is a curious ambiguity here that opens up a number of questions. For it is not immediately clear how these senses of the malign disposition of *diṣṭiya* in relation to the body could be employed interchangeably. Is there no difference between "having" a *diṣṭiya*, having a *diṣṭiya* "in" or "on" the body, or having a *diṣṭiya* "within" the body? If not, what kind of body is this that refuses these familiar distinctions and divisions?

To illustrate the problem further: One young woman who claimed herself to be afflicted with the *diṣṭiya* of the *yaksayā* named Kalu Kumāraya, the Black Prince (one story about whom I relate in the Appendix), was quite adamant that *diṣṭiya* does *not* go "inside" the body even though this might be how it is commonly put (she was responding to the question whether *diṣṭiya* goes inside the body—*äṅga ätulaṭa yanavā da?*). As she articulated it:

> *Diṣṭiya* does not go inside the body (*äṅga ätulaṭa yanne nähäyi*). When a *diṣṭiya* covers anyone's body, "*diṣṭiya* has covered the body" and "the body has a *diṣṭiya*" are said for that; otherwise "the body has a *diṣṭiya* inside" is said (*diṣṭiyak yamkisi kenekugē äṅgaṭa vähunahāma diṣṭiya äṅgaṭa vähilā tiyenavā kiyena ēkaṭayi, diṣṭiyak äṅgē tiyenavā nätnam diṣṭiyak äṅga ätulē tiyenavā kiyalā kiyanne*). Sometimes many people say "a *diṣṭiya* is inside the body" (*samaharaviṭa huṅgak minisu kiyanne diṣṭiyak äṅga ätulē tiyenavā kiyalā*).

The distinctions, one is tempted to say, are rather a Sinhala manner of speaking. One *ädurā*, Äddin Lokuvela, suggested as much:

> It is indeed "inside" that we are thinking (*ätula kiyalā tamayi api hitanne*). But that is common for wherever in the body (*namut ēka äṅgē koyibatat ekayi*). . . . Generally it [*diṣṭiya*] is an energy (*vēgaya*). So when a *diṣṭiya* falls on the body you can't say whether it is outside or inside (*itin äṅga ätulet äṅgaṭa diṣṭiya vätunāma ēka piṭa tiyenavā da ätula tiyenavā da kiyanna bā*).

Diṣṭiya, then, is an "energy." It is an intangible *force* that consists of the *yaksayā*'s essence, its malevolence. The Sinhala conception that the malevolent energy of eyesight "covering" the body, the body "having" this malevolent energy, and the body having it "inside," are virtually one and the same suggests, at the least, a body that is not organized as the same kind of spatial organism as is the Western body. It would appear that *diṣṭiya* does *not* go "inside" the body where this "inside" is understood as a place where, for example, food and drink go. This is in fact well illustrated in an very interesting way in the following passage about the relation between *diṣṭiya* and food. As Sinhalas have it, certain kinds of foods, specifically oil-mixed food (*tel misra kāma*)—such things as *kävun* and *kokis*, for example—are known to attract the *diṣṭiya* of *yakku* as a result of their pungent odor. In the course of talking about the relation between *diṣṭiya* and food, the young woman quoted earlier went on to emphatically deny that *diṣṭiya* could *enter* the body as through an orifice:

> "*Diṣṭiya* falling on food" means [that] if we, having eaten any food and gone here and there, that *diṣṭiya* covers that food (*kāmakaṭa diṣṭiya väṭenavā kiyalā kiyanne api yamkisi kāmak kāla ivaravalā ehe mehe giyot diṣṭiya väṭenne ara kāmaṭayi*). But a *diṣṭiya* cannot enter the body through the mouth, or nose, or any other means (*namut diṣṭiyak kaṭinvat nätnam nāsayenvat ehemat nätnam venat vidiyakinvat äṅga ätulaṭa yannama bähäyi*). It is only after eating food that the *diṣṭiya* falls (*kāmak kāvaṭa pasu diṣṭiya väṭenavā vitarayi*). But before we eat, *diṣṭiya* hasn't fallen on that food (*namut api kāmak kannaṭa issella diṣṭiya ē kāmaṭa vähilā tiyenne nā*). Because of that the *diṣṭiya* cannot go into a body through the mouth or nose (*ēka nisā kiyanne diṣṭiyakaṭa kaṭinvat nāsayenvat sarīrayakaṭa ätulu venna bähäyi*).[34]

Eating certain kinds of food, then, only *subjects* the body to a specific kind of vulnerability, that is, a vulnerability to the effects of malign eyesight. The surface of the Sinhala body therefore is not interrupted by a number of orifices which, acting as its structural weak points, so to speak, or as zones of a hypervulnerability, can potentially provide the *channels* of entry of a supernatural *presence*. This latter image, as familiar to us from

Christianity as from psychoanalysis, depends on a body whose surface is punctuated by orifices around which are constructed a whole discourse of danger, and which are central to its regulation and control. At the same time, however, if the metaphor "inside" or "within" (*ätulē*) *is* nevertheless employed, and if this usage is equivalent to those other forms of Sinhala utterance that convey the disposition of *diṣṭiya* in relation to the body, what positively is meant by it? In other words, what kind of "insideness" can there be that is not the inside of a cavernous, inhabitable space? Here we have to recall our discussion in chapter 1 of the theory of the regulation of the three humors (*tun dos*) and the kind of body it structures.

As I suggested in chapter 1, the Sinhala body is not a body with organs, that is to say, knowledge of the body's functioning is humor- not organ-based. The Sinhala body is constituted of three vital humors (*tun dos*): wind (*vāta*), bile (*pita*), and phlegm (*sema*). And these humors, contained in the blood (*lē*), flesh (*mas*), and skin (*sam*), are the fundamental elements of the body's energy system. Together they form the condition of the body's functioning, and the body must be maintained in such a state that these three humors remain in equilibrium. However, any disturbance to the person will result in their becoming "agitated." Now, as Sinhalas have it, the *diṣṭiya* that "falls" on and "covers" the body becomes "attached" (*sambandhavenavā*) to and "contained" (*aḍaṃguvenavā*) in it. Consider the following description, which, I think, vividly captures the relation between the energy of the "look" and the body's humoral system:

> "To be contained" means that [*diṣṭiya*] having come as though by the wind becomes attached to the body (*aḍaṃguvenavā kiyanne vātayen men ävillā sarīrayaṭa sambandhavenavā*). When it becomes attached to that one [i.e., to the body], because the power that it has is different to [that of] this person's body, a shaking results (*ēkaṭa sambandha unāma arayagē tiyenne balaya meyāgē sarīrayaṭa venas nisā calitayak ätivenavā*). . . . It is in the three, skin (*sam*), flesh (*mas*), and blood (*lē*), that this one [i.e., *diṣṭiya*] is contained (*sam mas lē tun denaṭa mēka aḍaṃguvenavā*). . . . Then when it [i.e., *diṣṭiya*] has touched the skin it penetrates (*etakoṭa dän samaṭa vädilā vinivida*).[35]

Notice the image of forces employed in this conception. Not only is *diṣṭiya* a force (the force of a certain kind of look), but the body too is constituted of forces—a system of energies or forces vulnerable to the play of other energies and forces in the cosmos such as *diṣṭiya*. Notice also that the presence of *yakku*—in the malign energy of their eyesight—does not enter the body as through an orifice, but "penetrates" or "perforates" it, as through the skin. The use of this metaphor—*vinivida*—may well be idiosyncratic, but the more important point is that in thinking this matter Sinhalas have to construct a relation between one kind of energy (*diṣṭiya*) and another (the system of the three humors). As one elderly *ädurā*, Saraneris Appu, rather straightforwardly put the matter: "If a *diṣṭiya* falls on anyone it is the blood-element that it influences (*koyi kenekuṭa diṣṭiyak vähunot mēka balapānne lē dhātuva*). It is the blood-element that is being controlled (*lē dhātuva tamayi mē palanayavenne*). . . . It is that blood-element that makes the body weak (*ē dhātuva tamayi mē sarīraya duruvela karanne*)."

The Sinhala body, we can see, is therefore dependent upon a distinctive set of metaphors. It is, in the first place, a system of *energies* regulated by the continuous innervation and distribution of the three humors, wind, bile, and phlegm. It is a body, therefore, potentially vulnerable to the force of other energies acting upon or coming into contact with it. One such energy is *diṣṭiya*, the malign energy of the eyesight of *yakku*. *Diṣṭiya*, as in the account just given, can be likened to the wind. When *diṣṭiya* "touches" and "covers" the body it becomes "attached" to and "contained" in the blood, skin, and flesh. And because of the difference in energy, its touching and becoming attached to the body disrupts the balance of the humors. It seems to me, therefore, that the metaphor of "possession" needs to be explicitly qualified to make it relevant to the Sinhala body. This body offers a conception of a spatial organism that cannot be assimilated to the possessed body of Christian and psychoanalytic discourse. The Sinhala body is an organism constituted by energies and normalized by an ethic of composure; it is differentiated not by a luminous inner essence radically marked off from an exterior materiality, but systemically by the regulation of levels and flows. It is a body vulnerable not to invasion as though it were a "house" or a "temple" whose owner could be usurped, but to a reconstitution of its elements precipitated by contact with other energies. Malevolence and benevolence are two such energies, and eyesight is their principal modality.

Diṣṭiya, *Tanikama*, and Composure

The idea of the regulation of the humors of the Sinhala body is important at another level. For this regulated body forms the condition for the constitution of a distinctively variable Sinhala subject, potentially exposed to, and disciplined by, the *subjectifying* force of eyesight.

Because Buddhism is classically regarded as that religion which rejects the notion of a real, permanent, self understood as the "agent" of thoughts and actions, it is probably useful to state clearly and precisely the sense in which I shall speak of a Sinhala subject or self. The view taken by Steven Collins in his reading of the canonical textual tradition of Theravāda is instructive here as a point of departure.[36] He suggests that it is only in discourse in which matters of theoretical or philosophical analysis are at stake that there occurs what he calls the "linguistic taboo" against speaking of the "self" (*anattā*) or "person" (*puggala*). "It is thought and discourse," he says, "in which a more or less definite theoretical system is in question, a system which has no direct link with any particular behavioural circumstances, but purports to offer a general and atemporal account of psychological structure and functioning" (p. 76). In representations of those more ordinary circumstances, on the other hand—those, for instance, in which *anattā* (self) is employed merely as a reflexive pronoun in narrative descriptions of behavior, or in kinds of religious exhortation in which no general or fundamental theoretical principles are at stake—there is no censure. At the same time, the analytical use of a concept of "self" does not necessarily commit one to the attempt to identify and represent, a priori, some essential, eternal, Sinhala Self, an immortal Soul inhabiting the body. The concept of "self" may mark out, analytically, specific formations of ways of speaking about moral dispositions, vulnerabilities, aptitudes, and the like. The important question, it seems to me, is not whether Sinhalas have or do not have a "Self," but rather what kinds of figures, statements, and so on, are employed pronominally to mark a distinctive mode of address within social life. My argument is simply that one of the elements that make up a distinctive Sinhala mode of address is *eyesight*.

Eyesight, I have suggested, is linked to the acquisition and organization of distinctive aptitudes and vulnerabilities, and it stands at the center of a whole radiating network of practices through which Sinhalas fashion themselves as, and recognize themselves in, particular kinds of subjects. Sinhala vulnerability to eyesight is connected to the organization of other vulnerabilities to which the Sinhala self is acutely disposed. Perhaps the most important such vulnerability is the vulnerability to the possible consequences of "being alone" (*taniyama*), or the "*condition* of being alone," or "aloneness" (*tanikama*: *tani* = alone, single; *kama* = occasion, act). Another, which is in fact inextricably linked to the condition of being alone, is the vulnerability to fright (*baya*), especially sudden fright (*hadissibaya*). What these bring sharply into focus is the importance to the fashioning of the Sinhala self of composure, a notion we have encountered in relation to the regulation of the body's humors. In this section I will discuss these—the potential danger of eyesight, the condition of being alone, and the disposition to fright—in their relation to the problem of formations and practices of the Sinhala self, particularly those in which it is composure that is involved.

In discussions of *yakku*, the malevolent effects of *diṣṭiya* are often linked to the predisposing condition or state known as *tanikama*. Indeed, this link is such that the ill effects of *yakṣa diṣṭiya* are themselves often referred to as *tanikam dōṣa*. It may be said, for instance, of the victim of *diṣṭiya* that a *tanikama* has touched him (*eyāṭa tanikamak vädilā*), or that a *tanikama* has occurred or happened (*eyāṭa tanikamak velā*). One of the earliest accounts of the relation between *yakku* and *tanikama* is again that given by the inimitable Dandris de Silva Gooneratne:

> When a man is frightened by a demon, and has the influence of that demon on him, it is called TANICAMA, which literally means "*loneliness*" or "*being alone.*" Fright is in most cases a necessary agent in bringing down *Tanicama* on that man; but it is also possible that a person, who has neither been frightened by a demon, nor been ten yards from his own door for five or six months, may also get the Tanicama influence on him. In this case, the explanation is, that the demon has taken advantage of some unguarded moment in the daily life of the man, as when he has been sitting in the open compound, or when he has happened to go to the back of his house at any of the Yamas, when a demon has happened to be in the vicinity; or when he has eaten roasted fish or eggs, while sitting outside in his Verandah on a Wednesday or Saturday. In this case the man is neither frightened by anything, nor even aware of his danger at the time.[37]

And he continues:

> The literal meaning of the word Tanicama gives us a key towards the understanding of many of the mysterious and wonderful circumstances connected with this part of our subject, especially when it is taken in connection with the other doctrine of Demonism already alluded to, viz., that, though a demon try his utmost by means of terrible apparitions or by actual seizure to frighten a man and give him the Tanicama,

> which results in sickness, yet the man will seldom get ill, if he do [*sic*] not get frightened. (p. 48)

These passages are extremely valuable, I think, because they make very clear the connection between *tanikama* and fright. Fright is typically a necessary condition for "a man to get the Tanicama influence on him." In a similar fashion, a practitioner of the arts of influencing *yakku* remarked the indispensable precondition of fright in the following way:

> At the time that you are going along, [*yakku*] are waiting to put the look on your body (*yana velāva obagē sarīrayaṭa bälma lāna innavā*). Without [your] seeing anything the look is put. However, without inducing fright (*baya karanne nätuva*) it [i.e., the *tanikam dōṣa*] can't be made regardless of the disturbance made by the *yaksayā*.

Fright, then—the suddenly precipitated onset of *dis*-composure, of agitation, the sudden loss of self-possession or equanimity—is a *condition* for the malevolence of the eyesight of *yakku* to have effects. And even where there is no clear instance of fright, the *yaksayā* has nevertheless somehow "taken advantage of an unguarded moment" in the victim's daily life. So that what is at any rate common to both situations is the sense of the suddenness of the *yaksayā*'s action (the swiftness of the malign glance), and the sense of the victim's *unpreparedness* and *exposure*.

It seems to me, however, that Gooneratne's insightful passages are misleading in at least one particular. It is an important one because it has been reproduced and elaborated upon in uncritical ways in the modern anthropology of *yaktovil*. Gooneratne translates the word "*tanikama*" as "loneliness" or "being alone," as though these two English expressions necessarily connoted equivalent conditions, equivalent states of subjectivity, and were, therefore, equally adequate to the translation of the Sinhala concept. But surely "loneliness" and "being alone" are not the same, and even if for the modern Western self they have come to denote almost indistinguishable modes of being this must be because of the specific conditions of formation of those selves. And these, needless to say, are not the conditions through which Sinhala selves are fashioned. It follows, therefore, that these two expressions *do not* both equally translate the Sinhala notion of *tanikama*. But more than this, I am not so sure that *either* of them is adequate. On the one hand, "being alone" is neither a necessary nor a sufficient condition for exposure to *tanikam dōṣa*; and on the other hand, it is not the bereftness that characterizes the Western condition of loneliness that is crucial to the Sinhala condition of vulnerability. (Lest I be misunderstood, I should emphasize that I am not committing myself to the idea that Sinhalas do not experience "loneliness," that is, a condition not only—not even necessarily—of being by oneself, but of a sort of bereftness. They may or they may not experience something that may be so described. What I am suggesting is that this is not what is meant by *tanikama*, and that therefore it is not the condition that exposes one to fright and the effects of malign eyesight.)[38]

Gooneratne's suggestion that *tanikama* involves a state of unpreparedness or exposure is nevertheless an important one, and I think that we may make use of it to begin to grasp something of this crucial concept. Note, though, that here unpreparedness and exposure are not mere lacks or absences (the absence of preparedness). Rather what is involved is something more like the production of a subjective state of apprehension. There is suggested in descriptions of *tanikama* a sense that it entails an uneasiness of mind, foreboding, expectancy, even perhaps anxiety. In those states the mind has formed an apprehension of some danger, a threat, so that the least noise or disturbance appears to be a calamity (*vipattiya*). Take, for example, the following passage. Discussing this concept of *tanikama* with Piyasena, I suggested a scenario in which three people are walking along when suddenly a noise (*sabdaya*) is heard by one—and only one—of them. How is it possible, I wanted to know, that in such a situation the condition of that one person who heard the noise could come to be described as *tanikama*, and that he or she should fall victim to a *tanikam dōṣa*. Piyasena responded in part as follows:

> When this noise was heard, one's mind ran to that side (*sabda ähenakoṭa tamangē hita ē ataṭa divvā*). The other two [persons] are not concerned about that noise. It is one's mind that became concentrated on it (*ēkaṭa tamangē hita yomu unā*). The mind is drawn to that side (*hita ē pataṭa ädunā*). It becomes startled (*gässilā*). Having heard that noise, that person's mind was shaken (*ē sabdaya ähilā tamangē hita hellunā*). . . . Having gone to the brain, that noise is contained there (*molayaṭa gihillā aḍaṃguvelā ē sabdaya*). Going along, you are still thinking about that noise. It has been taken to the brain, no? And you think straight away (*kelinma hitagannavā*) that this is a *yaksayā*, a *diṣṭiya* for me. Then, by thinking about that one the blood becomes agitated (*dän ēka gäna kalpanā kirīmen lē kupitavenavā*).

This passage, so characteristic of Piyasena's penetrating understanding, illustrates what is perhaps a basic cultural understanding of the relation between the mind and well-being: without turning the mind bad (*hita naraka nokarā*), a *yaksayā* cannot do any harm; and therefore if some calamity (*vipattiya*) is to be made to befall someone, the mind has to be made bad (*hita naraka karalā ōna*). In Piyasena's characterization, the mind is startled (*gäsenavā*) by the noise. But more than this, because the noise is not then merely swept away by other thoughts. Rather, as he put it, "it goes to the brain," and, moreover, is "contained" there. What is implied here is a condition of apprehension, even anxiety, which leads the person to a consuming worry about or preoccupation with (*yomuvenavā*) the noise, its meaning, its origin, its possible consequences. Even if the *yaksayā* "looks" at this person's companions, its malevolent energy can have no effect on them since it has not been able to take advantage of a preexisting condition of apprehension that would lead to a sustained fright.

On the Sinhala view, people preoccupied with acquiring money and other kinds of material wealth (a most un-Buddhist virtue) are likely candidates for *tanikam dōṣa*. But this is not because acquisitiveness is itself *pav* or "demeritorious"—or anyway, not directly so. Rather it is because aquisitiveness is likely to make one uneasy and fretful and suspicious; such a person, it is said, is always anxiously listening to hear if someone has suddenly come upon him to take what he has (whether someone has *pänalā giyā*, jumped and went, people like to say). This anxiety makes the mind "soft" (*lāmaka*) and thus particularly vulnerable to the swift, malevolent action of a *yaksayā*'s glance. This "softness" of the mind is said also to be particularly characteristic of young women, and this is why they are always afraid. Young girls, for instance, are constantly worried about being set upon or taken advantage of (or "jumped") by men. They too, like *mudalālis*, are vulnerable to the possible consequences of *tanikama*.

Moreover, as the last sentence of Piyasena's remarks above suggests—and as by now we would expect, given the nature of the relation between mind and body so far discussed—this consuming worry has consequences for the regulation of the body's humoral system:

> [The noise] is taken to the mind. And one's thoughts become solely about that (*tamangē kalpanāva nitarama ēkagäna*). When thinking about that one [the noise] one's blood becomes unclean (*ēkagäna kalpanā karanakoṭa tamangē lē apirisidu venavā*). That means the blood in the body becomes lifeless due to the state of fright in the mind (*kiyanne sarīraye lē hitē bayagatiyaṭa, aprānika venavā*). The phlegm (*sema*) becomes agitated.

> The wind (*vātaya*) becomes agitated. And having become agitated, fever results (*una hädunā*).[39]

Here the connection between the disturbance of the mind and the disturbance of the body's humoral equilibrium is clear. The consuming thinking that is brought about by the fright or startle makes the blood "unclean," makes it, in effect, "lifeless." It heats up the blood and results in fever (*una*), and the familiar *dōṣas*. Then one can say that one is "touched by an aloneness" (*tanikamak vädilā*), or else that "an aloneness has occurred" (*tanikamak velā*).

Clearly, then, it is not the aloneness by itself, nor even the startle or the fright, that are crucial—though (as was the case with "look" and *diṣṭiya*) all of them are useful shorthand ways of articulating the sense of *tanikama*. For of course each of these can and does occur without resulting in troubles or illnesses (*dōṣas*). Rather, I would like to suggest that it is the subsisting apprehension that turns a startle (*gäsma*) or sudden fright (*baya*) into a trouble (*dōṣa*)—that leads to the three humors becoming agitated. A startle that does not turn into a *dōṣa* may or may not have been the result of a *yaksayā*. If one had been walking by a cemetery or a crossroads or a pond when it occurred, it is likely to have been, but in fact there is no way to be certain. (A young woman I know and two of her female friends were walking down a lane one late evening—a most unwise thing for young women to be doing since the evening watch, *händāve jāmaya*, is well known to be a time when *yakku* aplenty are likely to be about. As they were going about, they saw, indistinctly, a curious light at the far end of the lane, and immediately became alarmed. *Yakku! Yakku ēvi!!* [*Yakku!* There may be *yakku* coming!!] shouted the woman I know, and in fright she turned and ran, leaving her friends. When she got home she was hot with fever [*una hädunā*]. *Yakku*? Likely, but there was uncertainty. An *ädurā* would have to have been called to make a precise diagnosis. Her father, an Āyurvedic physician's son, gave her a common medicinal decoction, *kasāya*, and by the following morning the fear and the fever had subsided. That the fright was sufficient to cause a fever suggests a subsisting *tanikama*, but if it had indeed been a *yaksayā*, it is clear that the "look" was not severe enough to cause a lasting disturbance.)

Maintaining the mind's composure, however, may be described as a more general Sinhala Buddhist self-fashioning practice. Certainly the unshakable composure of the Buddha (his fearless serenity in the face of

Ālavaka's or Aṅgulimāla's tempestuous behavior) is a recurrent feature in stories about him and forms part of the defining character of the virtue of his teaching. It characterizes the temper of life extolled by Sinhala Buddhists. As Gombrich and Obeyesekere remark, "The highest term of praise for someone in Sinhala society is *śānta dānta,* 'calm and controlled'."[40] And since it is culturally understood that troubles (*dōṣas*) are less likely to befall one if one's mind is kept properly composed, Sinhalas are wont to guard themselves against the possibility of a startle (*gäsma*) or fright (*baya*). Let me illustrate this Sinhala self-fashioning practice with a small but illuminating anecdote. It was related to me (in English) by a Sinhala friend, a young man in his early twenties. He had been on his way to his home in the hill country late one evening, he said. Getting off the bus in his home town he set off on foot for his house. It was dark by then, night having fallen, and there were no streetlights. Unfortunately, too, he had forgotten his flashlight and therefore had to make his way without even the company of light. Becoming a little worried at his situation, he said, he "took his mind in his hand" and proceeded on his way, secure in the knowledge that, so "holding" his mind, he was no longer in danger of being startled and therefore unsteadied by a sudden noise or sight. In this extraordinary metaphor, I suggest—keeping the mind in the sure grip of the hand—a distinctive practice of Sinhala self-fashioning is at work. The composure of the mind is vulnerable to being disturbed, disrupted, and therefore it must be protected. Putting his mind in the safety of his hand was a precautionary measure. By so doing, this young man had secured himself against his vulnerability to fright and therefore to the possibility of the malign energy of eyesight falling on him. With *tanikama,* the mind is already unsettled by apprehension or anxiety. It lacks the calm settledness of composure and is, as a result, in a fundamentally exposed and vulnerable condition.

It follows from what I have said that it is misleading to translate *tanikam dōṣa,* the ill effects of *diṣṭiya,* as "alone illness," as some anthropologists have done.[41] This is misleading not only because such a translation conveys too much of the flavor of the modern Western psychological condition of "loneliness" and the psychopathological disorders now associated with it. But more important, the *dōṣa* or ill effects in the case of *tanikam dōṣa* do not derive from the condition itself of being alone or of being by oneself (as is suggested in the Western conception of the psychological state of "loneliness"). Rather it derives, as I have sought to show, from the condition of *vulnerability* to which *tanikama* disposes one, specifically a vulnerability to a fright that, as we might say, catches one off guard and disturbs one's composure—a fright, of course, for Sinhala Buddhists invariably associated with the malign energy of the eyesight of *yakku*.

I have tried in this chapter to give an account of that concept which, as I understand it, is central to the way *yakku* transmit their malevolence, that is, *diṣṭiya*; to describe the broader cultural discourse about eyesight in which it participates; and particularly, to discuss its relation to what I have called a Sinhala Buddhist ethics of composure, a practice of care for the composure of the body and mind. Composure is a valued Buddhist good, and to cultivate it is a virtue. Monks, being committed to the Path, cultivate this ethics in a systematic and elaborated way. But it may well be said to constitute the modality of a Sinhala habitus, for in the practices of everyday life, composure is cultivated in the most common of habits—maintaining the body's humors in a state of relative equilibrium by eating the right balance of foods, avoiding inclement weather, expectorating excess phlegm in a regular and timely fashion, keeping the mind safe from the possibility of startle or fright, and so on. What *yakku* do is disrupt this composure—by precipitating fright and consuming worry, which give rise to fever and the agitation of the humors—and, as we will see in chapter 7, *yaktovil* consists in a strategy one aim of which is to achieve its restoration.

Chapter 3

Tovil Nätīma (The Dancing of *tovil*)

In October 1987 Lila Amma, a Sinhala woman in her mid- to late sixties, had a *yaktovil* ceremony performed—or "danced," *näṭuvā*, as is more properly said—for her.[1] In fact, she had not one but three ceremonies: a combined Prēta Pidēniya and Bahīrava Pidēniya (offering ceremonies for prētayō and bahīravayō) on one evening, and, the following day, an Iramudun Samayama or Midday Ceremony, and, some hours following, a Maha Kalu Kumāra Samayama or ceremony for the Great Black Prince.[2] The ceremonies took place over a period of two days in the yard of her home in the Matara district of the Southern Province of Sri Lanka. A descriptive consideration of these two ceremonies forms the central task of this chapter.

The story of Lila Amma's condition, as far as I could gather it, is fragmentary. Reconstructed somewhat on the basis of her own accounts, it is the following: In 1950 or thereabouts, a few years after her marriage and during her first pregnancy, Lila Amma went to a cemetery (*karakoppuva*) to see the cremation (*ādāhanaya*) of the body of a Buddhist monk. She had been sternly advised not to go, it being well-enough known to Sinhalas that pregnant women are particularly vulnerable to attack by *yakku*, and that, moreover, cemeteries are precisely one of those places infested with their malign presence. Lila Amma went, nevertheless, and, predictably, no sooner had she returned home that evening than she became ill. And that night the baby was lost (*babā näti unā*). During a succeeding pregnancy, the ceremony called Rata Yäkuma was performed for her. The Rata Yäkuma is a ceremony (or *yāgaya*, literally, "sacrifice") performed specifically for women who are either pregnant with child or in want of a child. Its chief purpose is either to protect the baby in the womb and ensure, at the appropriate time, its safe delivery, or to enable hitherto barren women to conceive.[3] The effort for Lila was in vain, however; her pregnancy failed to go the term. When subsequently she again became pregnant, another Rata Yäkuma was organized. In the course of its performance, however, it appears that one of the *ädurās* planted a *koḍivina* (sorcery) over which Lila Amma was caused to "step" (*ira pänīma*, literally, "stepping over the line"). In Sinhala conception, this kind of sorcery only becomes effective when the intended victim "steps" over it.[4]

That *ädurā*, the reason or reasons for whose maliciousness I was never able to determine, is said to then have told Lila's husband that nothing can be done about the sorcery—"even if one side is turned," he is said to have declared, "the other side can't be." And having so said he fled (*pänalā giyā*). Curiously enough, though, Lila Amma still encounters this by now aged *ädurā* who, she says, apologizes for what he has done, but insists nevertheless that try as one might the effects of the sorcery cannot be undone. "*Ammā maṭa kisi deyak karanna bā*," she says he says, "Mother, there is nothing I can do."

Sinhalas have a complex conception of sorcery. Note that the author of Lila Amma's sorcery maintained that even though *one* "side" of the sorcery might be "turned," the other side cannot be. Herein is contained the elementary principle of the *koḍivina*. According to Sinhala conception, the ill effects of the *vina diṣṭiya* (i.e., the distinctive *diṣṭiya* of the *koḍivina*) have to be "cut" (*kapanavā*), or again, "turned" (*haravanavā*) in order to stop its malign influence. It appears, however, that there are instances in which this is impossible, that is, when, because of the particular efficacy of the charms (*mantrayas*) employed, the *yakku* are "bound" too tightly to their destructive work to be deterred. In these instances it is considered that attempting to "cut" the *vinaya* or sorcery would lead to certain death, either of the *āturayā* or of the *ädurā* who attempts the *koḍivina käpīma* (the practice of "cutting" sorcery). As a result, at best only a partial and temporary amelioration can be effected, a "turning," as Sinhalas say, of but one "side" of it.

This was the unfortunate case with Lila Amma. Only one "side" of the *koḍivina* planted during the Rata Yäkuma could be "turned," and that by the judicious intervention of a skilled *ädurā*. He had been able to secure a "time limit" or *kāla sīmāva* during which Lila would be protected against the ill effects of the *vina diṣṭiya*. As the *sīmāva* waned, however, she would once again feel its malevolent influence (among the signs of which were burning sensations in the chest, and nightmares in which there appeared a large black figure), signaling the impending necessity for yet another *tovil*. Lila Amma had already had upwards of twelve *yaktovil* ceremonies danced for her.

The principal malign figure involved in Lila Amma's condition is the *yaksayā* known as Maha Kalu Kumāraya, the Great Black Prince. But for Sinhalas, as I have noted, where there is one *yaksayā* there are several. And the other main culprit in Lila's case is the Iramudun Rīri Yaksayā, the Blood Yaksayā of the Midday Hours. Thus the two *yaktovils* danced for her: the Iramudun Samayama, and the Maha Kalu Kumāra Samayama.

Iramudun Samayama

The Iramudun Samayama is a particularly interesting *yaktovil* ceremony for a number of reasons. First, comparatively little anthropological attention has been given to this *yaktovil* practice. One probable reason for this neglect is that it is the only large-scale *tovil* in which there are no sequences of comic drama (i.e., of the celebrated *Mangara Pelapāliya* and *Daha-aṭa pāliya*). These sequences have been at the center of anthropological examinations of the Sinhala *yaktovil*, the general thesis being that the comedy involved in them is the key factor in effecting cure.[5] Second, the Iramudun Samayama is the most compact and intense of *yaktovils*. It is the *tovil* of shortest duration—three or four hours—and the sequences run rapidly on one another, helping to create an atmosphere of acute, almost breathless intensity. Third, the Iramudun Samayama is interesting in that it is the *tovil* for that *yaksayā* that is considered the most fearful and dangerous of that malevolent assembly, the Iramudun Rīri Yaksayā (see chapter 1 for a discussion of the host of Rīri Yakku). At the same time, however, the practice of the Iramudun Samayama involves all the techniques and procedures generally employed in the "deflecting" or "stopping" of the malign effects of *diṣṭiya*.

The Lamp for the Four Warrant Gods (*Hatara Varam Deviyō*)

It is about 9:50 A.M., and Lila Amma is brought out of the house by her eldest daughter and accompanied to the makeshift shed, or *āturu pandala*,[6] where she will stay during performance of the *tovil*. (See Figure 1 for a schematic layout of the performing area.) Grave, she is dressed in a spotless white tunic and cloth. Äddin (or *Äddin māma*, Uncle Äddin, to some), the senior *ädurā* (*maha ädurā*), speaks to her in a voice barely audi-

Figure 1. Performance area for Iramudun Samayama

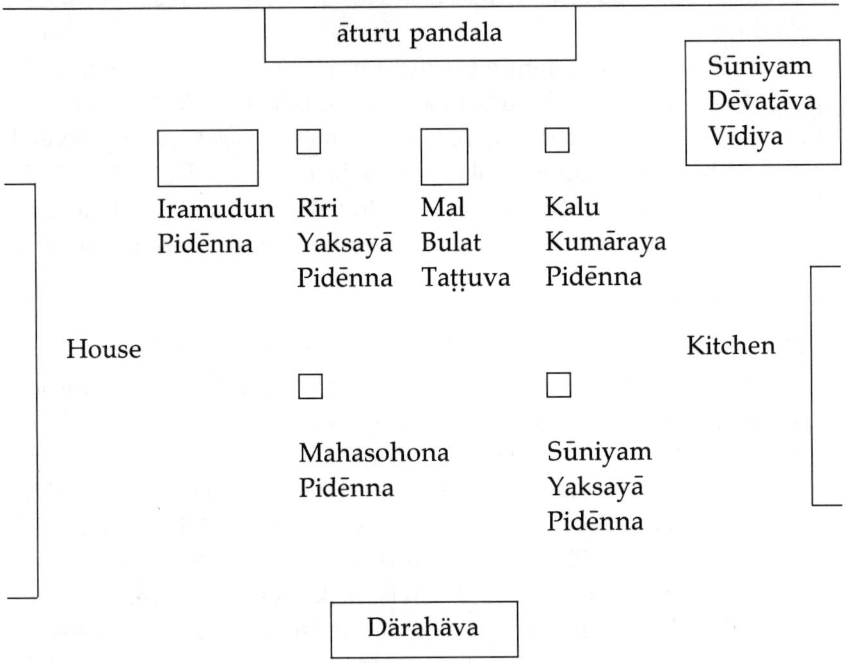

ble as she holds the lamp (*pahana*) of the Four Warrant Gods (*hataravaram deviyō*), Viṣṇu, Kataragama, Nātha, and Saman.[7] She is being told that she must concentrate on making her mind clear. She sits. A curtain (*kaḍaturāva*) is raised before her and held at each end by two young boys drawn from Lila Amma's household. The curtain separates her from the main activity of the performing area.

Sūniyam Vīdiya Käpakirīma (The Consecration of the Sūniyam Stand)

Almost simultaneously, as Lila is being seated, the first and inaugurating sequence of the *yaktovil* starts. This is the *Sūniyam Vīdiya Käpakirīma*, the Consecration of the Stand for the Godling Sūniyam.[8] This sequence, in which the godling Sūniyam (*Sūniyam dēvatāva*) is entreated to watch over the proceedings, and to keep their lives secure (*jīvita ārakṣāva tabāganna-vā*), is the opening sequence of all major *tovils* I observed. An *ädurā*, Samarapala, standing before the Stand (a sort of scaffold over which coconut leaves are hung), utters charms softly, shifting lightly from foot to foot. He holds several *pandams* (torches) in one hand, and a *baṭagaha* (a whistle made from a small species of bamboo), and *dummala* (a kind of harsh incense that produces a spectacular blaze when touched by a flame) in the other. An assistant stands nearby with a kind of small brazier or "fire pan" (*gini kabala*) of live coals (*gini an̆guru*) into which the *ädurā* periodically sprinkles some of the incense so that a thick pungent smoke sweeps over the Sūniyam Stand. *Yakku*, it is said, are particularly attracted to the sharp, acrid smell of the smoke of this incense (*dummala*), and the shrill sound of the whistle (*baṭagaha*). After five minutes or so the *ädurā* stops. The torches are planted on the Sūniyam Stand, one at each corner, and one in the middle. The cock (*kukulā*), its feet bound to prevent its escaping, is also placed on the Stand.[9] And once again the *ädurā*, Samarapala, begins uttering charms. This time, however, they are uttered quite audibly. There is apparently a difference between the charms uttered before the planting of the torches on top of the Stand and those uttered after. The first, as I understood it (there were contradictory reports on this matter), is the *ädurā*'s personal *mantraya*, or charm, with which he invokes the protection of Sūniyam; the second is the *diṣṭi mantraya*, the charm by means of which the *diṣṭiya* of Sūniyam is brought to the *tovil*.

Both drummers are beating a steady rhythm. Lila Amma, who has been swaying gently the while, suddenly lets out a loud, piercing scream, and begins to wail, swinging her head from side to side. Her daughter goes quickly to her assistance. Her feet are shaking. She is in evident distress. But the *ädurās* pay little attention to her. And now and again the piercing sound (*yakhan̆ḍa*, as it is called) of the whistle cuts through the drum rhythm, and the acrid smoke of the incense soaks up the air. (It was explained to me that three "characters," or *akuru*, are blown [*pimbinavā*] on the *baṭagaha*. The characters are *hū*, *vī*, and *ī*. They are necessary for "summoning" and "binding" *yakku* to the work at hand.) The Consecration of the Sūniyam Stand is a short, almost perfunctory, sequence. After five minutes or so, a large flame is thrown over the Stand, a short, tuneless sound is made with the whistle, and Samarapala, executing an elegant side step, clasps his hands, raises them at a slight incline, and bows in a brief, clipped, gesture of obeisance (*namaskāraya*) to Sūniyam Dēvatāva. The drums stop. It is just after 10:00 A.M. The torches are removed from the Stand.

Kattrīka Hatara Käpakirīma (The Consecration of the Four Offering Stands)

The following sequence, or better, set of sequences, is the *Kattrīka Hatara Käpakirīma*, the Consecration of the Four Offering Stands. It begins as soon as the necessary paraphernalia, already assembled, are put in their appropriate places. The offering stands are made of three slender sticks approximately four feet in height and tied together so as to be able to accommodate a small tray or *taṭṭuva* on top. The offerings (*dola pidēni*) are placed in them.[10] There is one offering stand each for the main *yakku* to be propitiated in this ceremony: Kalu Yaksayā, Rīri Yaksayā, Mahasōn Yaksayā, and Sūniyam Yaksayā. (Notice that this figure, Sūniyam, appears in *yaktovil* as both benevolent [i.e., as *dēvatāva*] and as malevolent [i.e., as *yaksayā*].) It is to these offering stands that the *diṣṭiya* or malign eyesight of these *yakku* will be "put" when the charms are uttered to summon (*an̆ḍagahanavā*), one after another, the presence of each of them. As I pointed out in chapter 2, the technique employed in this practice of invoking the presence of *yakku* is called *diṣṭi kirīma* (literally, the "performance" or "making" of *diṣṭiya*).

Lila Amma, in the meantime, has begun to wail once again, intermittently now, and with considerably less energy. The *ädurā*, Äddin, steps behind the curtain and cuts limes over her body. The cutting of limes (*dehi käpīma*) is one of several auxiliary practices employed by *ädurās* to effect the "binding" of *yakku*.[11] Generally, the lime is held in an instrument usually used to strip the husk away from the betel nut. While charms are uttered, it is passed over the length of the *āturayā's* body a few times before being cut at his or her feet. The number of limes cut depends on the *ädurā*'s judgment regarding the unruliness of the *yaksayā*. Meanwhile, the charms for summoning the malign eyesight of the first *yaksayā* to be called to the proceedings, Kalu Yaksayā, have started. A torch is planted on the offering stand for this *yaksayā*. The *ädurā* uttering the charms, Samarapala, shifts from foot to foot keeping time with the light rhythm of the drum. Small *gejji*, or bells, tinkle at his ankles. Every so often he sprinkles incense into the brazier held by the assistant, and a cloud of smoke lifts over the offering stand and *taṭṭuva* for Kalu Yaksayā. The cock is brought from the Sūniyam Stand and placed, squawking and flapping, at the foot of the offering stand. And in this manner the *ädurā* moves on, in turn, to the offering stands for Rīri Yaksayā, Mahasōn Yaksayā, and Sūniyam Yaksayā, summoning each to send their *diṣṭiya*, their malign eyesight, to the ceremony.

Iramudun Samayama Nätīma (The Dancing of the Midday Ceremony)

It is now about 10:35 A.M., and, after a barely noticeable pause following the end of the sequence of invocation, the *Iramudun Samayama Nätīma*, or Dancing of the Midday Ceremony, is about to begin. The presence of the *yakku* has been summoned. That is to say, their eyesight has been "caused to be brought" (*genvanavā*) to the *tovil* proceedings, and they have been "bound" to the work at hand, the *gurukama*. The Iramudun Samayama Nätīma is the main dance sequence of this particular *tovil*. Ariyadasa, a performer of incomparably charged movement, holds a torch and a handful of incense, and stands in the middle of the performing area. Then, with a sudden piercing shriek he executes a series of fierce, stamping movements. The *gejjis* at his ankles tinkle. He spins around and around the dance area. He shrieks again. Lila Amma's eyes are now wide open, her head rapidly shaking, shaking. And yet again Ariyadasa shrieks as he starts off once more with a fresh torch, the tender coconut leaf (*gokkola*) streamers of his headdress flying. Meanwhile Lila Amma has herself started to move her hands rigidly back and forth. There is a sort of rhythm to her rigid, jerky movements. Jaws clamped shut, her eyes are open but she appears little aware of anything but her own concentrated movements. And her daughter looks on with growing apprehension as, with a flourish, Ariyadasa throws a flame before the curtain and it is brought down, bringing Lila Amma into full view of the performing area. The dancing that now follows is even more fast and fierce.

Äddin, the senior *ädurā*, uttering charms, again cuts limes over Lila Amma's body. She appears to grow steadily calmer. The malevolence of the *yakku* is being restrained. But her eyes remain glassy, unfocused. And her face is tense with strain—*mūna tadavelā*, as people say. Her cheeks, too, are sunken, and the already accentuated appearance of pained distress is further set off by the silver-grey hair that, having come undone, falls disheveled about her shoulders. Soon, Ariyadasa throws a high, looping flame, to great shouts of *āyubō!*, *āyubō!!* (shortened form of "*āyubōvan*"—"Long life!, Long life!!"). He spins and stamps and, holding both torches, transcribes circular movements in the air. His whole body is in motion. . . .

It is now nearly 11:00 A.M., and time for the Iramudun Samayama to be formally introduced. Äddin, as "leader" of the performing troupe and as the *ädurā* who has had most to do with treating Lila Amma, makes the opening remarks. His manner is jocular, and at once authoritative and rhetorical. Although obviously speaking to the audience at large, he addresses himself to one of the drummers. He makes specific reference to Lila Amma's condition, and to the fact that many *tovil* ceremonies have been performed for her in the past. He is particularly concerned about her shaking (*calitavenavā*), he says, because she also suffers from high blood pressure (*preṣar ekak tiyenavā*). Nevertheless, he continues, in a tone of sure inevitability, having performed the necessary preliminary procedures, it was clear that a *tovil* was needed once again. The drummer, tapping lightly on his drum, agrees. "There are some people who play," Äddin then concludes with a sudden, deliberate sarcasm (someone in the audience having apparently made an uncomplimentary remark about him and his practice of *tovil*), "there are some people who play at cooking rice. *Those* are good works!"[12]

Two *ädurās*, Äddin and Samarapala, then take small portions of incense and, sprinkling it into the brazier, utter charms once more. Now the presence of *diṣṭiya* is not simply being generated, but also intensified. In other words, the procedures for intensifying *diṣṭiya* such that it induces the condition of *āvēśaya* (or trance) are being performed. This is because Lila Amma is going to be made to "dance and sing." A previously prepared necklace of flowers (*mal māle*) is held over the brazier, from which the incense rises thickly. Lila now begins to shake wildly, screaming, screaming. The necklace is taken to her and, in a loud voice, Äddin asks her whether she accepts it:

ÄDDIN: [*to Lila*] Do you accept (*piligannavā da*)?

LILA: The verses must be said (*kavi kiyanna ōna*).

ÄDDIN: Eh? [*as though not hearing*].

LILA: The verses must be said.

ÄDDIN: The verses must be said after it [the flower necklace] is bound. Do you accept? The verses must be said *after* it is bound. Or else it [the verses] can't be said, no.

Lila Amma howls loudly. With some difficulty Äddin manages to secure the necklace around her neck. The drums roll, and Lila howls again. Flower strands from the areca-nut palm (*puvak mal*) are placed in each of her hands. Then suddenly the drum rhythm rises in pitch. And the adorned Lila shuffles into the performance area to "dance and sing." Really, however, she sort of trots behind the *ädurā*, Ariyadasa, holding the arecanut flower strands aloft and nodding her head up and down. Little but tense weariness can be read in her immobile face. And Ariyadasa, in a stern, commanding, indeed almost rough manner, marks out with the *īgaha* (literally, "arrow tree") the path she is to follow. (The *īgaha* is made of a slender but sturdy stick of the banana plant. It is decorated at the top with loops of the tender coconut leaf, and a nail is stuck in the tip. It forms an indispensable part of the equipment by which the *ädurā* wields his authority.)[13] Lila obeys. And round and round the performing area they go. Then, on cue, both the drum and the *ädurā* stop. And propped up by another *ädurā*, Äddin questions Lila:

ÄDDIN: Are the virtuous commands (*aṇaguṇa*) of our omniscient All-Wise Buddha who crossed over the ocean of *samsāra*, the *tatāgata*[14] who attained *nirvāna*, valid for the *yakku* who are in this body?

LILA: Yes (*Eseyi*).

ÄDDIN: Now, I have been giving offerings (*dola pidēni*) for thirty-five, forty years. Once every five years you have accepted those offerings. Isn't that so?

LILA: Yes.

ÄDDIN: Now what I am asking is this. Aren't you going to go beyond five years (*avurudu pahen ehāṭa tamā yanne nädda*)? [Five years, recall, is the limit of the period for which the *tovil* will have efficacy for Lila. The *yakku* involved, principally Maha Kalu Kumāraya, have insisted on that *kāla sīmāva*.]

LILA: No [i.e., she wants to keep a five-year limit].

ÄDDIN: Now my life has surpassed (*atikrānta*) its expectancy and is going to end. Since that is so, won't you extend it beyond five years.

LILA: No.

DAUGHTER: [*To Äddin*] Ask why not.

ÄDDIN: [*To Lila*] Why? What is the cause (*hētuva*)? If the *vina diṣṭiya* [i.e., the *diṣṭiya* resulting from the sorcery] in your body was cut. . . . That day [i.e., the first time Äddin saw her for her condition] you said that, first of all, under no circumstances must the *vinaya* (sorcery) be cut. Didn't you say that if it is cut you will lose your life?

LILA: Yes.

ÄDDIN: Yes. Then, when I look I see that it has been thirty-five years since that time. Including today's there have been eleven [i.e., *tovil* ceremonies]. During those *tovils* you accepted the customary rites (*vatpilivet*)[15] that were done for you every five years according to the rule (*nītiyen*). . . .

Now, I had some trouble (*karadaraya*) last night [i.e., in the Prēta Pidēnaya, the offering ceremony to the *prētayō* who contributed to her affliction]. Why was there that trouble? Tell a little bit. . . .

LILA: I will tell later (*Passe kiyanavā*).

ÄDDIN: Can't! Can't! Not in that way. If there is any trouble you must tell. Now, were the rites and offerings that were given last night to the *prētayō, bhūtayō, bahīravayō,* and *yaksayō,* accepted (*bāragattā da*)?[16]

LILA: Yes.

ÄDDIN: Then, during this noontime period (*iramudun pālaya*) do you accept the rites and offerings that are being given to you?

LILA: Yes.

ÄDDIN: So have you done enough dancing and singing and so on (*nurtagīta ādiya karanavā*)?

LILA: Not enough (*madi*).

ÄDDIN: Now, in this . . . in this noontime, from the time we started, various offerings were dedicated (*käpa karuvā*). . . . When *diṣṭiya* was performed for [i.e., summoned to] one of the offerings, you had a greater shaking (*calitaya*) than us. Today there was no trouble, no? Did you have any trouble?

LILA: Why? I told [you] night before last.

ÄDDIN: Why? Then, according to what was told [to me] night before last I performed these rites and went away. Did you accept that (*piligattā da*)?

LILA: I accepted (*piligattā*).

ÄDDIN: So?

LILA: There are [i.e., more] (*tiyenavā*).

ÄDDIN: There are again (*āyemat tiyenavā*)?

LILA: There are.

ÄDDIN: So what should [we] do for that (*ēkaṭa mokada karanna ōna*)?

LILA: You should know to cut and go (*kapalā yanna*) [i.e., "cut" the effects of the *diṣṭiya*].

ÄDDIN: Very good (*bohōma hondayi*). . . . Now do you accept the rites and offerings that I am giving in this noontime period?

LILA: Yes.

ÄDDIN: If we are hampered (*avahira karanavā*) in the night, what should we do?

LILA: You should know to cut.

ÄDDIN: I won't trouble you any more. You are an ill person (*rōgāturayā*) [referring here to her high blood pressure, not to the effects of *diṣṭiya*]. Then, in the system of blessings (*sānti kramaya*)[17] that is performed for that period, the rites having been performed, are you going to dance and sing and so on?

LILA: Yes.

ÄDDIN: At what time?

LILA: At 9:00.

ÄDDIN: At 9:00 you can't (*namayaṭa bǟ*).

LILA: At 12:00.

ÄDDIN: 12:00 at night, and. . . .

LILA: At 9:00, 12:00, and 3:00.

ÄDDIN: There is no dancing at 9:00, no. When these offerings are given at the *āturu pandala* (the *āturayā*'s shed), you will dance and sing and so on. In that case, it is during the dancing of the *Maha Samayama*

Pelapāliya (the Great Ceremony of the Procession) that, having gone to the *raṅgamaṇḍala* (dancing area), you will dance.

LILA: [*Almost whispering*] Can't. [*Then more loudly*] At 9:00 also.

ÄDDIN: You want to dance at 9:00 also? Again?

LILA: At 12:00.

ÄDDIN: And again?

LILA: At 3:00.

ÄDDIN: After that?

LILA: After that . . . [*a terribly querulous note sounding in her voice*]?

ARIYADASA: The *diṣṭiya* [i.e., this *ädurā* prompts the crucial question].

ÄDDIN: At what time is the *diṣṭiya* being gotten rid of (*diṣṭiya maga haralā yanne koyi velāvaṭa da*)?

LILA: At 3:00.

ÄDDIN: Then, at 9:00 and 12:00 at night. . . .

LILA: At 3:00. . . .

ÄDDIN: At 3:00 . . . having danced and sung and so on. . . . It can't go at 3:00, no?

LILA: At 3:00. . . . At 3:00 [*insisting breathlessly*].

ÄDDIN: At 3:00 [*conceding*].

LILA: [*Very weakly, barely audible*] Yes.

ÄDDIN: Then, before 3:00, the dancing and singing and so on must be done. At 3:00, the dancing and singing and so on having been finished, these *yakku* are going to their residence (*yakvimānaya*) having given up this interior (*mē abhyantarē at häralā*). Aren't they?

LILA: Yes.

ÄDDIN: They are going forever, aren't they[18] (*jīvitāntaya dakvā yanavā ne*)?[19]

LILA: [*Forcefully*] No.

ÄDDIN: No? I asked it jokingly (*kaṭa boruvaṭa ähuvaṭa*). It can't be said in that way, no. It is always at five years that they are going. Why?

LILA: That is the order (*aṇa*) that was given.

ÄDDIN: So it is definitely [only] at five years that they are going?

LILA: Yes.

ÄDDIN: Then. . . .

DAUGHTER: It can't be done in that way, no. Always.

ÄDDIN: Generally, for at least one more year. . . .

MAN:[20] [*To Äddin*] Ask who gave that order (*aṇa*).

ÄDDIN: [*To the previous questioner*] It is King Vessamuni who has given that order. [*Then, irritably*] You stay away with that one until I ask. . . . [*Turning back to Lila*] It is definitely for five years that they are going?

LILA: Yes.

ÄDDIN: They won't go for even one day more than five years [he asks with a chuckle]? Have pity, a little (*anu kampā karanna, poḍḍak*). It is with these children and all the others who are here that, working very hard (*bohōma mahansi velā*), we perform this ceremony of blessing today. . . . So then, for us, won't you give a chance for at least one more year? For what that *gurunānse* [i.e., the man who planted the sorcery] said. . . . Offering flowers and lamps to gods is not for nothing, no. Having said "*Anē deviyō*," some benefit (*yahapatak*) should be received, no. . . . [*Silence. He is waiting for Lila to answer. Then, in an urging, sympathetic voice*] Say something, won't you (*kiyannako poḍḍak*)? [*Then, more harshly*] You won't say? They are going for five years?

LILA: [*Almost inaudibly*] Yes.

ÄDDIN: [*After a pause, sharply*] Good. Having performed dancing and singing and so on for those three *jāmayas* (watches), what kind of sign (*lakuna*) will indicate [that the *yakku* are] going to their residences?

LILA: I will give three hoots (*hū tunak kiyāgannavā*).[21]

ÄDDIN: Then what are we to do for you?

LILA: Water must be poured.

ÄDDIN: How much?

LILA: Seven.

ÄDDIN: Can't, no. These days there is an illness which has created trouble for your whole body no [i.e., the high blood pressure]. So at that time when the bathing (*nävili*) is done, is that good?

LILA: Good.

ÄDDIN: [*In a sympathetic tone*] Good? . . . Now, is the dancing and singing and so on enough?

LILA: Not enough.

ÄDDIN: Not enough? [*To another* ädurā *and the drummers*] Make her dance a little more (*tava ṭikak natavannā*).

And again Lila Amma trots behind the *ädurā* around the dancing area. The *ädurā*, Ariyadasa, making aggressive gestures and shouting abrasively, indicates with his *īgaha* the path she is to take and what actions she is to perform. Then again, when the drum stops, she is questioned:

ÄDDIN: Is the dancing and singing and so on enough?

LILA: [*In a weak, barely audible voice*] Enough (*äti*).

ÄDDIN: Then you will be dancing and singing and so on again at 9:00, 12:00, and 3:00 at night. Aren't you? [*He raises his voice*] Now in this noontime watch, having finished this dancing and singing and so on, during the dancing of the midday ceremony (*iramudun samayama*), you are going to the *purahala*, aren't you?[22]

LILA: Yes.

ÄDDIN: You can't go today, okay.

LILA: I must go.

ÄDDIN: You must go?

LILA: I must go.

ÄDDIN: Nevertheless, it is because your body has an illness that I'm telling you. Must you really go?

LILA: Yes.

ÄDDIN: Having finished dancing and singing and so on, you, and I also with a *purahala diṣṭiya* (the *diṣṭiya* that is taken to this structure), are going to the *purahala*.

LILA: Yes.

ÄDDIN: At that place, having tied the *sīma nūla* (literally, "boundary thread"), you are going to come to this house. . . . Having done dancing and singing and so on the way that you wanted, they are going for another five years.

LILA: Yes.

ÄDDIN: That's all, definitely (*sahatikayi*)?

LILA: Yes.

At this point—approximately 11:15 A.M.—Äddin begins saying charms inaudibly over a shallow pot, stirring its contents, a mixture of turmeric and water (recall that this is a "cooling" mixture). He tries to sprinkle a little in Lila Amma's mouth with areca-flower strands. But unexpectedly, in a show of resistance, she snatches the strands and throws them to the ground. Äddin, however, ever measured and sure in the authority he displays, takes another group of strands and patiently repeats the procedure. More subdued, she also drinks directly from the pot. And soon she appears much calmer, and is walked back to her shed.

Now the verses (*kavi*) for the *yakku* to whom offerings are to be made are about to begin. And Samarapala, holding the *īgaha*, dances before Lila Amma. Suddenly, though, she screams and starts a stiff jerky movement. And in the next moment she stands and again starts to dance. Äddin quickly intervenes and questions her again.

ÄDDIN: You gave a promise (*poronduva*), didn't you?

LILA: [?]

ÄDDIN: Ah, for now?

LILA: Now.

ÄDDIN: There is no trouble.

LILA: No.

ÄDDIN: Then while we are doing these rites and singing the verses for these offerings you will be dancing and singing and so on?

LILA: Doing.

ÄDDIN: You won't be harassed (*tamanṭa kisi hirihärayak venne nā̈*).

LILA: No.

ÄDDIN: Then, having given up this interior (*abhyantarē at häralā*) in the way you said earlier, at that night watch, having done dancing and singing and so on, [the *yakku*] having gone to their residences at 3:00, and having been bathed with seven pots of water, again, for how many years are they going?

LILA: [*Screaming almost*] They are going for five.

ÄDDIN: [*Plaintively*] *Anē,* say it is for one year more.

LILA: [*Shouting*] Don't create trouble (*karadara karanna epā*).

ÄDDIN: Don't? It is for five years that they are going?

LILA: Yes.

ÄDDIN: Then were the rites that I gave the *bahīravayō* (mean spirit associated with lower regions) and *prētayō* (mean spirits of deceased relatives) last night accepted?

LILA: Yes.

ÄDDIN: Were the *yantrayas* (protective inscriptions) that were arranged on your behalf to protect this yard (*bhūmiya*) accepted?[23]

LILA: Yes.

ÄDDIN: Then I will prepare and give [the rites] in that way. The way that you want [the rites performed] if someone makes an annoyance, that isn't accepted, is it?

LILA: [*After a short pause*] No.

ÄDDIN: No.

LILA: Cut (*kapanna*).

ÄDDIN: Are our commands (*aṇa*) valid? Will [the *yakku*] be obedient?

LILA: Cut.

ÄDDIN: Right. You are saying that . . . having cut the *diṣṭiya* in that way in those three watches, the dancing and singing and so on having been done, having been bathed at 3:00, it is not forever but for five years that they are going.

LILA: Going.

ÄDDIN: Definitely.

LILA: [?]

ÄDDIN: Now when those offerings are given. . . .

LILA: [*Weakly*] Those fellows are not singing [i.e., the verses]. Without singing. . . .

And so the verses continue, for each of the *yakku* in turn: beginning with Kalu Yaksayā, and followed by Rīri Yaksayā, Mahasōn Yaksayā, and Sūniyam Yaksayā. This is the main offering sequence in this *tovil*. The *taṭṭuvas* or offering trays placed on top of each offering stand contain the offerings to be made to the *yakku*. At the end of the verses for each *yaksayā* there are "head-to-feet" verses (*sirasapādaya*), the *ädurā* passing the *īgaha* down across Lila Amma's body to indicate (indeed to command) the direction of the descending *dōṣas*.[24] This is accompanied, as ever, by shouts of "*āyubō! āyubō!*" ("Long life!"). Then the appropriate offering tray is lifted by the assistant and held before Lila Amma. She places an offering of mixed flowers and betel leaves (*mal bulat*) and a coin offering (*pañḍuru*) in the tray. Then she enacts a significant procedure referred to as *mūna ata pisa gāsīma*, literally, "the wiping of the face with the hands" (see chapter 7 for a discussion). In this gesture Lila passes both her hands down her face three times, bringing them to rest briefly on each occasion on the outstretched offering tray. This gesture accompanies, and is indeed prompted by, the *ädurā*'s uttering of the following formulaic phrases:

The ten great troubles are finished (*daha maha dōṣa nivārnayi*).
The eighty great troubles are finished (*asū maha dōṣa nivārnayi*).
The million troubles are finished (*kōṭiyak dōṣa nivārnayi*).
Finished (*tīnduyi*). Finished (*tīnduyi*).

At the end, Lila herself says "*tīnduyi*" (finished).

This is done in turn for each of the offering trays. It were as though, in this procedure, the troubles or ill effects of the malign eyesight of the *yakku* were being transferred from Lila Amma's body back to their origin, back to the *yakku* themselves. Indeed, it is here that the activity of *diṣṭiya* is important and, with it, the concept of *sēman gänīma*, the taking of *sē-*

manaya (the substance of the food), by looking at it. As I described in chapter 2, the *diṣṭiya* that has been "summoned" (*diṣṭi aṇḍagahanavā*) by means of special charms, *diṣṭi mantrayas*, is what "takes" this substance. It is this imbibing through eyesight that provides the satisfaction (*santōsaya*) of the *yakku*.

Därahäva Pidēniya (Offering of the Bier)

In the meantime, it is now about 11:45 A.M. After the offerings are made, all the offering stands are removed to the *purālapala*, and preparations are made for the sequence to follow, the *Därahäva Pidēniya*, the Offering of the Bier. The *därahäva* is a "litter-shaped bier" made of stout stems of the banana plant and hung around with tender coconut leaf tresses. It will house the body of the *ädurā* in the ruse of death to be enacted in this sequence.

Äddin, a specialist in this sequence, takes a mat (*pädura*) and, holding it over his shoulders, begins uttering charms. He holds several lengths of cord over the brazier so that the incense rises around them. The other *ädurās*, in the meantime, seated off to the side, begin a fresh set of verses, verses that recount the story of the mat.[25] Almost immediately, Lila Amma begins to wail and flail her arms about. Äddin, with an air of complete unconcern, calmly places the cords on the ground. Charms, recall, summon *yakku*. It is therefore to be expected that when charms are being uttered and the presence of the eyesight of *yakku* is thereby generated and intensified, it will have effects on the afflicted person. And indeed it very often has effects on people in the audience. The most marked effect that *yakku* have is trembling and shaking. The spectators now begin to press closer in their effort to see. Again Lila Amma screams. With the mat slung casually over his shoulder, Äddin sings the verses accompanied by the other *ädurās* and the drummers.

Again Lila Amma wails. Now her movements appear more rhythmic. An odd smile is fixed to her lips. Then the verses stop, and she hangs her head to one side, exhausted. Äddin spreads the mat on the cords. Lila is made to lie down on her mattress. The *īgaha* rests at her side. A red cloth is then spread over her.

Then Äddin lies on the mat, taking the *īgaha*. Uttering the formulaic phrases "The ten great troubles are finished (*daha maha dōṣa nivārnayi*), the eighty great troubles are finished," and so on, Lila passes the red cloth from her head to feet and then hands it to Äddin. He covers himself. A large mortar and two pestles are placed nearby. Betel leaves, which have been passed over the brazier, are placed on Äddin's stomach. The mortar is placed on these leaves and held by assistants. Paddy (unhusked rice) is then poured in by Ariyadasa, and while *mantrayas* are being uttered it is pounded by two assistants. A chorus of *Apō!* (roughly, "Oh, my goodness!") accompanies the pounding. The paddy is taken out and sifted on Äddin's stomach. Replaced in the mortar, it is pounded once more. And again it is taken out and sprinkled over Äddin's stomach.[26]

Lila Amma seems visibly pleased. There is then a flurry of movement as Äddin is wrapped in the mat and lifted into the bier (*därahäva*). The remainder of the rice is taken to Lila, who scoops it into a small pot into which coconut water is also poured. The *därahäva* is then moved closer to Lila Amma and Äddin begins uttering charms, sprinkling incense into the brazier from time to time. A small effigy, or *pambayā,* is brought out of the house where it has been kept till now, and placed at the foot of the bier. An *ayila* (small offering tray) with a torch stuck in it is placed on it. Left for a while, it is soon taken back inside to Lila Amma's room. The cock is tied to the end of a stick at the other end of which is the pot of rice and coconut water. Hoisted onto the shoulder of an assistant, these are taken to the *purālapala*.

In a shallow pot on one side of the bier there is rice cooking over a small fire. In a similar pot on the other side is a skull fragment and an egg. These too are being cooked. The bright hibiscus-adorned offering for the Iramudun Rīri Yaksayā is placed on top of the bier. And now, in a hilarious drama of grief, two assistants begin to wail, "*ayyō Budutātti! . . . ayyō anē! . . . balannako mēka!* (oh, Buddhist father! . . . oh my! . . . look at this!)" The bier is doused with incense, and as the verses that recount its story are sung Lila Amma sways slowly from side to side. The verses over, she is made to sit up, and in turn she places in Äddin's hand *mal bulat* (a mixture of betel leaves and flowers), paddy, a ring, and a coin offering. She then repeats the gesture *mūna ata pisa gäsīma* ("wiping the face with the hands") to the familiar phrases signifying the removal or end of the effects of the eyesight of *yakku*.

By this time the assistant who had taken the cock and pot to the bier platform, the *purālapala,* has returned. The cock is taken and tied to the bier, and the contents of the pot are "read" for signs of the progress of the *tovil*. Satisfied, the rice is distributed around the bier in a number of small trays. Then Äddin, from his prone position, throws a flame and the bier is hoisted and taken around the house three times. At each of three trays staked in the ground, they pause to fan incense onto it. The bier with Äddin in it is then taken to the bier platform. It is now 12:50 P.M., and therefore, strictly speaking, the proceedings are running late.

Dekonavilakku Pidēniya (Offering of the Double-Sided Torch)

During the final stages of the Offering of the Bier, Ariyadasa has been preparing himself for the last and most dramatic sequence of the Iramudun Samayama, the *Dekonavilakku Pidēniya*, the Offering of the Double-Sided Torch. Standing at the Sūniyam Stand, Ariyadasa blackens his face with soot. He shuffles from foot to foot so that the ankle bells, *gejji*, tinkle. Feet spread apart, he leans against the Stand, shaking it. He inhales drafts of incense. The double-ended torch is fixed to his mouth and lit. He turns sharply, gives a short, clipped, perfunctory bow (*namaskāraya*) to the Sūniyam Stand and throws a flame. He moves then, staccato fashion, transcribing a half circle and waving both torches in Lila Amma's direction. Shuffles and steps are alternated with threatening, frozen stances. The gestures are aggressive; the glares, menacing. Doubling back to the Stand, he inhales more incense, replenishes the torches, and spins back into action. Another *ädurā*, Samarapala, assists him. His air of unconcern cuts a striking contrast to the high-pitched intensity of Ariyadasa's movements and the expectant gravity that hangs about the atmosphere in the "*tovil* house" (*tovil gedara*). Ariyadasa is indeed now shaking violently, pulling the Sūniyam Stand this way and that. He makes a sudden turn in Lila Amma's direction and instantly she stands and starts to "dance." From her he turns abruptly toward the house. He enters it through the open doorway. And Lila Amma follows. Going first into Lila's room, he throws a flame, then stands shaking with an outstretched arm waiting for his assistant to give him a lime and the lime cutter. These placed in his hand, he cuts the lime and drops them to the floor. Then, taking the *īgaha*, he holds it at various points of the door frame with menacing, admonishing gestures. Before leaving the doorway, he throws a flame and in like manner goes through the whole house. He is, as *ädurās* say, collecting the *diṣṭiya* and *dōṣa* from the house onto himself. All the while Lila Amma is shuffling at his side.

The house is then shut up and they return to the dancing area. Both

Ariyadasa and Lila Amma are shaking. Ariyadasa holds a lime at Lila's head and shufflles back and forth up to her with aggressive and admonishing gestures. The lime is cut. Then lime and lime cutter are dropped to the ground and he holds the *īgaha* to her in the same attitudes of threat and admonition. Presently he throws a flame in front of her. It is the sign to set off for the bier platform. With Ariyadasa and Lila Amma at the lead, a whole throng of people follow for the distance of about a quarter of a mile to the open area where the platform, or *purālapala*, has been constructed. At the platform, Lila Amma mounts it and collapses on Äddin (who had been brought there in the bier). Ariyadasa makes an effort to mount but is prevented, restrained by assistants. He falls against an assistant, is then lifted onto a mat, and immediately and very solicitously attended to. A great deal of urgency surrounds this procedure because the *ädurā* must be coaxed back to normal awareness. Samarapala utters the appropriate charms and sprinkles him with turmeric water. Gently he pries his mouth open just enough to take the double-ended torch. His face is cleaned, and he is helped out of his costume. In the meantime, Äddin is tying a fresh protective thread (*äpa nūla*) around Lila Amma's wrist and neck. It is about 1:20 P.M. The Iramudun Samayama is complete.

[There then follows a slow and filling lunch (*bat*, literally, rice), and a long rest for all. A few people mill around. By 4:00 P.M., the performers and their assistants have already made headway erecting the new structures for the next *tovil* ceremony. (See Figure 2)]

Maha Kalu Kumāra Samayama

A pyramidal structure elaborately decorated with loops of tender coconut leaves stands in the middle of the performing area. This is the Sanni Kalu Kumāra Pidēniya (Offering for the Illness-making Black Prince). It is the signature offering in this *tovil* which in many other structural respects differs little from other *tovil* ceremonies. At its apex are strands of the areca-nut palm. The central (or at least most imposing) structure, the *mal maḍuva* (literally, flower shed), stands opposite the *āturayā*'s shed. Bright red hibiscuses hang from some of the tender coconut leaf tresses, and small red flowers dot its outer sides. It is now evening. Clusters of people are gathered waiting for the proceedings to begin.

Figure 2. Performance area for Maha Kalu Kumāra Samayama

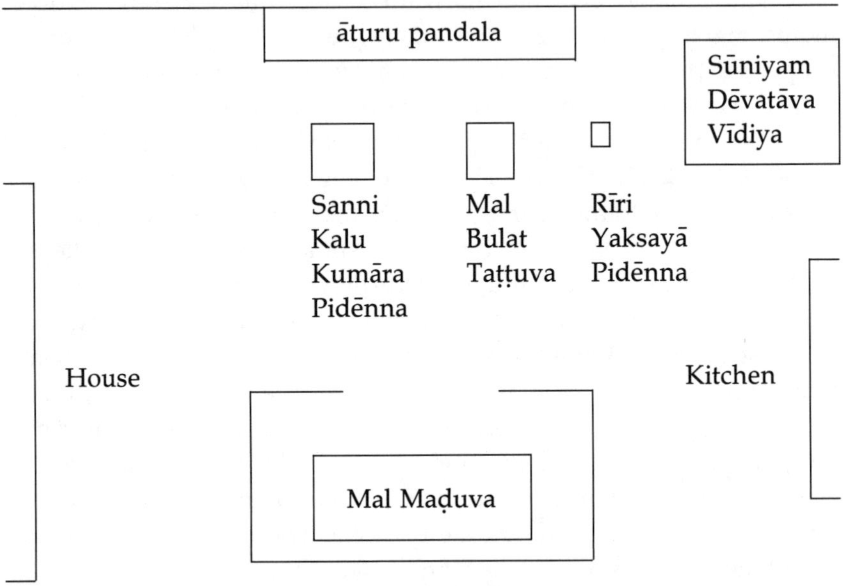

The Lamp for the Four Warrant Gods (*Hatara Varam Deviyō*)

Shortly after 6:00 P.M., Lila is led out of the house—in much the same fashion as in the earlier Iramudun Samayama. The lamp for the Four Warrant Deities, two of its small flames dancing in the overcast evening, is taken from her and hung from a rafter of her shed. She sits hands clasped, a little subdued, it would appear, as the curtain is raised hiding her from view.

Sūniyam Vīdiya Käpakirīma (The Consecration of the Sūniyam Stand)

It is about 6:15 P.M. The Consecration of the Sūniyam Stand (*Sūniyam Vīdiya Käpakirīma*) is beginning. The charms are said in a whisper. The torches are planted. Smoke from the *dummala* sprinkled in the brazier rises around it. Now and again the *ädurā* fans some of it unto himself. The *baṭagaha* is blown. The drumbeat rises, the *ädurā* throws a flame over the Stand, and the sequence ends. Meanwhile, an offering stand (with the offering tray for Kalu Kumāraya) and the Sanni Kalu Kumāra Pidēniya are placed immediately before the raised curtain.

Kattrīka Hatara Käpakirīma (Consecration of the Four Offering Stands)

After the inaugural invocation to the deity Sūniyam, asking for his permission to perform the ceremony and his protection throughout the night's proceedings, there follows the *Kattrīka Hatara Käpakirīma*, the Consecration of the Four Offering Stands. There is a slight difference between its performance in this ceremony and the earlier one. Three offerings are initially placed before the curtain. In addition to the two already mentioned—that is, the offering stands for Kalu Kumāraya and the Sanni Kalu Kumāra Pideniya—there is an offering basket for the consorts of Kalu Kumāraya, the Rid Yakṣanī (or Riddi Bisavun). This is called *mal bulat taṭṭuva* (the offering of flowers and betel). Torches are placed in each and Äddin begins the charms for calling the *diṣṭiya* (*diṣṭi karanavā*) of these figures. No sooner is this done than the verses about Kalu Kumāraya start. Wearing bright red bands around his white sarong and tunic, and layers of beads around his neck, Äddin steps slowly, elegantly, from foot to foot. There is a serene air about Uncle Äddin that must, no doubt, inspire confidence. He is joined by another *ädurā*, a deft and almost sensuous dancer, Samarapala Liyanage. They take turns executing steps around the dancing area. These verses finished, the *ädurās* turn sharply to the *maḍuva* and perform a salutation (*namaskāraya*).

Lila, in the meantime, lies calmly on her mattress. The red flower offerings at her side provide a startling aspect against her white clothing. After the verses about this figure, there follows the crucial "head-to-feet" verses (*sirasapādaya*). Äddin, holding a fresh torch, sings. This finished, the tray for Kalu Kumāraya is held before Lila, who makes the requisite offering of flowers and betel (*mal bulat*) and enacts the gesture of "wiping the face with the hands" and saying "*tīnduyi*" at the end of it. This is followed by the coin offering (*pan̆ḍuru*) in similar fashion. The same is repeated with the Mal Bulat Taṭṭuva for Kalu Kumāraya's consorts. Lila Amma, already tired, fails to repeat the important word "*tīnduyi*" and the *ädurā* shouts that it must be said. The offering stand for Kalu Kumāraya and the Mal Bulat Taṭṭuva are then removed (they are placed beside the Sūniyan Vīdiya) and the other three offering stands—for Rīri Yaksayā, Mahasōn Yaksayā, and Sūniyam Yaksayā—are brought and set in a line before the curtained-off Lila Amma.

Charming begins, Äddin holding a torch, the whistle, and *dummala*.

From time to time the offering stands are doused with smoke. After the *diṣṭiya* has been summoned, each of the stands is raised for a moment before the *āturayā*. The cock is similarly raised before her. It is now approximately 8:00 P.M. and the verses for Rīri Yaksayā are about to begin. As they do, Lila suddenly sits up. She shrieks and starts to shake rhythmically from side to side. But she soon collapses again, resting her head on her pillow. The drumbeats intensify and the steps of the dancing *ädurās* quicken. In duet now, the "head-to-feet" verses (*sirasapādaya*) start. As an *ädurā* approaches Lila Amma, pointing the *īgaha* down the length of her body, there are shouts of "*āyubō!*" At the conclusion of the *sirasapādaya* verses the offerings are made to the trays for Rīri Yaksayā and Mahasōna in the customary way.

Although there is one more offering stand to be "consecrated" (for Sūniyam Yaksayā), it is now close to 8:50 P.M., and preparations are being made for Lila to "dance and sing" at the appointed hour, 9:00 P.M. The Sanni Kalu Kumāra Pidēniya is placed in the center of the dancing area. The curtain is raised before her. She sits calmly; then lies down. The drumbeat intensifies once more. But Lila Amma does not respond. Äddin disappears behind the curtain to cut limes. Incense fills the air. The necklace of flowers is placed around her neck. Still she does not respond. The areca-flower strands are placed in her hands, but even now she seems unmoved. Then with a dramatic flourish a flame is thrown before the curtain and it is brought down. And Lila stands, but wearily. She is led round and round the Offering Stand for the main *yaksayā* involved in her affliction, Maha Kalu Kumāraya, and through the passageways of the Flower Shed before the drum stops and she collapses against her son. She is then questioned by Äddin:

ÄDDIN: Are the virtuous commands of our All-Wise, noble and Venerable King Buddha, the *tatāgata* who attained *nirvāna*, valid for the *dēvas*, *dēvatāvas*, and *yakku* who are in this body (*mē sarīra abhyantarē vāsaya karanne*)?

LILA: Valid (*valangu*).

ÄDDIN: Second, is the sermon (*dēsanāva*) and order (*aṇa*) of the god Sakra, leader of the gods of both heavens, valid?

LILA: Valid.

ÄDDIN: Third, are the qualities of the virtuous commands (*aṇaguṇa*) those who have attained the Path to nirvana (*aṣṭārya pudgala*), the Great Jewel of the Sangha, valid?

LILA: Valid.

ÄDDIN: If the virtuous commands of the Buddha and *dēvas* and *dēvatāvas* are valid, what I am asking is. . . . For a number of years I have known what *yakku* are in this body. Now the others who are in this place [i.e., the audience] will think that what this person [i.e., himself] is doing is a great big hoax (*loku boruva*). Because of that, I am asking what *yakku*, what *dēvatāva*, and what *kumbhāndaya* [are there in this body]?

LILA: [*At almost screaming pitch*] Venerable Kalu Kumāra Dēvatāva (*Kalu Kumāra dēvatāvun vahanse*).

ÄDDIN: Who else?

LILA: The Venerable Dēvatāva Mahasōna.

ÄDDIN: Who else?

LILA: Also Iramudun Rīri Yakā.

ÄDDIN: And also Iramudun Rīri Yakā was contained in this body (*sarīra abhyantarēṭa aḍaṃgu unā*) with an impediment of sorcery (*yam kisi vini tahanciyak*).

LILA: Yes.

ÄDDIN: Since that is so, the rites and offerings that were given here once every five years were accepted . . . were accepted, weren't they?

LILA: Yes.

ÄDDIN: Now, did the Iramudun Rīri Yaksayā accept the rites and offerings that were given at midday?

LILA: Yes.

ÄDDIN: Now, why I don't think I will harass you and make you dance and sing like on other days is because you have an illness in your body. Since that is so, have you performed enough dancing and singing and so on?

LILA: Not enough.

ARIYADASA: [*To Lila's daughter*] So you are telling me not to make her dance, not to make her perform dancing and singing and so.

ÄDDIN: [They] are saying "don't (*epā*)!"

ARIYADASA: [We are] not to harass.

ÄDDIN: [*To Lila's daughter*] So you are telling me not to make her perform this dancing and singing and so on.

ARIYADASA: They are saying "don't."

ÄDDIN: [*To the audience at large and emphatically*] She [i.e., Lila] is saying it is not enough. So I have to make her dance as much as she wants, no? It gives us a bad name, no (*ēka loku naraka nāmayak ne*)? When it happens like that, having gone and performed the ceremony of blessing (*sāntiya*), this person can be made to lie down, no? Then it is not good, no? Now it seems that the dancing and singing is not enough. So let us perform and sing and so on a little more. You [all] don't be afraid (*baya venna epā*). . . . [*Then, turning back to Lila*] Now, in the morning too I asked [i.e., about the dancing] because there is an illness in the body. . . . Early in the morning medicine was brought. . . . Now, if the dancing and singing for the *yakku* who are in this body was done in the way you wanted, will the body be disturbed?

LILA: No.

ÄDDIN: There won't be any trouble at all?

LILA: No.

ÄDDIN: [*In a sympathetic voice*] You should dance as much as you want?

LILA: Yes.

ÄDDIN: Let go her hand.

The drumming begins again and the *ädurā* leads Lila Amma round the dancing area. Presently they stop.

ÄDDIN: You promised that the virtuous commands of our omniscient All-Wise Venerable King Buddha who crossed over the ocean of *samsāra*, the *tatāgata* who attained *nirvāna*, is valid for *yakku* who are in this body.[27]

LILA: Yes.

ÄDDIN: Have you performed enough dancing and singing and so on?

LILA: Not enough.

So again, led by an *ädurā,* Lila Amma "dances and sings." This time they go up to the clay effigy (*baliya*) of Kalu Kumāraya. Lila bobs her head back and forth toward and from it. She is executing the gesture called "taking *sēman*." They circle the Sūniyam Stand, and then the Sanni Kalu Kumāra Pidēniya. Here again she pushes her face toward the offering, "taking *sēman*." They stop.

ÄDDIN: Have you performed enough dancing and singing and so on?

LILA: Not enough.

ÄDDIN: Not enough? That is not the way (*ehema nemē*). There are two more times for you to perform dancing and singing and so on. At 12:00 at night the dancing and singing and so on can be done. Don't you accept? You want to dance more?

LILA: Yes.

So again she dances. And again she is questioned.

ÄDDIN: [*Saying a charm first*] Now have you performed enough dancing and singing and so on?

LILA: Enough.

ÄDDIN: At what time will you perform dancing and singing and so on again?

LILA: At 12:00.

ÄDDIN: And after?

LILA: At 3:00.

ÄDDIN: At 3:00. Then at 12:00 and at 3:00, the dancing and singing and so on having been done, at what time will the *yakku* go to their residence, having given up this body?

LILA: At 3:00.

ÄDDIN: Will there be a sign (*lakuna*) when this *diṣṭiya* is being gotten rid of (*diṣṭiya maga haralā yana velāva*)?

LILA: Yes.

ÄDDIN: What kind of sign is it?

LILA: Hooting (*hū kiyanavā*).

ÄDDIN: So, then what must we do for you?

LILA: Water must be poured.

ÄDDIN: Water? How much?

LILA: Seven.

ÄDDIN: You should be bathed with seven pots of water?

LILA: Yes.

ÄDDIN: Then every time, these *yakku,* having given up the body, are going for. . . . This is the twelfth *tovil* as far as I can remember. You are going for five years. Is it for five years that you are going?

LILA: For five years.

ÄDDIN: You won't go a little farther? At least one month?

LILA: No. You were allowed [i.e., previously to extend the limit].

ÄDDIN: I was allowed. Why I was allowed is. . . . The one that was going for three years was extended to five years. . . . It is your children who have been caused trouble and harassment to drive away (*dakka gannavā*)[28] *yakku* who have fallen in this body. . . . They are going for five years.

LILA: Yes.

ÄDDIN: They won't go any farther than that?

LILA: No.

ÄDDIN: So . . . can't you move it up one year? Have pity (*anukampā karalā*). If that harasses you, don't do it. You said no, that if it was removed you would be harassed for the whole year. You said, "Without harassing me it is for five years that they are going," didn't you? You have promised that, no?

LILA: Yes.

ÄDDIN: Because of that, five years is enough. There is nothing I can do. I would be satisfied if they go until the end of your life. . . . On that day, having made an effigy for the eighteen *vīdiyas* (*dahāṭa vīdiya baliya*), a Maha Kalu Kumāraya effigy, and done a *tovil*, I asked whether they will go forever. So what can we do? . . . The dancing and singing and so on having been performed at 12:00 and 3:00, having hooted three times and been bathed with seven pots of water, the *yakku* who are in the body are going to their residences at 3:00.[29]

LILA: Yes.

ÄDDIN: After that [i.e., after the *yakku* go], shall we stop this ceremony of blessing (*sāntiya*)?

LILA: Don't (*epā*).

ÄDDIN: We should do the rites that we have to do?

LILA: Yes.

ÄDDIN: After that, when we are doing this ceremony of blessing, will there be any trouble?

LILA: No.

ÄDDIN: Definitely (*sahatika da*)?

LILA: Yes.

ÄDDIN: At this time, then, at 3:00, the dancing and singing and so on having been done, as on other days, do you give me a promise?

LILA: Yes.

ÄDDIN: Have you performed enough dancing and singing and so on now?

LILA: Enough.

ÄDDIN: So what more should I ask, eh?

VOICE: Don't trouble her any more. . . .

Lila Amma, having been given some turmeric water to drink, is led back to her shed. She lies down, exhausted, as the verses for Sūniyam

Yaksayā (the only *yaksayā* left to receive offerings) are sung; after the verses about him, the *sirasapādaya*. Then the offering tray is held out to Lila, who makes the usual offerings, gestures, and utterances. It is 9:35 P.M. or thereabouts, and a short break follows.

Däpavilla Pidēniya (Offering Made Lying Down) and the *Aṭa Kona Käpa Kirīma* (Consecration at the Eight Corners)

After about fifteen minutes, the performers sufficiently refreshed with tea, the sequence called the *Däpavilla Pidēniya* begins. The Däpavilla Pidēniya is an offering sequence in which verses are sung about the mat (*pädura*), the *diṣṭiya* of *yakku* are called from the eight corners (*aṭa kona*), and the *ädurā* lies on his back on the mat as though a death offering for the *yakku*. It is, principally, a sequence for one of the Rīri Yakku.

One *ädurā*, Ariyadasa, takes the mat and begins to sing verses. He holds it over the brazier so that incense rises around it. He waves it slowly before Lila as he sings. Then another *ädurā*, Samarapala, joins him, holding the *īgaha*. They sing the verses, alternating stanzas.

Lila Amma lets out two shrieks. Her feet move with an agitated rhythm.

The verses continue. Periodically one of the *ädurās* makes a gesture in Lila's direction, which is greeted with shouts of "*ayubōvan!*" (or sometimes lengthened to "*ayubōvēvan!*"), "Long life!" Ariyadasa passes the torch along the mat as he sings. The mat is then spread on the ground and a fierce dance follows. Ariyadasa races to the Flower Shed and shakes it, shrieking. Returning to the mat, he throws a flame, falling onto his back, crossing the torches. Getting up, he takes a few steps, then falls on his knees, crossing the torches and bringing them down at one corner of the mat. This is repeated at each of the four corners of the mat. This is the sequence called the *Aṭa Kona Käpa Kirīma*, or the Consecration at the Eight Corners. Between each "consecration" a comic sequence ensues in which Ariyadasa feigns chasing the assistant who holds the brazier. The audience delights in this.

Avamangalle Pidēniya (Funeral Offering)

The eight corners dedicated, the mat is spread closer to Lila Amma and Äddin lies on it. He covers himself to the neck with a sheet that Lila has passed down the length of her body three times. The *Avamangalle Pi-*

dēniya or Funeral Offering, a shallow, casket-shaped container, is placed on his stomach. In it there are nine offering trays, each with betel leaves, coins, a small bit of cloth, and a lime. A torch is stuck in the offering.

Holding the whistle in one hand and the torch in the other, Äddin utters charms. This is followed by verses. Periodically he blows the whistle. Presently the offering is lifted to Lila, who makes the necessary expressions of offering. The gesture of wiping the face and touching the offering is repeated. And repeated again, touching the cock. While uttering charms, Äddin throws a flame before Lila. This signals the end of the offering sequence. Lila Amma is led away briefly.

Mahasamayama (Great Ceremony)

The four offering stands and the various other offerings are taken away to the bier platform, and preparations are made for the sequence called the *Mahasamayama*, the Great Ceremony. The Great Ceremony is a sequence given over to elaborate expositions of dance. All the *ädurās* participate. Ariyadasa starts, shrieking, charging toward the Flower Shed. Then, all the *ädurās*, holding torches and to shouts of "Long life!," charge the Flower Shed and plant the torches. A torch is planted at the clay image of Maha Kalu Kumāraya.

At this point Äddin formally introduces the *tovil*:

ÄDDIN: Is there an *āturumahatmaya* (*āturayā*'s husband) here?

DRUMMER: No.

ÄDDIN: There is no one. Only she [Lila] as [both] *āturumahatmaya* and *āturuhāmini* (ill wife).

DRUMMER: Yes.

ÄDDIN: If there is anyone who is *āturumahatmaya* [i.e., a responsible male in the family], it is the two sons.

DRUMMER: Yes.

ÄDDIN: These two are very afraid to come to gatherings like this [i.e., *tovil* ceremonies. They were actually inside the house].

DRUMMER: Yes.

ÄDDIN: They are very innocent (*bohōma ahinsakayi*).

DRUMMER: Yes.

ÄDDIN: Because of that, although I have asked them to come I don't know whether they will come. . . .

DRUMMER: Yes.

ÄDDIN: Because we are given the command and authority (*aṇavaram*) to perform this ceremony of blessing (*sāntiya*). . . .

DRUMMER: Yes. . . .

ÄDDIN: We should get permission (*avasaraya*) from these two. If it is not gotten, it is not good, no.

DRUMMER: It is not good.

ÄDDIN: Permission should be gotten from these two. Do you know why?

DRUMMER: Yes.

ÄDDIN: Now, when I was dancing in the evening I was told, "Oh, Uncle, don't make her dance as much as this."

DRUMMER: Yes.

ÄDDIN: Because of that we have to make her dance at 12:00. Again, we should ask from these two [i.e., the sons]: "If we have to make her dance again, if there is a system like this, what should be done?" We can't in that way, no [i.e., without asking]. Without asking in that way the *leḍā* of others [i.e., a sick person who belongs to another family] can't be made to dance, no.

Child, come here [to one of the sons, the younger (*malli*), who has emerged from the house and is standing at the door]. It is to both of you that I spoke. Where is big brother (*ayyā*)? Now, I was told this evening too, at this watch, at 9:00, when she was made to dance, not to make her dance in this way. But I was not happy that she was made to dance even a little bit. [Yet] on every occasion that I ask she says it [i.e., the dancing] is not enough. At that time I made her dance. Now at the 12:00 watch in which she is to dance, the sequences (*kramaya*) having occurred, if mother says, "I didn't dance enough," there is nothing I can do. I have to make her dance, no? It is because of you fellows that I am asking.

First of all, I was told not to do it, no? . . . Where is big brother? I have to ask big brother too. . . . Without asking in that way, I can [i.e., in fact] perform. Without making her dance while it is like that, having prohibited the ill person (*leḍā hira karalā tiyalā*), I can perform the *tovil*. [But] this one is not a work like that. . . . Because of that, until the ill person says [i.e., to stop], we are going to make her dance. There won't be any trouble. This ceremony of blessing (*sāntiya*) is done in such a way that there won't be any trouble. It is not done [simply] in the way that we want. But you children have a determined mind (*hitē vēgayak tiyenavā*). But there is nothing I can do. This is not a *tovil* performed in order to learn. You both know, no? At that time, at the beginning when I was performing *tovils*, you weren't born. Because of that the *tovil* is performed in the way that I know.

It is to say this small matter that I spoke. Now, this evening it was once again said not to make this mother dance, wasn't it?

VOICE: Yes.

ÄDDIN: Then when she is made to dance at 12:00, if we want to make her dance in that way, what can we do? That's right. It is from your childhood that I have been performing *tovils*. Not only you, there is big sister (*akkā*), who is older than you. Since before that too I have been performing *tovils*. Because of that, if I am told to make her dance I will make her dance. I too am not happy, because she is an ill person. She has had an illness since those days, no? Medicine was taken for pressure, no? I too was afraid. If that happened in that way, we won't make her dance. But if we are told that she wants to dance we will make her dance. Now, in the evening at 9:00 when she was dancing, having done these things, I asked once every three minutes. She said she couldn't, no? She said she wants to dance, no?

I can only ask these two [i.e., the sons]. It is these two who are the heads (*mūlikaya*) [i.e., of the family]. So if the ill person says to me that she wants to dance, I will make her dance. Okay (*hari da*)? So you are not angry, no?

Then again the *ädurās* dance alternately through the Flower Shed and around the Sanni Kalu Kumāra Pidēniya. But it is rapidly approaching 12:00 and it will soon be time for Lila Amma to "dance and sing" once more. The curtain is raised before her, and she is made ready for the sequence. However, she seems barely able to rouse herself. Her disheveled hair accentuates the pall, the heavy weight that seems to hang over her.

The flower necklace is placed around her neck. Weakly, she takes the areca-nut strands. A flame is thrown and the curtain is brought down. Ever so slowly, then, Lila Amma gets up. An *ädurā* solemnly rests the *īgaha* on her forehead. Then off they start. Once at the Flower Shed, Lila leans against it, throwing her head forward in the action of "taking *sēman*." She is led to the clay image of Kalu Kumāraya where again she "takes *sēman*." The drums stop and she is questioned:

ÄDDIN: Did you dance enough?

LILA: Not enough.

ÄDDIN: Not enough? Were the offerings that were given in the evening to the *yakku* accepted?

LILA: Yes.

ÄDDIN: Yes? In the midday watch, did the *yakku* who are in the body accept the offerings that were given to the Iramudun Rīri Yaksayā and the Avamangala Rīri Yaksayā?

LILA: Yes.

ÄDDIN: Did they accept, giving a promise (*porondu velā bāragattā da*)?

LILA: Yes.

ÄDDIN: Now, for the time being have you performed enough dancing and singing and so on?

LILA: Not enough.

ÄDDIN: Why you can't do a lot of dancing and singing and so on is because you are ill, no? So won't there be trouble?

LILA: No.

ÄDDIN: More dancing and singing should be done?

LILA: Yes.

ÄDDIN: Make her dance (*naṭavanna*).

So again she dances, this time following behind a different *ädurā*. She is led to the clay image. Then she is made to climb on a pot of water placed on a chair. Weakly she climbs, falling backward. At this point her children intervene, protesting, imploring—her daughter in tears. In disgust, one of the *ädurās,* Ariyadasa, walks off. But Lila insists on continuing. Slowly she moves behind another *ädurā,* Samarapala. The drums stop.

ÄDDIN: [*A charm to begin with. Then*] From midday and from evening a promise was given to me that the virtuous commands of our Omniscient All-Wise Venerable King Buddha who crossed over the ocean of *samsāra,* the *tatāgata* who attained *nirvāna,* is valid for the *yakku, dēvas,* and *dēvatāvas* who are inside this body (*mē sarīra abhyantarē vāsaya karana yakun yakṣaniyanṭa devi dēvatāvunṭa*). It was given, wasn't it?

LILA: Yes.

ÄDDIN: Then I was told that the *yakku* who are inside you (*tamagē abhyantarē inna yakun yakṣaniyan*) want to perform dancing and singing and so on at 9:00 and at 12:00. According to the promise that was made there, we have performed it. Was it accepted?

LILA: Yes.

ÄDDIN: Now have you performed enough dancing and singing and so on?

LILA: Not enough.

So again she follows the *ädurā.*

ÄDDIN: You having performed dancing and singing and so on. . . . I was given a promise that having performed dancing and singing and so on again at 3:00 at night [the *yakku*] are going, having given up this interior for five years. Is it definitely at that time that they are going?

LILA: Yes.

ÄDDIN: Now should more dancing and singing be done?

LILA: Yes.

ÄDDIN: Really?

LILA: Yes.

ÄDDIN: A little more. Let go [her] hand.

And again she is led off. And a few moments later, again they stop.

ÄDDIN: Is the dancing and singing and so on enough?

LILA: Enough.

ÄDDIN: At what time will you dance and sing and so on again?

LILA: At 3:00.

ÄDDIN: Yes. Having finished dancing and singing and so on at 3:00, having hooted three times and been bathed with seven pots of water, for how long are these *yakku* who are inside, in this body (*mē abhyantarē inna, mē sarīra inna yakun yakṣaniyan*), going, having given up the inside of this body (*sarīra abhyantarē at häralā yanne*)?

LILA: For five years.

ÄDDIN: That's it, no? So that is the wrong story (*väradi katāva*), no? Every time you won't go farther than five years. It never goes farther than that?

LILA: No.

ÄDDIN: What is the meaning of that. Has a promise been given to you? . . . It is like this. The obstruction (*avahiraya*), meaning the sorcery, that one has been given with a promise (*ēka dīla tiyenne poronduvak ätiva*). . . . Either the ill person or the *ädurā* [i.e., will die if the sorcery is "cut"]. Because of that, it is having promised for [a period of] five years that they are going. That is what has to be understood. Like that. According to your promise, they won't go for even one year more than five years, [but] what I am saying is that I would be satisfied if they went not for five but for six years. . . . I am saying that this is the twelfth *tovil*. . . . They won't go?

LILA: No.

ÄDDIN: [That] means that you are saying that there is a sorcery (*vina*) *diṣṭiya* and I am being told to cut that sorcery *diṣṭiya*. If I can't cut . . .

LILA: It can't be cut.

ÄDDIN: Why? If I can't cut it, somebody else having been brought must cut it.

LILA: Can't (*bā*).

ÄDDIN: Why? What will happen if it is cut?

LILA: If [it is] cut, this human body will die (*kapuvot mē nara sarīraya yanavā*).[30]

ÄDDIN: If that sorcery (*vinaya*) is cut.

LILA: Yes.

ÄDDIN: If it is like that, that sorcery can't be cut, no. That means when they go, having given up the interior, when the sorcery is cut, what seems to be said is that her life will be lost. It can't be done in that way.

DAUGHTER: Can't it be done by giving another *billa* (sacrifice)?

ÄDDIN: [*Responding to daughter*] I was ready to give two sacrifices. Now, on that occasion I said that I would give two sacrifices instead of one. But I was told "don't!" It seems they [i.e., the *yakku*] don't want *billas* (sacrifices) either. . . . There is nothing I can do. . . . [*To Lila*] Is it enough?

LILA: [*Barely audible*] Enough.

A limp Lila is carried back to her shed. And the dancing of the Mahasamayama continues, each *ädurā* taking turns with a repertoire of steps. They sing verses.

It is about 12:00 A.M., and there then follows an interlude called *aḍavva* (dance) in which the drummer beats out a small rhythm and each dancer in turn provides accompanying steps ending it with a gesture of deference (*namaskāra karanavā*). A collection of money follows, first from the householders, and then from the audience.

Mangara Pelapāliya (Procession for the god Mangara)

After a break of roughly half an hour there is a short sequence for the *mal bulat taṭṭuva* (the flower and betel offering tray). It is then taken away. Immediately after the preparations begin for the next major sequence, the *Mangara Pelapāliya*, the Procession for the god Mangara. From here on in the *tovil* the comic sequences begin. The Mangara Procession concerns a letter received from someone that the god Mangara wished to see a *tovil*. The *tovil* performers are asked to arrange a procession for his amusement. There is a short comic dialogue with a drummer regarding the letter.[31] The procession is organized with a group of small children, each being given a particular item symbolizing royal paraphernalia. They are then marched through the Flower Shed and around the dancing area to the hilarity of the audience. There is a short juggling act by one of the *ädurās*, and a comic repartee between two of them. Then sequences involving a tusker, an ox, and last of all Kalu Vädi Dēvatāva, who "kills" a cock with his bow and arrow.

This long set of sequences is followed by an offering (of ten offering trays) to Mahasōn Yaksayā (in this sequence referred to respectively as *dēvatāva*) and his various *avatāras* or apparitions. (There is a legend that the Mahasōna was subjugated by the god Mangara.) The offering trays are then distributed around the Flower Shed.

By now it is approaching the crucial hour of 3:00 A.M. when the *diṣṭiya* is supposed to be removed, and the dancing area is once again being readied for the "dancing and singing." The Sanni Kalu Kumāra Pidēniya is again placed in the middle of the area and three torches are planted in it. Charms are uttered and the necklace and areca-flower strands are taken to Lila Amma. Two flames are thrown and the curtain is brought down. Lila Amma only barely responds. With effort she stands and follows the path marked out for her by the *ädurā*—up to the clay image, around the offering, through the Flower Shed. Then, as the intensity mounts, Lila Amma dramatically climbs the Flower Shed. The audience literally gasps—for, remember, she is a woman in her middle sixties—and presses farther upon the performing area. In a most precarious manner she walks across the top, pausing now and again to shake her feet and hands. Eventually she is helped down and questioned.[32]

ÄDDIN: Have you performed enough dancing and singing and so on?

LILA: Not enough.

ÄDDIN: Not enough? [*To the drummers*] Beat.

So again she dances. Refusing to follow the *ädurā*, she goes off to the Sūniyam Stand, then into the kitchen. The *ädurā* shouts out a reprimand and she returns to the path he marks out. Round the offering. The drum stops abruptly.

ÄDDIN: Enough?

LILA: Not enough.

ÄDDIN: In that case, having given answers for what I want to ask, do as much dancing and singing and so on as you want. . . . I was given a promise that the virtuous commands of our Omniscient All-Wise and Venerable King Buddha, who crossed over the ocean of *samsāra*, the *tatāgata* who attained *nirvāna*, is valid for the interior of this body. Then, when that promise was given you said that Kalu Kumāraya, Rīri Yaksayā, and the Venerable dēvatāva Mahasōna are inside your body (*tamagē sarīra abhyantarē*). We have done rites and given offerings to the *yakku* who are there. Were they accepted?

LILA: Accepted.

ÄDDIN: Then, you said that the *yakku* who are in the interior of your body are going to their residence at 3:00. That time hasn't yet come. Even though our exact time has come [i.e., by the clock it is now 3:00 A.M.], you still have time. At that time, with what kind of sign are they going?

LILA: Having hooted three times. Having hooted three times and been bathed with seven pots of water, they are going.

ÄDDIN: Going. Then, again, they are going to their residence for . . . years?

LILA: For five.

ÄDDIN: For five. A great trouble has come to me that they aren't going for more than this five years. Now, there was a small indication, but I am satisfied that any one of those gentlemen or whoever will say sometime [i.e., will cast suspicion upon his *tovil* performance]. Now, I am even ready to be hit. . . . It is not from this *tovil* alone that I am living. I will earn and eat well. This *tovil* is a *tovil* which is done once every five years. Anyone having been brought. . . . If there is any *yakädurā* gentleman (*yakädurā mahattaya*) who can make this ill person go farther than five years, having been brought, do so. I will pay their wage (*poliya*). Why is that? Having performed for twelve years, having performed twelve *tovils*, I have taken wages for that. For that one [i.e., for extending the five-year limit] I will give one wage to the gentlemen who spoke. Any, any gentleman. [This was very interesting. Evidently there were people who were suggesting that Äddin was not "cutting" the effects of the sorcery because he wanted to be assured of future *tovils*.]. . . . If it is done in that way I won't dance in this yard (*midula*) again even for an *ädurukama*, even if one of these children will be angry. Even if these fellows [i.e., the audience] will be angry. None of these fellows are angry. They would even come for a drop of oil to be charmed. If I am going to speak in that way I should say it to their face. To anyone. I also am doing this *tovil* with determination (*hari vēgayen karanne mē tovilaya*). That is it. . . .

[*Now to Lila*] Is the dancing and singing that was done enough?

LILA: Not enough.

ÄDDIN: Dance; [she] wants.

So they set off again. Lila takes the cock, holding it above her head. She leans against the Flower Shed, pressing the cock to her face. Leaving it on the Flower Shed, she turns back to the center of the dancing area. Then suddenly she lets out three piercing hoots—the signal she said would indicate that the *yakku* were gone—and collapses against someone. Immediately, the pots of water (already prepared) are emptied over her. One . . . then another . . . and another . . . all seven required. Lila Amma is soaked. But it is over. Her daughter accompanies her into the house.

Daha-aṭa Pāliya (Procession of the Eighteen Figures)

There then follows a quick offering to the eighteen Sanni *yakku*. And following that the *Daha-aṭa Pāliya*, the Procession of the Eighteen Figures. Lila Amma has now reemerged, dried and changed. She positively delights in the biting humor of this sequence—for the early part of it, at least. As is typically the case, only eight of the eighteen are presented. (Extensive excerpts of the humorous exchanges performed in this sequence have been provided by others, so there is little need to do so here.)[33] First, the magnificent Pandam Pāliya, the "spectacle of the torch" figure—grey-bearded, a distorted nose, streaming hair, throwing flames here and there after every couple of steps. He leaves the torch beside Lila Amma. Pandam Pāliya is followed by Salu Pāliya, the "spectacle of the shawl" figure—a humorously effeminate figure who, with hands akimbo, speaks in an exaggerated way with the drummer. He places the shawl around Lila and departs. At this point, though, Lila Amma's interest seems to be falling off. Much of the strain of the preceding hours is gone, though, and her face shows a relative calm, if also a weariness. The audience, anyway, is thrilled by the obscene banter between the performers, and there is much laughter around. There soon follows Keṇḍi

Pāliya, the "spectacle of the water pot" figure—a shaky old man with a walking stick and a water pot who dances a few steps, converses with the drummer, and departs, leaving the water pot beside Lila Amma. After him comes Kalas Pāliya, the "spectacle of the cooking pot" figure—a young woman carrying a pot who likewise dances a few steps, engages in a funny exchange with the drummer, and leaves after placing the pot beside Lila. Tämbili Pāliya, the "spectacle of the coconut" figure, is next—he carries a large "King" coconut (*tämbili*). The routine is the same as the others. There then follows Pañḍuru and Añguru Pāliya, the "spectacles of coin offering and charcoal." The "procession" is closed by the appearance of figures properly belonging to the group of Sanni *yakku*. First, Bille Sanni, and then, Bhīta Sanni. This concludes the Daha-aṭa Pāliya.

Baliya Pāvādīma (Offering of the Clay Image of Kalu Kumāraya)

As morning begins to show itself, the final sequence, the *Baliya Pāvādīma*, or the Offering of the Kalu Kumāra Clay Image, is performed. And once again the accent of the *tovil* returns to *diṣṭiya* (and *dōṣa*). Facing Lila Amma, the clay image is leaned against two chairs. At its base are placed three coconuts, a long pestle, *hāl* or unhusked rice, betel leaves, and a few small coins. A lime and red flower is attached by a thread to the image. A little oil is sprinkled on the face of the image (evidently to soften the clay), and with Lila standing before it, charms are uttered. (In the meantime, beyond this, the Flower Shed and other structures are being dismantled.) The charms close with the formulaic phrases, "The ten great troubles are finished/the eighty great troubles are finished/the thousand great troubles are finished/ . . . *tīnduyi*." Then Lila Amma throws the lime and flower at the image, where it sticks to the softened clay. Then the sheet that has acted as the curtain is similarly thrown so that it haphazardly covers the image. And then, finally, holding the lamp of the Four Warrant Gods and *īgaha*, and while charms are being uttered, Lila is led into the house. The *tovil* is complete. At least, in Lila Amma's case, it is over for the next five years—as long as the promises that have been secured are kept, and the *yakku* remain obedient to the virtuous commands of the Buddha.

In my description of the *tovil* ceremonies performed for Lila Amma, I have given much attention to those sequences in which the *ädurā* attempts by rhetorical strategies both to influence the demands of the disturbing *yakku* and to determine whether and to what extent the procedures of the *tovil*—the offerings and the "dancing and singing" especially—have been accepted. These sequences, as far as I am aware, have received but scant attention in the now quite significant anthropological literature on the Sinhala *yaktovil*.[34] It is arguable, of course, that this neglect has much to do with the local variation of the practice of *tovil* itself in the Western and Southern Provinces of Sri Lanka. The performance of *tovil* is indeed marked by variation determined by a whole range of factors—from the vagaries of individual financial considerations to differences in local traditions of performing styles to changes attributable to social and historical currents. Clearly, a careful study of such factors would repay the effort. However, it is necessary to at least raise the question whether this neglect may be understood less as some inherent "logic" in the Sinhala practice of *yaktovil* itself or its "context" than as something of an *effect* of assumptions and preoccupations in the *anthropology* of Sri Lankan "ritual." After all, it is anthropologists and not *ädurās* who produce and circulate them *textually* as part of the larger archive of the ethnography of "ritual." Certainly, much of the work on the *yaktovil* (or on related Sinhala practices)—that of Sarachchandra, Obeyesekere, Halverson, AmaraSingham, and Kapferer, for instance—has concentrated on a certain group of sequences: the sequences of comic drama and dialogue that form a highly expressive and visible aspect of *tovil* performances.[35] The question here is less about the fruitfulness or otherwise of this emphasis than about the extent to which it is informed by and embedded in a certain kind of anthropological problematic.

Part II

Colonial Discourses

Chapter 4

Exorcisms and Demonic Experience, Anthropology and *Yaktovil*

This chapter opens a critical inquiry into the way in which contemporary anthropology has analyzed and discussed *yaktovil*. To do so I will undertake a reading of one recent contribution to this anthropology, that of Bruce Kapferer, and particularly his ethnographic monograph, *A Celebration of Demons*.[1] In this reading my critical concern is with the *theoretical* and *ideological* constructions of this work's conceptual object—indeed, my concern is with the conditions in which these intersect. "In order to evaluate the theoretical limitations of contemporary anthropological knowledge, and its political implications," Talal Asad has suggested, "it is necessary to carry out detailed critical analyses of specific representative work. This is the only effective way of demonstrating the principle that the uncritical reproduction of an ideological object is itself ideological and *therefore* theoretically faulty."[2] This is a principle which my reading of Kapferer's construction of *yaktovil* as the object of an anthropological analysis will seek to elaborate.

The specific ideological formation that interests me is that of colonial discourse. Stated broadly, my concern is that the relation between colonial discourse and anthropology, while often enough recognized or asserted in a general sort of way, has not been adequately interrogated, indeed has not been adequately formulated. The question of how and in precisely what ways an identifiably *colonial* discourse continues to exercise a specifiably *discursive* hegemony in the *contemporary* construction of anthropological objects has, it seems to me, received far less analytical attention than it properly deserves.[3]

No one would wish to deny, I think, that anthropology today is an enterprise increasingly self-conscious about its colonial legacy, and as a consequence is less and less naive about the language of representation it employs. I shall wish to suggest, however, in the course of this chapter, that while it is indeed arguable that a humanism of nonpejorative terminology, and an impressive level of theoretical sophistication, has come to characterize the construction of anthropological objects, what bears more systematic investigation is really the question whether the colonial *problematic* itself—that is to say, the interrelated set of distinctive ideological or discursive presuppositions—that established the contours of visibility of native practices, and thus the possibility in the first place for their constitution *as objects of Western discourse*, has been effectively displaced. It is at this, as it were, internal and more fundamental level, the level of the *problematic*, that I wish to think the connection between colonial and anthropological discourses. For colonial problematics, I will argue, can and do travel—in a variety of updated conceptual languages—in contemporary anthropology.

As I have suggested earlier, the anthropology of *yaktovil* has, by and large, constructed its accounts and analyses in and through the conceptual metaphors of "demonism," "possession," and "exorcism."[4] In chapter 5 I will describe something of the founding moment of these metaphors in the *ideological problematic* of nineteenth-century colonial Christian discourse on British Ceylon. In sketching the outline of this problematic I shall argue that the evangelical practice of Christian conversion (which emerged as central to the practice of colonial governance in mid-nineteenth-century Ceylon) involved colonial discourse in a particular strategy of identifying and representing Sinhala "religion." In this strategy (which rested on certain Victorian presuppositions about "true"—that is, "vital"—religion and the authentic attitude of religious subjects), "demonism" was identified as the "darker" underside of Buddhism, a constant, more primeval and obtruding force exciting in the Sinhalas what one colonial authority described as "a deeper and more reverential awe" than the official but largely ineffectual religion, Buddhism.[5]

Obviously, however, what is most important is not the authoritative discourses of the past in themselves—crudely put, the issue of origins—but the question whether and *through precisely what concepts* the generative problematic of this founding discourse has been appropriated by, and reproduced in, such *contemporary* authoritative discourses as anthropology. As will be clear in this chapter and the following one, I am not interested in a social history of representations of Sinhala religion as such, but in a genealogy of a contemporary anthropological problematic. This is why it is necessary to begin by examining the anthropological text.

Kapferer's monograph, as I indicated, is of particular importance because it is the first (and to date still the only) modern, full-length anthropological study of *yaktovil* to be published.[6] All the more reason, therefore, to subject to a careful reading the kind of argument it employs. Kapferer, like many of those who have studied or observed *yaktovil*, unreflectively assumes that such conceptual metaphors as "exorcism," "demons," and "possession" are proper translations of the respective Sinhala words *tovil*, *yakku*, and *āvēśaya*. Now of course one might imagine an objection being raised here that the mere use of these English glosses cannot, in and of itself, prove that Kapferer is uncritically reproducing a colonial object. Fair enough (though I wish to point out that the glosses do participate in the construction of a very misleading ethnographic image, and for that reason alone stand in need of criticism). Yet the critical point here is not the mere use of the glosses themselves *but their distinctive place in a conceptual economy that reinscribes the ideological problematic that gave them birth*. What I shall endeavor to do in this chapter, therefore, is the following: First of all, I will inquire into some of the assumptions embedded in Kapferer's use of the theoretical construct of "experience" in conceptualizing *yaktovil* as a practice transformative of self, identity, and experience. In so doing I shall be particularly concerned to question his notion of a specifically "demonic experience" among Sinhalas, and I will suggest that this conception of his reproduces in a fundamental way aspects of the demonological problematic of colonial discourse on the Sinhalas.

I will not stop here, however, because it seems to me that this reinscription of a decidedly colonial object is not fortuitous; nor is it to be understood in merely biographical terms, but rather is symptomatic of the way in which (i.e., of the assumptions through which) anthropology typically goes about the production of the objects of its discourse. Secondly, therefore, I will attempt to show how this reproduction of an identifiably colonial object is related (at least in part) to the fact that in Kapferer's text the anthropological object itself—in this case "ritual"—is, in specific ways, an uncritically formulated one.

Let me hasten to emphasize, though, that my general point here is not to try to secure, by the strategy I have outlined, a simply determinate relationship between colonial discourse on the one hand and the concept of "experience" on the other. I do not wish, in other words, to be read as suggesting either that *every* anthropological use of a concept of "experience" necessarily reproduces a specifically colonial object, or, conversely, that *every* anthropological reproduction of an identifiably colonial object is necessarily articulated in terms of a concept of "experience." My general point is a rather different one, namely, that anthropological analyses of "ritual" (indeed, not unlike anthropological analyses of other sorts of cultural practice) have tended to take unproblematically and uncritically the objects identified and constructed in their own discourses. This, I wish to suggest, has consequences that are at once theoretical *and* ideological insofar as the objects so reproduced can be shown not only to be internally incoherent but also to reinscribe the presuppositions of a colonial problematic. Updated theoretical languages do not guarantee anthropology an immunity from colonial complicity. Indeed, this is precisely what they often serve to conceal. And this is why I wish to suggest that the theoretical level at which questions need to be put to anthropology is that of the construction of its object domains.

Ritual and the Transformation of "Experience"

The theme of "experience" is central to Kapferer's analysis of *yaktovil*. This is a theme, of course, that has become increasingly visible in contemporary anthropological discourse, much of it finding inspiration in Victor Turner's later work on theatre and social drama.[7] More generally, though, it participates in the renewal of the concern in anthropology with subjectivity, and forms one of the more recent elaborations of the preoccupation with cultural "meanings" in contemporary anthropology. The analysis of culture as a system of signs and symbols to be interpreted has seemed to many anthropologists to provide a more sophisticated way of speaking about such domains as "self," "mind," "emotions," and "experience."[8] Needless to say (and here is the thrust of an anthropological criticism), one question that these anthropologists never bothered to ask themselves is what the historical conditions are that have facilitated this turn in their own discourse. What changing practices of the *Western* self (as, for instance, Asad has asked) have made this preoccupation necessary, or indeed, possible?[9] The point is not that this kind of question would necessarily have preempted the concern with subjectivity, nor indeed do I suggest that it *should* have, but it might at least have cautioned a considered reflection on the *conceptual* premises of their theoretical enterprise.

What, then, is the anthropology of "experience"? Wherein lies its distinctiveness, its special claim on our attention? It will be useful to follow Edward Bruner's formulation of this enterprise in his Introduction to a collection of essays entitled, precisely, *The Anthropology of Experience*, which he edited with Victor Turner, and in which, notably, Kapferer himself has a contribution.[10] "The anthropology of experience deals with how individuals *actually experience* their culture, that is, how events are *received* by consciousness" (p. 4, emphasis added). The explicitly stated assumption in this perspective is that "What comes first is experience" (p. 4); or again that "Lived experience . . . as thought and desire, as word and image, is the primary reality" (p. 5). Acknowledging that "we can only experience our own life, what is received by our own consciousness" (p. 5), Bruner suggests that the way to "overcome" this "difficulty" is through the interpretation of "expressions"—that is, the interpretation of "representations, performances, objectifications, or texts" (p. 5). These two domains, that of experience and that of expression, are said to be in "dialogic and dialectical" relationship, experience structuring expression and, vice versa, expression structuring experience. "The critical distinction here," says Bruner, "is between reality (what is out there, whatever that may be), experience (how that reality presents itself to consciousness), and expressions (how individual experience is framed and articulated)" (p. 6).

Now of course it is one thing to talk about "experience," one's own or, by inference, that of others, in statements claiming no special *theoretical* status. But it is quite another to turn these into ontological statements regarding the supposed *latent* ground or *foundational* truth of behavioral domains, and to then see systematic discourse epistemologically, in terms of its privileged access to this ground. Certainly this is the kind of foundationalism that a number of philosophers—Richard Rorty and Ian Hacking among them[11]—have recently been arguing against. Yet this conception of experience as the source and guarantee of conceptual certainty is precisely the view taken by Bruner and company. For them, "experience" (something supposedly inner and unobservable), is the foundation or ground of a corresponding domain of "expressions" (supposedly outer and, in virtue of this, observable), which are its several forms of—as they variously put it—materialization or objectification or representation or enactment. The field of determinations having been so constructed, the claim will then be made for the "anthropology of experience" that it can achieve a closer proximity, a more authentic relation, to the latent truths of the native's culture:

> The advantage [Bruner says a bit later on] of beginning the study of culture through expressions is that the basic units of analysis are established by the people we study rather than by the anthropologist as alien observer. By focusing on narratives or dramas or carnival or any other expressions, we leave the definition of the unit of investigation up to the people, rather than imposing categories derived from our own ever-shifting theoretical frames. Expressions are the peoples' articulations, formulations, and representations of their own experience. (p. 9)

What is astonishing about this passage is not so much the tone of deference in the apparent bestowal upon the native of this singular prerogative (defining the units of anthropological investigation), but the assumption that anthropology is thereby secured against the claims of ethnocentrism. This aside, however, it may be an uncontroversial matter that expressions articulate experience; but it would be only reasonable to ask the advocates of this anthropology of experience how the anthropologist can be sure that he or she is reading the "experience" independently of its "expression." In fact, as we shall see in Kapferer's work, this is one conceptual ambiguity in which this sort of approach to the analysis of social discourses never ceases to entangle itself.[12]

The primacy and authenticity of experience; the transparency of expressive practice; the epistemological privilege of the anthropological vista—these indeed are all themes that recur in Bruce Kapferer's work on Sri Lanka. In Kapferer, however, what is of primary concern is what he calls the "transformation of experience," and the special ability or "power" of ritual to effect this transformation. Kapferer, in fact, would seem to have two general objections to contemporary anthropological conceptions of ritual, both centering on this question of the "power" of ritual. The first of these objections is directed against what he calls "structuralist and symbolicist studies," which, concerning themselves with "an often esoteric level" of analysis of "the meaning of symbol and act," are unable to adequately answer the question of how so-called rites of passage (as *yaktovil* is said to be) effect their transformations (*ED* 109). The questions that, so to put it, inaugurate Kapferer's analytic engagement with *yaktovil* are explicitly concerned with how the effects of transformations in experience are brought about in ritual. In an early article on *yaktovil*, Kapferer, having made a few general introductory remarks, pauses to raise the following questions:

> How does a healing ritual cure? Or better: how does the performance of a healing ritual facilitate the transition of a patient from an agreed state of illness to a publicly recognized condition of health? What is it in the performance of a ritual, in the organization of word and action, in the manner and form of presentation of magical incantation, in the gesture and style of dance, in the rhythm and cadence of music, which effects and eases the way for a patient and audience to reach an agreement that a cure has been achieved? (*ED* 108)

Thus Kapferer, in keeping with the concerns of the anthropology of experience, argues for a focus on ritual as performance.[13] However, it will immediately be evident from the quotation above that what we have here are the production of social discourses, social practices, and processes of negotiation—in which case it may well be asked: where is "experience" in all this?

Kapferer's second objection is rather more implicit than explicitly stated—if nonetheless significant for that. In foregrounding his notion of the "power" of ritual, Kapferer would appear to be taking issue with an anthropological argument of late particularly associated with the work of Maurice Bloch.[14] Bloch too has been much concerned with the theme of power and ritual. His perspective, however, is markedly different from Kapferer's. For Bloch ritual, far from being a source of transformation, or even in itself a transformational process, is but a site of repetition. As he says, for instance, in an almost epigrammatic phrase regarding ritual communication: "A frozen statement cannot be expanded, it can only be made again and again and again."[15] Certainly this is a conception against which the tenor and argument of Kapferer's analysis of the *yaktovil* is turned.[16] (It is a curious and noteworthy fact, however, that while making such seemingly divergent claims about ritual [ritual as transformative and ritual as the embodiment of the absence of transformation], both Kapferer and Bloch begin with the same set of assumptions about the formalized character of ritual.)

The elaboration of this theme of power in Kapferer's work on ritual may be said to fall along two distinct if related axes. On the one hand, he is concerned to extend and develop the ideas of Arnold Van Gennep and, particularly, of Victor Turner, on the processes of transformation in rites of passage.[17] Kapferer is indeed an intellectual heir to an anthropological tradition much preoccupied with the relation between ritual and forms of transformation. Although Turner's familiar conception of the key transformational moments of ritual (articulated through such seminal categories as "liminality," "communitas," and "anti-structure") is admiringly regarded as an advance on Van Gennep, he is felt nevertheless to fall somewhat short of an adequate consideration of what is termed the "dynamic" of transformation itself.[18] Kapferer, for his part, wishes to explore precisely the "transformational process within ritual":

> This is important [he says], for many rituals derive their power to transform identities and contexts of action and meaning, which are located in the mundane order of everyday life, through effecting transformations within the organization of their performance. (*RPTC* 3)

In this analysis, Kapferer continues, it is necessary to inquire into

> The nature of ritual performance, and the expressive or performative modes in which ritual symbol and action is organized in effecting ritual transformations of meaning and action. This will also involve a discussion of the transformational properties of specific symbolic elements in ritual, and the role of particular "cultural logics" as they are produced and revealed through performance, in facilitating some of the transformational work of ritual. (*RPTC* 3)

In his analysis of what he later calls the "transformational logic of exorcism" (*CD* 180), then, Kapferer attempts to demonstrate the "transformational properties" of music, dance, song, and comic drama.

On the other hand, Kapferer is concerned with how the "transformational efficacy" of ritual "is communicated to and made part of the experience of participants" (*RPTC* 3). Here the theme of subjectivity enters explicitly into his analysis. Specifically, Kapferer wishes to argue that in such rites as *yaktovil*, "self," "identity," and "experience" undergo transformation. In this argument the ideas of George Herbert Mead (and, more generally, a social phenomenology inspired by Alfred Schutz) are employed to demonstrate the "construction" and "negation" of "self" in the course of ritual performance. Thus, for Kapferer, the "power" of ritual consists in that it *transforms*; and what it transforms are what are referred to as "identities and contexts of action and meaning" (*RPTC* 3).

The link between these respective foci on ritual is, of course, to be founded on the conceptual terrain of "experience." The supposed "properties" of certain "symbolic elements" will be perceived by Kapferer to have determinate effects on the "experience" of participants in the ritual. As he puts it:

> The thesis I develop is that transitions and transformations in meaning and experience are communicated, received, and engendered among ritual participants through the dynamic properties of the major aesthetic modes of exorcisms and by the way participant standpoint or perspective is ordered in ritual action. (*CD* 178)

This idea of the relation between "experience" and ritual, of course, bears much resemblance to Turner's conception of the relation between "experience" and aesthetic forms such as drama. In a lyrical passage from his late work, for example, Turner writes:

> Theater is one of the many inheritors of the great multifaceted system we call "tribal ritual," which embraces ideas and images of cosmos and chaos, interdigitates clowns and their foolery with gods and their solemnity, and uses all the sensory codes to produce symphonies in more than music: the intertwining of dance, body languages of many kinds, song, chant, architectural forms (temples, amphitheaters), incense, burnt offerings, ritualized feasting and drinking, painting, body painting, body marking of many kinds including circumcision and scarification, the application of lotions and the drinking of potions, the enacting of mythic and heroic plots drawn from oral tradition—and so much more.[19]

Kapferer would endorse this view: "Exponents of the arts and scholars in the East and West," he writes, "have long related artistic forms to their roots in ritual" (*CD* 178). Kapferer too is explicitly arguing that ritual, specifically *yaktovil*, has an aesthetic aspect (or perhaps more strongly *is* an aesthetic mode). And as such, ritual employs special devices to organize "experience" toward the specific end it "intends." My principal concern in the rest of this section of my chapter will be to critically discuss this theme of the transformation of "experience" in Kapferer's work. I shall first sketch out some of the conceptual assumptions inscribed in it, and then point to its implication in a demonological problematic inherited from colonial missionary discourse on the Sinhalas.

At the outset of his discussion of the "aesthetic of exorcism," Kapferer states explicitly his guiding assumption: "My analysis is based on the assumption that possibilities for the ordering of experience and its meaning inhere in the structure of artistic form" (*CD* 178). This assumption, I shall argue, is a fundamentally misguided one. However, before tackling it directly, let us follow Kapferer in the development of his argument. Art, he continues, invoking interestingly enough the authority of T. S. Eliot,[20] can "evoke among those who are embraced by it a subjectivity appropriate to the emotion and feeling which art formulates" (*CD* 178). In other words, art—or, more precisely, artistic *form*—is invested with the inherent cognitive quality of being able to "formulate" not only specific human emotions, but "appropriate" ones. And note that what is "appropriate" in this usage has nothing to do with a set of social conditions which have *made* that particular response apt or fitting in this situation or that, but with a determining quality *essential* to artistic form itself.

"Exorcisms," Kapferer maintains (referring to *yaktovil*), are transition rites having the structure described by Van Gennep and Turner. Specifically, they are divided into three periods, namely, the evening, midnight, and morning "watches":

> In these, respectively, the patient is separated from the mundane world, then placed in a liminal world of the supernatural where demonic and divine forces are fully elaborated and joined in struggle, and then replaced within the paramount reality of everyday life in which the patient is freed from demonic control and returned to normality. (*CD* 179)

This "triadic phasing" Kapferer will call the "objective structure of major demon ceremonies" (*CD* 180).

Such rites as these, Kapferer continues (drawing here on the work of Terence Turner),[21] "effect a passage between two states of person," a movement described as one from a "lower possibility of being to a higher"—or, where exorcisms are concerned, from a "lower demonic possibility of being to a higher nondemonic being" (*CD* 179). The "objective structure" of exorcism is then said to "model the vertical order of relations in the cosmic hierarchy along a horizontal plane," so that as the patient moves temporally through the rite he or she is "progressively reordered" in terms of the cosmic hierarchy. Now for Sinhalas, Kapferer continues, the cosmic hierarchy is one in which "demons" are at the base and the Buddha and deities are at the apex. The three periods of exorcism can therefore be restated in terms of this movement:

> The separation phase (the evening watch) encompasses a period when the demonic is largely dominant and, because demons constitute a low level of ordering, cannot constitute the everyday world of human beings within it. With the emergence of the divine in the liminal or marginal period of the midnight watch, the reconstitution of an everyday world within the context of ritual action becomes possible. This is fully realized in the reaggregation phase (the morning watch), which objectively asserts the dominance of the divine and the subordination of the demonic. (*CD* 180)

This is the "transformational logic" of exorcism. The sequences of the exorcism ritual through which the patient is moved have a correspondential relation with the cosmic hierarchy of the Sinhalas. On Kapferer's view, however, this level of analysis still leaves unanswered the question of how the "transformational efficacy" of the ritual is "communicated to and made part of the experience of participants" (*CD* 180). Kapferer's answer, of course, already adumbrated, is that this efficacy is achieved through the symbolic forms of the ritual:

> The symbolic forms of the rite are the media by which ritual participants become subjectively oriented in the ritual process. They link the inner experience of the subject with the objective structure of the rite. Through the manipulation of these mediating symbolic forms, the inner experience of the subjects can be made to parallel the transformations taking place in the objective structure of the rite. (*CD* 180)

Exorcism, Kapferer argues, is a "communicational field." And what is communicated in this field,

> and the transformations it may effect as these are revealed to participants, occurs on at least two planes: that of experience, the immediately felt individual subjective encountering of a context of meaning and action, and that of the conscious reflective grasping of this experience in terms of the idea constructs and typifications of the culturally objectified world. (*CD* 180)

So that Kapferer's conception of *yaktovil* is that of a field of messages which get transmitted to subjects at two different levels: a primary one of "experience," and a secondary one of conscious reflection. This Experience/Reason opposition echoes, and is indeed a particular elaboration of, that other, as it were, master opposition, Nature/Culture, through which the whole of Kapferer's argument is cast.[22] Experience, like Nature, is supposedly an unmediated domain or zone, being in some sense what comes *before*—both temporally and ontologically—Reason and Culture. As with Bruner's, examined earlier, this assumption of an inner authentic region of subjectivity ("experience") anterior to its cultural "typification" (or "expression") will then offer itself up as a theoretical guarantee of Kapferer's conception of the "dynamic" of transformation in ritual.

Now specifically, in his concern to elucidate what he calls the "aesthetic of exorcism," Kapferer maintains that this artistic form, exorcism, has "inherent possibilities for experience and meaning" (*CD* 180). Music, dance, and comic drama, are identified as its signal and constituent aesthetic modes, and these, moreover, are invested with certain essential qualities and potentialities. Again I quote Kapferer:

> In their form, the music, dance, and comic drama of exorcism organize perception in distinctive ways and, through this, the meaning and experience of what is presented in them. Essentially, music and dance have their meaning constituted in the directly revealed experience of them. Their form is such that they can potentially achieve an existential unity with their subject. They can produce in experience what is already integral to their form. Exorcists are concerned to construct in ritual that which they aim to transform. Music and dance have the capacity to engender in experience that which is objective in the rite and, at the same time, subject those who are embraced in their realm in a process of change which the rite intends. However, the unity which the musical or dance object achieves with its subject can place that which is directly revealed or disclosed in subjective experience beyond the objective grasp of those who are engaged in the immediate process of experiencing music and dance. Hence the movement to comic drama in exorcism. Drama, and comic drama in particular, places the object at a distance from its subject and, further, in its specific dynamic . . . tests and explores the objective truth of that which was revealed directly in the music and dance. (*CD* 181)

Music and dance, then, the forms that are elaborated most fully in the early sequences of *yaktovil*, are said to "have their meaning constituted in the directly revealed experience of them" (*CD* 181). They are, one might say, less cerebral, more visceral. Music and dance, Kapferer proposes, have the capacity to "engender in experience" what is "objective in the rite," and in so doing, "subject those who are embraced in their realm in a process of change which the rite intends" (*CD* 181). This curious notion of the ritual "intending" a process, a notion that recurs Kapferer's discussion of ritual, is left unclarified. One is left with the puzzling impression that *yaktovil* is itself a sort of conscious subject, with attributable volition and agency.

More important, however, I want to note two ideas. The first is the idea that music, as he puts it elsewhere, *"demands the living of the reality it creates"* (*CD* 187, his emphasis). This is clearly unfounded. The very fact that Kapferer himself is not enveloped in the "experiential possibility" of *yaktovil* music is reason to think that what is important is not some supposed essential quality of music (or dance, for that matter) but the formation of specific dispositions to subjective states that count for Sinhalas as distinctive kinds of experience. And if it were to be objected here that the argument is not about some universal essence of music but about the specific potential of *cultural* music for *cultural* subjects, Kapferer would still need to specify the authoritative discourse by which Sinhala subjectivities are formed to respond appropriately to certain kinds of music in certain kinds of situations.

The second thing to note is the distinction Kapferer makes between the "experience" of the subject on the one hand, and the "objectivity" of the ritual on the other. Music and dance are supposed to produce a correspondence between the two, or rather, to create in the former what is already present in the latter. There is at work here a curiously ambiguous notion of "objectivity." In talking about the "objective structure" of *yaktovil* it is never altogether clear whether the attribution of this "objectivity" is supposed to be the anthropologist's (e.g., in terms of Van Gennep's and Turner's theory of the stages of rites of passage), or the native's (e.g., in terms of the indigenous cosmic hierarchy of the Sinhalas). In either case, however, it ought to be understood that what is made to *count* as the "objectivity" or true knowledge of a Sinhala practice is a product of strategies of authorization, not the inherent principles of an essential reality. What is left unexplained in Kapferer's text, and indeed *what cannot be explained,* is how these periods of *yaktovil* (the evening, midnight, and morning watches) *come to be inscribed with the authoritative meanings ascribed to them.*

Connected with this, it is also necessary to point to the questionable conception of "subjectivity" employed by Kapferer. For Kapferer (as for Bruner), the subject has a passive and an active side, corresponding to "planes" of experience and reason, respectively. On the one hand, the passive subject receives the impress of the outer, supposedly objective world, in the form of unmediated experience (the figure, in other words, of the subject "enveloped" in music); on the other hand, the active subject takes stock of this experience in the rational categories provided by culture (the figure of the subject of a sovereign reason stepping back to "test and explore" the "objective truth" of experience). But surely this is implausible, since for experience to be known *as experience* it has already to have been cognitively and therefore discursively organized as such.[23] As Vološinov has argued: "*not only can experience be outwardly expressed through the agency of the sign* (an experience can be expressed to others variously—by word, by facial expression, or by some other means), but also, aside from this outward expression (for others), *experience exists even for the person undergoing it only in the material of signs*. Outside that material there is no experience as such."[24] And he goes on to draw the important conclusion that therefore "there is no leap involved between inner experience and its expression, no crossing over from one qualitative realm to another. The transit from experience to its outward expression occurs within the scope of the same qualitative realm and is *quantitative* in nature (p. 28, his emphasis).

I have been saying that Kapferer's argument regarding "experience" is not a very coherent one. What I want to notice now is how these supposedly authentic aspects of the Sinhala self are arranged hierarchically so that "experience" is assimilated to what is "lower" and reason to what is "higher." The ideological ramifications of this conception become clear when seen in terms of Kapferer's notion of a specifically "demonic experience" among the Sinhalas.

Whereas music and song characterize the performance of the "evening watch" of *yaktovil*, dance characterizes that of the "midnight watch." Dance, Kapferer maintains, is like music in that it "can draw those who are attending to it into the realm of its creation" (*CD* 193). Dance, like music, is an experiential mode, but one in which there is an "externalization of the existential properties of music" (*CD* 192), and a loss of formal "flexibility":

> The music of the evening watch has a degree of flexibility which can move the patient in and out of the demonic, a movement which nonetheless is productive of instability. The demonic music of the dance, however, loses its flexibility and is dominated by the beat. (*CD* 193)

It is in this period that the "demonic" is said to be developed to the point of trance by dance's "inherent capacity to limit perception and to inhibit the subject's ability to reflect upon himself or herself at a distance" (*CD* 196). And as a result, subjectivity is said to collapse into an almost totalizing "experience." As Kapferer puts it,

> trance . . . is the point when the object of the demonic enters into a direct communion with the subject. Trance is the dissolution of any subject/object distinction, and in exorcism emerges as a natural gesture out of the virtual gesture of the dance. It is in trance that the nature of the object as directly experienced discovers its validity, a validity which is defined in the subjectivity of the subject. (*CD* 195)

The trance marks for Kapferer the crucial moment of the "transformation into a demon self" (*CD* 196). In order to illuminate what he calls "the possible experiential process leading to trance" (*CD* 198), Kapferer draws on the ideas of George Herbert Mead. Specifically, he takes up the notion that the "Self" emerges in a process in which a subjective "I" interacts with an "Other" such that a "me" is produced. This "me," the reflection of the "I" in the "Other," is then in a constant relationship or dialogue with the "I." This dialogue is the supposed space of the "Self." Now, this Meadian dialectic, it is necessary to note, its sense of process and interaction notwithstanding, is problematic by itself inasmuch as it assumes that the constitutive spaces of the "I" and the "Other," that is, the loci out of which the supposed objective referent—the "me"—is formed, are at once unitary and given in advance.[25] According to Kapferer, however, in the "midnight watch" of the exorcism there is a breakdown or what he calls a "negation" of this Meadian process of "Self" formation. In this breakdown or negation, it is argued, the multiplicity of Meadian selves is reduced to a single Self, said now to be completely dominated by demons that have, as it were, erupted from their place outside of culture. Kapferer writes:

> The multiple selves of a "normal" and healthy individual become suspended and the process of self construction in the mundane world is reversed. The self of the patient is reduced to a single demonic mode of being, which is dangerously outside cultural constraint. Demonic possession is the emergence to dominance of nature over culture, nature in its disorderly aspect, as the display of aggression, passion, and violence, often appearing in the behavioral display of demonic trance. (*CD* 201)

Or, as he has written elsewhere:

> Demons in the mind of the patient are no longer distanced from the world of human beings, but have directly and illegitimately entered it,

> threatening the patient with their unrestrained capricious, lusty, greedy, grasping, and bloodthirsty natures. (*MSO* 115)

Here he has suggested that this demon-dominated Self is to be better understood as a "basal Self," "equivalent to the Jungian 'shadow' " (*MSO* 118)—that is, a Self representing "the dark characteristics of the human personality that are normally suppressed by culture and social convention" (*MSO* 118).[26] It is interesting, parenthetically, that, attempting as he does to formulate his notion of a suppressed but always latent, precultural "self" in terms of this curious mixture of Meadian and Jungian categories, Kapferer lapses into the very subjectivism that he would claim to have avoided by his social-phenomenological approach.

"Demonism" in this scheme now stands fully revealed as the latent potential, the deep inner core or "basal" aspect of the Sinhala self. For Kapferer the "demonic" and "experience" are assimilated to each other. The "demonic" is represented as occupying a special relation to subjectivity, a relation characterized by "direct communion." The "demonic" is, then, a kind of primeval force, unreflective, dormant, and anterior to rationality, a force brought to the surface (or made to "emerge," to use Kapferer's expressive metaphor) by the peculiar reason-suspending qualities of music, song, and especially dance. The whole conception rests, as I have already shown, on an assumption of a domain of authentic subjectivity. Kapferer does not pause to ask himself, as well he might have, how the disposition to this ("demonic") experience is produced and effected as an appropriate response, in particular conditions, to music and dance. Such a reflection might have led to the theoretically more relevant inquiry into the formation among the Sinhalas of specific aptitudes, habits, and dispositions—that is, the formation of a specific cultural habitus.[27]

As I shall spell out at length in the following chapter, this representation of the essential experience of the Sinhalas in terms of a "demonic mode of being . . . dangerously outside cultural constraint" is not new in Western discourse on Sri Lanka. Its roots are at once colonial and Christian. This conception of the essential "underside" experience of the Sinhalas has its founding moment in Victorian Christian discourse on British Ceylon. To anticipate my argument a bit: In this evangelical discourse, "demonism" is represented as the ineradicable subterrain of Sinhala religion, as a level akin to "nature," and thus essential to the latent core of Sinhala subjectivity. Moreover, this demonism—the natural or true religion of primitive or pagan peoples—was represented as being "outside" (in the sense of being temporally prior to, and continuously resistant of) that "superior" (albeit limited and flawed) reason and culture which Buddhism attempted to introduce. And it would remain, for the Christians, the essential reality of the religious "genius" of the Sinhalas inasmuch as it would constantly "reemerge," no matter the labor employed to erase or suppress it, to threaten the order which Christian conversion attempted to impose.

The point here, of course, is not that Kapferer is a conscious accomplice to colonial Christian ideology. The point rather is that in employing a *problematic* in which *revealed experience* is assimilated to demonism, and demonism to the latent underground of Sinhala subjectivity, he reinscribes the conceptual presuppositions and thus the problematic through which colonial Christian discourse in nineteenth-century British Ceylon attempted to identify and represent the latent truth of Sinhala religion. This raises a more general point, however, namely, that anthropological discourse that does not inquire into the ideological conditions that make its specific objects possible, visible, seemingly self-evident, that is to say, that does not inquire into both its conceptual and ideological presuppositions, must inevitably find itself reproducing the assumptions of those discourses its self-conscious humanism and its updated language would claim to have supplanted.

Constructing Anthropological Objects

If, as I suggest, this anthropological reinscription of a colonial object is not fortuitous but rather a consequence of questionable anthropological assumptions regarding the objects of its discourse, and thus the problematic which makes them thinkable, it is necessary, I submit, to inquire into at least some aspects of the formation of the theoretical object of Kapferer's text. By so doing, it will be possible to show how certain assumptions (which Kapferer, needless to say, is not alone in holding) about the making of anthropological objects work to preclude precisely an interrogation of the generative problematic in which they are embedded.

One of the things that Kapferer is concerned to specify at the outset of his discussion of *yaktovil*, as a way of setting the stage, so to say, for his analysis of this practice, is the *object* about which his discourse will speak: that is to say, "ritual." As one of a growing number of theoretically self-conscious anthropologists, Kapferer is concerned to state explicitly the general conceptual arena in which his arguments are to take place. This is especially pertinent to note since Kapferer does not intend his study of the Sinhalas to have a merely parochial relevance, but rather sees it as informing more generalizable theoretical claims about ritual. His analysis of *yaktovil*, in other words, is at least in part employed as *an exemplary instance* of how certain kinds of social and cultural practices might (indeed, *should*) be studied.

As with many other contemporary anthropologists, ritual in Kapferer's view is essentially to be understood on the model of ideology, that is, of mystification.[28] Discussing *yaktovil*, Kapferer speaks of ritual as a form of social practice that involves the "production of ideas which are illusory and mystifying of the objective conditions of human existence" (*CD* 4). "Ritual," he says, "makes statements about the world and achieves resolutions and transformations in terms of ideas which disguise the real and objective conditions of existence from its participants and/or is integral in the reproduction of those conditions the effects of which the ritual is directed to alleviate or overcome" (*CD* 4). On this view, in other words, "human existence" has "objective conditions" that ritual ideas veil or distort or otherwise conceal from those who actually produce and live them. More than this, however, ritual does not merely "disguise" the "real," it at once reproduces the mystification *and* addresses itself to "overcoming" what this mystification supposedly produces (in the Sinhala case, forms of suffering), but still in a mystified idiom.

Now, what is important for us to notice first of all is that these purportedly "objective conditions of human existence," which the ritual is said to "mystify," are explicitly claimed as the privileged domain of anthropological discernment—anthropology, that is to say, understood as an "objective" or at least a somehow unimplicated discourse. It is, at any rate, anthropology which (or the anthropologist *who*) is said to have a privileged *access* to these "objective conditions of human existence." "Anthropologists or observers whose own conditions are not those of the people whom they study," Kapferer continues, "may be able to discover such illusory and mystifying processes in the cultures they examine" (*CD* 4). Of course the idea that the anthropologist is better placed to understand another people's culture than the natives themselves is a recurrent theme in Western discourse, and one that has been offered on a variety of grounds. Bryan Wilson, for instance, gives a representative summary of some of these when (picking up on some of Robin Horton's ideas) he contrasts the African diviner and the "western scientist" in terms of the former's "limited opportunity for empirical observation," "less developed objectivity," "lesser prospect of abstract thought," and "lesser likelihood of distinguishing factual and evaluative elements, and of separating emotional from cognitive orientations."[29]

Of course, Kapferer might want to disavow any connection to these blatantly ethnocentric notions, but his vague conception of the differential "conditions" of anthropologist and native is certainly couched in terms of the privileged rationality of the former. I do not wish to be uncharitable. The observation that the "conditions" of the investigator are somehow linked to the creation of specific knowledges is doubtlessly a potentially useful one. It might enable one, for example, to begin to problematize questions about the *location*—particularly the discursive and institutional locations—of systematic discourse, that of anthropology in this case. Certainly this is one of the pressing contemporary questions for anthropology, as for other theoretical knowledges. We notice, however, that for Kapferer, the only "conditions" that are seen to be operating upon the formation of knowledges are those of being inside (as the native is) or outside (as the anthropologist is) the culture under investigation. And it is precisely because the native is inside his or her culture that Kapferer sees him or her as being subject to (in fact virtually encumbered by) specifically "mystifying" conditions. The "conditions" of his own position and discourse remain unproblematic, or more precisely, they are assumed to rather *facilitate* than hinder the production of objective knowledges. The anthropologist (and, generously, the occasional native) can, from his or her vantage, discern the means "whereby they [the Sinhalas, in this case] delude and mystify themselves." And, so doing, they are able to disclose the supposedly "real conditions" of Sinhala culture.[30] In Kapferer's discourse, therefore, anthropology is able to claim for itself a unique and asymmetrical relation to the object of its gaze, an epistemological privilege denied the hopelessly mystified native. His assumptions, however, do not allow for the recognition that this very vantage from which his anthropologist or enlightened native accedes to the truth of Sinhala culture is not neutral but an always discursively and therefore ideologically produced site. (Indeed, parenthetically, it would be interesting to know what the specific conditions are that make it possible for some natives *and not others* to enjoy the anthropologist's privileged vantage! In the absence of an explicit explanation, is it not tempting to hear in this formulation an echo of the paternalist Western narrative of the native who learns to see as the master does?)

The problem with Kapferer's conceptualization, it is easy to see, is that it turns on a confused notion of "objectivity" and, consequently, on a very questionable conception of the construction of adequate theoretical discourse. For Kapferer, "objectivity" evidently consists in a place (*that of his own discourse*) from which it is possible to decipher the *true* meanings of other places and practices. Recognizably, this is a conceptualization founded on the premise that anthropology is an epistemological discourse concerned with making foundational statements about the true or ultimate nature of the social realities of others. Whether one accepts such a definition of the anthropological project or not (and I count myself among the latter), what is significant—and especially so where a comparative discipline like anthropology is concerned—is that these kinds of claims about the "objective conditions" of the social and cultural realities of others are typically nonreciprocal; that is to say, they are made, and, moreover, they accede to an authority that is secured by the West about the non-West. The point, in other words, is that theoretical claims about the adequacy of knowledges are inseparable from the power relations in which these knowledges are embedded.

At least one consequence of these kinds of assumptions about the status of anthropological knowledges is that for Kapferer, as indeed for many other anthropologists, the objects which anthropology takes up in its discourse—"religion," "ritual," "social structure," "kinship," or what have you—are treated as self-evident, as transparent and therefore unproblematic. Not surprisingly, then, "ritual" is always found to occupy a predeterminate site—that is to say, a site which is representable precisely in virtue of a set of features identifiable and verifiable in advance, in advance, one might say, of the anthropologist's very arrival in the field. And indeed, Kapferer joins other recent anthropologists who would propose a priori definitions of what "ritual" *is*, and who are concerned to identify, in advance of the discourses and practices that locally constitute it, its supposedly universal features.[31] Setting aside his own warning that "the definition of cultural phenomena is always a hazardous activity," Kapferer proposes the following definition:

> I define ritual as a multi-modal symbolic form, the practice of which is marked off (usually spatially and temporally) from, or within, the routine of everyday life, and which has specified, in advance of its enactment, a particular sequential ordering of acts, utterances, and events, which are essential to the recognition of the ritual by cultural members as being representative of a specific cultural type. (*CD* 2)[32]

Even granting that we accept this comprehensive definition as being a more or less adequate *characterization* of those practices that anthropologists are accustomed to identifying (in the field) and representing (in their texts) as "ritual," it is not at all clear what *analytically* is to be gained by it. Even if *yaktovil,* the specific practice with which Kapferer is concerned, can be described in the general terms he proposes, this hardly enables us to grasp how these practices are locally produced to have their essential effects. What I am getting at can be made clearer by attending to certain aspects of Kapferer's definition.

The definition specifies a demarcation between "ritual" and the "routine of everyday life." The point to note here is the implicit authorization of this demarcation. In its assertion there is a hardly noticeable operation at work by which the *identification* of what is to count as "ritual" is made simultaneously a function of the anthropologist's discourse ("I define ritual . . . ") and of the native's (" . . . essential to the recognition of the ritual by cultural members as being representative of a specific cultural type"). The ambiguity in Kapferer's conceptualization arises once again from the confused notion of objectivity employed. The unique validity of his definition of ritual is supposed to inhere in its conformity with the native's point of view. Recall that this is the general case that Bruner makes for the authority of the anthropology experience. Yet of course the *place* where the truth of *yaktovil* is here authoritatively produced is unambiguously Kapferer's text. More important, however, the distinction upon which his formulation rests—a version of the emic/etic distinction—assumes a conception of culture (whether theirs or his) as an identifiable a priori system of essential meanings. A "ritual," then, is ever in advance of the anthropologist's arrival. It is, so to speak, already *there* in the field, anticipating its formulation in the conceptual scheme of the imaginative anthropologist and its final realization in the anthropological text. And this is the critical point. For what cannot be accounted for in the problematic organized by this definition of ritual is the extent to which certain local practices are "spatially and temporally marked off" *as an effect of the production of local authoritative discourse*. Once this becomes the anthropological question, one need no longer be preoccupied with attempting to establish the universal grounds of a general theory of ritual.[33]

It is clear, therefore, that on a view such as Kapferer's the only kind of problem that is perceived as being of any anthropological significance has to do with the argued or arguable claims of divergent theoretical perspectives–psychological, semiological, sociological, and so on. What remains altogether unattended to, however, is that each of these perspectives, in as like a manner as the other, *has always already assumed the coherence and self-evidence of the object as identified and represented in the anthropological text*. This, it seems to me, represents another aspect of the typically unquestioned discursive and institutional nexus of power and knowledge in which anthropology participates, and in terms of which it arrogates to itself (more often than not, of course, in virtue of its continued ability to maintain a silence about its own assumptions) the privileged space of authoritative identification. And therefore, the *prior* question of the *founding visibility* of these objects is neatly occluded. The question of the way in which these objects come to be identified and represented *as such* in anthropological discourse is suppressed or elided. So that by the closing narrative sequences of its privileged discourse/text, anthropology as the science of cultural truth will have uncovered a latent or anterior native reality that was, in any case, already there, as if always awaiting an adequate interpretation.

Let me emphasize at this point that my criticism of Kapferer's construction of the anthropological object is *not* the hermeneutical one elaborated recently by a number of writers, most notably perhaps Charles Taylor and Clifford Geertz.[34] Geertz, for instance, in his well-known essay, " 'From the Native's Point of View': On the Nature of Anthropological Understanding,"[35] was concerned to indicate a path out of that variously stated but perennial anthropological problem of (to use Richard Bernstein's, not Geertz's, terms here) "objectivism" versus "relativism."[36] He suggested that anthropological understanding is most fruitfully pursued by a "continuous dialectical tacking" between "experience-near" and "experience-distant" concepts. But if this notion of a "tacking" between anthropological and native categories is thought to be one possible path out of a dilemma such as Kapferer's, I would like to suggest that in fact this is far from being the case, and that, to the contrary, it can easily be shown that Kapferer and Geertz both participate in the same set of questionable assumptions. In a passage worth quoting in full, Geertz relates and distinguishes these concepts in the following way:

> Confinement to experience-near concepts leaves an ethnographer awash in immediacies, as well as entangled in vernacular. Confinement to experience-distant ones leaves him stranded in abstractions and smothered in jargon. The real question, and the one Malinowski raised by demonstrating that, in the case of "natives," you don't have to be one to know one, is what roles the two sorts of concepts play in anthropological analysis. Or, more exactly, how, in each case, ought one to deploy them so as to produce an interpretation of the way a people lives which is neither imprisoned within their mental horizons, an ethnography of witchcraft as written by a witch, nor systematically deaf to the distinctive tonalities of their existence, an ethnography of witchcraft as written by a geometer. (" 'From the Native's Point of View,' " p. 57)

It is well to note that part of the apparent appeal of this formulation of Geertz's has to do with its sense of movement, its nonfoundationalist approach to anthropological knowing, and its seeming ability, as at least one philosopher has suggested, to work in a nonreductionist way with the problem of "incommensurability."[37] But allowing this for the sake of argument, is it acceptable for that? To begin with: Why should an ethnography of witchcraft written by a witch be less than adequate conceptually, *in virtue of its being written by a witch*? This is, of course, the same point that Kapferer makes, except that for him the native is "mystified," whereas for Geertz he or she is "imprisoned" within his or her "mental horizons." But the trouble is that the formulation itself is a spurious and therefore question-begging one since, of course, anthropologists are generally *not* witches (indeed, still, rarely even natives) and so could not in any case be "imprisoned [whatever this means] within their mental horizons." Rather, the anthropologist might *construct* his or her text on witchcraft *as though* he or she were so "imprisoned," *as though*, in other words, it were written by a witch.

And this brings me to the central problem, which is that Geertz's "dialectical tacking," for all its apparent subversion of the objectivism/relativism couple, remains a movement between two supposedly *given* discursive spaces—as it were, *his* and *theirs*. And therefore his own argument (like Kapferer's) remains, if I may, "imprisoned" at the level of a quarrel about appropriate ways of interpreting an object whose status as such is never questioned. For what is completely obscured in the passage quoted is the fact that in every historical instance the two conceptual sites (note, of course, that they are, self-consciously, *conceptual* sites)—"experience-near" and "experience-distant"—between which the nimble anthropologist tacks are never essential, a priori, but constructed. My more general point is that *this construction, precisely because it is always embedded in discursive and institutional networks of power and knowledge, has to be interrogated, and this interrogation itself incorporated in a problematized way into our own systematic deliberations.*

We can now see that one of the things that Kapferer's (and Geertz's) strategy tidily obscures is the specific ideological/discursive determination of the object of his own (i.e., anthropological) discourse. For if *yaktovil* is merely the Sinhala name for an authentic "ritual," then it must of course already accord with what is (anthropologically) known about "ritual," in some sense perhaps exemplify it. But if, on the other hand, *yaktovil* is not only a practice constructed within a terrain of local historical conditions, but one that comes, in a determinate genealogy of *Western* knowledges, to be constituted within the anthropological discourse of "ritual," then it is necessary both to argue against any a priori definitions of "what ritual is about" (Kapferer's phrase) and to begin with a very different sort of question entirely.

This question, I would suggest, would be concerned with the specific ways in which *yaktovil* has been constructed as a visible object in that archive of Western knowledges to which anthropology is heir. Here the kind of question to be asked might run as follows: What made the constitution of such an object of knowledge possible for Western discourse, and what kind of problematic did it establish? In other words, "ritual" is, if anything, an area of *anthropological*, not local, knowledge. And the (anthropological) assumption that there is "ritual," one instance of which is the Sinhala *yaktovil*, makes it impossible to ask a question regarding the relation between Western power/knowledge and local discourse, namely, how the practices under the observation of the former, and the discourses to which it so meticulously attends, have come, *as discourse*, to form an area both solicitous of scrutiny and possible of inquiry.

Clearly this raises the question of the complicitous relation between anthropology and colonial discourse (and specifically, where Sri Lanka is concerned, orientalism). At this level, needless to say, the theoretically relevant questions have little to do with the politics or moral attitudes of this or that individual anthropologist. Rather, what is at issue here is the question of the reproduction of a distinctively colonial *object*. For anthropology, after all, is only the latest Western discourse to concern itself with Sinhala (religious) practices, and not the first to presume in so doing a privilege in representing its supposed truth. Part of the dilemma of contemporary anthropological discourse surely centers on its failure to interrogate, much less rethink, its relation to the economy of discourses—military, administrative, missionary, and so on—through which various practices of the colonized and ex-colonized came to be identified, demarcated, and subjected to inscription at the level of Western knowledge. Colonial discourse is a practice of appropriation. Through its devices not only is an area *of* knowledge organized, but an area *as* knowledge is instituted. Insofar as anthropology, taking up its place in the genealogy of the great Western discourses of difference (and indeed, as I have suggested, acceding to a privilege within it), does not reflexively inquire upon those objects that inform its analytic accounts, their inception in the colonial economy of power and knowledge, their deployment in fixing the essential truth of the colonized, it is reproducing a colonial problematic and is, *therefore*, theoretically faulty.

In concluding, let me reiterate that what is most fundamentally questionable in Kapferer's argument regarding self, identity, and the transformation of experience in *yaktovil* is not simply the misguided demonology (though this in itself should not be minimized), but its reliance on the conception of a relation between anthropology and its objects that works to preclude the effective displacement of ideological, and in this case colonial, problematics. For Kapferer, as for so many contemporary anthropologists, this relation is in fact always a straightforward and transparent one. My argument is simply that so long as anthropology proceeds in this fashion—that is to say, so long as anthropology presumes that the objects of its discourse are not only self-evident but entirely *outside* the genealogical network of discourses within which it (anthropology) participates, and are in fact simply waiting there at the dusty edge of a village to be approached, to be represented and interpreted within its texts—then irrespective of the updated theoretical language it employs it must inevitably reproduce ideological (and more often than not, colonial) objects. If, on the other hand, anthropology abandons altogether its faith in this assumption of a fixed and transparent relation between itself and its objects and takes as its point of departure precisely *this* discursive relation itself (what Michel Foucault called the study of "modes of problematization" of practices: *its own, as well as and in relation to, those upon which it inquires*), a rather different, and I would say, a rather more fruitful field of anthropological questions will present itself. Let me turn now to a genealogy of the colonial problematic which this anthropology has assimilated.

Chapter 5

Colonial Christian Discourse, Demonism, and Sinhala Religion

The early formation of Western knowledge about the Sinhala *yaktovil* was largely the work of British Protestant missionaries and Christian colonial administrators in Ceylon in the nineteenth century. Knowledge about *yaktovil* (such as it was) was itself part of the larger colonial production of knowledges regarding the religious doctrines and observances of the Sinhalas. This production of knowledges formed an important part of the practice of nineteenth-century British colonialism in Ceylon. One of the things that this chapter will examine is the conditions of the production of these colonial knowledges—the political and ideological conditions, more specifically.

My general concern is to argue and demonstrate that discursive objects—in this case "demonism"—treated within disciplines such as anthropology are not arbitrary. They have a determinable history, that is to say, following Foucault, a "genealogy." This genealogy gives shape to the general problematic in which these objects of knowledge are produced and reproduced (in reflective, but also in unreflective discourse). And "demonism" is a conceptual metaphor that has been central to the organization of the anthropological study of the *yaktovil*. This chapter has two aims. First, it seeks to inquire into some aspects of the genealogy of this notion of "demonism" as it has informed Western ideas of what Sinhala "religion," and the Sinhala subjects who practice it, are all about. Second, it seeks more generally to trace the formation of the problematic in which the "religion" of the Sinhalas is understood as being comprised of "two systems."

Genealogies of Empire

Tracing the conditions that produced a demonology of Sinhala religious practice requires a grasp of the general conditions in which the island was incorporated into the framework of British colonialism.[1] This is important not only for the obvious sociological reason that ideas are informed by their context, but more critically because it is not often enough appreciated that that "context" which is in question – here, British colonialism – did not constitute an internally unvarying unity. British colonialism itself constituted a changing practice of power, and therefore produced and organized historically varying conditions and effects of knowledge. I shall, for instance, particularly wish to differentiate the practices of power and knowledge in the "Old" and "New" (or First and Second) British Empires.[2] What I am suggesting more generally, then, and indeed wish to emphasize, is that the play of power and knowledge in colonial practice must also be approached genealogically.

British Ceylon formed part of the New or Second Empire, the reconstituted British colonial enterprise that began to take shape at the end of the eighteenth century in the wake of the irrecoverable loss to England of the North American colonies. Although Parliament abolished the then-existing administrative instruments of colonial policy in 1782,[3] and there appeared to commence a period of administrative if not political uncertainty regarding the colonies, by 1812–15 with Lord Bathurst as Secretary of State for War, the modern, more organized, more efficient Colonial Office had come into being. And England – that least ungenerous of mother countries[4] – was already moving swiftly to recover the influence she appeared in danger of losing as premier colonial power. The East would be an important, if not necessarily central, element in that design.

On the morning of 16 February 1796, the British took possession of the Dutch East India Company's garrison at Colombo on the southwest coast of Ceylon. It marked the final capitulation by the Dutch of the Maritime Provinces of the island, which they themselves had captured from the Portuguese a century and a half before, in 1656.[5] Before the end of the Seven Years' War (1756–63), the British had scarcely shown any serious interest in Ceylon. Following the formation of the East Indies Squadron in 1744, the British had been content to have the Dutch provide British ships with access to the harbor at Trincomalee on the eastern coast of the island.[6] However, the Anglo-French struggle for control of South India, and the seeming possibility that the Dutch, whose power and influence were declining, might transfer their allegiance to the French, forced the British to take more substantial notice of the island.[7] At the end of 1795, taking advantage of the weakened and anomalous position of Dutch colonial power, the British began the occupation of the island.[8] Not until the Peace of Amiens in 1801, however, was the British claim to the island officially recognized. The Maritime Provinces of Ceylon became British possessions, then, because of the strategic position of Trincomalee for the defense of colonial interests in India. The strategic value of Trincomalee would sharply decline, however, after 1805 when the British finally became undisputed masters of Eastern waters. But even then it would be another twenty years before a settled and committed policy toward British Ceylon would emerge.

The Second Empire differed in important respects from the First, the so-called Old Colonial System. A full account of these differences is outside the scope of this chapter. Suffice it to sketch something of the general outline and to highlight those aspects most germane to my present concerns.[9] The Second Empire may be said to have transformed the old colonial relation between power and wealth in which the value of overseas possessions was conceived in terms of the exclusive control of resources out of which the state could enhance and exert itself. This idea of commercial monopoly, which informed the mercantilist desire for a "self-sufficient Empire,"[10] was overthrown by the resilient ideology of free trade being advanced by the new captains of industry. A more disseminated thrust toward commercial power was advanced. At the same time, there was a more deliberate move to formulate a coherent imperial policy for the governance of the increasing diversity of peoples being brought within the purview of colonial rule.

More important for our consideration, the Second Empire involved what we might call a transformation in the "political technology" of colonial control. The First Empire of the great sugar plantations of the West Indies rested on the application of a mute physical force applied directly to the bodies of uprooted African slaves. The whip is the symbol of this exercise of power. The Second Empire, by contrast, while never entirely relinquishing its ability to take physical hold of the body of the colonized, reduced its proximity to it. It was concerned rather to develop techniques of subjectification, surveillance, and discipline. The colonial missions are the emblems of this civilizing project.[11] Indeed, critical to this new modality of colonial power in the nineteenth century was the rise of "vital religion" and its corollary, Evangelicalism, as social and political forces in England.[12]

The "Evangelical mind" (to borrow a phrase from Eric Stokes)[13] rejected the prevailing practice of Christianity, in which God appeared all too marginalized. It sought to invest Christian practice with an earnestness and conviction, with an urgent sense of the depravity of man, and the need for salvation through an intensely individual and, as Stokes puts it, "transfiguring religious experience" (p. 29) of conversion. Conversion, in fact, was central to the expressly simple but powerful message of the Evangelicals. As Ian Bradley has argued: "The doctrines of the depravity of man, the conversion of the sinner, and the sanctification of the regenerate soul represent virtually the sum total of the theology of early nineteenth-century Evangelicalism."[14]

From the outset "vital religion" demonstrated an evangelizing or missionary impulse. If the Evangelicals were concerned with the individual experience of salvation, with being reborn, they were equally preoccupied with the dissemination of the Word. As Stokes comments: "The communication of the saving knowledge to the millions that dwelt in darkness could only be accomplished by preaching the word among them in a direct assault on their mind" (p. 30). And this assault was soon to extend beyond the home constituency. The Evangelicals—William Wilberforce and Charles Grant prominent among them—early demonstrated a keen interest in the fate of the "heathen races" in the far-flung outposts of the ever-expanding colonial Empire. Mired in the abominable worship of false gods as the natives were, the Evangelicals felt an acute sense of responsibility for the reformation of their souls. And by the first decades of the nineteenth century, Evangelicalism had begun to exert a material and political influence in shaping the colonial enterprise. The same religious fervor that spearheaded the attack on the slave trade and slavery itself in the West Indies found expression at the other, "fag" end of the Empire, in Wilberforce's celebrated call for an Evangelical mission to the East.[15] It is largely in the context of this "mission," as it took form in Ceylon, that the British colonialists encountered the practices of the Sinhalas.

It is with this encounter that I am concerned in this chapter. Principally, I am concerned with the knowledges about Sinhala religion, and, at a particular stage, about the *yaktovil*, that this encounter produced. As I indicated in chapter 4, my concern is to suggest that anthropological discourse in general, and, more specifically, anthropological writing on the *yaktovil*, has neglected to inquire into the ideological determination of the objects that it constructs for, and considers in, its discourse. Anthropology as an authoritative discourse of "cultural difference," in other words, has need to be self-reflexively cognizant that its knowledges are always produced through, and inscribed within, relations of power. These relations of power and knowledge are, of course, always simultaneously several and intersecting. And one aspect of their (over)determination has a specifiably *colonial* location. Colonial power in British Ceylon, I wish to argue, produced, as part of its multifaceted practice, a "political economy" of constructions of Sinhalas and their society—an interconnected archive of ideas, images, themes, narratives—through which their practices could be made manageably visible, could be fixed and named, that is to say, could be brought more or less securely within a horizon of Western knowledges. In short, colonial power produced a *discourse*;[16] and specifically, as I shall try to show, British colonial power in Ceylon produced a *demonological* discourse. This demonological discourse established the stereotypical modalities through which the "religions" of the Sinhalas would be marked out and experienced (i.e., by the West). And it is this *discursive* relation (between colonial power and the fabric of colonial knowledge as it related specifically to the British colonial encounter with the practices of Sinhala "religion") that is the subject of this chapter.[17]

Indeed, nowhere is the process of the production of colonial knowledges more evident than in the colonial encounter with the practices of "exotic" religions. In fact, "religion" was central, in an almost inaugural way, to the tropic economy of colonial representation. From the outset of their Renaissance voyages, Western Europeans were compelled to find ways of assimilating the exotic peoples they were encountering at what, from their point of view, were the outer margins of the world. They did so first and foremost, Michael Ryan argues, through the readily available trope of "paganism."[18] "As a focus for assimilation," he writes, with specific reference to the sixteenth and seventeenth centuries, "paganism was timely, unambiguous, and emotion laden. More important, it was familiar" (p. 525). The colonial mode of this assimilation was to change historically with changes in the practices of colonialism. This figure of the exotic as heathen would be now the past of Europe, now its unregenerate Other (a shift that will in fact form part of my concern in this chapter).

Religion, however, would remain a constant point of reference in colonial attempts to manage the world of the colonized.

The point I want to emphasize, however, is that what was constructed *as* "religion" in colonial discourse was itself subject to change. So that part of the problem to be sketched and investigated has precisely to do with the instability of what gets identified and counted by authorized knowledges as "religion": how, by whom, and under what conditions of power. In other words, the determining conditions and effects of what gets categorized as "religion" are historically and culturally variable, a fact which anthropologists too often ignore in their attempts to identify universal effects and essential processes.[19] In this respect, anthropologists are not unlike the Evangelical Christian missionaries in nineteenth-century Ceylon who had their own assumptions about what "religion" was all about, and who, in their mission of conversion among the heathen, were much concerned—and for very practical reasons, too—to discover, identify, and represent the prevailing "religion" of the Sinhalas.[20]

Orientalism, Religion, and British Ceylon

With the exception of Philip Almond's little-noticed but very fine study, *The British Discovery of Buddhism*,[21] the place of Buddhism in the discursive economy of British orientalism has unfortunately been the subject of little scholarly attention. The place of British Ceylon even less so. Why this should be so is not immediately discernible.[22] However, in his recent work on the hitherto neglected but quite remarkable career of the Pāli scholar Thomas William Rhys Davids, *The Genesis of an Orientalist*, Ananda Wickremeratne has made a welcome contribution to an inquiry that intersects precisely these areas.[23] T. W. Rhys Davids, ill-starred in his comparatively short career as a member of the British Ceylon Civil Service between 1866 and 1873, was nevertheless to make a most distinguished mark on the early study of Buddhism.[24] I do not wish to discuss Wickremeratne's significant study at length here, however. Rather, my immediate interest concerns some very pointed remarks of his on the attitude of the British toward Buddhism in the nineteenth century. Discussing the differential in responses to Buddhism and Hinduism on the part of the British colonialists, Wickremeratne suggests that more than anything else it was the atheism of the Sinhalas as that aroused the sustained and peculiarly vituperative indignation of the Protestant missionaries and colonial administrators. In contrast to Hinduism, Wickremeratne writes,

> Buddhism . . . was a different kettle of fish. Christianity and Buddhism were totally divergent faiths. Ethically there seemed to be common ground, but the ethics sprang from widely dissimilar assumptions. Small wonder that Christian Protestant missionaries in South Asia should have hurled their bitterest shafts at Buddhism rather than Hinduism, although the latter—no doubt on account of political reasons connected with the British presence in India, especially in the time of the East India Company—loomed larger in the picture. The moral was plain. Buddhism, the personification of atheism, was deadlier than Hinduism. (p. 180)

Although this observation has a certain substance, it stands in need of careful qualification. That British colonialism adopted different attitudes toward the various religious practices—Islamic, Buddhist, Hindu—that it encountered in South Asia is an important point and one perhaps not often enough recognized. However, it is a point that requires studied analysis and elaboration. For it is far from clear that the British were not deeply antipathetic toward Hinduism, or that Hinduism was compared favorably with Buddhism. Consider, for example, the following passage from an early Wesleyan missionary whose work we will examine more closely later:

> Compared with the prevailing religion of the Hindoos, Buddhism wears an aspect amicable and humane. Unlike the worship of *Juggernaut*, (to instance one Hindoo deity only) whose rubric prescribes impurity and blood, as acceptable and even essential *acts of worship*, the worship of Budhu is simple and inoffensive. The sacred books of this system forbid cruelty, dishonesty, unchastity, and falsehood; and inculcate kindness, sympathy, and subordination in civil society. The system tends to correct the inveterate prejudices of *caste*; and has even produced institutions of benevolence and mercy in different parts of the island. On such a system the infidel looks with complacency; and latitudinarian, in the exercise of a spurious candour, pronounces it to be *safe*. But the believer in Divine Revelation, while he admits its comparative excellence, when weighed in the balance with the impure and sanguinary systems of India, and other Pagan lands, beholds written on its portals in the indelible characters of inspired truth—"WITHOUT GOD IN THE WORLD."[25]

Moreover, it seems to me that whereas it is certainly arguable that the "atheism" of the Buddhists did serve as a measure of Buddhism's "inferiority" to Hinduism in the evaluation of the British (as we shall see), Wickremeratne's remarks miss at least two important points. And both these points turn on the necessity for an adequately historical (or again, genealogical) conception of the production of British colonial knowledges about Sinhala religious practice.

The first point is that Wickremeratne's comparative assessment assumes a homogeneous colonial history. It assumes that the conditions that produced the hostility toward Buddhism in the nineteenth century were the same as those that produced the keen interest in Hinduism in India in the eighteenth. But this assumption is an ahistorical one. As I shall try to show, the nineteenth-century Victorian Evangelicalism whose presuppositions and colonial project played such a vital role in producing Western knowledges about Sinhala religious practice were not identical to the late-Enlightenment eighteenth-century discourse that produced the classical Orientalist work on Hinduism.

The second point is that what was so discrepant and unaccountable to the Victorian English Christians in Ceylon in the mid-nineteenth century was, it seems to me, more the observable popular *practices* of the average village Sinhala than the avowedly lofty and metaphysical precepts of the Buddhist Canon. To be sure, the colonial Protestants ridiculed and disparaged the principles of the Buddhist Canon (that is, as far as they could gather them at the time). But even here they could often allow themselves some small gesture of appreciation. What was irreconcilable, however, were the popular practices. For these practices seemed to the Christians to countenance a range of what they perceived and *named* as "demonism" or "devil worship." What is more, these practices appeared to them frustratingly impervious to the great civilizing work of Evangelicalism. And for them, the Evangelical Christians, these practices would define the "real," as it were, of Sinhala religion.

The rest of this chapter is organized around the problems posed by these two points. I shall suggest that one can roughly plot two phases in the early (1796–1850) production of British colonial knowledges about Sinhala religion. These phases, I shall propose, are related to changes in British colonial practice in Ceylon, changes that can, in a qualified way, be conceptualized within the historiographical distinction between Orientalists and Anglicists. I now turn briefly to a consideration of the conceptual appositeness of this distinction to our purposes.

A discussion of the orientalism in which Sinhala religion was initially inscribed in British colonial discourse necessarily requires a reflection on the Orientalist/Anglicist distinction so critical to the historiography of British India. Indeed, it seems to me that British Ceylon is particularly interesting for a discussion of this distinction because it was inserted into the web of British colonial practice precisely in the transition from the one to the other.

In a recent debate, the question has arisen whether Said's *Orientalism* is adequate or even pertinent to the comprehension of this distinction. David Kopf, for instance, whose work on modernization in India turns on this distinction,[26] has criticized *Orientalism* for what he perceives as its lack of "historical precision, comprehensiveness, and subtlety."[27] Central to Kopf's argument is that Said takes no cognizance of the historiographically significant Orientalist/Anglicist controversy of the 1830s around colonial cultural policy toward India. So doing, says Kopf, he fails to recognize the specificity and difference of what he calls "historical Orientalism," a "concrete reality" which, as he would have it, was "born in Calcutta in 1784" (p. 499). Kopf's main purpose is to maintain that Said's choice of the term "orientalism" is misleading because it is rather the anti-Oriental and anti-Orientalist Anglicists who are the real "villains." "It is *their* ideology," writes Kopf, "and not that of the Orientalists which Said reviews in his work" (p. 503, his emphasis).

Without belaboring the point, I think it may be said that Kopf, in his enthusiasm for that singular quartet of William Jones, H. T. Colebrooke, Charles Wilkins, and H. H. Wilson (whose contributions no one would wish to deny), has completely missed Said's point. *Orientalism* is not about discerning where and when "low esteem of Orientals . . . originated" (p. 506); and thus "orientalism" is not merely a "sewer category for all the intellectual rubbish Westerners have exercised in the global marketplace of ideas" (p. 498). Rather, "orientalism," as Said deploys it, is above all a politically invested theoretical category concerned to facilitate a mapping of those economies of representation by means of which colonialist/imperialist power constructs essential and authoritative knowledges about what the East is supposed to be. In this sense, the rise of the Anglicists—foreshadowed in the influence of Charles Grant and William Wilberforce and culminating in Macaulay's Education Minute of 1835—did not signal the beginning of "orientalism" (as indeed it did not the complete demise of the concerns of the Orientalists—a fact which the career of T. W. Rhys Davids well illustrates). What it did signal rather was a *refiguration* of the point of intersection of power and knowledge in the discourse of orientalism.

Thus the distinction between the Orientalists and the Anglicists remains useful, and the historical displacement critical to bear in mind (this particularly in attempting to understand the colonial *inscription* of Ceylon), because they indicate a moment of redistribution of colonial power and a transformation in the technique(s) of colonial practice. Henceforth British orientalism would answer different imperatives, would be differently empowered, would engage a different object, and would operate through different channels of force. More precisely, it would cease to be a means through which (in the manner inaugurated by Warren Hastings [1772–85] and institutionalized by Marquess Wellesly [1798–1805]) a secular Company official-cum-scholar could acquaint himself with the languages and cultural traditions of the people over whom he ruled in order (at least theoretically) to make himself a more responsive and efficient administrator. Rather, British orientalism would become the means through which Victorian missionaries and civil servants would attempt to exert and exercise control over the ruled people. Orientalism, in other words, became part, perhaps the most significant part, of the Evangelical Christian technology of subjectification and colonial discipline.[28]

It is precisely at the inchoate beginnings of this transformation in the economy of orientalism that Ceylon becomes inserted into British colonialism. And the effects on colonial knowledge were considerable. The absence, for instance (with one or two notable exceptions—e.g., George Turnour in the early period, and Hugh Nevill in the later), of a cadre of scholar-civil servants in British Ceylon, to which Vijaya Samaraweera has referred, was hardly fortuitous.[29] By the middle of the nineteenth century the missionary-scholar (such as Daniel J. Gogerly) and the Evangelical-minded administrator (such as Sir James Emerson Tennent) had effectively supplanted them.

Buddhism and Hinduism: Orientalism and Asiatic Chronology

The Asiatick Society of Bengal was founded in Calcutta in 1784, in years when British colonial interest in Ceylon was just taking shape. Although the scope of the Orientalists' concerns (as defined in the opening address to the Society by William Jones) was almost breathtaking in its comprehensiveness,[30] their relation to the East India Company made it almost inevitable that, initially Persian, and a little later Sanskrit, were their principal foci. Persian, as the language of the Mogul court, and Sanskrit, as the language of the texts that codified Brahmanic law, were crucial to the administration of the Company's commercial interests.[31] (This, it is important to bear in mind, was to change as the extent and character of British colonial interests in India changed in the early nineteenth century and it became necessary to give emphasis to the vernaculars, in particular Hindi.) It is understandable, then, that neither Buddhism nor Pāli, the language of its canonical texts, formed part of their central concern.

At the time of the arrival of the British in Ceylon—in early 1796—therefore, the Orientalists at Calcutta knew very little either about the doctrines of Buddhism or about the historical personage Gautama the Buddha, its founder.[32] Because of their trade relations with Southeast Asia and China they were aware of the geographical spread of the doctrines associated with its name. And there was even speculation that knowledge about Buddhism could potentially fill in some of the gaps in their knowledge of what they called "Asiatic history." The most authoritative and celebrated of the Calcutta Orientalists, Sir William Jones, for example, had expressed the opinion that the philosophy of the Buddha was "connected with some of the most curious parts of *Asiatic* history."[33] For want of material evidence, however, he did not (partly because he could not) elaborate. Speculative conclusions were informed by, and arrived at, through readings and interpretations of the ancient Sanskrit texts and conversations with Brahman pundits. Consequently, the Orientalists were anxious for information regarding the religious doctrines and observances of the neighboring island of Ceylon.

One of the great tasks that preoccupied the Calcutta Orientalists was the construction of a proper "chronology" of the Hindus.[34] This, in fact, was the subject of a seminal lecture by Sir William Jones in 1788 in which the great Enlightenment belief in "sound reasoning from indubitable evidence" was to be exercised upon the East. In the name of those "who seek truth without partiality," who neither suffer themselves to "be dazzled by a false glare, nor mistake enigmas and allegories for historical verity," Jones wished to construct a "concise account" of the "Chronological System" of the Hindus, who professed themselves to be of "great antiquity."[35]

Thus, not unexpectedly, one of the critical Orientalist problems regarding Buddhism concerned its place in "Indian" chronology.[36] This question of the age of Buddhism, obviously turned on another, equally puzzling question, that of the historicity of its founder, Gautama the Buddha. As J. H. Harington (jurist, active and highly esteemed member of the Asiatic Society of Bengal, and resident of Colombo for a short period in 1797) put it:

> The real time at which BUDDHA, the son of SUDHODUN . . . propagated the heterodox doctrines ascribed to him by his followers, and for which they have been branded as atheists, and persecuted as heretics, by the Brahmens, is . . . a desideratum which the learned knowledge, and indefatigable research, of Sir W. Jones have still left to be satisfactorily ascertained. (p. 531)

To have been able to decide the "real time" of the Buddha, the Orientalists reasoned, would have enabled them to determine the original time of Buddhism, and thus too its chronological relation to Brahmanism. The issue was complicated, however, by another aspect, that of references in the ancient texts to a certain "Budha." The question thus arose, Harington continued, "whether BUDDHA, the ninth *Avatar* of the *Hindus,* be the same with the heretic BUDDHA, now worshipped at Ceylon, and in the eastern peninsula; as well as in China, Bootan, and Tibet" (p. 532).

In his early and classic essay "On the Gods of Greece, Italy, and India" (originally written in 1784), Sir William Jones had written tentatively: "As to the Buddha, he seems to have been a reformer of the doctrines contained in the *Vēdas;* and though his good-nature led him to censure those ancient books, because they enjoined sacrifices of cattle, yet he is admitted as the ninth *Avatār* even by the *Brāhmans* of *Cāsi.* . . . "[37] This view, however, seeming as it did to collapse the doctrines of the contemporary followers of the teachings of the Buddha with the illusive figure of the Brahmanic texts, was contradicted by Brahmans. And therefore, in an essay written some four years later, "On the Chronology of the Hindus," Jones offered the modified view that there was a second Buddha who assumed the character of the first and attempted in his name to overthrow the system of Brahmanism.

With the conquest of the Maritime Provinces of Ceylon, then, it was anticipated that "the authentic materials for a history of the Singalese, their religion, manners, and customs"[38] would be communicated to the Asiatick Society of Bengal, and thus enable a resolution of these issues. Three articles were published on Ceylon in the journal of the Calcutta

Orientalists, *Asiatick Researches,* in the early years of British rule. And in keeping with the prevailing interests of the Orientalists, these were concerned largely with the Buddhism of the Sinhalas and, more specifically, with the chronological relation between Buddhism and Brahmanism.

The first of these articles, entitled, "Remarks on Some Antiquities on the West and South Coasts of Ceylon," was written by Captain Colin McKenzie in 1796.[39] McKenzie, who was a functionary of the East India Company and an avid Orientalist, was part of the British forces occupying the Maritime Provinces.[40] He tells us himself that it was while "employed on objects of a very different nature" that he availed himself of the unprecedented opportunity created by the "late reduction [of the island] to our power" of promoting "the interesting objects of the [Asiatic] society" (p. 425). His principal object of interest (informed clearly by the Orientalist preoccupation with chronology) was the supposed "remains of *Hindu* antiquity" in the island. This interest rested on his assumption that Hinduism rather than Buddhism was the original religion of the Sinhalas. His visit to the southern town of Devundara or Devinuwara—"Dewunder-head, or Divi-noor (called in the charts Dunder-head)"—provided him with evidence (in figures carved on stone pillars and scattered objects "indicating some connexion with the *Lingam* and *Phallus*") to confirm this theory. The captain advanced the opinion that in the "revolutions of religion" Buddhism had displaced Hinduism and in the process destroyed "almost every vestige of its worship" (p. 441). This view of the relationship between Hinduism and Buddhism, however, would soon be eclipsed by the first adumbrations of the progressivism that was to dominate the nineteenth century, and according to which Buddhism, lacking as it did a supreme godhead, was judged the more primitive of the two religions.

Captain McKenzie's visit to the southwest, this time to Weligama ("Belligam or Velli-gam") also afforded him the opportunity of meeting a Buddhist monk. This must have been his first meeting of this kind, and something of its novelty tells in his description of the event:

> At the gate, to which we ascended by some steps, the priests received and conducted me to the door of the temple; they were bare-headed, and their hair cut close; they had none of the distinguishing marks worn by the Hindus, on the forehead; their garment consisted of a cloth of a dusky snuff colour, which folded round the body and descended to the feet; their dark complexion, and inanimate features, exhibited no

> symptom of superior intelligence, of deep penetration, or of keen genius; nor did any of that mild cast of countenance, or chastened resigned features, which sometimes distinguish the recluse, or devotee of every nation, appear here; neither severe, nor shy, their looks rather indicated a kind of apathy, or indifference. (p. 435)

The studied sense of discrepancy is barely disguised. Notice how his expectation has been framed by his perception of the Hindu. The Buddhist could only be described in negatives. The last passage, moreover, with its theme of complacency, that trait which the Victorian sensibility was to find so unaccountable and irredeemable in the Oriental, already anticipates the nineteenth-century image of the Sinhala perhaps best exemplified in the writings of Sir James Emerson Tennent. Yet, on the other side, there is a measurable mixture of captivation and solemnity in his description of the image of the Buddha:

> The countenance was mild and full, and the top of the head painted to represent the hair in several small curls of black colour. This was the grand idol of the place, but on it, placed thus at full length on a raised terrace on which several lamps and a profusion of flowers were placed, no external signs of adoration or respect were shewn by the priest. (pp. 435–436)

The second article, "On Singhala, or Ceylon, and the Doctrines of Bhooddha," was also written by a military man, a Captain Mahony.[41] This Captain Mahony, it appears, was an "officer of the *Bombay* establishment."[42] Unlike the somewhat superficial and impressionistic McKenzie, however, Mahony was more explicitly concerned with a consideration of the "Doctrines of Bhoodha." He seems to have acquainted himself more carefully with some of the details of Sinhala Buddhist cosmology and mythology, and even to have secured translations of passages of "some books of the Singhalais."

In his account, Mahony describes at some length the cosmological system of the Buddhists and the Buddha's place within it. He notes the number and names of Buddhas and of the "heavens" in the Sinhala system; he comments on the fact that "Bhoodha is not properly speaking considered a god," on the Sinhala's "denial of a Supreme Power," and on the indifference to "what is understood by us under the term of Paradise"; and he notes the hierarchical arrangement of "the characters in their mythology" (pp. 32–37). He then goes on to offer a few cautious but sensitive remarks on what he understands to be the main precepts of the doctrine:

> The religion of BHOODDHA, as far as I have had any insight into it, seems to be founded in a mild and simple morality. BHOODHA has taken for his principles, Wisdom, Justice, and Benevolence; from which principles emanate Ten Commandments, held by his followers as the true and only rule of their conduct. He places them under three heads; thought, word, and deed; and it may be said that the spirit of them is becoming, and well suited to them whose mild nature was first shocked at the sacrifice of cattle. These commandments comprise what is understood by the moral law, which has been generally preached by all the BHOODDHAS, in the empire of Raja GAHA NOOWERAH. (p. 40)

Also included in Captain Mahony's article is a translated extract from a text entitled *Maha Raja Wallieh* (i.e., the *Rājāvaliya,* a seventeenth- or eighteenth-century text written in Sinhala). In this extract there is recounted a version of the great origin story of the Sinhalas. This must have been the first appearance in English translation of any portion of this now well-known legend.

If Mahony did not seem interested in the chronological preoccupation with the relative historical priority of Buddhism and Hinduism, his article could nevertheless not conclude without addressing the perplexing and related Orientalist question, "how far this BHOODDHA [of the Sinhalas] is the one of the Hindoos" (p. 52). Mahony is worth quoting at length here because it is interesting that in arriving at what appears to be his conclusion—the refutation of this claim—it is the authority of Hindus in the island rather than Buddhists that is to determine the identity of the latter's Buddha:

> Having always conceived, from what I had an opportunity of reading and hearing, that BHOODDHA was one of the nine *Avataurams,* and that, notwithstanding his having contradicted, in his doctrines, some of the most essential points in the divine authorities of the Hindoos, his praises were nevertheless sung by some of the first order of Brahmins, I stood forth in asserting his dignity to the persons above-mentioned [i.e., some "learned Hindoos whom I lately met on *Ceylon*"]; when I was informed, that he was not included in the nine *Avataurs.* . . . The incarnation of BHOODDHA, it was added, arose in the following circumstances: "In former ages there were three giants, named *Trepooras,* (so entitled from their cities of iron, brass, and gold, which cities had wings, and were ambulatory,) who were votaries to SEVA [Siva], and continued to adore his sacred emblem, *Lingam,* so that they were invin-

> cible. They often oppressed the Gods, who having besought VISHNOO, he assumed a form under the title of BHOODDHA, who entering the cities, wrought miracles, and preached his seducing doctrine to the inhabitants, who embraced his religion, and became in every respect his proselytes. By this stratagem the *Trepooras* fell into the hands of BHOODDHA, and were destroyed by SEVA. . . . Hence BHOODDHA is considered as the promulgator of an heterodox religion. The adherents to BHOODDHA are looked upon as infidels; and their religion, though commendable with respect to morality, yet is reckoned as one of the 339 sects, or branches of the well-known heresy, or rather schism, among the Hindoos." (pp. 55–56)

The third article on Ceylon to appear in *Asiatick Researches*, "On the Religion and Manners of the People of Ceylon," is perhaps the most interesting of the three.[43] Certainly, in treating as it did both the "religion" and "manners" of the "Singalese" it was the most comprehensive. But more important, because of the position of its author, it gives us a first hint at the emerging relation between colonial knowledge and local colonial practices in this early period of British rule in Ceylon. Joinville (his full name was Joseph Endelin de Joinville), described as a very "learned naturalist,"[44] was the only one of the early writers on Ceylon to actually reside in the island. He was in fact a Frenchman who had come out to Ceylon to join the administration of the first Governor, Frederic North, in 1798. And by the time of his article, he was Surveyor-General in the North Administration.[45] What is more, Joinville's article bears the authorizing imprimatur of an introductory letter by Governor North himself. In this letter, dated 27 September 1801, North is at pains to emphasize the seminal character of his Surveyor-General's researches on the "religion and customs of the *Cingalese*":

> It is necessary to mention, that this Essay was concluded before the arrival on this Island of the Embassy of Colonel Symes, and of the Account of the Religion and Customs of the Inhabitants of *Burmah* by Doctor Buchanan, contained in the Sixth Volume of the Researches of the Society.[46]

Indeed, Joinville himself was acutely self-conscious of inaugurating a whole new area of research. Mindful of the fact that his "information," as he called it, was "not altogether complete," he nevertheless waxed confident that it would "serve as a clue for further and deeper researches" (p. 397). "The first person who treats on such a subject," he declared, already looking ahead to his successors in the field, "labours under disadvantages, which succeeding authors know how to turn to their own account, by finishing what a former hand had sketched, claiming the merit of the whole work. Regardless, however, of this consideration, I have the consolation to think, I shall be useful to him who may next treat of the present subject" (p. 397).

Again the question of chronology was uppermost. The first section of the article was entitled "Antiquity of the Religion of Boudhou," and in it Joinville set out to resolve the puzzle of the historicity of the Buddha:

> If BOUDHOU be not an allegorical being, he was a man of genius, who made laws, established a religion, over a large tract of Asia. It is hard to say whether he, ZOROASTER, or BRAHMA, were the most ancient. (p. 397)

Joinville offers the suggestion that in order to decide the question it is necessary to establish whether "these three legislators had really existed, or rather if these names are not merely attributes" (p. 397). In fact, however, Joinville has little problem deciding in favor of the relative historical precedence of Buddhism over Brahmanism. "I am rather of the opinion," he writes,

> upon a comparison of the two religions, that that of BOUDHOU is the more ancient, for the following reasons. The religion of BOUDHOU having extended itself in very remote times, through every part of *India*, was in many respects monstrous and unformed. An uncreated world, and mortal souls, are ideas to be held only in an infant state of society, and as society advances such ideas must vanish. *A fortiori*, they cannot be established in opposition to a religion already prevailing in a country, the fundamental articles of which are the creation of the world, and the immortality of the soul. Ideas in opposition to all religion cannot gain ground, at least cannot make head, when there is already an established faith; whence it is fair to infer, that if *Boudhism* could not have established itself among the *Brahmins*, and if it has been established in their country, that it must be the more ancient of the two. (p. 400)

Of course it was not exactly "fair" to so "infer" since the premises themselves were ill-founded. But Joinville was simply applying the yardstick of an incipient progressivism according to which notions of creation and immortality necessarily belong further up the scale of civilization.

After these three articles, nothing of note (indeed, so far as I can tell, nothing at all) on Ceylon or Buddhism was published in the pages of

Asiatick Researches. What occasioned this curious abandonment of a field of such interest and potential for the Society is not readily apparent. It seems most likely that the British Government's decision to relieve the East India Company of administrative responsibility for the island in 1802 must have discouraged further investigation.[47] The Orientalists were first and foremost Company men, after all. Moreover, the whole Orientalist project itself was at that moment—in the face of the emergent Evangelical challenge—battling for its very survival.[48]

For the Orientalists, in summary, the question of Buddhism and of the Buddha were, for the most part, *exegetical* problems bearing upon the "chronology" of Asiatic religions and customs. "Religion" was the fundamental object of focus. And "Buddhism" as represented in these early articles derived from an interface between colonial assumptions about the authorizing emblems of "religion" (official institutions, clergy, texts) and those in Sinhala society who claimed for themselves the authority to represent Sinhala religion (the monks, and the canonical texts). Thus in these articles, whereas there is the reproduction of a temple scene, there is no mention of the *yaktovil*, or of those popular practices associated with the Sinhala pantheon of deities. But the Orientalist preoccupation had little or no immediate practical, that is to say, *political*, significance. And herein lies a (perhaps *the*) critical distinction between the Orientalists and the later Evangelicals and Anglicists. Indeed, when the latter took up what we might call the second phase of colonial writing about Sinhala "religion," other problems than the academic one of the chronological relation between Buddhism and Brahmanism were to come to the fore.

Buddhism and Demonism: Conversion and Colonial Knowledge

In what I am proposing to call the second phase of colonial writing about Sinhala "religion," the political and ideological atmosphere of colonial rule in Ceylon was very different from what it had been in the earlier phase. There were at least two reasons for this. First of all, the British had by this time committed themselves not only to keeping the island but also to exploring ways of developing it economically and improving the efficiency of its administration. This became particularly evident with the increasing consolidation of colonial rule that followed the ceding of the Kandyan Provinces in 1815 and the suppression of the Great Rebellion of 1818 in the Kandyan Provinces.[49] And if neither economic solvency nor administrative reform were to be achieved until the 1830s–with the coffee boom on the one hand,[50] and the implementation of a diluted version of the Colebrooke-Cameron recommendations on the other[51]–there were nevertheless signs by the 1820s that the island was now more than a mere strategic outpost for the protection of British possessions in India.

Second, Evangelicalism was beginning to exercise an influence on the determination of colonial policy, and missionary organizations had begun to play a prominent role in the shaping of colonial society. Responding to William Wilberforce's rousing call for an Eastern mission, there was a general Evangelical interest in those "neglected regions of the Eastern World." The idolatry of India was, since Grant's famous 1793 treatise on "the state of society among the Asiatic subjects of Great Britain,"[52] uppermost in the minds of the Evangelicals. But Ceylon was, in many ways, a particularly attractive prospect to the missionaries. There were, first of all, reports of large numbers of nominally Christian natives in the island who were, as a result of a want of proper instruction, in imminent danger of relapsing into their former idolatry.[53] Moreover, and this must have been a weighty consideration, there was the anticipation that, Ceylon being a Crown Colony, there would be a greater degree of tolerance toward missionary work than existed in the Indian territories under the control of the East India Company.[54] The Baptist Mission began their work in 1812, the Wesleyan Methodist Mission soon after, in 1814, and the Church Missionary Society in 1818.[55]

These two factors–the movement toward the liberal political and economic development of Ceylon, and the growth of the missionary enterprise–intersected in a paradoxical but significant way in the problems that arose out of the celebrated fifth clause of the Kandyan Convention of 2 March 1815, by which the provinces of the Kandyan Kingdom were ceded to the British.[56] They constituted two sides, as it were, of the transformation of the "political technology" of British colonial practice, and they made for a change in the way Sinhala religion was identified and represented. The fifth clause of the Kandyan Convention stipulated that

> the Religion of Boodhoo professed by the Chiefs and inhabitants of these Provinces is declared inviolable, its Rites, Ministers and Places of Worship are to be maintained and protected.[57]

If British rule in Ceylon may be said to only really begin with the extension of political and territorial control over the entire island after the cession of Kandy, then the British colonial encounter with Buddhism—or at least this more significant phase of it—was inaugurated in unprecedented compromise and curious ambivalence. It was in order to mollify the Kandyan chiefs, Governor-General Robert Brownrigg assured the Secretary of State, Lord Bathurst, in defense of the wording of this clause of the Convention, that he had had to agree to the maintenance of the traditional Sinhala relation between the state and religion.

Not unexpectedly, the Evangelicals in England, William Wilberforce particularly, objected strongly to the wording of the fifth clause, feeling that it could be interpreted as being prejudicial to the active Christian proselytization of the Sinhalas. However, as K. M. de Silva has suggested, in 1815 Evangelicalism lacked the influence it would later wield in matters of colonial policy.[58] As this political influence grew, however, especially during the long term of office of James Stephen as Permanent Under-Secretary at the Colonial Office, this relation with Buddhism would become the object of considerable missionary agitation. British accession to colonial dominance in Ceylon in the nineteenth century, therefore, immediately involved them in a *political* problem regarding native "religion" that the emergent Evangelicalism would both define and endeavor to resolve.[59]

In one of the early nineteenth-century works on Sinhala religion, Edward Upham's *History and Doctrine of Budhism*, published in London in 1829, there is a vivid and dramatic representation of Sinhala worship remarkable for the fact that it was unrepeated (because perhaps already unrepeatable) in the Orientalist literature on British Ceylon. For in it, precisely at a time when colonial rule in the island was relatively settled and even advancing toward its review and progressivist rationalization in the 1830s,[60] we are presented with an imagined colonial "scene" (Upham's word) of singular ambivalence: both dark and light. An Oriental scene which, while explicitly inscribed within the Evangelical and Anglicist endeavors then taking root, simultaneously called up the comparativist and classicist preoccupations of the late Calcutta Orientalists. This scene Upham sets before us thus in the concluding paragraph of the Introduction to this work:

> We have now before us a map of the vast portion of the human race, who derive their opinions and faith from Budhist doctrine, who profess to regulate their hope and notions of future bliss wholly by its moral instructions and rules. These important and striking considerations (for so every cause operating on millions of human beings may justly be deemed) will convert into matters of deep interest the most minute details, and secure patient attention to the astrological puerilities of their demon worship, and to their opinions on the character of infernal punishments. All these matters supply traits, without which the picture would be imperfect; and it may be considered a very useful lesson to set before the pride of man, that, in reference to the most important of subjects, the state and quality of future existence, the most refined Greek philosophers, and the darkest and most ignorant of the followers of the Budha, were much on a par as to external religious observances, and any advantageous views of what becomes of the soul after death. It seems, therefore, to warn us that, on these great subjects, very little advantage can be gathered from the utmost stretch of the human understanding; *the teacher must be divine*. However high his intellectual attainment, philosophy could not lift her greatest follower, at his death, above the standard of the humblest disciple of the Budha, whom, sacrificing a cock to the Bali, or planetary influences, as he lay languishing under sickness amid the woods of Ceylon, we see under the same vow, and offering the same tribute to the Deity, as marked the last hours of Socrates. "Uncovering his head, for his head was covered, that nothing might trouble him, 'Crito,' says Socrates (these were his last words), 'we owe a cock to Esculapius, discharge this vow for me, and not forget it'." A midnight scene, which was witnessed in the forests of Ceylon, wherein a magical practitioner was addressing the sparkling host of heaven, "the Bali," in behalf of an unfortunate individual languishing under sickness, will demonstrate how precisely this last act of the greatest philosopher of the Athenian school sprung from the same root of doctrine as that of the sick Singalese. (p. 15)

We cannot read this long passage without being astonished by its serenity, its lack of animus. It has not yet been overcome by what Homi Bhabha has referred to as "those terrifying stereotypes of savagery, cannibalism, lust and anarchy which are the signal points of identification and alienation, scenes of fear and desire, in colonial texts."[61] Upham is not unwilling to raise a warning about the "pride of man" by elaborating a cross-cultural affinity incompatible with the missionary Evangelicalism that had already begun to disfigure and efface it. His text rings perhaps one of the last notes of the theme of the noble savage. But what is of particular interest for us here is the very setting of the scene itself, "the woods of Ceylon."[62]

If the knowledges of the Orientalists at the end of the eighteenth century derived in the main from their prodigious translation and examination of texts, that of the Evangelical missionaries of the nineteenth was fashioned in large part through their actual contact with the everyday practices of broad sections of the native population. The production of colonial knowledge depends on the constitution of privileged "scenes" where what counts as "true" knowledge is to be found. The physical and symbolic place of this "scene" shifted according to the imperatives of the colonial enterprise. That, for instance, Calcutta once constituted such a "scene" was the reason for the establishment there of the College at Fort William in 1800. That it had already effectively ceased to be so early in the nineteenth century, and particularly after 1813 with the change in the East India Company's policy toward missionaries, was the reason for its decline. In these years colonialism became authorized through a discourse of subjectification and discipline—in short, the "civilizing mission"—requiring a different modality of power, and a different site of application. And what emerged as one of its privileged techniques was the Evangelical practice of *conversion*. With the emergence of conversion as distinctive to the micropolitics of colonialism, the "scene" of the production of knowledges about native religions, languages, and customs moved from the conclave of scholars in the commercial and administrative centers to the "outstations," the villages, "hamlets," and isolated mission houses that regulated the round of solitary labors of the intrepid missionary.

The practice of missionary conversion in British Ceylon changed the problematic of orientalism, and with it the productive gaze of colonial knowledge. And transforming this productive gaze, it brought into play, into the field of what was visible to colonial discourse, a new object: *demonism*.[63] As long as orientalism had a purely scriptural site, and as long as Orientalist knowledge about native religion was conceived to have a secular and educative effect *on the colonizer rather than the colonized*, it could, as it did for the Orientalists, preoccupy itself solely with the authorized texts and their select interpreters. Once the missionary had set himself in the "moral wilderness" of the natives themselves, however, with the task not of understanding their popular discourses and practices but of militantly confronting and *changing* them, the "gloomy" and "monstrous" observances before his eyes destabilized the received boundaries of the textual tradition and transformed the identified object, Sinhala religion.

This is not to suggest that the textual project and the object it identified declined. Far from it. As Philip Almond has well argued, during the first half of the nineteenth century, "Buddhism" became established as a textual object:

> By the beginning of the 1850s, a discourse about Buddhism had developed. "Buddhism" by this time described and classified a variety of aspects of Oriental cultures. Moreover, it had been distinguished from the religion of the Hindus, and had come on the whole to be viewed as having begun with Gautama (at some as yet unspecified time), and as having originated in India. Most of these opinions of it were only able to gain a foothold as a result of Buddhism having come to be viewed as an object determinable primarily by the collection, and editing, of its own texts. By the 1850s, the textual analysis of Buddhism was perceived to be the major scholarly task. Through the West's progressive possession of the texts of Buddhism, it becomes, so to say, materially owned by the West; and by virtue of this ownership, ideologically controlled by it.[64]

And this is precisely my point. Whereas what was called "Buddhism" was constructed as a textual object, Sinhala "religion"—the religion observed among the Sinhalas—was constructed as *both more and less* than this: more, insofar as Sinhalas were said to have *two* systems of religion; and less, insofar as the predominating one of these two was not Buddhism but demonism. This privileging of the textual in the construction of "Buddhism" was to have far-reaching consequences for later attempts to think the relation between "Buddhism and society."

The first articles on Sinhala religious practice, as we have seen, make no mention of demonism. Admittedly, the writers, some of whom were visitors based in India, must have had only the slightest acquaintance with the range of practices of the people who had so recently "passed beneath British rule" (to use A. J. Arberry's infelicitous phrase). In the post-1815 period, however, when colonial rule in Ceylon had become more settled and regulated, and when the missionaries of the various denominations (particularly the Wesleyans) had established themselves in village areas, the whole character of writing about Sinhala religion changed. The question of the relation between Buddhism and Hinduism, though by no means resolved, gave way to a concern with the relation between Buddhism and demonism.

The Rev. William Martin Harvard's *A Narrative of the Establishment and Progress of the Mission to Ceylon and India,* published in London in 1823, provides one the earliest Evangelical representations of Sinhala religion. Harvard had been a member of the first group of Wesleyan missionaries to set out for Ceylon, arriving in February 1815. He was stationed at Colombo. Setting the tone of nineteenth-century missionary writing on Sinhala religion, his *Narrative* provides not so much a considered description of Sinhala practices as a militant declamation of them. In it, nevertheless, we can discern the emergence of something new in the field of Sinhala religion.

In the section of his Introduction entitled "Ceylonese superstitions and idolatrous ceremonies," Rev. Harvard maintains that there are "two principal religious systems" prevailing among the Sinhalas—"Kapooism, or, the worship of Demons; and that which inculcates the superstition of Budhu" (p. xlix). These were both "systems of heathenism" and, as he continued, represented "another district" of that vast "empire of darkness" which was beginning to yield to the "cheering and vivifying beams of THE TRUE LIGHT" (p. xlix). In a conception different to that of the Orientalist's, Sinhala religion is now represented as double, as consisting of two forms or "systems"—Kapooism or demonism on the one hand, and Buddhism on the other. It was not the first time that Sinhala religion had been so represented (Governor North had actually used similar terms in 1799).[65] But now, in different conditions of colonial practice, it would be endorsed, repeated, and elaborated. And indeed, it would become the defining feature of Sinhala religion.

In his account of these "two religious systems" Harvard turns first to that of Kapooism. This strategy of representation is not accidental. Harvard wishes to ascribe a certain differential status to Kapooism and Buddhism, and underline a very particular kind of relationship between them. Kapooism, Harvard claims, consists in "the worship of evil spirits" and is, according to the "ancient Singhalese records," the "primitive religion of the Singhalese" (p. 1). In other words, for Harvard, as for many early nineteenth-century European Christians, the "superstitious fear and worship of evil spirits, is in fact the universal *religion of nature*" (p. 1, his emphasis). This meant at least two things. First of all, it meant that Kapooism could be assimilated to the Christian view of pagan practices as Satanic. Ceylon, Harvard charged, was one of those "benighted lands" where "the sovereignty of that malignant spirit, known among us by the name of the devil, (because in the Scriptures is so termed), is openly and officially proclaimed" (p. 1):

> The ascendancy of Satan is THERE not merely *intimated* by the features of human conduct, as they are opposed to virtue and goodness. It is *avowed* in the most unequivocal manner. The visible kingdom of the Wicked One stands THERE erected, with unblushing front—in frightful images—in venerated temples—in an order of priesthood—in a round of ceremonies—in A DIRECT WORSHIP—in a series of terrifying fears and apprehensions—in amulets, and offerings—and in various abominable evils! (p. 1, his emphasis)

And he continues, giving an account of its nature and functions:

> This gloomy system is founded on the supposition, that all the pains and sufferings to which man is exposed, are occasioned by the baleful influence of daemons on his person and concerns. Every misfortune and disease has its presiding daemon; and prayers are offered, and sacrifices made, to avert the evils which they are supposed to inflict. Their images represent Satanic beings, of the most horrible forms and propensities. Some of them have the semblance of men, of gigantic size, with several hands, each armed with an instrument of torture. Others are represented as monsters with tremendously large eyes, mouths, and teeth, in the act of devouring a human being; holding several more, suspended by the hair, in readiness for the same fate: and some are pictured as feeding on the reeking entrails of expiring men, whom they have massacred for the purpose. There are others of a character which forbids description! (p. li)

Second (and a point that was critical for the practice of Christian conversion), it meant that Kapooism was older, more original, and thus more "real" to the Sinhalas than Buddhism. One of the textual authorities on which Harvard relied for his *Narrative* was Dr. John Davy's *An Account of the Interior of Ceylon and of its Inhabitants*.[66] Finding in some of Davy's remarks on the word "Kapooa" a substantiation of his own conception, Harvard noted that

> according to Dr. Davy, this word is derived from *kapu*, proper, and *ralle*, chief. If this be its real derivation, may it not be considered as indicative of the "proper," or legitimate claims to ascendancy and influence which the Singhalese assign to this order of native priests; and thus afford a strong presumptive evidence of what the Author assumes

> to be the fact, that the worship of daemons is the primitive offspring of the imagination of fallen man: and hence the "proper," or real and actual, religion of nature? (p. lin)

Only after discussing Kapooism does Harvard turn to Buddhism, the position of which is, in turn, described before his discussion of the virtues of Christianity and the difficulties faced by its missionaries. This "superstition," he says, is the "established religion of the Singhalese" (p. lii). His discussion of it is concerned with two issues primarily—the "introduction" of Buddhism into the island, and its "principal doctrines." When Buddhism was introduced into Ceylon has not been satisfactorily determined, he writes, and indeed the circumstances of its introduction are "set forth by the Singhalese histories, in all the extravagant hyperbole of an Eastern fable" (p. liv). Nevertheless, Harvard asserts, divested of the "absurdities in which it is clothed," it is gathered from these "fables" that the Buddha was a religious reformer, who, finding the Sinhalas

> devoted to the Kapooa system of demon worship, endeavored, by preaching some portion of truth, though mixed up with much error, to raise their minds from the degraded and enslaved state in which they had been held for ages; success followed the persevering promulgation of the system; until it gained the ascendancy, and became the established religion of the island. (p. lv)

As always, colonial missionary representation entailed the appropriation and assimilation of indigenous discourses. The story of the relationship between Buddhism and demonism is thus cast by Harvard in an Evangelical language familiar to the missionary and his audience. The Sinhalas, in their original state, and for ages, were "enslaved" to "demon worship." At a later, and as yet undetermined period, however, the Buddha, "religious reformer" that he was, had attempted to "raise their minds" from its "degraded" state, and had, after much perseverance, achieved a measure of success. Indeed, was not this just what the colonial Christian missionary was now attempting to do? So that in Evangelical discourse, Buddhism is made to stand in the relation to demonism that it accords to its own relation to both. For note that Buddhism is assigned "some portion of truth," though a truth that is, nevertheless, "mixed up with much error." The authority and justification that the program of Christian conversion could therefore claim for itself was the benevolent one that it set out to complete a task ineffectually started by

Buddhism. For, after all, "civilization and Christianity" were the "most powerful counteractions" against all vestiges of superstition. Moreover, Buddhism was a false and anomalous doctrine. Not only did it profess to be godless, but the very founder of that doctrine was himself transformed into a god. Harvard wrote, affecting a sort of ironic astonishment:

> Budhuism, in its original form, is probably the only system of undisguised Atheism ever promulgated; and presents the curious anomaly of the founder of a system (who himself denied a Creator) being at length constituted a god by his own disciples. He who rejected all religious worship, as vain and foolish, has now temples reared to his name, in which he is worshipped: and his image is reverenced as a deity, wherever it is seen! (pp. lvi-lvii)

This theme of the failure of Buddhism to overcome the deep-seated vice of demonism among the Sinhalas was to repeat itself throughout the nineteenth century, and it still lingers in the twentieth-century anthropological idea that an abstract Buddhism was forced to accommodate itself to popular supernaturalism. In fact, this latter idea is more directly related to the adjunct and more important missionary theme regarding the character of the relation between these two systems. If Kapooism, as it was conceived by the Evangelical mind, was older, more primitive, and more original to the Sinhalas than Buddhism, and if it had been supplanted by it as their "established religion," it had also formed a curious yet very visible connection to it. The precise formulation of this connection, however, was open to some dispute. Here, for example, the Rev. Harvard disagreed with Dr. Davy. Davy had suggested that it was "not merely tolerated, but *quite orthodox*" to have a *dēvālē* (shrine-house for a god) and a *vihāra* (Buddhist temple) "contiguous, or even under the same roof." Harvard begged to differ:

> The general correctness of this respectable and learned author . . . cannot be questioned; but I apprehend him inadvertently to have adopted a mistake in supposing that the worship of either the Brahminical gods, or the Kapooistic daemons, is consistent with pure Budhuism; than which nothing can be more *heterodox*. It is true, the followers of Budhu, and even the priests themselves, will perform acts of worship to the Kapooistic deities, and have figures of daemons painted on the walls of their own temples. But this, so far as I have been able to learn, is a corruption of the Budhuist system. (pp. lv-lvi)

Writing somewhat later, the noted missionary and scholar of Buddhism, Daniel J. Gogerly, was to offer this connection on slightly more "sociological" grounds (grounds, in fact, prefiguring those of latter-day anthropologists). Gogerly made a distinction between "the views of the learned and reflecting part of the Buddhist community" and those of "the great body of the people" who, thinking little on the subject, "merely tread in the footsteps of their forefathers." [67] These latter, he asserted, had "united demon-worship with Buddhism." But this was "in direct opposition to the system" (*Ceylon Buddhism*, p. 4), that is, to the views and practices of the "reflecting" Buddhists. In short, Gogerly argued significantly that "The practical working of Buddhism is essentially different from its system" (p. 6). Or, as he had put it, and somewhat less elegantly, in the pages of *Friend*, the Wesleyan propaganda journal:

> whatever opinion there may be formed of the morality of some of its precepts, or the refinement of its metaphysics, no one conversant with the people can fail to observe that its effects are to render them earthly, sensual, and devilish.[68]

This linking of Sinhala character with their religious practices, and particularly with their *resistance* to conversion, became a preoccupation of mid-Victorian Evangelical writing on the practices of the Sinhalas.

The explicit object of the colonial Evangelical project was *conversion*, not knowledge; its concern was to *displace*, not understand, the religious practices of the Sinhalas. Yet within a short decade of the inauguration in the island of that inspired civilizing enterprise it was clear to the most sanguine of Christian protagonists that it was little more than a dismal failure. Indeed, a recurrent theme in missionary writing of this period is the profound dismay and bewilderment over this fact, which they attributed to the "character of the Singhalese people" and the peculiar "genius of their religion."

One of the most illuminating expressions of this idea is to be found in Sir James Emerson Tennent's *Christianity in Ceylon*, published in 1850.[69] (Tennent was Colonial Secretary to Viscount Torrington and was recalled with him after the debacle over his handling of the "rebellion" of 1848.)[70] Nineteenth-century literature on Sinhala religion and Christian conversion is replete with the theme of the extreme apathy and pliancy of Sinhala character. To be sure, all "Asiaticks" were, to an excessive degree, "apathetic," in contrast to the bristling "vigor" of the European. But the

Buddhist character, according to Tennent, appeared peculiarly marked by a deceptively *yielding* quality, which differentiated it from the Brahmanic character, and which had definite implications for the colonial Christian practice of conversion. Whereas the Brahmanism of the Tamils of the Jaffna peninsula, for instance, was "exclusive and fanatical," the Buddhism of the Sinhalas, in its singular "self-righteousness," extended a "latitudinarian liberality to every other faith" (p. 191). Paradoxically, however, this served to make the Buddhists, with their "habitual apathy and listless indifference" not less but *more* resistant to conversion. In "the hands of the Christian missionary"—and the metaphor is instructive for the image of molding so central to the micropolitics of conversion—the Sinhalas were not "plastic," but, "a yielding fluid which adapts its shape to that of the vessel into which it may happen to be poured, without any change in its quality or any modification of its character" (p. 193).

Another, earlier, writer had recorded his impression of this curious facility in a slightly more exasperated tone:

> No race of people appear so easily convertible to Christianity as the Singhalese; for they have no fixed principles or prejudices. . . . They have *no objection* to the Christian religion; but for their amusement are apt to attend the Budhuist festivals. Numbers of them make no difficulty in asserting that they are *both Budhuist and Christians;* and are willing to be sworn *either way,* or *both ways,* in a court of justice![71]

The Evangelicals found this a "perverse" and "embarrassing" obstacle to the advance of Christianity in Ceylon. They were better prepared to deal with the direct opposition they perceived among the Hindus and Muslims. It was something of a paradox because, at the same time, Tennent repeated Harvard's view that Buddhism was, in the ethical content of its doctrine and the ascetic restraint of its practice, "superior" to Islam and Hinduism. The British appear indeed to have conceived a curious regard for the ethic of Buddhism.[72] Buddhism was given neither to the "fanatical intolerance" of Islam nor to the "revolting rites" of Hinduism. On the contrary, it seemed characterized by a benevolence, a modesty, and a severity that appealed to the Evangelical Christian. But the strategy of the Buddhists of nominally acceding to Christianity while continuing their indigenous practices struck at the heart of the Evangelical conception of the inner experience of conversion. And this, moreover, confirmed the Evangelical idea that the "Buddhism" of the Sinhalas was only a superficial veneer covering a deeper, more entrenched reality. As "religion," in other words, Buddhism was an ineffectual failure. As Tennent wrote: "No national system of religion, no prevailing superstition that has ever fallen under my observation presents so dull a level, and is so pre-eminently deficient in popular influence, as Buddhism amongst the Singhalese" (p. 229).

Among the Sinhalas, Buddhism had followers enough, but few "votaries." Here was a conception, that of the votary, the devotee, that was central to the Evangelical identification of "religion" and the religious subject. The "warmth," "fervor," and "earnestness" that were to the Evangelical Christian of the nineteenth century the definitive indices of individual "faith" and religious commitment were "utterly foreign and unknown to the followers of Buddhism in Ceylon" (p. 229). And this fundamental inability to evoke the visible signs of Victorian religious desire was, for the Evangelical, the reason for Buddhism's supposed lack of influence. "Beautiful as is the body of its doctrines," Tennent wrote, "it wants the vivifying energy and soul which are essential to ensure its ascendancy and power" (p. 226).

If the sincerity of Tennent's estimate of the aesthetic value Buddhist doctrine is not doubted, what nevertheless needs to be appreciated is the discursive strategy in which it functioned. It was meant to underline an essential discrepancy between the claim Buddhism made for itself and its actual condition. Buddhism had been able to achieve only an "ostensible prevalence" among the Sinhalas. Indeed, this exalted doctrine, which lacked even the power to "arrest man in his career of passion and lust," was, when subjected to the discerning scrutiny of the Christian, found to reveal beneath it a whole underground of darker idolatry. It was this idolatry that really commanded the "reverential awe" of the Sinhalas. It was this idolatry to which those Sinhalas who professed Christianity inevitably returned. And therefore, it was reasoned, it was this idolatry that was the true religion of the Sinhalas. Wrote Tennent:

> Yet, strange to tell, under the icy coldness of this barren system, there burn below the unextinguished fires of another and darker superstition, whose flames overtop the icy summits of Buddhist philosophy, and excite a deeper and more reverential awe in the imagination of the Singhalese. (p. 229)

This "darker superstition" consisted, of course, in the "worship of demons." After a masterly demonstration of the seeming virtues of an elaborate doctrine, then, the Evangelical Christian calmly but resolutely flings away the superficial deception to disclose the horrible reality of demonism. So that, in fact, Tennent inverts the earlier strategy of Harvard of presenting Sinhala religion developmentally, or, chronologically, from Kapooism through Buddhism. Tennent, concerned less with chronology than with revealed truth, presents first the surface, Buddhism, and then proceeds to uncover what lies smoldering beneath it, demonism.

In summary, the Evangelical project of converting the Sinhala natives produced a dilemma which colonial Christian discourse attempted to resolve. This dilemma grew out of a perceived discrepancy between the "doctrine" of Buddhism (as authorized by the canonical Buddhist texts, and the Buddhist clerics in the Sangha) on the one hand, and the popular "practices" of Sinhala Buddhists as witnessed in their villages and hamlets on the other. This was a dilemma which had not arisen for the Orientalists in the first years of British occupation of Ceylon. Demonism, therefore, was at best marginal to their identification and representation of Sinhala religion.

For the Evangelicals, however, demonism was at the heart of Sinhala religion. The practice of missionary conversion involved colonial discourse in a particular kind of strategy of identifying and representing Sinhala religion. This strategy rested on premises about "true" religion and the authentic attitude of the true religious subject. These premises, in turn, were important for the practical reason that they enabled the Evangelical to distinguish the merely nominal from the authentic Christian convert. Applied to the Sinhalas, the Evangelicals did two things: First, they assimilated the canonical Buddhist representation of the "establishment" of Buddhism in Lankā to the nineteenth-century European conception of the historical evolution of religion. Sinhala supernaturals were not only older and more primitive than Buddhism, they were identified with demonism. Second, Buddhism was represented as admirable but, in the end, ineffectual. Beneath it the Christian revealed the latent actuality of the Sinhalas: *demonism*.

In this chapter, I have been concerned with the formation and production of colonial knowledges about the "religious" practices of the Sinhalas. It has been my aim to show that specific anthropological objects have determinate histories, even specifiable inaugural moments, and that these need to be traced out if we are to fully appreciate the ideological conditions of the conceptual metaphors we employ in our cultural analyses. In the instance I have considered, my aim has been to show that "demonism"—that figure through which much of the contemporary anthropological description and analysis of certain Sinhala practices has been framed—is not a merely innocent classificatory term, a convenient gloss, but a conceptual metaphor that is founded upon and operates within a distinctive discursive economy, or problematic. It should be clear that the sources of the view (which I examined in Bruce Kapferer's work) that demonism forms the deep, latent, and recurrent self of Sinhalas, a self that emerges eruptively through the surface of a Buddhism unable to hold it completely at bay—the one related to the other as nature is to culture—are colonial Christian ones.

In arguing as I have in this chapter, I hope it is clear that I do not claim that this discursive economy was the *only* one in which the trope of "demonism" operated. Doubtless, in the various locations that describe its colonial topoi, missionary discourse operated the trope of "demonism" in quite different economies of representation, differences that would depend, of course, on the ideological and material conditions of their local production. Nor, by the same token, do I claim that *every* anthropological use of the conceptual metaphor "demonism" is *necessarily* participating in the *same* colonial problematic as the anthropology of the Sinhala *yaktovil*. For surely this is a matter for careful, empirical investigation. What I *do* claim, however, is that if we are to subvert the reproduction of colonial representations in our analyses of the practices of others, we must submit the conceptual metaphors by which we work to scrupulous and critical inquiry—and one aspect of that inquiry, it seems to me, must be concerned with a genealogy of their ideological determinations.

But something else should be equally clear, namely, the founding of the general problematic in which the generative question about the religion of the Sinhalas is whether or not, or to what extent, or in what admixtures it is in fact "Buddhism." The Sinhalas were identified by the Victorian Christians as having two distinct religious systems, "Buddhism" and "kapooism" (or demonism). And the distinction was drawn, as we have seen, by constructing "Buddhism" as a "system" or "doctrine" represented by the canonical texts which they were busily setting about translating and interpreting, and then marking the proximity to it of the observable practices of the Sinhalas in the villages where the missionaries found them going about their everyday lives. This doctrine, it is true, was one that Christians like Gogerly and Tennent could congratulate for the high tone of its moral principles or the remarkable character of the Buddha. But, of course, these Christians would find that, in the end, the Sinhalas were really votaries of the "kapooist" system, not devotees of the Buddha's precepts. And they would conclude that "Buddhism" in Sri Lanka was a project that had failed. Now anthropology, when it came a little more than a century later to reconstitute this object—the religion of the Sinhalas—would answer that generative question founded by the Victorians differently, *but it would, nevertheless, find the need to answer it.* As much an heir to, as a critic of, the Victorian Christians, modern anthropologists of "Buddhism and society," as we will see in the following chapter, would retain the question—whether or not, or to what extent, or in precisely what admixtures Sinhalas are Buddhists—and the associated idea of two systems of religion, but they would invert the privilege between Buddhism and demonism.

Part III

Reconstructing Anthropological Objects

Chapter 6

Historicizing Tradition: Buddhism and the Discourse of *Yakku*

With this chapter the thrust of my inquiry again shifts registers somewhat. In chapters 4 and 5, my concern with the relation between power, knowledge, and Sinhala religion centered on those authorizing discourses through which Sinhala religion was inaugurated and reproduced as a visible area of a specifically *Western* knowledge. In general terms, my endeavor was to provide a genealogical investigation into the ideological and conceptual *sources* of an anthropological object. That investigation will have significant effects in this chapter.

The kind of investigation I undertook in Part II, I would insist, is necessary for a critical anthropology. However, it is important to realize, I think, that in unmasking colonial discourse, in making visible the specifically *colonial* space of a theoretical object, the *anthropological* problem is not thereby exhausted. The interrogation of the *Western* texts in which non-Western practices are represented should, I would argue, form one axis—and an important one—of such an anthropological investigation. But at the same time, it seems to me that the familiar antiessentialist criticism (of Edward Said, for instance)—that it is necessary to avoid the assumption that there is, as it were, beyond representation, a "real" East—while legitimate in an obvious way, is not itself unproblematic.[1] For this kind of criticism often tends toward an oversimplification of the problems of ethnographic representation. It tends to preclude, for instance, any discussion about the *adequacy* or otherwise of particular attempts at representing societies and cultures. Surely not all representations are equal or equally admissible. Moreover, such criticism tends to retain a conceptual and ideological location in an argument whose principal preoccupation is the *West's* reading and writing. It were as though the whole problem of anthropology, whether positively or negatively, was altogether *about* the West. And even though I argue the importance of calling the West's representational practices into question, and this precisely *because* of anthropology's conceptual and ideological location, what we would still have failed to properly appreciate in the construction of our theoretical objects is that authoritative discourse is not restricted to colonial practice; the theme of power and knowledge has a specifiably *local* register as well. Therefore, the interrogation of colonial theoretical spaces must have as well a constructive, positive yield: the production of the space of other anthropological questions—questions, for example, regarding the local production of local authoritative constructions of what counts as (in our case, religious) "reality" and (religious) "truth."

In this chapter, then, I re-site the focus of my concern at a level of *local* relations, taking up an inquiry into the conceptualization of relations *among Sinhala* religious discourses and practices. As we will see, however, the problem that I shall attempt to elucidate here—the problem of an anthropology of the Buddhism of the Sinhalas, and within this, of the discourse of *yakku*—remains fundamentally one of an analysis of relations between power, knowledge, and religion.[2]

In writings about Buddhism in Sri Lanka there is often an implicit counterpositioning of Buddhism and Christianity such that the former, Buddhism, is represented as the "true" or authentic religion of the Sinhalas, and the latter, Christianity, as an "alien" or imposed religion, the religion of the erstwhile colonizers. Both are of course acknowledged to have originally been "foreign" to Lankā, the one from India, the other from Europe. But the Sinhalas are typically thought of as having *adopted* Buddhism (from about the third century B.C.E.), as though from below, whereas they were *subjected* to Christianity (from the sixteenth century C.E.), as though from above. There is perhaps a more or less discernible politics served by the construction of this opposition. For it would seem clearly to participate in the narrative strategy of a nationalist historiographical mapping, one which no doubt has its origins in the late nineteenth century in the Great Buddhist Revival that explicitly defined itself in opposition to the Christianity of British colonialism. The rhetorical construction of the idea of the authenticity of Buddhism to Sinhalas, therefore, enacts a story which has been central to the making of the modern interleaving of politics and religion in Sinhala life. The problem I am interested in here turns on the fact that the naturalization or reification of this polemical construction has often tended to obscure—at least in such systematic discourse as anthropology is – the historical and ideological character of the Buddhist tradition in Lankā itself, its construction, that is to say, within a shifting field of power and knowledge.[3]

For, of course, if colonial Christian practice – discursive as well as nondiscursive – effected in the nineteenth century a radical refiguration of relations of (religious) knowledge and power in British Ceylon, putting in place a dimension of cultural difference and social and political force hitherto unprecedented in the island, it was by no means the first institutional (religious) practice to constitute itself in a (political) space of authority. A self-consciously *Buddhist* discourse (or anyway, a discourse representing itself as the authorized adjudicator of the Buddha's *dhamma*) had, since its ancient "establishment" in Lankā, been much concerned to preemptively authorize what *counted* as the truth of Sinhala religion, and what did not. And for much of Lankan history this discourse has occupied a privileged relation to the structures of state power, and has been associated with distinct symbols (e.g., the Tooth Relic), institutions and spokespersons (e.g., the *sangha*, or Order of Monks, and the monks belonging to one or another of its fraternities), and events (e.g., the Äsala Perahära) of public sanction and authority. The general point I want to make here is perhaps an uncontroversial one, namely, that the relation between religious discourse and Sinhala religious identity is a *historical*, not an essential, one – and this is no less the case whether one is talking about Buddhism or Christianity. I think this is important for any concern to constitute Buddhism as the object of an anthropological inquiry, but my reason for thinking this is not the familiar one that it will facilitate a more social-historical understanding of religious change (important as that is), but that it will open up the possibility of an understanding of Buddhism as a "discursive tradition" traversed by positions constituted by varying social projects and social uses. I will try to spell out what I mean by this in the course of this chapter.

Buddhism as an Anthropological Object

The particular problem with which I am concerned in this chapter, then, has to do with the conceptualization of the relation between Buddhism and those popular Sinhala observances in which knowledges about, and techniques for the control of, malevolent supernatural beings such as *yakku* are produced. The Western inception of the distinction between a "real" Buddhism (the textual Buddhism of the Pāli Canon) and a corrupt one (the practical Buddhism of everyday life) in nineteenth-century colonial Christian discourse about "demonism" has already been discussed. In that Victorian discourse, I suggested, this relation was thought more or less straightforwardly in terms of a structure of separable, hierarchically ordered, and historically sequenced layers: a pre-Buddhist "animism" beneath a later "pure" or authentic Buddhism.

What I wish to examine here is the more recent *anthropological* construction of Buddhism as a theoretical problem, the problem, as it is sometimes glossed, of "Buddhism and society." (Note how the conjunction "and" in this phrase forces us to think of these as separate entities, requiring a feat of theoretical labor to conceive their interaction. The *Buddhist,* it may be objected, *is* a social way of life.) This anthropology emerged in the late 1950s and early 1960s, in part as a corollary to the growing field of anthropological studies of "village" South and Southeast Asia—itself, of course, a field of investigation with roots in the nineteenth century.[4] Where Sri Lanka is concerned, the work of Gananath Obeyesekere, Michael Ames, and Nur Yalman is central to this inaugural moment when "Buddhism" was first constructed as a specifically anthropological object.[5]

Something of the nature of the conceptual space into which these anthropologists were inserting themselves can be gathered from Manning Nash's Introduction to a volume of essays, *Anthropological Studies in Theravada Buddhism,* that grew out of the seminal "Conference on Theravada Buddhism" held at the University of Chicago in May 1962.[6] Two points are worth mentioning by way of situating and gauging the concerns of these anthropologists. The first is the self-consciousness of a shift in the kinds of societies U.S. (and U.S.-trained) anthropologists were studying in the years following the Second World War—"peasant" rather than "tribal" societies—and the theoretical significance of this for how the "unit" of anthropological study was conceived. All the participants had done fieldwork in a Theravāda country—Burma, Cambodia, Sri Lanka, Thailand (there was no study of Laos)—and so had first-hand acquaintance with the round of life among ordinary Buddhist peasants. "Where in older anthropological writings," Nash wrote, "description and analysis of the bounded, located social system observed and reported by the field-worker himself had usually sufficed, these papers exemplify the shift from the study of tribal to peasant peoples. All the authors show an awareness of the fact that their unit of study forms part of a larger social and cultural system. One of the repeated themes in this volume is the attempt to take systematic account of the 'part-whole' problem which arises in the study of civilizations and their peasantries" (p. vii). Robert Redfield's vastly influential *Peasant Society and Culture* had sought to provide the theoretical concepts with which to think this "part-whole problem" in his formulation of the idea of the great and little communities and traditions.[7]

The second point turns on the existence by the 1960s (and indeed long before this) of an established tradition of historical and textual scholarship in Buddhist studies. As we have seen, "Buddhism" for this tradition was what was to be found in the texts of the Theravāda Canon, and scholarship was interested in a certain kind of question: the identification of the particles of historical truth in the legends of the Buddha, the relative age of the Pāli and Sanskrit sources, the precise relation between Brahmanical and Buddhist ideas, the correct interpretation of *nirvāna*, and so on.[8] There was no connection to a living tradition of religious practice (or rather, since the collection, translation, and interpretation of Sanskrit and Pāli texts had become by the end of the nineteenth century an undertaking of secular academics like T. W. Rhys Davids rather than missionaries like D. J. Gogerly, this connection, such as it was, had been broken); and where living people who called themselves Buddhists were not openly disparaged for corrupting Buddhism, their practices were simply neglected. Thus the anthropologists who gathered at Chicago that spring at the request of Professors Manning Nash and Nur Yalman were confronting an old and authoritative tradition. The framing device which the anthropologists introduced—of an interaction between parts and wholes, between peasants and civilizations—opened up a whole area of "religion and society" questions neglected by (or not visible to) the Indologists: the interaction of "pre-Buddhist and non-Buddhist elements with the traditional Buddhism," between "text and context," and more generally "the relations between the ongoing behavior of the ordinary Buddhist (both monk and laity) and the voluminous canonical (in the Tipitaka) and semicanonical literature of Theravada Buddhism" (*Anthropological Studies*, p. ix).

The construction of Buddhism as a theoretical object for anthropology, therefore, was something of a conceptual intervention in a field virtually constituted by Indology.[9] In relation to both of the conceptual sites from which it took its bearings, however—the anthropological and the Indological—the new object inherited as much as it displaced. As is perhaps necessarily the case with any tradition of discourse, its strengths as well as its weaknesses are a consequence of the very conjuncture that gave it birth. For the anthropological analysis of "Buddhism and society" has remained largely functionalist in the character of its theoretical concerns. What has preoccupied this now not inconsiderable body of work is the attempt to reconcile the seeming contradiction between a radical ascetic discourse of otherworldly salvation (represented by Theravāda Buddhism) on the one hand, and a popular discourse of this-worldly gratification (represented by the propitiation of supernaturals) on the other. These attempts, to be sure, have by no means been identical. But what is interesting to note is that whereas in the progressivist historicism of nineteenth-century Evangelical discourse, the story of Sinhala religion was cast as one of an antagonism which ended in Buddhism's dismal failure to overthrow the reigning worship of devils, modern anthropology takes refuge in a cautious functionalist allegory according to which Buddhism has not so much failed as *adjusted*, making allowances at various levels of its doctrine and practice for the indispensable role played by the supernaturals in ministering to the compelling worldly affairs of their constituents. "Buddhism" and "society" seem parts whose interconnection has to be thought. The trouble with the anthropological approach as presently conceived, I shall try to show, is that even as it departs in important ways from the colonial model, it too relies on the construction of an authentic Buddhism. As Kitsiri Malalgoda put it in his illuminating reading of Gombrich's *Precept and Practice* (significantly the first full-length study of Buddhism in Sri Lanka to appear since Copleston's *Buddhism Primitive and Present in Maghada and in Ceylon* at the end of the last century),[10] the question that this anthropology addresses is the same as has been raised "again and again since the days of the pioneer works of the nineteenth century: are Sinhalese who call themselves Buddhists in fact Buddhist?"[11] However, whereas Malalgoda's very learned view seems to be that the problem with this question is that it has not been "adequately discussed or analysed" (p. 156), my own view is that there can be *no* adequate discussion or analysis of it, and that therefore the question itself should simply be dropped.[12] This chapter tries to say why I think so, and what kinds of question I see as more fruitful in constituting Buddhism as an anthropological object.

To my mind, the most nuanced and suggestive attempt to think about Sinhala religious discourse and practice in terms of a critical engagement with, and reformulation of, the great/little tradition metaphor has been that of Gananath Obeyesekere. Already in the late 1950s, in his sharply critical review of Bryce Ryan's *Sinhalese Village*,[13] Obeyesekere had questioned the sociological soundness of an approach that sought to "isolate Buddhism from non-Buddhist beliefs."[14] This kind of approach, he suggested, had the effect of doing "injustice to both systems of behaviour." "Though it is possible to isolate these two for purposes of study," he went to say, "it is not possible to treat them as relatively airtight compartments with few inter-connections. Both these form one interconnected system which may profitably be studied as Sinhalese Religion" (p. 259). This is a formulation which has had, needless to say, a profound and productive impact on the anthropological construction of Buddhism in Sri Lanka. My own doubt, though, if I may call it that, is with the theoretical justification for identifying authentic "systems of behaviour."

I would like to examine closely the structure of Obeyesekere's argument in its first formal elaboration in "The Great Tradition and the Little in the Perspective of Sinhalese Buddhism," and in its most recent reworking, in the book co-authored with Richard Gombrich, *Buddhism Transformed: Religious Change in Sri Lanka*.[15] This is not, I should say, because I wish to criticize Obeyesekere, but on the contrary, because I believe that any path beyond the problematic of the "part and the whole" or the "great and the little" has of necessity to pass *through* his thought. The early essay, "The Great Tradition and the Little," is still unsurpassed more than a quarter of a century after its pointed intervention in the debate about religion in Buddhist societies of South and Southeast Asia. This essay, it seems to me, provides a particularly useful textual vantage from which to think about the anthropology of Sinhala religion because its deliberately conceptual character is worked out precisely in the attempt to reformulate—at a specific theoretical juncture—this anthropological problem.

In this essay, as we know, Obeyesekere is concerned to take issue with a compartmentalizing conception of Sinhala religious practice in terms of "levels" or "strata"—"the image being that of horizontal layers, one on top of the other" (p. 141). Important to note is that in this kind of conception, Obeyesekere, anticipating in fact my own argument in chapter 5, himself discerns elements of a missionary fable couched in terms of a curiously lingering "animism." He writes:

> The image of cultural layers has led in turn to the notion of a supernatural or "animistic" residue. The bogey of "animism" has long haunted missionaries and intellectuals interested in peasant communities in South Asia. To most people, the practices and beliefs of the village seemed flagrantly to violate the ideologies of the great tradition of the area. Although subscribing nominally to a great tradition, these people were "animists." Rarely was the term animism clearly defined; it became a convenient label under which one could subsume beliefs or customs he did not fully comprehend or was impatient with. . . . The social scientists wedded to the image of cultural layers have perpetuated the "animistic myth"; the residue of beliefs and rituals which could not be subsumed under a single great tradition or traditions were conveniently lumped together as animism, or supernaturalism. (p. 141)

Against this kind of view Obeyesekere argues cogently that, at least "synchronically" and "behaviorally" (i.e., "from the actor's standpoint"), such dichotomies as Buddhism/animism and Hindu deities/Sinhala Buddhism are neither tenable nor indeed relevant since, observably, Sinhalas participate in a continuum of religious practices conceived within a "framework" of Buddhism. Obeyesekere, it is well to stress, does not want to abandon the Great/Little Tradition metaphor so much as to reconceptualize it systemically. To be useful to a Sri Lankan religious context, he maintains, the metaphor needs to be rethought in terms of a distinction between a Great Tradition of Theravāda Buddhism (Pāli texts, temples, monks) and a Little Tradition of *Sinhala* Buddhism. This latter, consisting of the practices of lay villagers (and forming the typical domain of ethnographic description), is to be understood as a culturally integrated "whole" structured by an hierarchically organized pantheon:

> As we see it, in any civilization there is a great tradition and a great community, and on the other hand, many peasant societies or little communities. In Ceylon, the religious great tradition of the civilization is Theravada Buddhism, with its corpus of Pali texts, places of worship, and a great community of monks. The doctrines of Theravada Buddhism are embodied in this corpus, and their expositors are the Buddhist order of monks. But what about the little community or the peasant society, which is after all the focus of anthropological inquiry? Could we view its culture as compounded of a great tradition and a little tradition? Methodologically, nothing is gained by approaching the religion as Buddhist in a great traditional sense. It is best to see what

> the existent reality is, for it is too much to hope that the speculations of orthodoxy would be the equivalent of the whole or part of the religious tradition of the masses, whether of the village or the town. (pp. 141–142)

He then goes on to suggest that

> it would then be desirable to approach the religion of the Burmese or Thai impersonally or holistically, simply as Thai or Burmese Buddhism, and the religion of the Sinhalese as Sinhalese Buddhism. Viewed in this perspective, Thai or Sinhalese Buddhism is the little tradition—that is, the religion of the masses (little community) in these countries, whereas the great tradition of Theravada Buddhism is really the religion of the greater community of monks, intellectuals, and scholars. Such a conceptual separation has its utility, for it follows from this line of thinking that the religions of the masses in these countries may be vastly different from each other, whereas the great tradition they all share (Theravada Buddhism) is the same. (p. 142)

Sinhala Buddhism, then, as Obeyesekere argues, is a "single religious tradition." And the remainder of the essay is devoted to demonstrating the integrated character of this tradition. For example, he shows that the Sinhala "theory of causation" is articulated at a number of interrelated levels, drawing on the great tradition concept of *karma*, as well as non-great tradition concepts of astrological, demonological, and divine causality.

This is perhaps the central argument: the main problem with the Buddhism/animism dichotomy, Obeyesekere maintains, is that it "results in a failure to see the religious tradition of a people as a coherent whole" (p. 146). The heterogeneity of Sinhala religious discourse and practice, he therefore proposes, is underlined by a "core of shared meanings" or a "common cultural idiom" that gives to the whole culture a cohesion and unity. As one might put it, it is not (Theravāda) Buddhism that determines Sinhala religion so much as the *idiom* of Sinhala culture that determines the character of a properly or distinctively Sinhala Buddhism. This idiom, to be sure (that of "salvation," for instance), is in some sense derived from the great tradition, but it is always "refashioned to fit the peasant world view" (p. 153). It is by invoking this concept of cultural unity—"a shared commonality of meanings which define the central values of the people and constitute their governing ethos" (p. 153)—I would suggest, that Obeyesekere succeeds in transcending the Buddhism/animism dichotomy.

One can hardly overemphasize the importance for the anthropology of Sinhala religion of this intervention and conceptual remapping that Obeyesekere undertakes. It is one, however, which (despite the fact that it is a much-cited text) has generally gone unrecognized; and this, I think, for precisely the reasons pointed to in the two previous chapters regarding the chronic failure of anthropology to critically examine the ideological conditions and implications of its own discourse. The anthropology of Sinhala religion has, to this point (and Obeyesekere gives examples relating to Thai and Burmese Buddhism as well), been defined in terms of the essentially colonial Christian idea that Sinhala religion consists of two separable parts, one "Buddhist" and the other "animist." And these two parts are thought to occupy a curiously hierarchical relation to each other. In two senses: First, Buddhism is associated with the religion of the elite, the intellectuals, and animism with the religion of the peasant, the unlearned. This assumption, of course, replays the familiar colonial assumption that Buddhism was ethically higher, historically more recent, and therefore more civilized than animism. Second, animism is designated the "real" religion of the Sinhala masses and Buddhism but a superficial veneer to which people had only a nominal allegiance. This assumption similarly replays the colonial conception that Buddhism had never been able to win a real place in the heart of the Sinhalas. It is these entrenched colonial views of non-Western (and indeed non-Christian) practices that Obeyesekere's essay at once unmasks and displaces. And by arguing that the religion of the Sinhalas constitutes a "single tradition" of Sinhala Buddhism linked but not reducible to Theravāda Buddhism, the image of authentic and inauthentic layers of religion through which the object of Sinhala religion has been constructed is replaced by one of cultural cohesion.

My own concern, as I have stated, is to try to understand the relation between religious power and religious knowledge. More specifically, my concern is that the representation of Sinhala religion as constituting a single tradition consisting of systemically and functionally integrated aspects tends to preclude an analysis of the theme of power and knowledge in Sinhala religion. And the questions that I have in mind have to do with the general problem of the *formation* and *authorization* of specific Sinhala religious knowledges and specific Sinhala subjectivities. Accordingly, I will attempt to draw out some further implications of Obeyesekere's essay.

In making his argument, Obeyesekere sharply criticizes what he sees as "historical-diffusionist" approaches which, in their preoccupation with the "origins" of contemporary religious symbols, confuse historical with behavioral perspectives:

> It is certainly legitimate (and often necessary) to study the origin of various beliefs in a given religious tradition, but in doing so one must maintain a strictly historical perspective. In confusing the historical dimension with the behavioral, these writers [i.e., those who speak about such things as Hindu deities in Sinhalese Buddhism] have posed a fundamental methodological dilemma. (pp. 140-141)

The criticism is important because Obeyesekere is attempting to separate out levels of conceptual confusion in the anthropology of cultural phenomena, the confusion between how social practices come to be as they are or come to be composed of their distinctive elements (the problem of historical origins), and how individuals in a specific social setting observably conduct their lives (the problem of the integration of social functions). It is interesting, however, that the historical problem in Sinhala Buddhism is not thereby resolved. For I want to note that in his own essay, in which it is *function* and not *history* that is the defining theoretical concern, the *historical* problem emerges again and again, sometimes marginally, sometimes not. For example, when Obeyesekere speaks about the important concept *varama* (warrant) as enabling the "*incorporation* of a supernatural being *into* the Sinhalese Buddhist pantheon," or when, in the same breath, he goes on to refer to the "*proselytization* of 'non-Buddhist' supernaturals" who accept "the suzerain position of the Buddha in the pantheon" (p. 146, emphasis added), or again, when he states unambiguously that "Sinhalese Buddhism cannot be equated with Theravada. Instead it should be seen historically as a fusion and synthesis of beliefs derived from Theravada with other non-Theravada beliefs to form one integrated tradition" (p. 146), is there not an allusion to, or indeed a positive evocation of, a *process* whereby supernatural beings are, over time, *made a part of* a Sinhala Buddhist pantheon in which the Buddha has *been secured* a "suzerain position"? For what these passages allude to, evoke, but do not really specify, is a historical intervention by which a now unreadable past (populated by anonymous figures and crossed by irretrievable discourses and practices) was *reconstituted* in/as a (Sinhala)

Buddhism; *and,* a radical disparity of power in the confrontation of knowledges which eventually *authorized* and *secured* the Buddha's "presidential status." Submerged, in other words, is a silent history of the "establishment" of Buddhism in Lankā.

Yet Obeyesekere's essay does explicitly raise the question of religious authority in a very interesting way. Indeed, the concept *varama* (warrant) is central to the argument he outlines precisely inasmuch as it is one of those "mechanisms," as he puts it, that facilitate the "linking" of elements or levels in the hierarchical structure of the pantheon—a linking through what he calls a "distribution of power and authority." The argument is in fact crucial to an understanding of popular Sinhala religious discourse. In Sinhala Buddhism, it is the Buddha that "is the ultimate repository of power and authority possessed by deities and demons; these latter have their power relegated to them by the Buddha. In other words, these beings have a *varan* or 'warrant' from the Buddha to accept sacrifices from humans and bring relief from their woes" (p. 145). Thus the malign figures, *yakku*, are linked to the Buddha through the concept of *varama* (as indeed through others, such as *aṇaguṇa* or "authoritative efficacy"). The idea of a delegated authority, Obeyesekere continues (and it is this that is critical to our question),

> is surely an attempt made by Sinhalese Buddhism to meet a great-traditional assertion: the demons, by virtue of the supremacy of the law of universal causation (karma), have no real power. Sinhalese Buddhism, like any other institutional religion, could not dispense with supernatural beings possessed with power (or capacity to do good or ill), and it meets the doctrinal challenge by stating that these beings do not intrinsically have power but derive it directly or indirectly from the Buddha. (p. 145)

The question that I would raise here, however, is the following one: why should "Sinhalese Buddhism" *need* to "meet a great-traditional assertion" about the proper status and character of demons? Or what precisely does it mean to say that Sinhala Buddhism was unable to "dispense with supernatural beings possessed with power" and therefore had to state that this power was derived from the doctrinally authorized source, the Buddha? Indeed, Obeyesekere himself points us toward the answer when he alludes to the question of "institutional religion." In other words, I am trying to suggest that the fact that demons have to be *defined* and *represented* as submissive to the Buddha and dependent upon his *varama* surely implies the *ideological* construction and resolution of a specific danger to Buddhism in Lankā, and *therefore* implies relations of power in the constitution and consolidation of the *authority* of Sinhala Buddhism. This, I think, opens up an area of potentially interesting questions for a historically informed anthropological analysis of Sinhala religion. For it might well be suggested, therefore, that there is a "history" that is not reducible to a preoccupation with the disclosure of originary sources but rather with the relation between (religious) power and (religious) knowledges. The question here would have nothing to do with either the historical priority of "Buddhist" as against "Hindu" practices (an issue that, as we have seen, fascinated nineteenth-century observers) or the systemic relation between two seemingly contradictory religious practices (the twentieth-century anthropological solution), but rather would concern itself with the conditions—ideological and political—through which (religious) power authorizes certain (religious) discourses and practices as *true*, as, in this case, authentically and meaningfully "Buddhist." And such a history might be considered in terms of (*a*) the specific institutional and ideological conditions in which Buddhism emerged in Lankā, conditions which gave to it a particular ecclesiastical character, and a particular relation to the institutions of secular power; (*b*) the main locus of what counted (and for whom) as authentic Buddhism and as an authentic Buddhist, that is, the monasteries with their inculcation of programmatic rules of obedience, habits, the learning of specific texts, and so on; and (*c*) the political and ideological conditions under which Buddhism began to extend the terrain of its authority, to enable it to impinge on, regulate, and direct the formation of specifically Buddhist subjectivities, identities, and dispositions—a process that would not only have brought it into direct contact with already existing practices, but would have forced upon it the necessity of defining the proper place for these practices, devising strategies for incorporating, transforming, and excluding them from the field it authorized as authentically Buddhist.

Buddhism Transformed, a full-length monograph, is, to be sure, interested in "history," but not of this sort. Rather, the effects of that anthropological self-consciousness of a concept of "history"—to which Sherry Ortner has referred as characterizing U.S. anthropology in the 1970s—is registered in this book in terms of a concern with the problem

conception of Buddhism as one "religion" (*buddhāgama*) among other "religions" (*āgamas*)—distinctive yet related to them in being identifiable as of the same genre of discourse—does not appear to predate the British missionary encounter with Sinhalas. The use of the term *āgama* as a generic equivalent of "religion," Malalgoda has argued, was introduced by Protestant missionaries in the nineteenth century. "*Buddhāgama,*" he maintains, "was the term that the missionaries used to refer to Buddhism; it was only later that it gained acceptance among the Buddhists themselves as a term of self-reference."[17] John Carter seems to suggest a somewhat earlier date: "It is probable that the use of the terms *āgama* and *buddhāgama* to represent 'religion' and 'Buddhism' respectively antedates the debates mentioned [i.e., the debates between representatives from the Christian and Buddhist communities from about the middle 1860s to the 1890s]. By how many years? I would suggest by about one hundred years at most."[18] Nevertheless, he concurs that these terms emerged in a more or less direct way from the Christian encounter: "I would suggest . . . that Sinhalese Theravāda Buddhists have become acquainted with the concepts 'religion' and 'Buddhism' and have either attempted to coin Sinhalese terms to match the concepts or decided to adopt new terms and/or new meanings first proposed by Westerners, perhaps by Christian missionaries" (p. 272). The point here, at any rate, is that defined principally in textual terms, in terms of "doctrine" (supposedly "what the Buddha taught"), it was only natural that Buddhists were taken by Western observers to be those who could be said to "believe" in, to adhere to, the propositions of that doctrine. Everything else was animism, or at least *non*-Buddhist. Moreover, that Buddhists in Sri Lanka *themselves* came to espouse this text-privileging view in the Revival has much complicated the matter. For this social fact is then taken unproblematically as ratifying the anthropological view of the authentic distinction between the "great" and the "little" traditions, between two systems of religious practice. It is often enough said these days that, after all, Buddhists themselves make the distinction between their "religion" (i.e., "Buddhism") and all else (spirit religion), or again between true Buddhism and village Buddhism. Now, of course, Buddhists may well argue about the true parameters of their religion, and the ways these are to be determined. Indeed, without such argument it is difficult to speak of a religious—as of any—tradition.[19] But the *anthropological* problem, it seems to me, is not to seek to adjudicate between the various claims made by Buddhists about their tradition, that is, to itself try to discover by an ever more ingenious interpretive model which, in the final analysis, is the more adequate claim, and where the distinction between Buddhism (however defined) and what it is not is to be drawn. Rather, I think the anthropological problem is to seek to understand such matters as the conditions that made for the emergence of differential claims within traditions, and the social, political, and other uses to which these claims are (and have been) put.

This view—that Buddhists themselves make a kind of great/little distinction—is, of course, connected to another, namely, that the Western misinterpretation of Buddhism is shaped not only by a colonial misreading but by the selective and biased account in the authoritative texts themselves.[20] However, what is curious about this view is that it presumes that Western interpretive discourse occupies the same conceptual relation to Buddhist tradition that canonical or semicanonical—or indeed *any*—Buddhist texts do. Again, it is of course the case that canonical texts do not present a "view from nowhere," that they are employed to make claims for what the *dhamma* is, how it is to be interpreted, and so on. It is precisely my argument that it is *this* internal argument as a discursive—if nonunitary—whole that should form the object of the anthropological investigation. The texts form part of a tradition and as such are integral to arguments within that tradition, and to positions regarding what correct views and practices are. The Western dilemma arises only insofar as *its* discourses seek to adjudicate what the truth of that tradition is. And it is this preoccupation (indeed this presumption) that I am suggesting anthropology give up.

Even if we were to take the Canon as the authentic word of the Buddha, why should anthropology take *this*—the Buddha's word—as constituting the *anthropological* object "Buddhism"? This is not to say that one should do the inverse and take what this is not—that is, "village Buddhism"—as authentic Buddhism. Indeed, to take something called "village Buddhism" as "true Buddhism" is as conceptually flawed as taking "Modernist Buddhism" as authentic. What I am in fact suggesting is that this whole problematic—in which the great/little paradigm struggles to correct the privileging of nineteenth-century textuality by asserting different features as authentic Buddhism—is worth abandoning altogether. I can state my disagreement another way if I say that my argument is not the one that Southwold advances—namely, that it is not "belief" but something else ("moral conduct") that is the "fundamental basis of religion"—but rather that what is taken as fundamental to religion, what defines its basis and parameters, depends on the discourse employed to identify it. And anthropology, I say, should abandon the preoccupation with producing new ways of identifying and specifying such things as the "fundamental basis of religion."[21]

So, I agree with Obeyesekere that observable practices are what anthropologists need to look at, but I do not think that envisioning the Buddhism of the Sinhalas as a "whole" or as a behavioral continuum entails positing a unifying ethos or idiom to support it. Rather, it seems to me that this "whole" might more usefully be thought of as a discursive tradition composed of discursive positions differently articulated to the sources of religious authority and power.[22] So understood, we might ask: How does power authorize what kinds of knowledges can count as "Buddhist"? How is the line between "Buddhism" and what it is not drawn and by whom? What kinds of virtues, duties, obligations—what kinds of subject—can count as authentically and meaningfully "Buddhist"? What kinds of statement, uttered by whom, when, under what conditions can count as "Buddhist"? In what kinds of social project are purportedly Buddhist knowledges used? These kinds of questions, I think, work to displace essentialist assumptions about authentic Buddhism because rather than beginning with claims about what Buddhism is or is not, they seek to describe the varied discursive positions that constitute the field of a "discursive tradition."

Conceived in this way, the Sinhala discourse of *yakku* is, anthropologically, most usefully understood as a distinctive discursive *position* within the Buddhist tradition in Sri Lanka. However, if this discourse about *yakku* (about their origins, their character, their modes of influence, the nature of the afflictions they cause, etc.) is a Sinhala Buddhist discourse, it has to be understood that it occupies a social space constituted by contemporary Buddhist orthodoxy—that complex of religious power organized through the *sangha*—as heterodox, or at least as inauthentic. At the same time, not only is the discourse of *yakku* marginalized by the canonical practices of Sinhala Buddhism, but it also in turn "deterritorializes" the authorized religious discourse, appropriating its major figures, employing them for its own arts and uses, in its own social projects. Needless to say, this discursive position does not see itself as marginal or inauthentic but only as different; it does not seek to claim for itself (as the orthodoxy does) a preemptive position within the Buddhist tradition.

I think something of what I mean about differential discursive *positions* in a discursive *tradition* can be seen if I contrast two stories about the same event, and the kinds of social project into which they are drafted. The event I have in mind is the "establishment" of Buddhism in Sri Lanka. This is interesting because it is an event that turns on an encounter between the Buddha and *yakku*.

The "Establishment" of Buddhism in Lankā

The authoritative narrative account of the introduction of Buddhism into Lankā is, of course, to be found in that extraordinary Sinhala text, the *Mahāvaṃsa* or Great Chronicle. The *Mahāvaṃsa* was written, it is estimated, about the sixth century C.E. by the monk Mahanāma of the preeminent Mahavihāra fraternity in Anuradhapura. It is, by and large, the account of the *sangha* and its relation with contemporary kings.[23] The *Mahāvaṃsa*, indeed, is the principal literary source for the historical reconstruction of ancient Lankā.[24] All of the major descriptive representations of the early political and religious history of Lankā—that is, the period of the political dominance of Anuradhapura, from roughly the third to tenth centuries C.E.—depend on the account provided by the *Mahāvaṃsa*. This is important to bear in mind because the *Mahāvaṃsa* narrates a very particular kind of account of the founding of Buddhism in Lankā.

This has not always been appreciated in nationalist historiography. In an essay on the "introduction" of Buddhism into Lankā written a generation ago, the very distinguished Sri Lankan scholar Senarat Paranavitana suggests that it is possible that Buddhism was known in Lankā before the arrival of Mahinda in the third century B.C.E. since there was constant trading contact between India and Lankā. However, he goes on:

> From the evidence now available . . . it cannot be stated that any considerable group of people were adherents of Buddhism in Ceylon before the middle of the third century B.C., though there might have been, here and there, individuals who had some knowledge of its tenets, and had inclinations towards them. At any rate, there do not appear to have been Buddhist *bhikkhus*, leading a corporate existence, in those early days, and the establishment of the *Sasana* from the Buddhist point of view, is synonymous with the establishment of the *Samgha*. And this took place, for the first time, in the reign of Devanampiya Tissa.[25]

What is interesting about this passage is not the issue whether or not there were actually Buddhists in Lankā before the establishment there of the *sangha*—for to determine this, in any case, depends not simply on more "facts," but on the authoritative discourse by which one *identifies* a true Buddhist. Rather, what is interesting is Paranavitana's assumption that there is a historically *unvarying* "Buddhist point of view" from which it could be held that the establishment of the *sāsana*[26] was synonymous with that of the *sangha*, and therefore that *what* counts as Buddhism and *who* counts as a Buddhist in Lankā has always been the same. Surely the significance, for instance, of Gombrich and Obeyesekere's *Buddhism Transformed* is that it can be read as recording contemporary changes in precisely this. Paranavitana's assumption, in other words, is the ahistorical one that the "tradition" authorized by the *sangha* in Lankā and narrated by the *Mahāvaṃsa* at a particular historical moment (i.e., in the sixth century C.E.) is a unitary and timeless one.

In the *Mahāvaṃsa* the inauguration of Buddhism in Lankā is represented as, on the one hand, a victory of the Buddha over a race of beings called *yakkhas* and, on the other, as the rise and struggles of institutionalized religion. In his splendid work, *The Story of Ceylon*, the late Sri Lankan critic and historian E. F. C. Ludowyk has closely examined the stages through which this epic retrospectively authors the founding episodes of Buddhism in Lankā. Ludowyk's thoughtful work is especially interesting because he is particularly concerned with the *constructed* or *positioned* character of the *Mahāvaṃsa*'s point of view. What he says, therefore, is very instructive.

Ludowyk suggests that in these founding episodes, in which we are given to believe that the inaugural moment of Buddhism in Lankā is to be traced to Mahinda's arrival in the island at Aṣōka's behest in the mid-third century B.C.E., "*more than the introduction of a new religion* to Ceylon is at issue" (p. 44, emphasis added). From the consecration of Tissa (250–210 B.C.E.) as King by the Mauryan Emperor Aṣōka (269–232 B.C.E.) to the latter's exhortation to the former to accept the "religion of the Sakya son," to Mahinda's mission to Lankā and the instantaneous conversion, first of King, then gods, court, and people, to the King's donation of a park as the physical site of the new religious order, what is most noteworthy is that the *Mahāvaṃsa* is less concerned with the probable impact made by the new doctrine on the people at large than to inscribe an intrinsic connection between Buddhism and (state) power. The idea that people simply flocked to Buddhism functions as a rhetorical or textual device within the authoritative point of view inaugurated by the *Mahāvaṃsa*. What is at issue in the *Mahāvaṃsa*, Ludowyk (quoting from Rahula's *History*) maintains, is the establishment of a *state* religion—that is to say, the *fixing* of Buddhism in Lankā in an inaugural register of power. As Ludowyk cautions in this immensely illuminating reading,[27] it is necessary to keep firmly in mind that the narrative and dialogue of this founding discourse were "framed" by a "later age," by "the commentator's clear understanding of the particular position of Buddhism in Ceylon at his own time" (p. 48)—that is to say, "when the early stages of missionary zeal and conversion were long past, [and] when what was important was not a message which the hearer had to understand, but institutionalized religion which had left its mark on the history of the island for over seven hundred years" (p. 49). The *Mahāvaṃsa*'s account of the Buddha's encounter with the *yakkhas* in Lankā has to be read against this background of a situated point of view.

The account itself is the first major episode recounted by the Chronicle. It comes after a cursory overview of the Buddha-to-be's resolve to become a Buddha (1.5), his homages to the twenty-four previous Buddhas (from Dīpamkara to Kassapa [1.6–10]), his own "supreme enlightenment" at Uruvelā (i.e., Bodh Gayā) (1.12), and his subsequent travels in India (1.14–18). At this point the narrative shifts from India to Lankā, when "the Conqueror, in the ninth month of his buddhahood, at the full moon of Phussa (the tenth month of the lunar year), himself set forth for the isle of Lankā, to win Lankā for the faith" (1.19):

> For Lankā was known to the Conqueror as a place where his doctrine should (thereafter) shine in glory; and (he knew that) from Lankā, filled with the yakkhas, the yakkhas must (first) be driven forth.
>
> And he knew also that in the midst of Lankā, on the fair river bank, in the delightful Mahānāga garden, three yojanas long and a yojana wide, the (customary) meeting-place for the yakkhas, there was a great gathering of (all) the yakkhas dwelling in the island. To this great gathering of the yakkhas went the Blessed One, and there, in the midst of that assembly, hovering in the air over their heads, at the place of the (future) Mahiyangana-thūpa, he struck terror to their hearts by rain, storm, darkness and so forth. The yakkhas, overwhelmed by fear, besought the fearless Vanquisher to release them from terrors, and the Vanquisher, destroyer of fear, spoke thus to the terrified yakkhas: 'I will banish this your fear and your distress, O yakkhas, give ye here to me

> with one accord a place where I may sit down.' The yakkhas thus answered the Blessed One: 'We all, O Lord, give you even the whole of our island. Give us release from our fear.' Then, when he had destroyed their terror, cold, and darkness, and had spread his rug of skin on the ground that they bestowed on him, the Conqueror, sitting there, made the rug spread wide, while burning flame surrounded it. Daunted by the burning heat thereof and terrified, they stood around on the border. Then did the Saviour cause the pleasant Giridīpa to come here near to them, and when they had settled there, he made it return to its former place. Then did the Saviour fold his rug of skin; the devas assembled, and in their assembly the Master preached them the doctrine. The conversion of many koṭis of living beings took place, and countless were those who came unto the (three) refuges and the precepts of duty. (1.20–32)

As compared with the *Dīpavaṃsa*'s account of the same episode, which stretches on for more than sixty verses, the *Mahāvaṃsa*'s account is short, compact, and straightforward.[28] It is not only sparer and less long-winded; more important, the attitude of the Buddha constructed in the *Mahāvaṃsa* preserves throughout the encounter an unambivalent singleness of purpose absent in the earlier Chronicle. The *Mahāvaṃsa*, moreover, has nothing to say about the character of the *yakkhas*, whereas the *Dīpavaṃsa* waxes energetically on their maleficent nature (and interestingly, too, there is in the *Mahāvaṃsa*'s account a noticeable absence of any reference to the Buddha's likeness to a *yakkha*).[29] The entire episode, in other words, is narrated in a lower key and a flatter tone, and therefore it tells a more convincing story about power and civilization. So much so, in fact, that one is left with the impression that the later Chronicle constructs the image of a Buddhism with a surer and more unequivocal estimate of its capacity to displace as authoritative ideology whatever discourses and practices it encountered in Lankā.

The *Mahāvaṃsa*'s Buddha is represented in no-nonsense terms: he is full of vigorous might, irrepressible, uncompromising. Indeed, as some historians have pointed out, in this regard the Chronicle departs significantly from representations of him in the Pāli Canon and commentarial works where, as in the story of Ālavaka, for instance, it is the Buddha's persevering kindness and profound compassion *alone* that eventually secure conversion.[30] In the *Mahāvaṃsa*'s account, however, it is not so much conversion as *submission* and indeed the extension of territorial power that is represented as the Buddha's aim. It is not difficult to see that the *Mahāvaṃsa*'s narrative of the Buddha's subjugation of the *yakkhas* is inscribed in a political project, namely, that of clearing a social and physical space for political power, and this by the establishment of a fixed and intrinsic relation between the Buddha's doctrine and the legitimacy of an expansionist state. As R. A. L. H. Gunawardana has put it, the *Mahāvaṃsa*'s Buddha is "clearly a conqueror who has time for compassion only after a kingdom has been annexed."[31] So that on the *Mahāvaṃsa*'s account the great episode of the subjugation of *yakkhas* by the Buddha forms the initial moment of the fable that recounts the rise and stabilization of a political order. Enacting a triumphalist epic in which the *dhamma*'s mission against rival doctrines is to be established and secured even at the cost of contravening such canonical moral principles as nonviolence, it inaugurates the theme that the Buddha acquired an unchallengeable right over the island. And in postcolonial Sri Lankan history, where ethnicity and religion have become sides of a coin, this theme has been drafted into the service of legitimizing a modern ethnic politics that seeks to guarantee the claim that the island of Lankā is exclusively the land of the Sinhalas and of the Buddha's *dhamma*. The interrogation of the political projects into which the *Mahāvaṃsa* has historically been drafted has recently become a focus of some scholarly attention.[32]

This, at any rate, is the authorized narrative. Epic in its structure, it may be said to authorize the canonical representation of the installation of Buddhism as the true religion of the Sinhalas. In so doing it attempts to preempt the space of potentially competing discourses. However, the *Mahāvaṃsa* cannot be read as constituting the *entire* space of Sinhala conceptions of *yakku*. There are other narratives. The discourse of *yakku* produces one such alternative narrative, differently cast, differently emplotted, differently flavored, and which forms part of rather different sorts of social project. One instance of such narrative is the following, the more elaborate version of two similar stories related to me by two different persons regarding this inaugural event—the Buddha's subjugation of *yakku* in Lankā. It was told by S. A. Piyaseṅa, a man—as must now be quite obvious—of a seemingly inexhaustible store of stories.

The story as told was situated in the context of an exhaustive narrative recalling, in turn, the birth of the hosts of *yaksayās* (*yakṣa samūhaya*) in the Great City of Visāla (*Visāla Maha Nuvara*);[33] their destructive rampages; the inability of the *dēvas* and *dēvatāvas* to put an end to this reign; their appeal to the would-be Buddha or *Bōdhisattva* then in the divine world (*divya lōkaya*) called Tav Tissa; the latter's decision to be born in the human world (*naralōkaya*) and his selection of a suitable mother and father to be born to, and a suitable place, day, and time; the celebrated three dreams of the Great Queen Maya, and the Brahmana's equally celebrated interpretations of them; and the birth of Prince Siddhartha, who, in time, becomes Gautama, the fourth Buddha in the current Bhadrakalpaya (the period in which the doctrine of a Buddha prevails). It is at this point, then, that our story begins, for the *dēvas* and *dēvatāvas* again approach the now Enlightened One, exhorting him to intervene upon the desecration being wrought in Lankā by the *yaksayās*. And the Buddha agrees to do so. This is the story:

> The Buddha, getting ready to go to Mayyanganaya[34] to subjugate the *yaksayās*, asked who will go with him. He called Viṣṇu. But Viṣṇu exclaimed, "Appo!, we can't go to the place where those *yaksayās* are!"[35] Then he called the Mahabrahmaya, but he too exclaimed, saying, "Appo! I can't go." The gods (*dēvas*) and godlings (*dēvatāvas*) too, having been called, said they couldn't go. Then the Great Venerable rahat Ananda got ready quickly, saying, "I am coming."[36]
>
> The Buddha then took two robes (*sivuru sangala*) and the alms bowl (*patraya*). At that point, the god Sakra also got ready, saying, "I too am coming." He took the book and the umbrella. With Ananda too taking an alms bowl, they all set off for the place where the *yaksayās* lived.[37]
>
> Seeing them coming, the senior *yaksayās* said to the junior *yaksayās*, "Look at those three people going along the street below. Seize them and bring them here to be eaten (*Allanvara mehāṭa kanna*)!" But when these junior *yaksayās* looked they recognized that these were not simply three ordinary people. Those *yaksayās*, having been born in previous Buddhist epochs (*Buddha sāsanaya*), had heard sermons (*bana*) of Buddhas. And although the period of suffering the effects of their wrongdoing (*pav*) had not yet elapsed, upon seeing, these *yaksayās* realized that this was no one but a Buddha.[38]
>
> [The Buddha asked them:] "Why did you come?"
>
> [The *yaksayās* replied:] "We have brought a message (*panivuḍaya*) from the godling Rakusa[39] that the three of you are to come."
>
> At that point [the Buddha] said: "Good, we will come." Having dispatched those people, the Buddha asked Ananda, "Are you going?" But Ananda replied, "I can't." [The Buddha then asked Sakra,] "Sakra, are you going?" But Sakra also replied, "I can't." So the Buddha said, "Then not a soul must come. I will go simply in the costume of a decrepit old man." Then the Buddha created the costume of an old man, an old man who has become decrepit, wears rags (*värahäli*), and carries a walking stick (*häramiṭiya*) like a beggar (*hinganna*).

Then [that is, having gone, the Buddha] said, "Anē *yaksayās*, in order to receive divine possessions in the divine world, seven divine possessions in the seven divine worlds, and human possessions in the human world, give us a little space for today."[40] So said the old man (*mahallā*). "Give the three of us a little space for today."

At that point the *yaksayā* asked [the Buddha], "From whom are you asking like this for lodging?! Do you know who I am?"[41]

So the Buddha asked a second time, "Anē *yaksayās*, in order to receive divine possessions in the divine world, seven divine possessions in the seven divine worlds, and human possessions in the human world, give us lodging for today."

The *yaksayās* are [by this time] becoming increasingly angry, and make to hit him [i.e., the Buddha] with dead bodies.

The lodging is still not given. So the old man asked a third time, "Anē *yaksayās*, in order to receive Brahma possessions in the Brahma world, seven divine possessions in the seven divine worlds, and human possessions in the human world, give us lodging for today."

Now it had become a little clearer to those [junior] *yaksayās*. The old man had said the same thing three times using the same words. So the power was being recovered little by little (*pavar ṭika ṭika honda venna enne*).[42] It became a little bit valid due to the authoritative efficacy (*aṇaguṇa*) [of the Buddha].[43]

At that point, the chief godling, Rakusa, said to those *yaksayās*, "Tell him to stay in a corner. Having allowed him [to stay], chase and beat him with a switch in the morning."[44] *He* did not know the power of the Buddha.

So they then gave [the Buddha, Ananda, and Sakra] permission to stay (*inna avasara dunnā*).

At that point [the Buddha thought], "Now I want to show my power to these people.[45] It is the power of these people that has been shown to me as many times as this. Now I want to show my power." Then the Buddha resolved (*adhisṭhāna kalā*) that the rocks of Rock Sakwala (*Sakwala Gala*) should be become hot (*rat venna*).

"Ammata uḍu!"[46] [the *yaksayās* exclaim]. The rocks having become hot, they can hardly stand. They can't endure it (*inna bā*). [The ground] is ablaze because of the increasing heat. "Budu ammā!"[47] [the *yaksayās* exclaim again]. These *yaksayās* attempted to go through the air (*udin yanna bäluvä*). But they cannot go through the air (*uḍin yannat bā*). They attempted to go around (*vaṭin yanna bäluvä*). But around is also ablaze (*vaṭet gini*). They can neither see nor go (*pēn nā yanna bā*). And now when they looked again at the place where the old man had been he is no longer there. When they looked up the old man was above like a golden statue.

At that point the *yaksayās* paid obeisance (*namaskāra karanavā*), keeping their hands at the top [i.e., clasped just above the head]. And they said [pleading], "Anē Swamini, we are the people who did wrong in those days, who did wrongs formerly. Because we did wrongs in this life too we couldn't know that you are Gautama Buddha. Because of that, for the ill that happened due to us, don't end our lives.[48] We are obedient to you, Lord." Crying, they repeated this three times.

Then the Buddha, smiling (*hinā velā*), said [reprimandingly], "Wrong-doing *yaksayās*, don't do wrongs (*pāpakarma yaksayā pav karanna epā*)! I am not giving you authority until the period for which wrongs have been done has elapsed."

Then god Sakra was sent for and he brought a handful of rice produced from hill-paddy (*äl vī*). The rice was cooked, and a cone of blue rice (*nil bat goṭuvak*), a cone of red rice (*ratuven bat goṭuvak*), and a cone of yellow rice (*kaha bat goṭuvak*) were made. Having placed the seven cones of rice separately, this sanction (*vivaranaya*) was issued [to the *yaksayās* by the Buddha]: "Until the 5,500 years of my epoch (*sāsanaya*) have elapsed, if a *yakṣa ädurā*, a *yakṣa väḍakaruva*, or a *yakṣa kaṭṭāḍiya*[49] came and uttered my Authority and the Name, or even if a *rēphaya*, a *pāpilla*, an *älapilla*, an *ispilla*,[50] or a character was uttered, take these roasted offerings (*dola pulutu*) which are being given, and give up (*at harinavā*) entirely the illness (*leḍa*) that has been made by you."

That sanction having been issued, those *yaksayās* were put into the island of Yak Giri (*yak giri diva-ina*), into the city of Yak Giri (*yak giri patanaya*).

The narrative enacts a popular version of the Sinhala story about the confrontation between the Buddha and *yakku*. The power of the Buddha is always most vividly represented in his confrontation with, and victory over, *yakku*. As in the canonical narrative of the *Mahāvaṃsa*, it is story about the defeat of *yakku* by the Buddha. But, noticeably, it is one performed through a very different strategy of representation. The story is not plotted as an epic in which the Buddha is cast as the leading figure and force in the great teleologically assured establishment of Civilization. This, recall, is the tropic structure of the *Mahāvaṃsa*. The latter is an undisguised master narrative and that, of course, is consistent with the institutional and ideological *position* from which it is enacted—the position of the state extending the political terrain of its authority. Piyasena's narrative does not occupy any such relation with secular power.

In this narrative Lankā is represented as being overrun by *yakku*. The Buddha is asked by the gods to subjugate them, no doubt because they themselves are incapable of accomplishing this. Indeed, they do not even want to accompany the Buddha on the mission. Only the Buddha, therefore, is ultimately able to triumph against *yakku*. In embarking on his mission, however, the Buddha goes incognito, as a beggar looking for a night's lodging. In contrast to the narrative of the *Mahāvaṃsa*, he does not present himself directly, transparently. Rather, he assumes a disguise in order to dramatize his power over *yakku*. The junior *yakku*, knowledgeable about the *dhamma* from previous Buddhas, suspect that this must indeed be a Buddha but nevertheless first attempt to attack him with the dead bodies they have accumulated round and about them. Dead bodies are, of course, the mark of their unworthiness (see chapter 1). When at last the Buddha decides to unveil himself by direct use of a show of spectacular power, he immediately secures their obeisance. In proscribing their wrongdoing (i.e., their cannibalism), however, the Buddha nevertheless allows them a restricted and diminished power. They can no longer kill and eat people (as Rakusa and company wanted to do with the Buddha), but only make them ill. And to this are attached conditions, a whole area of sanctions. According to the Buddha of this narrative, if a *yakädurā* utters his name or his authority, the *yakku* are bound to accept the proffered offerings and, as they say, "give up" the illnesses they caused.

The point that I want to emphasize here is that this is not the "Buddha" of the *Mahāvaṃsa*. In this narrative the Buddha figure is appropriated for uses and practices which authoritative positions within the discursive tradition of Sinhala Buddhism exclude from the circle of "real" Buddhist practice—specifically those called *gurukama*. And it is this local practitioner of the specialized techniques for influencing the ways of *yakku* who will invoke and utter the name and authority of the Buddha not, that is to say, the canonically authorized monks of the *sangha*.

The way in which the discourse of *yakku* constructs a direct link between *gurukama* and the Buddha is made more explicit in the following fascinating story, also told to me by Piyasena. The history of the *yaktovil* and the techniques of charming (*mantra sāstraya*) are not readily reconstructed. Once again, however, there is a story, a *katāva*—indeed, there are perhaps several—told about the origins of this knowledge and practice. One of them is the following. It is the story about an enigmatic group known as the Isivarayō and Rusivarayō. The story:

> In Dambadiva [India] there lived the nine Isivarayō and the nine Rusivarayō. They were skilled in the whole arts (*sāstraya*). These eighteen fellows, having bound the knowledge (*vijjāva bändalā*) and the

characters (*akuru bändalā*), made these arts (*sāstraya häduvā*). They were written in palm-leaf books (*puskola pot*). They were written separately (*vena venama*), line by line, one by one (*pelin pelaṭa ekēka*).[51]

These Isivarayō and Rusivarayō learned the arts of charming by taking and putting together the characters of the *pirit* (protective charms) and *bana* (sermons) of the Buddha. It is that doctrine [i.e., the Buddha's] that made these charms. It is also according to the sermons preached by the Buddha that these fellows made *vedakama*.[52] The Isivarayō and Rusivarayō were the original leaders (*mul nāyaka*) in the arts of charming, and it was they who taught the arts to the Brahmanas in Dambadiva.

These Brahmanas were coming to Lankā from Dambadiva to perform *yāgayas* (sacrificial rites) for the Kings. Having performed these *yāgayas*, *hōmas* (fire-offering rites), and *sāntiyas* (rites of blessing) for the King, shiploads of gifts (*tägi bōga nävganan*), goods (*baḍumūṭṭu*), wealth and grain (*dhana dhānya*), money (*milamudal*), and cloth (*redi pili*) were taken away to Dambadiva.

During that time, while this was happening, it occurred to the monk Sri Rāhula of Totagamuva, a wise and educated man, that, "having come every day as often as this a great amount of the wealth of this country is taken away. It is our wealth (*ē apē dhanaya*). Because of that I must become learned (*puhun venavā*) in this one [i.e., in the arts of charming]. But even though we asked these fellows [i.e., to share this knowledge] they aren't giving, aren't giving anything at all (*mē golangen illuvaṭa denne nā̆, mokutma denne nā̆*)."

At that point one Vidāgama from Totagamuva called out, "Rāhula!" In other words, this monk Rāhula is the disciple (*gōlayā*) of Vidāgama. And the disciple is more skilled in everything than the teacher.[53] So Vidāgama said to the disciple, "Gōlanma, get ready (*lāhasti karanna*)! Take the stylus (*panhinda*), palm-leaf books (*puskola pot*), and leaves (*kola*) and tell the Brahmanas to perform these things [i.e., a ceremony]." Then a *yāgaya* was caused to be performed (*kärevva*), a complete *yāgaya*. The monk Rāhula then wrote down everything they said and did.

The book that was written was big; a big *yāgaya* book (*yāgē visāla potak*). It had been a seven-day *yāgaya*. The *yāgaya* and the book having been finished, the monk from Totagamuva said, "Here, Brahamana, I also have one of those books. I still haven't applied *kalu*.[54] I brought it to see if it really is about this *yāgaya* (*mē yāgaya da kiyalā balanna genaya kiyalā*)." Having been brought, it is shown to the Brahmanas. "This is it!" [they think in dismayed surprise]. Then these Brahamanas saw stars (*mē Brahmanyinṭa taru penuna*)! They became very ashamed (*visāla lejjāvakaṭa päratunā*) and frightened (*baya-unā*). And the monks considered

> throwing them over the precipice (*mun prāpate damanna mēka api karanna ōna kiyalā*).
>
> Then the monks in all the temples were told to study what had been written [i.e., about the ceremonies]. And having studied, they performed *sāntiyas,* without asking for payment [i.e., as distinct from the practice of the Brahmanas]. Moreover, the monks thought that the power of the Brahmanas should be reduced even more, so the lowest [caste] section, the drumbeaters (*bera vayana*) were also instructed in the arts. And it is from that time that the arts of *mantraya* and *vedakama* have existed among us [i.e., Buddhists in Lankā] from generation to generation (*paramparāven paramparāvaṭa*).[55]

As in many Sinhala stories, India (Dambadiva) provides the originary setting. A group of eighteen, the artful and resourceful Isivarayō and Rusivarayō, extract certain characters (*akuru*) from the discourses of the Buddha. With these they construct another knowledge and practice—a sort of para-Buddhist knowledge and practice. Since the Brahmanas then learned this—note—Buddhism-derived, knowledge from the Isivarayō and Rusivarayō, it may be said that what they performed for the Kings of Lankā were already, in some sense, *Buddhist* practices. Thus the monks of Lankā (that rightful home of the *dhamma*) had, so to speak, more claims than one to this knowledge and practice. These unscrupulous Brahmanas were, after all, also extracting the very wealth of the country!

What is also interesting about this story is its foregrounding, and indeed celebration, of one of the most famous poet-monks of fifteenth-century Lankā—the Kōṭṭe period—Sri Rāhula Thera of Totagamuva. Piyasena's story makes Sri Rāhula not only a wise and educated man who knows more than his teacher, Vidāgama of Totagamuva, but a monk with a passionate, quasi-nationalist feeling for his homeland, Lankā. What seems to upset him is not so much the lack of the Brahmanas' esoteric knowledge as such, but the fact that this knowledge is used to deplete the country of wealth that legitimately belongs to "its" people. Piyasena's narrative obviously depends on the emergence of certain modern conceptions of state, territory, and citizen, but what is notable is the place it gives to a monk more esteemed in contemporary Lankā for his literary contributions than his Buddhism. The Kōṭṭe period was one of considerable debate and argument within the Buddhist tradition about what constituted the parameters of allowable Buddhist practice. It was also a period in which the literary genre *sandesa kāvya* flourished.[56] Sri Rāhula was a foremost exponent of this genre and his most outspoken opponent was the monk Maitreya Thera of Vidāgama. There were at the time, as Martin Wickremasinghe writes in his valuable study *Landmarks of Sinhalese Literature,*[57] two major schools of (scholarly) thought on what counted as correct Buddhist practice: that represented by the *Vanavāsi Nikāya* (or forest-dwelling sect), and that represented by the *Grāmavāsi Nikāya* (or village-dwelling sect). "Sri Rahula," maintains Wickremasinghe, "as a leader of the Gramavasi Nikaya did not hesitate to write poetry dealing with the physical charms of women, and he believed in certain pseudo-sciences condemned by the Buddha. He accepted, moreover, the worship of gods as part of Buddhist ritual. The monks of the Vanavasi Nikaya, on the other hand, were as vehemently opposed to the worship of gods as to the writing of poetry. . . . Vidagama was violently intolerant of the superstitious beliefs of the Brahmins" (p. 142). Indeed, as Wickremasinghe continues somewhat later, "It is not unlikely that Vidagama's spirited defense of Buddhism against such intrusions [i.e. the so-called Brahminic practices] was indirectly an attack on Rahula himself" (p. 149).[58]

At any rate, be this conflict and the interesting historical question it raises as they may, what I want to emphasize is that the narrative is manifestly more concerned to appropriate this estimable "Buddhist" figure than to authorize a specifiably "Buddhist" space for positioning the discourse of *yakku*. The first practitioners of the arts of *mantraya* were Buddhist monks. (Indeed, it is said that some of the most powerful *mantra*-books are still to be found in certain temples. And, moreover, there are, it is said, still monks who practice these arts on a small scale.) But somehow they did not maintain the knowledge. It was passed on to *yakädurās,* who therefore stand in a direct line of descent from the original practitioners of these arts—*paramparāven paramparāvaṭa.*

I have been arguing in this chapter that even in its significant departures from the colonial problematic of two kinds of Sinhala religion, the anthropological construction of Buddhism as a theoretical object has retained the essentialist preoccupation with identifying the supposedly authentic parts of Sinhala religion—"the strictly Buddhist and spirit religion"—and with representing their (more recently, changing) interaction. If colonial discourse constructed a vertical model of Sinhala religion in which one part lay on top of the other and in which no internal relations connected them, anthropological discourse, so to speak, turned this model on its side (one might almost say, democratized it) and introduced the idea of internal, functional links between them. I have suggested that this approach should now be dropped, and that we rather concern ourselves with trying to map the kinds of social projects in which religious discourse comes to be positioned and employed. In this I have suggested, further, that the discourse of *yakku* is employed in a distinctive kind of social project, namely, *gurukama*; I would like to turn to this in more detail in the next chapter.

Chapter 7

The Ends and Strategy of *Yaktovil*

The general aim of this final chapter is to suggest an approach to the analysis of *yaktovil* that does not depend on such notions about the fundamental experience of Sinhala Buddhists or the supposed intrinsic qualities of their cultural practices as I have earlier (in chapter 4) shown to be theoretically unsound, and (in chapter 5) to be implicated in an ideological, more specifically a colonial, history.

It is worth repeating that my critical disquiet is not so much with the analytical interest in symbols as such, as with those kinds of anthropological analysis that traffic in their supposed essential meanings. However, the sort of analysis I shall pursue in this chapter is not concerned with a symbolic analysis of *yaktovil,* nor with an analysis of its social functions. My concern rather is to explore what I shall call its "techniques" and "strategy," and in so doing I will endeavor to elucidate some of the ways in which the practice of *yaktovil* relies on those knowledges regarding *yakku*—their nature, their mode of malevolence, and their place in the moral universe of Sinhala Buddhism—examined in chapters 1 and 2, and described in the context of one observed performance in chapter 3. In particular I shall be concerned to demonstrate the role in this practice of that family of Sinhala concepts (and the ideas and images adhering to them) which we have encountered in those earlier chapters: *varama, aṇaguṇa, diṣṭiya,* and *dōṣaya.* As I have indicated, I understand these to constitute an interrelated semantic field, and to be central to the way in which *gurukama* in general, and *yaktovil* (one of its constituent practices) specifically, are taken by their practitioners to produce effects, both on *yakku* and the persons (*āturayās*) afflicted by them. Clearly, one of the things I want to insist on is that any anthropological analysis of such complex practices as *yaktovil* surely needs to situate itself among the concepts that propel or constitute the practice, and this not as a way of discovering through the aegis of some transcendant theory "what they mean," but as a way of grasping what *work* they perform in the fields in which they are composed.

The Ends of *Yaktovil*

Yaktovil is the most complex and elaborate of an interrelated group of esoteric practices commonly known, in and around Matara, as *gurukama* or *ädurukama*, "the work of the teacher"—that is, the work of practitioners known as *äduräs* or *yakäduräs*. The *yaksayā*—to recall the sequence—characteristically swift in the execution of its wrathful misdeeds, is understood to have taken advantage of an "unguarded moment" (in Gooneratne's apposite phrase) in the person's life and to have cast a severe "look" (*bälma*) upon him or her. Because this person is already in a vulnerable psychological state by virtue of a preexisting mental apprehensiveness, that is, a *tanikama*, the malign energy of this "look"—the *diṣṭiya*—that "falls" on him or her has the effect of causing a spasm of fright, a *gäsma*. This is the precipitating moment. The consequence of this conjunction of a subsisting mental unease and sudden fright is a consuming worry, which, given the indivisible or mutually reciprocal relation between mental and physical constitutions of Sinhalas, leads invariably to a rise in the body's temperature and therefore to an agitation of the bodily humors, *vāta*, *pitta*, and *sema*. A *diṣṭiya*, it will now be said, has "covered" this person; a *dōṣa* or "trouble" has "touched" him or her.

Yaktovil is an intervention that seeks to undo this affliction. The work of this intervention consists of two objectives: the first is the removal of the influence of *yakku* from the bodies of afflicted persons known as *āturayās*, an influence, as we have seen, transmitted in the medium of the energy of their eyesight, *diṣṭiya*. *Yaktovil* is concerned with "deflecting" *diṣṭiya* and removing *dōṣa*. But *yaktovil* has, as well, another objective, one that situates it within what I have called (in chapter 2) a Sinhala ethics of composure. The general aim of an *ädurukama*, Piyasena once remarked, is to inspire *seta*, that is, tranquillity. Thus *yaktovil* is also concerned with creating the conditions in which the afflicted person, the *āturayā*, can be restored to mental calm and humoral balance.

Let me elaborate this a little further since this notion of a double objective will inform in a decisive way the conception of *yaktovil* I construct in this chapter. As my description in chapter 3 of the two ceremonies performed for Lila Amma will have indicated, the object of *yaktovil* entails a more or less protracted encounter with *yakku* (and, of course, the other lesser malign beings involved—*prētayō, bahīravayō,* and so on—as well) in which they have to be coaxed, bribed, coerced, and so forth, into obedience to the Buddha's virtuous commands, his *aṇaguṇa*. Gaining the obedience of *yakku* and removing their malign influence, the *diṣṭiya*, and the *dōṣa* it has caused, is the very heart of the hard work of *yaktovil* practice. It is here indeed, in the procedures through which this work is carried out, that there are potential, even life-threatening, dangers—from sorcery, for instance, or from mere errors made in charming—and it is for this aspect of their work that *ädurās* seek the protection of Sūniyam *dēvatāva* in that opening *tovil* sequence known as the Sūniyam Vīdiya Käpakirīma or The Consecration of the Sūniyam Stand. But the accomplishment of this work of gaining the compliance of *yakku* and ridding the afflicted person of the malign disturbance caused by them is not the end of the matter—in almost every kind of *tovil*, at any rate. There is still left the less difficult (at least technically so) but nevertheless important therapeutic task of "pleasing the mind"[1] (*hita santōsakaranavā*) of the afflicted person and of creating the conditions that enable a return to that state of calm and composure—*śānta dānta*—so extolled by Buddhists. The exception to this of course is the Iramudun Samayama, The Ceremony of the Midday Hour performed for afflictions caused by the Iramudun Rīri Yaksayā. In this case the *yaktovil* ends sharply with the "stopping" of the effects of the *diṣṭiya* at the *purālapala* at the end of the sequence known as the Dekonavillaku Pidēniya (see the section in chapter 3 that discusses this sequence). But it is necessary to repeat that this *tovil* is rarely performed by itself. It is typically followed by a Mahasōn Samayama, a Sanni Yäkuma, or a Maha Kalu Kumāra Samayama.

What I would like to do in this chapter is to examine in some detail each of these ends of *yaktovil* in relation to the "technique" and "strategy" employed to achieve them. I do not propose to undertake an analysis of *yaktovil* pratice in its entirety, nor do I propose an analysis of the performance I have recorded (though I shall certainly make use of it illustratively); rather I propose to undertake a close examination of a small number of those "techniques" or "chains of technique" that constitute the "strategy" *yaktovil* employs to achieve its ends. These are the questions that interest me: How does *yaktovil* control—or as *ädurās* say, "bind"—*yakku*? How does it effect the removal of the malign energy of their eyesight, *diṣṭiya*, and the precipitated *dōṣa*, from the bodies of afflicted persons? And how, finally, does it seek to return the *āturayā* to a wholesome state of psychological calm? First, though, a word about my uses of the concepts of "strategy" and "technique."

Strategy and Technique in *Yaktovil* Practice

The use of a concept of "strategy" in the analysis of social practices is, of course, not altogether new. Let me try to indicate briefly some of the senses it has acquired in recent theoretical discourse, those anyway that are useful to my purposes. In anthropology, for instance, Pierre Bourdieu has recently made a strong and persuasive argument in support of its use, and since for him "strategy" is a key concept in a more fundamental theoretical displacement, it may be as well to consider it as a point of departure. On Bourdieu's account (scattered across a number of interventions), the concept of "strategy" is the theoretical means by which he seeks to dispense with a structuralist objectivism without at the same time slipping into an agent-centered subjectivism.[2] "The notion of strategy," he says, "makes possible a break with the objectivist point of view and with the agentless action that structuralism assumes (by appealing for example to the notion of the unconscious). But one can refuse to see strategy as the product of an unconscious program without making it the product of a conscious and rational calculation. It is the product of a practical sense, of a particular social game."[3] This, I think, is a useful theoretical move. Strategy is meant to form a generative conceptual moment in Bourdieu's concerted effort to leave the field of that recurrent family of oppositions in social analysis: subjective versus objective, individual versus social, freedom versus necessity, and so on. And in this, of course, it is linked to his use of the notion of *habitus* (that is, system of dispositions). Indeed, the two concepts, *strategy* and *habitus*, are necessarily interconnected for Bourdieu because strategies operate not upon essential subjectivities but precisely upon dispositions, vulnerabilities, and aptitudes constituted within the field of the social discourses and practices in which its (that is, strategy's) instrumental procedures are implicated.

Bourdieu, however, has another, related target, and it is in fact this one he says, that precipitated the concept into the foreground of his thinking. The concept of strategy, he maintains, enables one to distinguish between "theoretical aims" and "practical aims." As he suggests, it was his awareness of "a gap between the theoretical aims of theoretical understanding and the directly concerned, practical aims of practical understanding, which led me to speak of matrimonial *strategies* or *social uses* of kinship rather than rules of kinship. This change of vocabulary is indicative of a change of viewpoint. It is a matter of not grounding the practice of social agents in the theory that one has to construct in order to explain that practice."[4] In sum, then, the concept of strategy is concerned to elucidate the "practical sense of things," "a feel for the game," as he further puts it, a "practical mastery of the logic or immanent necessity of a game, which is gained through experience of the game, and which functions this side of consciousness and discourse."[5]

It seems to me that Bourdieu's is a theoretical move of much potential value, but there is one area of his formulation that I think is open to some reservation. The idea of practices operating "this side of consciousness and discourse" (much like de Certeau's famous image of the "common man" who in all ages "comes before the text") seems to me, unless adequately qualified, to stand in danger of suggesting too much of an unconstituted domain of pure practical activity (a sort of counterpart to the now familiar phenomenological assumptions about a domain of pure "experience"). From Bourdieu's remarks, for instance, it is not clear to me what the value is of talking about "matrimonial strategies" without implicating some notion of "rational calculation," without, say, the notion of a field of possible marriage alternatives or possible rivals, and thus without some notion of the discursive and other means of negotiating these alternatives and rivals. This would entail, certainly, some notion of stakes and risks involved in adopting one path as opposed to another—so as to preempt, perhaps, the objectives of one's rivals, and so to enhance the chances of achieving one's own ends. Surely, in any case, "rational calculation" need not necessarily imply systematic theory. It is perhaps in this regard that Talal Asad has raised some doubt about Bourdieu's sharp dichotomy between "theoretical aims" and "practical aims." Referring to the famous nineteenth-century work on the theory of war by Karl von Clausewitz, Asad argues that "strategy" presupposes not just any practical aim but a "special kind of practical aim": "of antagonistic wills struggling for supremacy over a terrain that may not always be delimited, with forces that are not always constant, in conditions whose changing significance cannot always be anticipated. Such an aim *does* require some theoretical understanding and knowledge of rules, although of course that is not all it requires."[6]

This is closer to the sense in which I wish to employ the concept. For the strategy of *yaktovil* practice, I would argue, surely does entail some sort of rational, even "theoretical," understanding of such things as the medium of the malevolence of *yakku*, the relation between this malevolence and the disturbance of the bodily humors, and the status of *yakku* in relation to the moral authority of the Buddha. Such a view too, one might add, is closer in many ways to the conception offered by Michel Foucault some years ago when, employing the images of games and war, he wrote of the concept of strategy being employed in three ways:

> First, to designate the means employed to attain a certain end; it is a question of rationality functioning to arrive at an objective. Second, to designate the manner in which a partner in a certain game acts with regard to what he thinks should be the action of the others and what he considers the others think to be his own; it is the way in which one seeks to have the advantage over others. Third, to designate the procedures used in a situation of confrontation to deprive the opponent of his means of combat and to reduce him to giving up the struggle; it is a question therefore of the means destined to obtain victory.[7]

The analysis of such social practices as *yaktovil* in terms of a concept of "strategy" is potentially useful therefore for at least two principal reasons. The first is that such a concept need not rely on the old dichotomy (especially prominent in anthropological analyses of ritual) between agentless structures (the objectivism of the so-called instrumentalists interested in the underlying logic of technical procedures) and structureless agents (the subjectivism of the so-called expressivists concerned with the "language" of expressive performance). Rather, the concept of strategy speaks to the procedures involved in the organization, regulation, and reorganization of socially conditioned bodies and subjectivities. The second reason is that the concept of strategy focuses on the specifically practical uses of rationalities and procedures operating in a field of differential moral forces or in a field of power. Strategy operates, in other words, in a domain of confrontation of socially constituted forces in which the outcome—failure or success, loss or victory—is not given in advance. I wish to propose that rather than undertaking an analysis of *yaktovil* in terms of the familiar metaphor of a "communicational field" in which effects are said to be dependent upon the correct interpretation of "experience," we might more adequately employ the concept of strategy.[8]

Yaktovil consists of a number of named sequences: Sūniyam Vīdiya Käpakirīma, Kattrīka Hatara Käpakirīma, Avamangalle Pidēniya, Baliya Pāvādīma, and so on (see chapter 3). These sequences themselves are made up of a combination of operations—which we may call "techniques"—operations which are characterized by the fact that they have have more or less delimited, instrumental objectives: charming (*maturanavā*), for instance, in the Sūniyam Vīdiya Käpakirīma to invoke Sūniyam Dēvatāva's protection during the *yaktovil* proceedings, singing verses (*kavi kiyanavā*) and dancing (*naṭanavā*) during the Mahasamayama to entertain the *yakku*, and giving offering (*pidēnna denavā*) during the Kattrīka Hatara Käpakirīma to appease them. *Gurukama* also has at its disposal a number of other techniques (as I will discuss in a moment)—the tying of threads (*äpa nūl bändīma*), the cutting of limes (*dehi käpīma*), and the charming of oil (*tel matirīma*)—which are strictly techniques of "binding" and "limiting" the effects of *yakku* (i.e., of their *diṣṭiya*). These are palliatives, typically employed prior to the staging of a large-scale *yaktovil* ceremony, though often employed in them as well.

These—techniques—are the elements or components of the strategy of *yaktovil*. They do not constitute the strategy itself. For *yaktovil*, though involving all of these operations, is not their mere assembly, but their combination in an overall plan, an overall strategy. *Yaktovil*'s strategy is to combine these techniques in such a fashion as to alternate between summoning and encouragement (in the Kattrīka Hatara Käpakirīma), trickery (as in the Avamangalle Pidēniya), pleading (as in those sequences of questioning), and appeasing (in the various offering sequences). This strategy derives from the fact that *yaktovil* is a contest of forces, *moral* forces—between *ädurās* on the one hand, whose labor, as we saw in chapter 6, is sanctioned by the Buddha, and *yakku* on the other; it derives from the fact that *yaktovil* is a game, if you like, constructed by *ädurās*, in which what is at issue is how to get the better of their opponents, *yakku*. Part of the point, of course, is that there is no final victory over *yakku*—not through *yaktovil* anyway. Only the Buddha can change the path on which these figures are working out their *karma*—as he did with Ālavaka and Kālī. And therefore what is at stake in *yaktovil* is in a sense only how to strike the best deal with *yakku*, how to give up the least for the most favorable outcome.

The techniques involved in influencing and gaining some measure of control over *yakku* are principally techniques about "binding" *yakku*. More specifically, *gurukama* is employed to "bind" *yakku* in order to "take work" from them: *yakku bändalā väḍak ganna,* as *ädurās* say. This work (*väḍa*) which is taken from *yakku* can be of two sorts: it can be beneficent or maleficent, that is to say, it can be used either to cure (*suva karanavā*) or to harm (*upadrava karanavā*). The *yakädurā* can bind *yakku* to make them remove the malevolent effects—the *dōṣa* caused by their *diṣṭiya*—from the body of someone they have afflicted; or, conversely, they can bind *yakku* to make them carry out an act of sorcery (*koḍivina*) against someone, an act that will ensure the ill effects of *diṣṭiya* on them. In either case, however, *yakku* must be "bound" by an *ädurā,* and this in a precisely Sinhala sense. For "binding" (*bandinavā*) indeed is a resonantly expressive Sinhala metaphor: fences and couples and parcels and *yakku* are all spoken of as being "bound" after some fashion. And this metaphor of "binding" turns, it would seem, on a certain image of the nature of relationships between elements or objects that is both one of a spatial proximity and one of a regulatory adhesive energy or force. This, as we will see in a moment, is precisely what uttering *mantrayas* produces—an adhesive energy or force known as *ākarṣana*.

The practice of "binding," then, forms perhaps the most elementary aim of any *gurukama,* and it is carried into effect by an *ädurā* uttering powerful charms (*mantrayas*) in specific sorts of context and with the appropriate accessory paraphernalia. Often, in fact, the specific charms or *mantrayas* are actually themselves called *bandanayas* (or *bandhanayas*); thus, for example, Rīri Bandanaya is a *mantraya* employed in binding one or more of that feared and recalcitrant group of Rīri Yakku. As we will see, these binding techniques of charming (*mantra sāstraya,* generally) constitute a practice of *securing* the obedience of *yakku,* of *restraining* their lawless and bloodthirsty extravagance, of *limiting* their field of movement and activity, and of *compelling* them to perform the "work" required of them.

I have said that in their beneficent aspects these techniques of binding *yakku* are concerned with the "removal" of the effects of *yakṣa* eyesight, *diṣṭiya*. Actually, however, the metaphor of "removal" is only a partially correct one. More properly speaking, this *diṣṭiya* is spoken of as being "deflected" (*maga harinavā,* literally, "to turn from the way") from the bodies of afflicted persons. Sometimes too the phrase *ivat karanavā,* "to put out of the way," is used. Both metaphors recall the way the eyesight of the Buddha-image is "deflected" in a mirror in the *nētra pinkama*, and the way Uppalavanna/Viṣṇu's eyesight was "deflected" from the bodies of the Portuguese, when its legs were cut by them. This notion—*diṣṭiya maga harinavā*—is therefore consonant with what I said in chapter 2 about the Sinhala conception of eyesight as an extruding flow of energy connecting with objects. But *diṣṭiya* is not only deflected; its malevolent influence is also spoken of as being "stopped" (*natara karanavā*). In point of fact, these practices—the deflection and stopping of *diṣṭiya*—go hand in hand.

In their beneficent form, these techniques of *gurukama* define a wide range of specific practices that can be brought, separately or in combination, to bear on the malign action of *yakku*. The first that might be mentioned is the practice of tying "security" threads (*äpa nūl bändīma*).[9] Once an *ädurā* has ascertained that the *dōṣa* (trouble) is in fact the result of malign *diṣṭiya*, the first thing to be done is to tie a "security thread." This is, as people say, an *ārakṣāva* or "protective" measure. The practice of tying such threads typically involves a short ritual, and those I saw proceeded more or less as follows: A cut *tämbili* (young drinking coconut) will be brought, and a little white sandalwood (*sudu handun*, an auspicious ingredient) sprinkled in it while the *ädurā* utters charms over it (*maturanavā*). A little of this will be given to the afflicted person to drink. Then a length of newly bought white thread will be cut and smeared with a turmeric paste (*kaha*). While charming, the *ädurā* ties nine knots on the thread and passes it through the smoke of resin (*dummala*). Finally, the charms continuing, he ties it around the neck (sometimes the wrist) of the afflicted person, periodically snapping his fingers at his legs as he does so. The tying of an *äpa nūla* is the most elementary practice by which a *yaksayā* may be bound. Typically, it will have protective efficacy for only a specific period of time—from several days to a few months. It serves as an assurance to the *yaksayā* (or, if many, *yakku*) that either offerings (*pidēni*) or even a *yaktovil* ceremony will be forthcoming.[10] This suggests a very interesting notion regarding *diṣṭiya*, namely, that *yakku* can, and can be made to, intensify or diminish its effects. This is most important for understanding the work of *gurukama*.

Then there is the practice of "charming oil" (*tel matirīma*). This is a small method or technique (*poḍi kramaya*) employed for very minor complaints. It may—but need not—accompany the tying of a protective thread. The practice as I observed it in Matara proceeds more or less as

Wirz describes it:[11] Over a small amount of coconut oil (*pol tel*), mixed sometimes with a little *sudu handun* (white sandalwood), the *ädurā* utters charms (*tel maturanavā*) and blows periodically on it. (The significance of this blowing—an omnipresent accompaniment to all *mantraya*—will become clear later in my discussion of how *mantrayas* produce effects. I would only say here that blowing transmits the power of the words that constitute the charm.) While still charming, he dips his fingers into the oil and dabs the *āturayā*'s forehead and temples. Another small technique or intervention, though one with more extensive and varied application, especially in crisis situations, is that called the "cutting of limes" (*dehi käpīma*). The "cutting of limes" has perhaps more a "limiting" than a "binding" function (as in the marking out of a *sīmāva*—though again it must be emphasized that these two functions are intertwined). Limes are often cut at points representing the four or eight directional corners (say, the sides of houses), at entranceways (doors, gates, for example, or steps), at crossroads, on tracks leading away from cemeteries—to limit (*māyim karanavā*), one might say to hold at bay, the field of efficacy of the malign *diṣṭiya*. During the extraordinary *yaktovil* sequence called *dekonavilaku pidēniya*, for instance, the *ädurā* goes through the *āturayā*'s house and other buildings on the premises deflecting the *diṣṭiya* and *dōṣa* onto his own body, and at each entranceway he cuts limes so as to make a sort of *sīmāva*. Very often too when a person who has been the victim of *diṣṭiya* is in an acutely agitated situation, trembling and shaking, whether during a larger ceremony or not, limes will be cut while uttering *mantrayas*, the lime cutter being passed several times over the length of the person's body (see chapter 3).

The techniques discussed so far—the tying of a protective thread, the charming of oil, and the cutting of limes—are all palliatives. They lack one element central to the understanding of what it takes to control *yakku* or to get work from them: offerings. For recall the Buddha's warrant (*varama*): *yakku* may enjoy the liberty of casting their malign glances on people, but this liberty is limited by the fact that they must acccept the offerings made to them. These offerings are called *dola pidēni*, and the elementary practice in which this takes place is called a *pidēnna dīma* ("the giving of offerings"). The practice of giving offerings may be performed on its own as an independent technique, or it may be a constituent practice in the larger strategy of a *yaktovil* ceremony. Since in either case the technique of the practice is the same, I will describe it below in my discussion of the *yaktovil* sequence in which it is a central element, Kattrīka Hatara Käpakirīma, the Consecration of the Four Offering Stands.

Finally, the most elaborate and complex practice which *gurukama* defines is the practice called *yaktovil*. *Yaktovil*, or the practice of "dancing *tovil*" (*tovil nätīma*), is the most powerful intervention upon the malign effects of *yakku* available to *yakädurās* because it combines a number of discrete *gurukama* techniques into an overall strategy. *Yaktovil* constitutes the most painstakingly orchestrated display of techniques necessary to bind *yakku*, employing strategies of appeasement (with song and dance and food); of coaxing to more reasonable demands; of ruse (to distract and deflect their attention and *diṣṭiya* from the afflicted person); and of coercion to force them to acknowledge and accept the virtuous commands (*aṇaguṇa*) of the Buddha.

In the sections that follow, I propose to focus not on *yaktovil* as a whole, or rather not on each and every sequence in the long chain that constitutes it, but on a number of its techniques—in a few of its sequences—that are crucial in advancing what I am calling its overall strategy. Specifically, as a way of trying to answer the question of how *yaktovil* works to bind *yakku* to remove their malign influence (their *diṣṭiya* and the *dōṣa*), I will look closely at the procedures employed in the sequence known as Kattrīka Hatara Käpakirīma or Consecration of the Four Offering Stands and try to elaborate the cultural principles that propel it; then, as a way of elucidating some aspects of the encounter with *yakku* which *ädurās* stage in their attempt to secure their compliance, I will look at extracts from those sequences of questioning from Lila Amma's Maha Kalu Kumāra Samayama recorded in chapter 3; and finally, as a way of trying to understand how *yaktovil* seeks to restore composure to the mind of the *āturayā*, I will attempt to elucidate the cultural principles involved in the sequence involving the lamp for the Four Warrant Gods, the Mangara Pelapāliya, and the Daha-aṭa Pāliya.

Deflecting *Diṣṭiya*, Removing *Dōṣa*

In "On Demonology and Witchcraft in Ceylon," Gooneratne maintains that "in every demon ceremony, which is performed either to cure or inflict sickness, or to protect a person from becoming liable to any 'demon sickness' at all, the effective agents, which influence the demons, and through them, the disease, are CHARMS or spells, Invocations, and

Dolla or offerings, especially the first with or without the two last" (p. 51). This view of the principal "effective agents"—what I am calling "techniques"—of *gurukama,* was confirmed to me often enough by the *ädurās* I worked with: charms (*mantrayas*), invocations (largely embodied in verses or *kavi*), and offerings (*pidēni*) are the means by which the work of removing the influence, the *diṣṭiya* and the *dōṣa,* of *yakku* is effected.

In this section I propose to focus on one major sequence of *yaktovil* practice in which these techniques are employed as an interconnected part of the strategy of "binding" *yakku.* The sequence I have in mind is that known as Kattrīka Hatara Käpakirīma, the Consecration of the Four Offering Stands. It is, perhaps, an almost prosaic *tovil* sequence, long and repetitive (lasting anywhere from a little over half an hour to two-and-a-half hours, and each of its procedures generally has to be repeated for each of the main *yakku* being propitiated with offerings), and devoid of the wonderful drama of such later sequences as the famous Daha-aṭa Pāliya. I think, though, that by looking closely at the chain of techniques that constitute it—summoning *yakku* through *mantrayas,* singing verses (some to invoke certain gods, some to flatter *yakku*), invoking the virtues of the Buddha to impel *yakku* to heed his commands, making offerings—we can see the connections among those concepts and images through which *yakku* and their malign effects are understood, and understood to be brought under control. Specifically, I mean here the image of a body as a system of energies and humors whose balance has been disturbed by an external malevolent energy—the "look" of the *yaksayā*—becoming "attached" to, and "contained" in it; the idea that this energy of the "look" is of the nature of a manipulable substance, which it is possible to "move" from one place to another, and being an energy, possible also of increase or decrease in intensity; the notion, moreover, of *yakku* as morally subordinate beings given to base pleasures, but existing nevertheless on "warrants" from the Buddha and thus bound to "listen" to his commands.

The Kattrīka Hatara Käpakirīma consists, as I have said, of a number of basic techniques. They are as follows: *diṣṭi kirīma* ("the making of *diṣṭiya*"); *kavi kīma* ("the singing of verses"); *pidēnna dīma* ("the giving of offerings"). I shall discuss each one of these in turn.

Diṣṭi Kirīma. The control—or "binding," we should more properly say—of *diṣṭiya* in *yaktovil* involves, in the first instance, its "generation" (*diṣṭi* *karanavā*). The opening sequences of the Kattrīka Hatara Käpakirīma or Consecration of the Four Offering Stands are concerned with this fundamental procedure of "generating" *diṣṭiya*. What does this mean? The transitive verb *karanavā* literally means "make" or "do." However, *diṣṭiya* is not really "made" (say, in the Sinhala sense of *hadanavā*); rather it is, as *ädurās* will sometimes say by way of explanation, "caused to be brought" (*genvenavā*). Essentially, therefore, to say that *diṣṭiya* is "generated" means that the presence at the *tovil* proceedings of *yakku* (who, recall, on the Buddha's injunction can no longer make themselves present in Lankā except in their eyesight) is brought about.

The generation of the presence of this malign eyesight, *diṣṭiya*, is effected by *ädurās* who "summon" *yakku* from the eight directional corners (*aṭa kona*) of the world to put their "look" (*bälma*) on the *yaktovil* proceedings: *diṣṭi aňḍagahanavā, ädurās* say. This notion is a highly interesting one, and at first sight a quite curious one in view of the fact that the *āturayā* already "has" *diṣṭiya*, indeed is literally "covered" with it. But two things need to be borne in mind. First, the active influence of *diṣṭiya* on someone upon whom it has "fallen" is not continuous but periodic. The bodily symptoms (Lila Amma's burning sensations, for example, or her trembling), or the psychological ones (such as Lila's dreams of a large, dark, manlike figure), are typically recurrent but not uninterrupted. There are thus periods when the presence of *yakku* is, so to speak, a "live," immediately disturbing one, and other periods when it is not. And in order for it to have efficacy *diṣṭiya* has to have "life" (I will return to this in a moment). Thus for the practice of *yaktovil*, what is necessary is that it be generated and—in fact, literally—given this life. By contrast, of course, when an *ädurā* is called to attend to a person in an acute situation—a person who is losing conscious awareness, shaking, shouting, and so on—*diṣṭiya* does not have to be "generated"; its active presence is only too manifest, and the intervention that is immediately required will consist largely in those techniques—the cutting of limes, for instance—that have the effect of quickly reducing or limiting its disturbing energy. (I might add parenthetically that this is also the case in the context of a *yaktovil* performance where the effects of *diṣṭiya* suddenly intensify at inappropriate times and the *ädurā* is forced to intervene [see chapter 3].)

Which brings us to the second point. If the work of *gurukama* is, as I say, conducted in the medium of *diṣṭiya*, what this means is that the strategic aim of its practice is to shape or determine the effects of this malign energy. This, after all, is precisely why one is said in a *gurukama* to "get work" from *yakku*. Lila Amma's case is illustrative here. Whereas the *diṣṭiya* that fell on her body at the funeral of the monk, precipitating the initial trouble or *dōṣa*, was the design of *yakku* themselves on, so to say, their own malicious initiative (of which, as we know, they have plenty), the *diṣṭiya* that "fell" subsequently as a result of the sorcery was deliberately generated in the practice of a *gurukama* and was therefore the *ädurā*'s regulatory production. Similarly, in *yaktovil* the accent on causing *diṣṭiya* to be brought is on its regulatory uses (as we shall see in the following section in the making of *āvēśaya*). And this is why the "generation" of *diṣṭiya* is simultaneously the "summoning" of *yakku*, and why this "summoning" is at the same time a "binding" of *yakku*. To explain this, I need to turn now to a discussion of charms (*mantrayas*).

The "summoning" of *yakku* is produced, as I said, by the uttering of special charms. These are called *diṣṭi mantrayas*. To understand what is entailed in "summoning" *yakku* we have to grasp how charming (*maturanavā*) works. Gooneratne (here as elsewhere our *guruvaraya*) has provided what is perhaps still the most comprehensive discussion of the practice among Sinhalas of using charms (*mantra sāstraya*).[12] He speculates on their origins in India; he gives a precise description of the several categories into which they are divided;[13] and on what makes them work, their efficacy, he has the following to say:

> The virtue and efficacy of a charm . . . consists, it is said, not so much in the meaning of the language used, as in a peculiar arrangement and combination of certain letters, each having its own peculiar power. According to this classification, some letters are called *poisonous*, others *deadly*, a third class *fiery*, a fourth *quarrelsome*, and a fifth *causing banishment*. On the other hand there are others called *prosperous*, some *pleasure-giving*, a third and fourth class *health-giving* and *friendly*, and a fifth *divine*; while a few are called *neutral*. Then again, these letters, when arranged and combined in a certain order, have different virtues—virtues much stronger, than those of single letters. Each of these combinations of letters is sacred to a certain demon, for whom it has an unaccountable, mysterious, and irresistible fascination, from which he cannot free himself. The mysterious virtues of all these combined characters in a charm, are sufficient to overpower and enslave the most powerful demons to the will of the Cattadiya. ("On Demonology," p. 53)

Mantrayas consist therefore of characters (*akuru, akṣara*) which are "brought together" (*ek karanavā*). The *mantraya* is a "word group" (*vaccana mālāvak*) made from this arrangement of characters (and on the account of the discourse of *yakku*, we saw in chapter 6, a word group derived from the Buddha's very sermons). And the efficacy of a *mantraya* lies not in the "intelligibility" of the language used—that is to say, whether the *ädurā* can give a coherent definition of the words he utters is immaterial, to him at least and to his practice—but in the *arrangement* of the characters that constitute the text, and particularly of certain of these characters called *ghana akṣara* or auspicious characters (for instance: *ōn, rīn, srīn, an*; these must be combined with other characters).

It would perhaps be more accurate to say here, though, that it is the *potential* efficacy of the *mantraya* that lies in the arrangement of the characters in the text, because the real efficacy of a *mantraya*, I think, is more properly understood to lie rather in the *relationship* between that, as it were, merely textual arrangement and the *sound* of the human voice (*haṇḍa ṣabdaya*) giving utterance—and therefore, most importantly, *energy*—to it. This sound is understood to impart to the characters that constitute the *mantraya* text what one might call a sound- or sonic-energy, a vibration, or to use a more Sinhala metaphor, the adhesive force of an *ākarṣana*.[14] The nature of this energy is of course one we have encountered before in connection with the *dōṣas* discussed in chapter 1: it is that of "life breath" or *prāna*, which is, I have said, essentially a function of the bodily humor of *vātaya* or wind. *Vātaya*, the bodily instance of the cosmic principle of movement, is, so to put it, the medium in which the *mantraya* works. (Now it will be understood why the *ädurā* blows as he utters the *mantraya*.) And so yet again we have an instance of that very fundamental notion of a constellation of energies in the moral world of Sinhala Buddhists that work their effect on each other.

This becomes clearer, I think, in the notion of the necessity of "vitalizing" *mantrayas* in the technique known as *jīvam kirīma*. In order to perform the work for which they were designed—in the instance at hand, summoning *yakku*—these charms have first to be "endowed with vitality." "Though a charm be ever so good in the number and proper disposition of those peculiar combinations of letters we have already mentioned," continues Gooneratne, "and though it be complete in all other respects, yet it can have no power for any practical purpose, unless it be subjected to a certain process or ceremony called JEEWAMA, which literally means, 'the endowing with life.' This it is that makes a charm efficacious for good or for evil" ("On Demonology," p. 56). As I observed it in the Matara area, this is indeed the case, and *jīvama* is perhaps most often—though not necessarily—a separate technique outside *yaktovil*. I can think of several occasions when, arriving at an *ädurā*'s house, I was told that he was in the middle of a *jīvama* and thus could not immediately be disturbed.

The procedure itself is of varying danger and complexity (depending on the object of the *mantraya*: vitalizing a *mantraya* to cure a headache is, as Gooneratne says, an altogether different matter than vitalizing one to cause death), but usually it involves repeating the text of the *mantraya* without interruption an auspicious number of times—first 108 times, then 21, then 7, for example—so that the energy or vibration or *ākarṣana* of the words imparted through uttering them strikes the smoke of the *dummala* or resin as it rises from the fire pan. It is, as one *ädurā* put it, when the *mantraya* is said that the auspicious characters are fixed in it (*mantraya kiyanakoṭa tamayi ghana akṣara pihiṭuvalā tiyenavā ē mantrayē*). In his reflections on the matter, Piyasena suggested what I take to be the more general cultural principle involved—that is, the relationship between the energy of sound and the production of effects—when he said that vitalizing a *mantraya* is in a certain sense merely the literal *utterance* of the text, which, before it is given voice, is useless. In their ordinary state, he said, the characters in a *mantra* book are dead characters (*mala akuru*) written in a dead book (*mala pota*); dead characters written on a paper that has no life (*prānayak näti kolayak liyapū mala akuru*). These characters cannot go anywhere (*kisima gaman kirīmak ē akuraṭa bā*). Thus by itself the *mantra* book is a dried leaf, lifeless (*vēlicca kolayek, aprānika*):

> *Jīvama* is the system that is used to take work from these characters (*mēken väḍaganna kramayaṭa tamayi jīvama kiyanne*). It is having taken from that book we keep it in our mind (*etakoṭa ē poten aragena tamayi api hadavata tänpat karaganne*). Those few words have to be put together at the place where the *gurukama* is being performed. What is meant by saying charms is reading those few (*kiyavanne ē ṭika*). When it is said, due to the sound made by those *ispillas*, *pāpillas*, *rēpayas*, and *kombuvas*, the binding is done.[15]

Note too that by performing *jīvama*—by combining (*galapanavā*) or fixing (*pihiṭuvenavā*) the characters by means of the sound of the voice—*yakku* are bound. The point, then, is that the "summoning" and the "binding" of *yakku* are actually sides of a single operation because it is this procedure of vitalizing a *mantraya* that ensures it the power to secure control of *yakku*. (Piyasena went on later to suggest two other instructive examples of the general principle or method [*kramaya*] involved in *jīvama*. The first was the example of a child with a schoolbook. Until the book is "read" by making sounds touch the words, what is written there on the page is without power [*bala nätuva*] and the book therefore is merely a "dead thing" [*mala deyak*]. Understanding, therefore, like so much else, is an effect that depends on the movement of energies. The second, more vivid still, involved the use of filthy words [*kunu vaccana*]. These too, said Piyasena, are characters. But they only become harsh [*sära*] when they are used to abuse [*baninavā*], because then they actually "hit" the ear [*kanaṭa gahanavā*].)

In this part of the Consecration of the Four Offering Stands, then, the presence of *yakku* is "summoned" to the *yaktovil* and "bound" by uttering *mantrayas* that generate the presence of their malign eyesight. It is an engagement of the first importance if the work of *yaktovil* is to be performed and its strategic objective achieved.

Kavi Kīma. Once the presence of *yakku* has been summoned to the *yaktovil* proceedings by the *diṣṭi mantrayas,* they have been "bound" to a work. This in itself is half the task accomplished. What summoning *yakku* does not itself ensure—at least not entirely—is that the *yakku* will not resist, will not be uncooperative. Two techniques are employed in this sequence to *encourage* the compliance of *yakku*. They are both embodied in verses, *kavi*. The first of these are verses that seek the assistance (*pihiṭavenavā*) of some relatively minor god or gods—such as Mangara *deviyō*—who have delegated jurisdiction over various *yakku*. These are called *kannalavva,* invocations, supplication. The following example of *kannalavva* is taken from those recorded for a Mahasōn Samayama by the late Michael Egan:

> More than five thousand people said, "sadhu, sadhu," and worshipped. Some worshipped by bowing down, some by bowing their bodies, some joining their hands together bent in worship, some worshipped holding their right hand up, others worshipped holding up the left, some worshipped with their hands raised together over their hands; all having taken permission to perform ceremonies in this world or in another.
>
> To you Lord god Siddha Mangra, to you who has the mark of a conch shell on your foot, the mark of the moon on your forehead, the mark of

> the rainbow on your right shoulder, you who trace your line from the sun, we offer this prayer of supplication.
>
> O venerable Siddha, in the name of this invalid, I, the ädurā, after having cleaned my hair, having brushed my teeth, having stood on a bed of nā [ironwood] leaves, and then on a bed of bō leaves, and finally on a bed of beautiful flowers, and then having bathed, now stand purified in front of you to perform this supplication.[16]

The second technique involves singing verses about (and for) *yakku*. As I said in chapter 1, *yakku* are beings much given to the enjoyment of song and dance. These verses are designed to, as it were, accommodate this predilection for entertainment. Singing verses (*kavi kiyanavā*), it is important to understand, does not "bind" *yakku*. Whereas there are in fact verses that have a power similar to that which *mantrayas* possess—*sirasapādaya*, for instance—praise verses (*āsīrvāda*) do not. They serve rather to appease (*sansiňdu karanavā*) and flatter (*iccā karanavā*) them. So that typically these verses address *yakku* in high terms (giving them titles such as Venerable [*vahanse*] or Great [*maha*] or referring to them as higher beings such as "godlings" [*dēvatāvas*]); representing them as beings born of high birth ("born from the womb of Maha Kalu Kiri Amma"); exhorting them in sometimes imploring tones to accept the delicious offerings being made to them and make the ill person well, and so on. The following are fragments of praise verses for Kalu Kumāra or Kalu Yaksayā, again taken from Michael Egan's collection:

> Queen Karanda Banada lived in a
> great grass palace,
> That grew upon a rocky island,
> Somewhere across the Seven Seas.
>
> In that palace,
> Queen Karandu Banada conceived
> a child,
> And after 10 months,
> A prince was born.
>
> Seven months later,
> This prince was publicly given
> The name of
> Maha Kalu Dēvatāva.
>
> Daily growing,
> Shining like the new moon,

With the god Ridī, he observes
the human world,
Looking from afar through his
divine power.[17]

And so on. The point of the *āsīrvāda kavi* is to gain the cooperation of the *yaksayā*, to encourage him to have pity on the *āturayā* and to take away the afflictions he has caused.

Pidēnna Dīma. It remains now to describe the concluding sequences of the Kattrīka Hatara Käpakirīma in which the actual offerings are given to *yakku*. Two questions interest me here. First, how precisely does the practice of giving offerings effect the removal of the disturbing affliction? And second, how are these offerings actually taken by the *yakku* to whom they are given? The answer to each of these questions turns, as the reader will no doubt anticipate, on the nature of *diṣṭiya* and its relation to other practices: in the first its relation to the practice referred to as "*mūna ata pisa gäsīma*" ("the wiping of the face with the hands"); in the second, to that known as "*sēman gänīma*" (which I will gloss roughly as "the feasting with the eyes").

Mūna ata pisa gäsīma: All illnesses, I have already said, involve a disruption of the three humors (*tun dos*) of which the body is constituted and which regulate its functioning. What the person who has been afflicted by *yakku* actually suffers from is a specific kind of humoral agitation or imbalance caused by the *diṣṭiya*. The *diṣṭiya*, to use one *ädurā*, Saraneris Appu's, wonderfully vivid metaphor, "wraps" (*paṭalanavā*) the "blood element" (*lē dhātu*) in the body, and disturbs the homeostasis of the humors. *Yaktovil* must therefore be concerned not only with getting *diṣṭiya* "out of the way" but with removing the *dōṣas* caused by the *diṣṭiya*—moving them from the head down to the feet, and from there out of, or perhaps, off of the body.

The technique known as "wiping the face with the hands" is, it seems to me, one of the most significant operations in the whole of *yaktovil* practice. This is a procedure by means of which the *dōṣa* is systematically removed from the body of the *āturayā*. As I described it in the Iramudun Samayama and Maha Kalu Kumāra Samayama (chapter 3), it is always situated at those crucial moments in *tovil* practice when offerings are being made to *yakku*. It consists of a number of repeated actions each of which is highly significant. After the *ädurās* have sung the "head-to-feet" verses (*sirasapādaya*), the tray (*taṭṭuva*) with offerings for a *yaksayā* is held before the *āturayā* by a *tovil* assistant. The *āturayā* places the requisite offerings (coins [*pañḍuru*], and flowers and betel leaves [*mal bulat*]) in the tray, and having done so, she (in the case I described) brings the palms of her hands up to her face (*mūna*) and, with a motion downward so that they pass over the length of her body, brings them to rest momentarily on the outstretched tray. This action is repeated three times as the *ädurā* utters the significant phrases, the last and most important of which the *āturayā* must also repeat with him:

> *Daha maha dōṣa nivārnayi* (The ten great troubles are finished)
> *Asū maha dōṣa nivārnayi* (The eighty great troubles are finished)
> *Kōṭiyak dōṣa nivārnayi* (The million troubles are finished)
> *Tīnduyi, tīnduyi* (Finished, finished).

It is necessary to repeat this entire procedure, "wiping the face with the hands," on every occasion on which some item is being passed on, that is, offered, to *yakku*. So that, for instance, it concludes all offering sequences including those when the cock is touched in the same manner as the *taṭṭuva*; during the *avamangalle pidēniya* when the red cloth is passed to the *ädurā* by the *āturayā* after she has passed it down her body; and similarly during the penultimate sequence of *yaktovil*, Baliya Pāvādīma, when the curtain (*kaḍaturāva*) is thrown over the clay effigy again after the *āturayā* has passed it down her body. Its importance, in fact, is such that whereas many procedures in the *tovil* can be accomplished with the *āturayā* asleep—"generating *diṣṭi*," for instance, or singing the verses (*kavi kiyanavā*) that recount the origin of a *yaksayā* or some item such as the mat—this one requires that the *āturayā* be awake and actually complete the procedures *herself* as required. No one else can make the offerings for her, or repeat the significant words, "*tīnduyi, tīnduyi*" ("it is concluded, it is concluded"). I witnessed many occasions when an *āturayā* would be roused insistently from sleep to "wipe the face with the hands."

This procedure—"wiping the face with the hands"—rests on a number of principles the elements of which we have already discussed, principles that have to do with the nature of the Sinhala body and with the nature of illness. First of all, it will be noted that "wiping the face with the hands" typically follows the "head-to-feet" verses (*sirasapādaya*). These verses, as I indicated in chapter 1, are sung in order to make the *dōṣa* descend (*dōṣa bassanavā*) from the upper to the lower regions of the body. *Sirasapādaya* literally means head (*sirasa*) and feet (*pādaya*). One *ädurā* explained that the *dōṣa* moves downward from the head (*isa*), the forehead (*nalala*), the two eyes (*äs deka*), the mouth (*mukaya*), the cheeks (*kammula*), the neck (*bella*), the two shoulders (*devura*), the two elbows (*devälamita*), the ten fingers (*dasängilla*), the chest (*lamäda*), both sides of the body trunk (*dävara*), the stomach (*baḍa*), the hip (*ukula*), the genitals (*rahasa*), the thighs (*kalava*), the shanks (*kenda*), the two ankles (*devalukara*), the instep (*piṭi patula*), the ten toenails (*dasaniya*). The following are the first and fifth stanzas of a *sirasapādaya* collected by Michael Egan:

> Having obtained varam from King Vessamuni,
> He grabs humans and with great glee makes them sick;
> O honorable, handsome prince,
> Please expel all the diseases from the head.
>
> Lurking near ponds where people bathe,
> He makes them delirious and insane.
> Think of the command and great power of dēvaguru Buddha,
> And without fail expel all the diseases you have caused
> from the neck.[18]

Sirasapādaya are sung therefore in order to make the *dōṣa* descend from the upper to the lower regions of the body. Second, the verses make reference to the virtuous commands (*aṇaguṇa*) of the Buddha, and these have efficacious effects. In two senses: on the one hand, generally the invocation of the Buddha has the beneficial effect of exercising some control over *yakku*—the Buddha as the embodiment of the Truth; on the other hand, as I discussed in chapter 1, the inverse side of the *varama* that the Buddha allowed *yakku* is his *aṇaguṇa*, and *yakku* are bound to "listen" to and "obey" his commands. As one *ädurā* put it, these verses address *yakku*, telling them that having seen the *dola pidēni* that is being offered, and having been satisfied (*santōsavelā*), they should come flying from the head (*sirasin igila varen*) at the order (*aṇa*) of the Lord King Buddha (*budurujānan vahanse*).[19]

Sēman gänīma: Even after the *diṣṭiya* or malign eyesight is "summoned" by means of the *diṣṭi mantrayas* from the eight corners and "bound," however, it itself must still be prepared in yet other ways for the work it is to perform. The procedures by which the *diṣṭiya* is prepared are of intricate complexity involving several stages of charming, each one having a specific emphasis. Essentially, however, the *diṣṭiya* which is summoned and bound has also to be given "life" (*prānaya*). And this introduces another concept indispensable to the practice of *yaktovil*, the concept of *sēman gänīma*, or "the taking of *sēman*." Often in the course of certain sequences of *yaktovil*, specifically those in which the afflicted person is entranced and "dancing and singing," the *ädurā* will be heard to admonish him or her sharply, saying, *sēman ganna vitarayi!* ("take *sēman* only!"). This concept of "taking *sēman*" turns on the relation between offerings (*dola pidēni*) and *diṣṭiya*.

As we have just seen, one of the principal constituent practices of *yaktovil* involves making offerings to the *yakku* responsible for the affliction of the *āturayā* and whose presence is summoned to the *tovil* proceedings. A *taṭṭuva* or tray of offerings (*dola pidēni*) will generally consist of a small measure of rice (*bat*), vegetables (*elōlu*), a mixture of leaves, coconut, salt, chili peppers, and rice (called *mällun*), *roṭi* (a kind of bread), sesame seeds (*tala ätē*), green grams (*mun ätē*), paddy seeds (*vī ätē*), dry fish and meat (*goḍa diya mas*), an assortment of roasted foods (*puluṭu*), several kinds of sweets (*kävili*), and flowers (*mal*). But recall that *yakku* can only be made present in their malign eyesight, in their *diṣṭiya*. And indeed, strictly speaking, it is only *diṣṭiya* that is present at *yaktovil* ceremonies. Therefore it is *diṣṭiya* that must somehow "take" the offerings that are presented. And in order to do so it must be given "life" (*prānaya*). This endowment of *diṣṭiya* with "life" consists in fact in a grant of permission (*avasaraya*) to take the offerings, and thus again inscribes the authority of the *ädurā* over *yakku*. As Piyasena remarked, "giving life (*prāna karanavā*) means this person [the *yaksayā*] is given a permission to eat this (*avasarayak denavā mēka kanna*). . . . If he is not told to eat he doesn't have permission (*eyāṭa avasara nā̄ nokivvot kanna*)."

The taking of the offerings by means of the malign eyesight or *diṣṭiya*, then, is what is referred to in the curious but important phrase *sēman gänīma*. This richly colloquial phrase actually has the sense of "feasting with the eyes."[20] Note again the metaphor of eyesight. The satisfaction given to *yakku* is, like the perpetration of their malevolent actions, restricted to the register of eyesight. The *diṣṭiya* of the *yakku*, having been summoned, bound, and endowed with life, is authorized by the *ädurā* to "feast" on the offerings but only by "imbibing the taste" (*rasa uranavā*). As Piyasena put it, "Having come to this place and climbed up [i.e., upon the stands holding the offerings] the vitality (*ōjasaya*)[21] of it, the taste that it has, is imbibed (*mēke tiyenne rasaya uranavā*)."

Interestingly enough, while the phrase *sēman gannavā* appears not to have a wide and frequent application, it is at the same time not unknown in *gämibhāsāva* (village or colloquial speech). Its connection here (with food again providing the basic image) is with desire (*āsāva*) for something which cannot be actually taken and eaten, and so has merely to be looked at.[22] So, for instance, a person hovering about casting covetous glances at the food one is eating may be confronted abrasively with the question: "Are you waiting expecting to take the *sēman* of this (*mēke sēman ganna balan innavā da*)?" In this case the hapless person is left to satisfy his or her desire by imbibing the "tasty" appearance of the food.

It should be clear from the foregoing that this sequence, Kattrīka Hatara Käpakirīma, is a comprehensive one. It is obviously not the whole of *yaktovil*, but in the engagements that comprise it—those of using *mantrayas* and making offerings in particular—it embodies a major part of its strategy of removing the afflictions, the *diṣṭiya* and *dōṣa*, caused by the *yakku*.[23]

Āvēśa and Questioning *Yakku*

The ability of *yaktovil* (or any *gurukama* for that matter) to accomplish the removal of *diṣṭiya* and *dōṣa* and to create the conditions for the restoration of a pleased and calmed mind depends in turn on the ability of the *ädurās* performing its sequences to make *yakku* heed the *aṇaguṇa*, the virtuous commands, of the Buddha. *Yakku*, recall, exist by virtue of the *varama* ("warrant") they obtained from the Buddha and which they exercise within the jurisdiction of King Vessamuni. This *varama* allows them, at certain periods, to cast their glances (*bälma*) on people, thereby making them ill. But the "warrant" also clearly stipulates that this allowance is wholly conditional, that it rests on the understanding that having afflicted people with troubles, they "listen" to—that is, obey—the *aṇaguṇa* of the Buddha, accept the offerings made to them by the afflicted persons, and remove their malign influence.

However, *yakku* are a notoriously unruly, intractable, and intransigent group of beings. They are, as we have seen, the very incarnation of what has not been tamed by the Law or Dhamma. Moreover, they are insatiable in their greed ("Lord," says Kālī, to the Buddha, "formerly I ate living beings just to satisfy my stomach and yet I was never full");[24] and they are incorrigibly wrathful, seeking at all costs to satisfy their chief craving, which is for human flesh and blood. While impermissible and outside the parameters of the *varama* they received, anything short of flesh and blood is disagreeable to them, and obstinate as they are, they resist. In consequence, *yaktovil* is ever a field of contestation of forces: *yakku* on the one hand, greedily seeking flesh and blood or their nearest equivalents; and *ädurās* on the other, seeking to compel them to make do with what is being offered—the *pulutu*, or burnt offerings. The strategy of *yaktovil*, therefore, entails finding the means of getting the better of *yakku*. In the confrontation each side is often forced to compromise. And as a result the actual outcome of a *yaktovil* ceremony can never be a foregone conclusion. Indeed, where *ädurās* are unable to make *yakku* heed the authority of the Buddha and remove their influence, a *tovil* may be unsuccessful.

It is this notion of *yaktovil* as a field of contestation of opposed forces, and as the putting into play of a strategy by means of which to secure the best possible outcome in the encounter with *yakku*, that makes the case of Lila Amma—described in chapter 3—so interesting. For Lila Amma's case is an instance where there is *both* success and failure, where in fact compromise has come to constitute the permanent condition of ceremonies performed for her. The case therefore nicely illustrates the idea that *yaktovil* entails a confrontation of "antagonistic wills" in a situation where the balance of forces is fluid enough to make for surprises. In this case the *ädurās* were able to "bind" *yakku* to their will, but only after a protracted series of "engagements," and even then, only partially so.

Recall the circumstances: in the course of the performance of a Rata Yäkuma for a pregnant Lila Amma now more than thirty years ago, one of the *ädurās* involved worked a piece of sorcery (*kodivina*) on her. I have already explained what this is. Such was the degree to which the *yakku* (the Iramudun Rīri Yaksayā and the Maha Kalu Kumāraya in particular) were "bound" to their malevolence by the *mantrayas* employed—in short, such was the strength of the sorcery—that it could never be totally undone. At best, only one "side" of it could be "turned," and even this would require a certain amount of skill. At the outset, the then young but already well-known and widely regarded *ädurā*, Äddin Lokuvela, was able to get the *yakku* to leave Lila alone for three years—to "turn" one side of the sorcery, in other words, and to "bind" the *yakku* to a *kāla sīmāva* or "time limit" of three years. Given the nature of sorcery, this in itself was a substantial victory. Subsequently, and apparently only after great effort, Äddin was able to get the *yakku* to agree to a longer *sīmāva*—a duration of respite lasting five years. By the time of the *tovil* ceremonies I described (October 1987), this five-year *sīmāva* had been in force for many years—and many *tovils*—and Äddin, not getting any younger (as he said himself), was keen to encourage the *yakku* to keep their influence at bay for longer than this period. This, then, was a major object of the *tovil*. What I want to be concerned with in this section is an examination of the rhetorical techniques by means of which—in those sequences in which Lila Amma was questioned by Äddin—this strategy is carried into effect. How is this confrontation staged? What knowledges of *yakku* are brought into play?

In these sequences, as I explained, a condition of *āvēśaya* is induced in Lila Amma by means of techniques used to intensify the presence of *yakku*, to intensify, in other words, the presence of their *diṣṭiya*. It is a condition, I said, induced in order to elicit a certain kind of speech from her. When questioned, she is said to speak *with* the *āvēśa diṣṭiya* of *yakku*. In the sequences I described, when this condition of *āvēśaya* was induced, the *ädurā* utilized various rhetorical strategies to determine (1) whether the offerings were satisfactory, (2) whether the Buddha's virtuous commands (*aṇaguṇa*) were taken as valid, and (3) whether the *yakku* could be persuaded to extend the period during which Lila Amma was untroubled by their *diṣṭiya*.

Once the condition of *āvēśaya* has been induced, the first thing the *ädurās* have to establish is whether the virtuous commands (*aṇaguṇa*) of the Buddha are accepted as valid by the *yakku* (and the other malign beings—*prētayō*, *bhūtayō*, and *bahīravayō*) who have afflicted Lila Amma's body. In a general sense, it cannot *not* be the case that the Buddha's commands are valid, but the *tovil* has to have a public acknowledgment (and the promise of compliance it entails) from the *yakku* themselves, as it were, that this is indeed the case. This having been ascertained (and recall that like almost every other procedure in *tovil* practice, this one is repeated at several points in the course of the performance), the *ädurā* then seeks immediately to find out whether the *yakku* would increase the *kāla sīmāva* or time limit of five years:

ÄDDIN: Now what I am asking is this. Aren't you going to go beyond five years (*avurudu pahen ehāṭa tamā yanne nädda*)?

LILA: NO.

ÄDDIN: Now my life has surpassed (*atikrānta*) its expectancy and is going to end. Since that is so won't you extend it beyond five years.

LILA: No.

Note the tone of sincere appeal, of entreaty. The *ädurā* makes out a case that he will not be alive much longer to keep making these offerings. Elsewhere, Äddin even asks for pity (*anu kampā karanavā*). But the *yakku*—again, the *diṣṭiya* of whom is the force by which Lila is giving these answers—are not moved to sympathy by the appeal and remain unwilling to extend the time limit. They are adamant that five years is their maximum. At this point the *ädurā* puts the matter aside for the while; or rather he undertakes a different path, by first determining whether the offerings of the night before—to *prētayō, bahiravayō*, and *yaksayō*—were accepted.

ÄDDIN: Now, were the rites and offerings that were given last night to the *prētayō, bhūtayō, bahīravayō*, and *yaksayō* accepted (*bāragattā da*)?

LILA: Yes.

ÄDDIN: Then, during this noontime period do you accept the rites and offerings that are being given to you?

LILA: Yes.

They were. In the combined Prēta Pidēniya and Bahīrava Pidēniya, the various malevolent beings involved in the affliction have accepted the offerings. But even so the "dancing and singing" are insufficient:

ÄDDIN: So have you done enough dancing and singing and so on (*nurtagīta ādiya karanavā*)?

LILA: Not enough (*madi*).

Yakku, as I said earlier, are creatures who delight in extravagant entertainment, and particularly "dancing and singing and so on." They seem indeed never to have had enough of it. But insisting on more of it—and again more of it—seems also to be their way of resisting the claims of the Buddha's *aṇaguṇa*, which in general they accept (since it is the very assurance of their existence) but which they ever seek to manipulate to their own advantage. So they seek to exact as much of it out of the *āturayā* as they can. And, in our case, driving her in the process near to exhaustion.

It will be recalled that this in fact was later—in the Maha Kalu Kumāra Samayama—the source of a highly interesting exchange between two *ädurās* and Lila Amma's daughter. This exchange is worth pausing over because it illustrates something of the way in which the stamp of the *ädurā*'s authority is visibly and sometimes dramatically imposed on the *tovil*'s proceedings. The daughter had been very concerned about her mother being made to "dance and sing" as often as she was since she suffered from high blood pressure, for which in fact she was receiving treatment. The *äduras*, Äddin in particular, were themselves concerned about her *preṣar*, but wanted to insist—and significantly, both to Lila's daughter and, more generally, to the audience—that the *tovil* could only be performed in the way they were undertaking it:

ÄDDIN: Now why I don't think I will harass you and make you dance and sing like on other days is because you have an illness in your body. Since that is so, have you performed enough dancing and singing and so on?

LILA: Not enough.

ARIYADASA: [*To Lila's daughter*] So you are telling me not to make her dance, not to make her perform dancing and singing and so on.

ÄDDIN: [They] are saying "don't (*epā*)!"

ARIYADASA: [We are] not to harass.

ÄDDIN: [*To Lila's daughter*] So you are telling me not to make her perform this dancing and singing and so on.

ARIYADASA: They are saying don't.

ÄDDIN: [*To the audience at large and emphatically*] She [i.e., Lila] is saying it is not enough. So I have to make her dance as much as she wants, no. It gives us a bad name, no (*ēka loku naraka nāmayak ne*). When it happens like that, having gone and performed the ceremony of blessing (*sāntiya*), this person can be made to lie down, no? Then it is not good, no? Now it seems that the dancing and singing is not enough. So let us perform and singing and so on a little more. You [all] don't be afraid (*baya venna epā*).

[*Then, turning back to Lila*] Now in the morning too I asked [i.e., about the dancing] because there is an illness in the body. . . . Early in the morning medicine was brought. . . . Now if the dancing and singing for the *yakku* who are in this body was done in the way you wanted, will the body be disturbed?

LILA: No.

ÄDDIN: There won't be any trouble at all?

LILA: No.

ÄDDIN: [*In a sympathetic voice*] You should dance as much as you want?

LILA: Yes.

ÄDDIN: Let go her hand.

The exchange was instructive for all because it positioned the *ädurās* both as humane, that is, interested in Lila's well-being, and as authorities in a practice whose successful outcome often necessitated temporary discomforts.

It must then be established at what times exactly the "dancing and singing" is going to be required, and also when the *yakku* are going to be satisfied and take their influence and depart of their residence:

ÄDDIN: Then, in the method of blessings (*śānti kramaya*) that is performed for that period, the rites having been performed, are you going to dance and sing and so on?

LILA: Yes.

ÄDDIN: At what time?

LILA: At 9:00.

ÄDDIN: At 9:00 you can't (*namayaṭa bā*).

Notice here the attempt to impose a restriction on the times for "dancing and singing" and thus to deny the *yakku* their desire. They want to dance at 9:00 P.M. The *ädurā* says it is not possible. The tone is no longer one of entreaty but one of stern, if nevertheless conciliatory, admonishment. The *yakku* insist, however. The *ädurā* yields:

LILA: At 12:00.

ÄDDIN: 12:00 at night, and. . . .

LILA: At 9:00, 12:00, and 3:00.

ÄDDIN: There is no dancing at 9:00, no. When these offerings are given at the *āturu pandala* (the *āturayā*'s shed), you will dance and sing and so on. In that case, it is during the dancing of the *mahā samayama pelapāliya* (the great ceremony of the procession) that, having gone to the *raṇamanḍala* (dancing area), you will dance.

LILA: [*Almost whispering*] Can't. [*Then more loudly*] At 9:00 also.

ÄDDIN: You want to dance at 9:00 also? Again?

LILA: At 12:00.

ÄDDIN: And again?

LILA: At 3:00.

These three times were the "dancing and singing" times in all the *tovils* in which I saw these sequences. However, the rhetorical strategy appears to be to suggest that the *ädurā* is yielding a position. It is as though it is, after all, not worth quarreling over, though the point is made to *yakku* that a gesture of compromise and appeasement can—but need not—be adopted. Lila Amma is "allowed" to dance at 9:00. However, it is still important to determine when the *yakku* are going to leave:

ÄDDIN: After that?

LILA: After that . . . ? [*a terribly querulous note sounding in her voice*].

ARIYADASA: The *diṣṭiya* . . .

ÄDDIN: At what time is the *diṣṭiya* being gotten rid of (*diṣṭiya maga häralā yanne koyi velāvaṭa da*)?

LILA: At 3:00.

ÄDDIN: Then, at 9:00 and 12:00 at night. . . .

LILA: At 3:00. . . .

ÄDDIN: At 3:00 . . . having danced and sung and so on. . . . It can't go at 3:00, no?

Again the *ädurā* insisting that too much is being asked for. But when Lila insists, again he yields:

LILA: At 3:00. . . . At 3:00 [*insisting breathlessly*].

ÄDDIN: At 3:00 [*conceding*].

LILA: [*Very weakly, barely audible*] Yes.

ÄDDIN: Then, before 3:00, the dancing and singing and so on must be done. At 3:00, the dancing and singing and so on having been finished, these *yakku* are going to their residence (*yakvimānaya*), having given up this interior (*mē abhyantarē at härala*). Aren't they?

LILA: Yes.

And once again the *ädurā* tries unsuccessfully to encourage a longer *sīmāva*:

ÄDDIN: They are going forever, aren't they (*jīvitāntaya dakvā yanavā ne*)?

LILA: [*Forcefully*] No.

ÄDDIN: No? I asked it jokingly (*kaṭa boruvaṭa ähuvaṭa*). It can't be said in that way, no. It is always at five years that they are going. Why?

LILA: That is the order (*ana*) that was given.

ÄDDIN: So it is definitely [only] at five years that they are going?

LILA: Yes.

There is apparently no way that the *sīmāva* is going to be changed.

Enough has been quoted to give a flavor of the range employed in the confrontation staged in the ceremony. As Äddin Lokuvela rightly says, offering flowers and lamps to gods cannot be for nothing. Something must be received in return – a point that nicely underscores the very practical, quid pro quo relation Sinhalas have with their gods. In this case, however, what is received turns out to be rather less than the *ädurās* would have liked, for it is in fact no more than has already been received for some time now – a *kāla sīmāva* of five years. For all the appealing and admonishing and the "dancing and singing and so on," the *yakku* steadfastly refuse to yield more than they have yielded before. Still, their techniques cannot be accounted a failure since they have, at the same time, achieved *no less* than has been achieved before. And perhaps—especially in view of the nature of the sorcery performed (the *ädurā* had made it clear that at best only one side could be "turned")—this in itself is something. Anyway, Lila Amma seemed to think so. After all, the *yakku* were successfully "bound" once again to remove their malevolent effects from her now aging body; and they had once again been deprived of what they would have most desired—her very flesh and blood; and they had of course once again been made to heed—at least with a modicum of fidelity—the virtuous commands of the Buddha.

The Pleasing of the Mind (*Hita Santōsakirīma*)

Finally, in the conduct of *yaktovil* the concepts of *diṣṭiya* and *dōṣa* are linked to another field of concepts that I have already discussed (in chapter 2) in relation to the ethics of composure and the well-being of the mind (*hita*)—those concepts, for example, of fright (*baya*) or sudden fright (*hadisibaya*), or sudden shock (*gassanavā*), or of course that elusive concept, which so often forms an intersecting point for these others, *tanikama*, which I have glossed as a vulnerable state of anxious apprehension.

I have suggested that maintaining the composure of the mind is important to everyday Sinhala life. A mind that has been shaken can have serious consequences for the well-being of both the mind and the body of the Sinhala person. Composure is a cultural value. Countless are the stories told of people suffering a fright and fainting, and no sooner were they roused and taken home than they had come down (to use an admittedly un-Sinhala metaphor) with a fever (*una*). With such a conception we can well appreciate the good sense of keeping one's mind in the tight safety of one's hand in circumstances in which one is in doubt as to the preservation of its well-being, its composure. The important point to grasp here is the central place of the mind in the regulation of well-being (*säpa-sanīpa*, literally, "happiness and health"). The malevolence of *yakku*, as I described it earlier, has an effect of transforming an anxious vulnerability (a *tanikama*) into a consuming worry, and consequently into a *dōṣa*. There then exists what Sinhalas often call a *leḍā-duk*: an illness-sadness. Thus not only does the precipitating *diṣṭiya* have to be controlled and removed from the body (by those remarkable techniques of manipulation and confrontation I have just discussed), but the mind has to be recomposed for well-being to be restored. This is what I suggest is the second target of *yaktovil*'s overall strategy. And it is in this sense of the practice that Piyasena's remark, noted earlier, has to be understood—that as a general concern the object of *ädurukama* is to inspire *seta*, that is, tranquillity of mind, or peace, or calmness.

Yaktovil, then, is about pleasing the mind (*hita santōsa karanavā*) of the afflicted person, about restoring to him or her "happiness and health." This restoration of well-being is the task of two kinds of technique in *yaktovil* practice: one is properly Buddhist; the other, though related to the first, is part, I think, of a broader Sinhala (perhaps South Asian) understanding of the relation between giving the senses—particularly the sense of sight—pleasure or delight and general well-being.

Significantly, the first of these techniques actually frames the *tovil* performance as such, being the first and last operation performed on any *tovil* occasion. The procedure I have in mind, of course, is that in which the *āturayā* holds the lamp—a powerfully evocative Buddhist metaphor—of the Hatara Varam Deviyō, the Four Warrant Gods of Buddhist Lankā, as she or he enters the performing area from the house at the formal beginning of the ceremony, or enters the house from the performing area at the formal end of it (see chapter 3). In this very brief, sometimes hardly noticeable procedure, lasting in fact no more than a few somber moments, an *ädurā* (usually the *maha* or senior *ädurā*, the one commanding most authority, and perhaps too the most merit) instructs the *āturayā* to fix her or his mind on the Buddha and on the four principal gods in the Sinhala Buddhist pantheon, that is Viṣṇu, Kataragama, Nātha, and Saman.

There is a passage in the thirteenth-century monk Dharmasēna Thera's story of Maṭṭakuṇḍalī (Flat-Earing) that is worth recalling here because it nicely illustrates the Buddhist principle underlying this procedure. In the story (picking it up some way into the narrative) the young son of a miserly Brahman lies dying on the porch under the eaves. He is beyond cure. The Buddha, meditating at the time, cast his Omniscient Eye of Compassion over the world and seeing Maṭṭakuṇḍalī decides to go to him. He approaches the boy, intending by his mere presence to give him tranquillity and enable him thereby to attain such merit as would furnish him with a rebirth in the Tavtisā heaven. And, as though observing the scene of this approach from elsewhere, Dharmasēna Thera writes didactically regarding the relation between the earnest mental evocation of the Buddha and the meritorious balm of tranquillity:

> Maṭṭakuṇḍalī saw the Buddha, who soothes the eye of those who look upon him, calms the mind of those who think of him, soothes the ear of those who hear him, whose goodness, acquired through one hundred million eons, was as if moulded together and sculpted into a single form. Then he thought, "Alas, because of the unfortunate association with my foolish father, for eight of the past sixteen years, I was unable to go to the Buddha, or worship him, or offer alms, or listen to a sermon. Now my legs are too weak even to walk up to him and greet him. Even if I were to get to him, my hand is already too stiff to lift in the gesture of worship. What else is there to do? At this point, since it is not too much effort to activate one's thoughts, I can at least make my mind tranquil. I will therefore do so." Thus, he made his decision and, though he was not destined to cure himself, he was destined to see the Buddha. He looked up, made his mind tranquil, and the purpose of the Buddha's visit was achieved.[25]

Or again, in the "story of the present" of the first *Jātaka*, the Buddha says to a group of his followers: "One thing there is, Brethren, which, if practiced and developed, conduces to utter loathing of the world's vanities, to the cessation of passion, to the end of being, to peace, to insight, to enlightenment, to Nirvana. What is this one thing?—The meditation on the thought of the Buddha."[26]

There are, it seems to me, three principles of Sinhala Buddhist understanding at work here. The first is the notion of the power of mental resolve: *adhiṣṭhānaya,* the idea that by fixing the mind on an object or goal real effects—mental and/or physical effects—will be produced. (This, recall, is also the principle involved in the fervent rebirth wish, *prārthanāva* discussed in chapter 1, and also in the vow—*pranidhānaya*—that one makes to obtain enlightenment or become a Buddha.) The second is the notion that by evoking (in a resolute, purposeful way) beings of inestimable virtue—first and foremost the Buddha (the store of whose virtue is of course an incalculable), and by extension those in a proximate relation to him like the Four Warrant Gods—the mind will be purified (*suddha kara gannavā*) and attain to tranquillity and composure. And third, the notion that tranquillity and composure are in themselves therapeutic, that is, that they make for "happiness and health" (*säpa-sanīpa*), in itself a sought-after Sinhala good. And this last reconnects us with the mind's relation to the bodily humors: a mind unsettled by fear or fright or worry will have unsettling consequences for the three humors that regulate the body's function; and conversely, a body whose humors are agitated will result in a state of mental unease. By the same token, a settled mind will be a condition for balanced humors, and balanced humors a condition for a calm mind. The lighting of the lamp for the Buddha and the Warrant Gods at the opening of the *yaktovil* ceremony, and at its close, therefore, is a technique that positions the practice within the larger strategic frame of a Buddhist psychology. Here it is *buduguṇa* not *aṇaguṇa* that is efficacious for the practice; it is the efficacy for a healing calm of the Buddha's presence, not the efficacy of his authority over the malevolent beings in the pantheon.

The other kind of technique for restoring the well-being of the afflicted person is that in which comic drama is employed. In all the major *tovils*—again, the one significant exception being the Iramudun Samayama—there are two main sequences in which comedy is employed for pleasing the mind of the *āturayā*: the Mangara Pelapāliya, in which there is a procession of comic acts, and the Daha-aṭa Pāliya, the procession or spectacle of the (formally eighteen but typically between eight and ten) figures (see chapter 3). As I indicated at the end of chapter 3, it is this sequence that has caught the attention of most anthropologists who have been interested in *yaktovil*, the general view being neatly summarized in AmaraSingham's handy phrase, "laughter as cure."[27] I myself, as we shall see in a moment, share the view that the sequence is of therapeutic significance, but I am less inclined to accord it the almost singular priority these scholars do in explaining how *yaktovil* accomplishes its work. It was in any case typically downplayed by the practitioners I worked with, who saw it as an entertaining but not indispensable feature of their practice. (Some spoke of it as a relatively recent innovation in *tovil* practice.) To be sure, comic drama has its role in inspiring what Piyasena called *seta*, but they constitute sequences that can without too much trouble be foreshortened when other contingencies—time, the need to question the *āturayā*—arise. What is indispensable, most insisted, to avert the danger (*upadravaya*) in which the *āturayā*'s life has been placed by the *diṣṭiya* is the ability to bind and control *yakku*, the ability to exert authority over *yakku* and make them heed the commands (*aṇaguṇa*) of the Buddha. And it is in the charming, invocation, and offering sequences that this strategic end is secured. Therefore, it seems to me more plausible to see such sequences as the Mangara Pelapāliya and the Daha-aṭa Pāliya not as negligible, to be sure, but as *one* distinctive kind of technique in an overall strategy to accomplish the aim of cure, and one, moreover, that comes into play at a moment when the primary work of controlling and binding *yakku*, and removing their *dōṣa*, has largely been effected.

By the Mangara Pelapāliya in Lila Amma's Maha Kalu Kumāra Samayama, most of the hard work of binding *yakku* is over. The main sequences concerned with the removal of *diṣṭiya* and *dōṣa* from her body—the offerings to the major *yakku*, the Däpavilla Pidēniya, the Därahäva Pidēniya, and so on—have been completed. However, the *yakku* have not yet completely removed their influence. They had indicated that 3:00 A.M. would be the hour at which they would do so. So a sort of anticipation hangs over this sequence, which otherwise is full of ribald humor. Once Lila Amma has hooted three times and been "bathed" with the seven pots of water, however, the *diṣṭiya* and the *dōṣa* are gone—*nivārnayi, tīnduyi*. Yet there is *gurukama* work left to be done. When Lila Amma returns to the performing area, dry and in fresh clothing, she seems less tense and there is an air of relief about her. And well she might be since the *yakku* have (in the turn of phrase used by the *ädurās*) returned to their residences with their afflictions—even though temporarily, for the space of five years. There is little left for her to do now but to enjoy the procession of comic figures. And indeed, the Daha-aṭa Pāliya, as it was explained to me, is like a show (*ṣō eka*) or a movie (*citrapaṭiya*), something to be watched and enjoyed in a secular sort of way. It is not a means of influencing *yakku*—whose malign presence has, after all, now been removed—but a form of entertainment (*vinōdaya*) to generate satisfaction (*santōsa ätivenavā*) in the *āturayā*, and to awaken in her joy (*prītiya*) and pleasure (*säpa*).

The conception underlying its practice would appear to be a more secular and inclusive version of the same principles as those discussed in relation to the lamp for the Hatara Varam Deviyō. Now clearly Lila Amma watching the comic antics of Pandam Pāliya or Salu Pāliya or listening to the punning obscenities of Kenḍi Pāliya, and delighting in them, is a rather different order of event than Maṭṭakuṇḍalī seeing the Buddha approach, but I think that the underlying conception of the relation between taking pleasure from the senses and the well-being of the mind is not a dissimilar one. The transcendent tranquillity and equanimity that Maṭṭakuṇḍalī attains from contemplating the Buddha's approach is, of course, derived both from the fact that the Buddha is the embodiment of moral perfection and from the earnestness and resolve with which he, Maṭṭakuṇḍalī, fixes his thoughts on him. But this perfection of the Buddha, it is important to see, is not merely an internal attribute (what Sinhalas would call *gatiya* or *gatiguṇa*) but is quite literally *embodied*, that is, is manifest on his physical person. For recall that Dharmasēna Thera says, in the passage quoted earlier, that the Buddha's "goodness, acquired through one hundred million eons, was as if moulded together and sculpted into a single form." So that the Buddha (with his thirty-two auspicious marks, according to other sources) is also—and in consequence of his vast merit—an embodiment of perfect *physical* beauty.

Thus one might say that there is a formal relation between the contemplation of the physical form of a figure and the potential wholesomeness or unwholesomeness of one's state of mind. Of course, not all physical forms are auspicious (*subayi*) in the sense of occupying some positive, proximate relation to the production of Buddhist virtues. But this by itself does not necessarily render them inauspicious (*asubayi*), at least insofar as they do not violate the basic axioms of moral conduct, the Five Precepts (see chapter 1). So whereas it goes without saying that a "show" like the annual Äsala Perahära in which the Buddha's Tooth Relic is paraded is "higher" than the Mangara Pelapāliya or the Daha-aṭa Pāliya (in the way, for instance, that, as one *ädurā* put it, *pirit* is higher than *mantraya*) in virtue of its proximity to the Three Jewels (*tun ruvan*),[28] and thereby lends a morally elevating tone to its effects on the mind of the observer, the latter too can have at least morally innocuous pleasing effects and can therefore be, as we might say, therapeutic. Which is merely to say that, for Sinhalas, to be free from worry and fear is a more wholesome psychological state than to be oppressed by them. For though these sequences may not purify the mind (*hita suddha kara ganna nove*) in the way a *perahära* could, nor indeed account for much—if any—positive merit, they are likely nevertheless to reduce the fear (*baya aḍu karanna*) and so doing make the "lifeless blood" (*apprānika vecca lē*) come alive again (*āyet prāna venavā*). And this, surely, for the pragmatic ethics of everyday Sinhala life, is no more than one could ask for. Or, to put it another way, to do so, to ask for more than the salutary delight in such secular performances—as Upatissa and Kolita did in the story of The Chief Disciples—Lila Amma would, like them, have to renounce altogether the mundane pleasure taken in "useless spectacles" and pursue the more rigorous search for *nirvāna*.[29]

This, as far as I have formed an understanding of it, is the strategy of *yaktovil,* and those of its techniques employed to carry its overall aim into effect in which one can see clearly the working of those indispensable notions of *diṣṭiya, dōṣa, varama, aṇaguṇa,* and so on that position *yakku* in the moral universe of Sinhala Buddhists. No doubt attention to a much wider field of concepts would throw further light on this strategy. Nevertheless, I think it should be clear how far the conduct of *yaktovil* forms a coherent structure, how far its practice is dependent upon an ensemble of ideas regarding both the nature of *yakku* and the source and element of their malevolence, and the nature of the bodies and selves of Sinhala persons who become their victims.

Conclusion

The course of this book's deliberations has not been the straight and narrow. I have sought to employ a strategy that combines a number of levels of investigation, and it may be as well to say here, by way of some concluding reflections, why I have thought them important, important anyway for the kind of critical anthropological inquiry that has seemed—and seems—to me worthwhile. It is as well in part because this book has attempted to articulate a criticism which is at once de-constructive and re-constructive, at once de-centering and re-positioning.

Perhaps the argument most central to the structure of this book's project derives from my complaint regarding the relationship typically holding between anthropology and the objects of its discourse. My complaint is that this relation is more often than not taken as unproblematic, such that the objects constituted in its discourses tend to be treated as self-evident, as transparent, as requiring no discussion, let alone interrogation—in fact, therefore, as not being *constituted*, properly speaking. It seems to me that even anthropological arguments which are (social-) historical in orientation tend to see themselves as recording the history of an object that is itself always already *there*, merely awaiting another, and presumably a better, inscription. So that the question of the constitution of the object as an object as such—that is, as a conceptual (and perhaps ideological) object of theoretical (and ideological) discourse—is one that does not arise. The kind of anthropological self-consciousness that this book has sought to embody is one that attends to this level of the *making* of anthropological objects. I have suggested that the main problem with books like Kapferer's *A Celebration of Demons*—and there are not a few of them—is not so much the colonial demonology it reproduces as that *because* its theoretical object is an uncritically constituted one, the recognition of this ideological reinscription is precluded.

It should be clear from this that one of the things that I am advocating in this book is a certain kind of anthropological historicity. This is not the familiar call for anthropology to be more historical, but rather that it admit a genealogical self-consciousness. The crux of my argument is that our concepts and our problematics—and thus the objects that get constructed in them—have histories. And it is only with an understanding of where the questions we ask are coming from, and how the kind of problematic that generated—and generates—them came to govern our thought about the practices constituted in them, that we will be able to ask ourselves whether we want to continue to raise these questions, to continue to try more adequately to respond to them, or whether we want to drop them, lay them aside, and construct new ones to respond to. One of the things that I have suggested is that the anthropological problematic of the great and little traditions, while it displaced something of the structure of what Philip Almond calls "Victorian Buddhism," and while, moreover (particularly in the work of Gananath Obeyesekere), it facilitated a rich archive of ethnographic description, nevertheless retained the colonial preoccupation with marking the distinction between an authentic Buddhism and spirit religion, of gauging the proximity between them; therefore, the question whether and to what extent Sinhalas are really Buddhists continues to pose itself. I have suggested that it would be fruitful to put this problematic aside, and to begin asking other kinds of questions, questions having to do with the ways in which Buddhists in Lankā make claims about what Buddhism is, the kinds of social and political projects into which the figures of the Buddhist tradition get mobilized, and so on. In any case, I think that we should leave it to Buddhists (speaking *as* Buddhists) to say what it is Buddhism *is*.

If we take seriously—as I think we ought to—the antifoundational argument that theory can offer us no final guarantees of certainty, that it too, like any other discourse, is local and situated and historical, that it finds what it finds (insofar as it can be said to *find* at all) in virtue of the questions it asks—if this is so, then it seems to me that the consequences for the way anthropology makes its object are such as cannot be ignored. For if the privilege that (anthropological) theory supposed itself to have vis-à-vis the (native) discourses it seeks to inquire into is but an empty boast, then the relation between theory and these discourses must now be thought of as a more lateral, and a less vertical, one. Theory can no longer look down, so to say, at local discourses as a way of finding out what it is these discourses think they are up to, but must engage them as one kind of narrative operating with certain kinds of categories seeking out other narratives operating with their network of categories. Of course, this is easier said than done. But part of the problem of putting this thought to work, I think, derives from the difficulty theory has in conceiving of itself and its work as being part of an interconnected tradition of such work. The antiauthority rhetoric of ruptures and discontinuities and breaks, subversive as it has been against that kind of inquiry which Alasdair MacIntyre calls "encyclopaedia," has contributed to an image of itself as a lone transgressive signifier, oppositional but sovereign, unmasking will to power, but itself unwilled.

However, it may be said with MacIntyre that it is only as part of "traditions" that rationalities—social and political and intellectual and religious rationalities—produce discursive problems, that is, discursive objects. Narrative (or discursive) traditions constitute what one might call the historical-discursive field or context of a discourse, the field of arguments wherein power and knowledge intersect, in which rival claims are contested, in which positions are established, negotiated, overturned, and so on. There is, in short, no discourse that does not inhabit the field of a tradition. And what I wish to suggest, therefore, is that the relation between anthropology and the discourses it inquires into might more usefully be understood as a relation *between* narrative traditions—between, in my own case, the narrative traditions of anthropology and the Buddhism of Sri Lankans.

If we come at the matter this way, then the sort of relation usually constructed between theory and ethnography is likely to be a changed one. Theory, on the view I am offering, will be less concerned to go in search of explanations for practices ("ritual") or conditions ("possession") based on elaborate preconceptions about cultural subjects derived from its own tradition, and more inclined to invent such concepts—that of "strategy," for instance—as will be more appropriate for understanding the work performed by local discourses and practices against the background of their own tradition.

This is how I take my discussion of the Sinhala discourse of *yakku*—for here I have been interested in the concepts (*prārthanāva, karma, varama, aṇaguṇa, dōṣa*) through which *yakku* are positioned in the Sinhala Buddhist universe they inhabit. More to the point of my argument, though, is my discussion of the concept of *diṣṭiya*, and my talk of a Sinhala ethics of composure. For if the whole problematic of "possession" is dropped, and with it the kind of body Western discourse supposes forms its support and its ground, then it is necessary to *begin* by asking what kinds of Sinhala concepts regulate the relation between *yakku* and Sinhala bodies. And this, I believe, is precisely the occasion for changing the field of ethnographic questions. It is here, as I have suggested, that the distinctive Sinhala conception of eyesight—eyesight as an obtrusive energy consisting of the moral essence of the being it emanates from—is important. But then, having established the medium of this relation, it is still necessary to ask what kinds of concepts of body and self are structured through this discourse about eyesight in general, and malign eyesight in particular. Now needless to say, these concepts form a complex ensemble, and I make no claim in this book to having exhausted them (nor even to having exhaustively discussed the ones I mention). But what I think is important is that the ethnographic topography—the discourse of *yakku*—here is inserted into a new theoretical problematic, one that—on my reading of it, anyway—prepares the space for a more satisfying analysis of what *yaktovil* is employed to get done.

On the view of the anthropological projects offered in this book, let me end by reiterating, anthropology's responsibility to work out and make explicit to itself its own history, its own discursive conditions and assumptions, the context of its own tradition, does not preclude that engagement with the traditions of others that has seemed distinctive and worthwhile about ethnography's way of going on; it only repositions that engagement, and by so doing tries to make it more responsive to a less presumptive field of questions.

Appendix

The Story of Iramudun Rīri Yaksayā

The most dreaded of Rīri Yakku or "blood" *yakku* is the one known as the Iramudun Rīri *yaksayā* (the blood *yaksayā* of the noontime). For this *yaksayā* there is a separate *yaktovil* called the Iramudun Samayama, which, as I suggested in chapter 3, is one of the most remarkable of this group of ceremonies. Here is one version of his birth story:

The Iramudun Rīri *yaksayā* was born in Säwätpuranuwara in Dambadiva. His mother was the Venerable Queen Rangiri (*Rangiri bisavun vahanse*, literally, the Venerable Queen of the Golden Rock) who lived at Ratran Māligāva (Golden Palace) in Säwätpuranuwara. One day, having conceived an affection (*premayak karanavā*) for the Divine King Sūriya (*Sūriya divyarājaya*), it occurred to her to go and see him. Ordinarily the Queen is not allowed to leave the Palace. But at any rate it occurred to her to go and see Divine King Sūriya at the time of the rising sun (*pāyan ira*). When this desire (*āsāva*) occurred to the Queen she informed the King, who ordered the servants to make preparations for the journey. The Queen was adorned with a red cloth (*rat saluvak*) and a divine cloth (*diva saluvak*), and so adorned she was presented to the Divine King Sūriya. In his presence she bowed, hands clasped in a gesture of worship and respect (*namaskāra karanavā*). She bowed three times. As a result of her faith (*ṣraddhāva*) a child was conceived in her womb (*darugäbak hatagattā*). After ten [i.e., lunar] months the baby was born. It was born during the auspicious time of *Anura* (an auspicious period). When it was born the King had the Brahmanas come to tell him what lay in store for the child. Having looked at the signs on the baby's body, they said, "King, this prince is a fiery one, he has the countenance of a *yaksayā* (*yakves*)." They said that they were unable to save him. The baby, however, was cared for lovingly.

One day at the age of seven the prince asked, "Who is my father?" But the Queen cannot say who his father is. There is no father (*tātta kenek nā*). Then the Queen realized that it was as a result of her gesture of worship to the Divine King Sūriya that the baby was conceived. She had been desiring (*āsāvakin sitiyā*) him. The child, however, insists on her telling him who his father is. And when she can no longer evade the question the Queen tells him that his father is the Divine King Sūriya. She says to him, "Son, go to the Sūriya Audience Hall (*maṇḍalaya)* and secure (*il-lagannavā*) a warrant (*varama*) from your father."

Then at the age of sixteen this prince, having dressed in a red cloth (*rat saluvak*), covered one side with a blue cloth (*nilavārna saluvak*), and, bearing a death crown (*mini ottuvak*) on his head, a *cakrayudhaya* (discus) in his left hand, a large sword (*loku kaḍuvak*) in his right, he set out for the Sūriya Hall. His height was about three *gavvas* (approximately twelve miles). The prince climbed to the top of the death mountain peak (*mini-kūta pārvataya*) and asked for and received permission (*avasaraya*) from the gods in the divine world (*divya lōkavala*) to go to the Sūriya Hall. The Sūriya Hall had four doorways. At the north doorway he called three times. The Divine King, looking out and seeing a beautiful prince (*lassana kumāraya*), asked who he was and where he came from. The prince replied, "I am Prince Kantarāma (*Kantarāma kumāraya*) who was born on your behalf (*oba venuven upan*)." He then asked Sūriya to give him permission (*varama*) to go with him when he travels on his *ratacakraya* (spinning vehicle). This permission was given. And from that harshness (*tadaga-tiya*) the prince became a powerful (*balagatta*) and dangerous (*napuru*) *yaksayā*.

The Story of Maha Kalu Kumāraya

The other *yaksayā* for which I provided a *yaktovil* description is the Maha Kalu Kumāraya, the Great Black Prince. It is sometimes insisted that there are three separate figures known as the Black Prince: Kalu Kumāraya, Sanni Kalu Kumāraya, and Maha Kalu Kumāraya, and sometimes that they are merely *avatāras* of one figure. In any case, his main victims are young, and often pregnant, women. The following is one version of the story of Maha Kalu Kumāraya told to me by S. A. Piyasena:

In the territory of Sandagana there was a *kōvil* (Hindu temple) called Sandagana. It was made of very beautiful rock (*alankara pārvataya*). There were blue lotus ponds everywhere. It was a beautiful place, like a divine city (*divya purayak*). Here lived a Queen named Murtu Māla. This esteemed Queen Murtu Māla, having gotten married, conceived a baby in her womb (*kusa darugäbak hatagattā*). When the baby was conceived a desire (*dola duk*) not to see beautiful women occurred to her. As a result, no woman could come to that province. It was a very dangerous wrath (*bohōma darunu krōdayak*) that was generated by the Queen. This Queen Murtu Māla had very good qualities (*guṇa yahapat*), was obedient (*kī karu*) and peaceful (*sānta*). But after this baby was conceived, because of the wrath, she could not bear the sight of beautiful women.

After ten [i.e., lunar] months a Prince was born. He was a resplendently beautiful Prince. When the child was born the King was told to name him and feed him rice. The Brahmanas were called to give an account of his future. What they told the King was very frightening. They said that when this Prince grows up he will act in a hostile manner (*antima naturukam karanavā*) toward pregnant women and beautiful women. In whatever way he can, he will destroy pregnant women and babies. This is what the Brahmanas said to the King. However, because he is a Prince nothing could be done. He had to be brought up. At the age of seven years he began hiding in places where beautiful women come and go. Seeing them, he would frighten them and make them ill. Seeing a pregnant woman, he would touch her stomach, and so doing the baby would be lost. Or if the baby was born it would be blue (*nil pāṭa gahenavā*). It would die. It was then that the name Maha Kalu Kumāraya was given to this Prince.

He started to destroy the whole country. And it was from then that he had to be supplicated to (*kannalav karanavā*) and given all sorts of food and drink. Only then could the ill effects (*dōṣaya*) be put an end to (*nirvāna karanavā*). And since then the ceremony (*yāgaya*) called Maha Kalu Kumāra Samayama was performed.

Notes

Introduction

1. I am thinking, for example, of Stanley Diamond, "Anthropology in Question," in *In Search of the Primitive: A Critique of Civilization* (New Brunswick, N.J.: Transaction Books, 1974), and "Theory, Practice, and Poetry" in *Theory and Practice: Essays Presented to Gene Weltish*, Studies in Anthropology 7, edited by Stanley Diamond (The Hague: Mouton, 1980). I find it both curious and telling that Diamond's name appears only once in George E. Marcus and Michael M. J. Fischer's *Anthropology as Cultural Critique: An Experimental Moment in the Human Sciences* (Chicago: University of Chicago Press, 1986), p. 74, and then in a wholly derivative connection.

2. Borrowing the conception of the "inscription" of social action from Paul Ricoeur, Geertz, "Thick Description: Toward an Interpretive Theory of Culture," in *The Interpretation of Cultures* (New York: Basic Books, 1973), asks and answers his "generative" question: " 'What does the ethnographer do?'—he writes" (p. 19). For anthropologists, Derrida's most influential contribution in this regard is his early collection, *Writing and Difference* (Chicago: University of Chicago Press, 1978).

3. James Clifford, "Introduction: Partial Truths," in *Writing Culture: The Poetics and Politics of Ethnography* (Berkeley: University of California Press, 1986), p. 2.

4. Marcus and Fischer, *Critique*, pp. 15–16.

5. One interesting attempt to think about this idea of "bounded" culture is to be found sketched in Arjun Appadurai, "Introduction: Place and Voice in Anthropological Theory," *Cultural Anthropology* 3(1)(1988):16–20.

6. Clifford, "Partial," p. 10.

7. I take this theme up in a little more detail in my "Criticism and Culture: Theory and Post-Colonial Claims on Anthropological Disciplinarity," *Critique of Anthropology* 13(4) (1992):371–94.

8. Edward Said, *Orientalism* (New York: Vintage, 1978).

9. Edward Said, "Representing the Colonized: Anthropology's Interlocutors," *Critical Inquiry* 15(1988):205–225.

10. Talal Asad, *Man* n.s. 14(1979):607–627.

11. I am thinking, for example, of "Anthropological Conceptions of Religion: Reflections on Geertz," *Man* n.s. 18(2)(1983):237–259; "The Concept of Cultural Translation in British Social Anthropology," in *Writing Culture*, edited by Clifford and Marcus; and "Towards a Genealogy of the Concept of Ritual," in *Vernacular Christianity: Essays in the Social Anthropology of Religion Presented to Godfrey Lienhardt*, ed. W. James and D. M. Johnson (Oxford: JASO, 1988).

12. See Alasdair MacIntyre, "Epistemological Crises, Dramatic Narrative, and the Philosophy of Science," in *Paradigms and Revolutions: Applications and Appraisals of Thomas Kuhn's Philosophy of Science*, ed. Gary Gutting (Notre Dame: University of Notre Dame Press, 1980), p. 63.

13. See Gananath Obeyesekere, *The Cult of the Goddess Pattini* (Chicago: University of Chicago Press, 1984), pp. 5–9.

14. See Senarat Paranavitana, *The Shrine of Upulvan at Devundara*. Memoirs of the Archaeological Survey of Ceylon, vol. 6 (Colombo: Ceylon Government Archaeological Department, 1953).

15. Quoted in João Ribeiro's *History of Ceilão*, trans. P. E. Pieris (Colombo: Colombo Apothecaries Co. Ltd., 1909), pp. 76–77.

16. Daniel J. Gogerly, "The Wesleyan Mission Station, Matura," *Friend* 1(4)(1837):101.

17. This was in fact a critical political period in Sri Lanka. On the one hand, the conflict between the Sinhalas and Tamils in the North and East of the island was escalating rapidly, and the Sri Lankan government was in the middle of talks with the Indian government on a solution. The negotiations led to a Peace Accord between Sri Lanka and India (signed in the wake of considerable Sinhala opposition), which brought an Indian Peace-Keeping Force to the island. In the event, and for reasons that cannot be entered here, the Accord was a failure.

18. See, for example, Gananath Obeyesekere, "The Impact of Ayervedic Ideas on the Culture and the Individual in Sri Lanka," in *Asian Medical Systems: A Comparative Study*, ed. Charles Leslie (Berkeley: University of California Press, 1976), and Bruce Kapferer, *A Celebration of Demons: Exorcism and the Aesthetics of Healing in Sri Lanka* (Bloomington: Indiana University Press, 1983), p. 37.

19. See Kapferer, *Celebration*, pp. 37–48, for a discussion of the sociology of performing troupes in the Galle area of the Southern Province of Sri Lanka. Otaker Pertold, who visited British Ceylon between 1909 and 1910, and again between 1919 and 1921, has written in his *Ceremonial Dances of the Sinhalese* (Dehiwala: Tisara Prakasakayo, 1930) that "at present the *Yakun-natima* is regularly performed by a single dancer, only exceptionally a whole band of demon-dancers being engaged. Financial reasons seem to be decisive for this reduction of the ceremonial apparatus" (p. 100). I was in fact told by one *tovil* performer (who was actually known more as a mask maker) that he only performs by himself, dancing being an unessential part of the practice of *tovil*. But, he went on, for this very reason, he is only rarely engaged, because people now do not feel that a *tovil* is a *tovil* without dancing. I never saw this man perform, however, nor did I ever see a *tovil* performed by a single performer.

20. Asad's article is to be found in the seminal volume, *Anthropology and the Colonial Encounter*, ed. Talal Asad (London: Ithaca Press, 1973); and Johannes Fabian, *Time and the Other: How Anthropology Makes Its Object* (New York: Columbia University Press, 1983).

21. Kitsiri Malalgoda, *Buddhism in Sinhalese Society, 1750–1900* (Berkeley: University of California Press, 1976).

22. David Pailin, *Attitudes to Other Religions: Comparative Religion in Seventeenth and Eighteenth Century Britain* (Manchester: Manchester University Press, 1984); and Peter Harrison, *"Religion" and the religions in the English Enlightenment* (New York: Cambridge University Press, 1990).

23. Almond's study (New York: Cambridge University Press, 1988), nicely compliments P. J. Marshall's *The British Discovery of Hinduism in the Eighteenth Century* (Cambridge: Cambridge University Press, 1970). John Carter's article appeared in *Religious Studies* 13(3)(1977):263–287.

24. See especially Talal Asad, "The Idea of an Anthropology of Islam." Occasional Papers Series (Washington, D.C.: Center for Contemporary Arab Studies, 1986).

Chapter 1. Situating *Yakku*

1. As Richard Gombrich, *Precept and Practice: Traditional Buddhism in the Rural Highlands of Ceylon* (Oxford: Clarendon Press, 1971), p. 60, suggests, *dhamma* can be and indeed has been translated in many, many ways—Doctrine, Truth, Law, etc.—and it is most often best left untranslated.

2. I do not aim to be exhaustive in my account. There are now several anthropological or anthropologically informed studies of the Sinhala Buddhist universe. Some of the more notable include Gananath Obeyesekere, "The Great Tradition and the Little in the Perspective of Sinhalese Buddhism," *Journal of Asian Studies* 22(2)(1963):139–153; "The Buddhist Pantheon in Ceylon and Its Extensions," in *Anthropological Studies in Theravada Buddhism*, ed. Manning Nash (New Haven: Yale University South East Asian Studies); *The Cult of the Goddess Pattini* (Chicago: University of Chicago Press, 1984); Michael Ames, "Magical-Animism and Buddhism: A Structural Analysis of the Sinhalese Religious System," in *Religion in South Asia*, ed. Edward B. Harper (Seattle: University of Washington Press, 1964), pp. 21–53; Richard Gombrich, *Precept and Practice*; Bruce Kapferer, *A Celebration of Demons: Exorcism and the Aesthetics of Healing in Sri Lanka* (Bloomington: Indiana University Press, 1983); Richard Gombrich and Gananath Obeyesekere, *Buddhism Transformed: Religious Change in Sri Lanka* (Princeton: Princeton University Press, 1988); George Bond, *The Buddhist Revival in Sri Lanka: Religious Tradition, Reinterpretation and Response* (Columbia: University of South Carolina Press, 1988); and John Holt, *Buddha in the Crown: Avalokiteṣvara in the Buddhist Traditions of Sri Lanka* (New York: Oxford University Press, 1991). My understanding of the moral universe of Sinhala Buddhists is indebted to these studies, and the reader will profit from considering them in conjunction with my account.

3. I am indebted in this paragraph to Gail Sutherland's recently published study, *The Disguises of the Demon: The Development of the Yakṣa in Hinduism and Buddhism* (Albany: State University of New York Press, 1991). This stimulating work, which has sought to take up and elaborate upon Ananda Coomaraswamy's much-neglected study *Yakṣas* (New Delhi: Munshiram Manoharlal, 1971), is immensely important for the light it sheds on the iconographic and literary background of the *yakkha* figure. Also very useful are O. H. de A. Wijesekera, "The Philosophical Import of Vedic *Yakṣa* and Pāli *Yakkha*," *University of Ceylon Review* 1(5)(1943):24–33; and M. M. J. Marasinghe, *Gods in Early Buddhism* (Kelaniya: University of Sri Lanka [Vidyalankara Campus] Press, 1974).

4. The *Jātaka* stories constitute perhaps the most popular part of the Pāli canon. They—the 550 stories of the births of the Buddha-to-be—are contained in the *Sutta Piṭaka*, the second "basket" (*piṭaka*) of the threefold canon. In connection with stories in which the *yakkha* figure is not especially malevolent (if, nevertheless, human-eating), and is indeed helpful to the *bōdhisattva*, see *Mahāsīlava Jātaka* [no. 51], in *Jātaka Stories*, 6 vols., ed. and trans. E. B. Cowell (Delhi: Motilal Banarsidass, 1990).

5. In connection with the etymology of the word *yakkha*, T. O. Ling, in his *Buddhism and the Mythology of Evil* (London: Allen & Unwin, 1962), says the following: "The word yakkha, which is one of the commonest terms for a demon, is explained by the Pāli Buddhist commentators as being derived from the root *yaj*, to sacrifice, so that a yakkha is understood as a being to whom a sacrifice is offered. The etymology may be unsound, but it indicates that there was some connection between yakkhas and sacrifice in common practice" (p. 19).

6. G. P. Malalasekara, *Dictionary of Pāli Proper Names* (London: Routledge and Kegan Paul, 1974), p. 293.

7. See Marasinghe, *Gods in Early Buddhism*, p. 282. This text is very useful for its discussion of the place of deities in early Buddhism.

8. Sir M. Coomaraswamy, trans., *Sutta Nipata or, Dialogues and Discourses of Gotama Buddha* (London: Trübner & Co., 1874), p. 47.

9. In a footnote to her English translation of this *sutta* in the *Samyutta Nikāya*, Caroline Rhys Davids gives this information: "That the questions and answers had been handed down by the yakkha's parents (who had them from Kassapa Buddha), written on a golden leaf (patta) in red ink, are a quaint feature in the legend" (*The Book of Kindred Sayings* [a translation of the Samyutta Nikaya], Part I, trans. Rhys Davids (London: Oxford University Press for the Pali Text Society, 1917–30), p. 276f.

10. Coomaraswamy, *Sutta Nipata*, p. 152.

11. The story, in this tradition, typically combines a main narrative plot (the "story in the present" in which are related the circumstances in the Buddha's life that led to the encounter), a "branch story" (set prior to the first and organized around a different plot), and finally a short didactic summary in which the Buddha connects the events in both stories by identifying the characters in one as those in the other in a previous birth. The strategy forms a highly imaginative way of illustrating key principles of Buddhist ethics. For a discussion see Ranjini Obeyesekere, "Introduction," *Jewels of the Doctrine: Stories of the Saddharma Ratnāvaliya* by Dharmasēna Thera (Albany: State University of New York Press, 1991), pp. xiii-xxiii.

12. See Robert Spence Hardy, *A Manual of Buddhism* (Varanasi: The Chowkhamba Sanskrit Series Office, 1967 [orig. 1853]), pp. 249–253, for one telling of the story of Aňgulimāla.

13. Charles Godakumbura, *Sinhalese Literature* (Colombo: Colombo Apothecaries Co. Ltd., 1955).

14. See Hugh Nevill, *Sinhala Verse (Kavi)* (Colombo: Government Press, 1954), vol. 1, p. 189, and vol. 2, p. 185. The stanza reproduced in the first of these, given in the title as "Alawu katā" or "Story of Alawu," is as follows:

> Daily I will give human victims two by two,
> One by one I will give a dish of rice,
> Bringing betel leaves fittingly, I will offer,
> If released, I will give the Yaka this sacrifice.

Godakumbura's remarks on the historical context of the poem are worth quoting also: "The present poem is of special importance, as it belongs to a century when learning in Ceylon was said to have been at a low ebb, and when literary compositions were rare. The language of the poem, although simple, is correct in idiom; its vocabulary is profuse and its style chaste. The narrative is very lively and dramatic, and is interspersed with beautiful descriptive passages" (*Sinhalese Literature*, p. 176).

15. Much the same story was told to me by the late Venerable Vijayananda of Devinuvara. See also Hardy, *Manual*, pp. 261–265. In neither of these, however, is there the significant narrative of the former births of Ālavaka, the King, and the prince.

16. See Sutherland, *Disguises of the Demon*, pp. 26–29, for a discussion of the belief in the Buddhist tradition of trees as the dwelling place of *yakkha* (*yakku*). In Sinhala, *ruk devi* is a name for a tree deity.

17. The Sinhala: "*Buduhāmuduruvō adhisṭhāna karalā paya tiyenakoṭa ē dora ärunā.*"

18. This is the first of the four stages that mark the path (*mārga, mārgaya*) to *nirvāna*. The

other three are: Once-Returner (who has a last birth as a human being), Non-Returner (who will not be reborn before achieving *nirvāna*), and the stage of the Purified One or Arhat.

19. See Ranjini and Gananath Obeyesekere, "The Tale of the Demoness Kālī: A Discourse on Evil," *History of Religions* 24(4)(1990):318–334. The story of Kālī is one of the stories in Dharmasēna Thera's thirteenth-century *Saddharmaratnāvaliya* (*Jewel Garland of the True Doctrine*), ostensibly a translation of the fifth-century Pāli work, *Dhammapadaṭṭhakata* or *Dhammapada Commentary*. It is, as Ranjini Obeyesekere writes in the Introduction to her English translation of it, *Jewels*, "one of the best-loved books in the Sinhala literary canon" (p. x). One of the interesting features of the Buddhist story tradition – no doubt a crucial didactic device – is its intertextuality. Thus, for instance, the Kālī story makes reference to the Prince Alavi of our Ālavaka story and to the Senior Monk Aňgulimāla.

20. There is a related Sinhala word, *pätuma*, which has both the sense of a request or petition or beseeching, and hope or expectation.

21. It may be worthwhile to bear in mind that Gombrich's discussion of *prārthanāva*, very useful though it is, is inscribed in a different project than is my own, namely that of measuring the distance or proximity between the actual practice of the Kandyan villagers among whom he lived in the middle 1960s and the orthodox precepts of the Doctrine. His astonishing conclusion is too well known, and has been the subject of too many arguments, to need repeating here.

22. See *Karma: An Anthropological Inquiry* (Los Angeles: University of California Press, 1983), ed. Charles Keyes and E. Valentine Daniel, for a good discussion of uses of *karma* in South and Southeast Asia.

23. For a good general discussion of the Buddhist concept of merit see John S. Strong, "Merit: Buddhist Concepts" in *The Encyclopedia of Religion*, vol. 9, ed. Mircea Eliade (New York: Macmillan, 1987). Another common way of influencing one's *karma* is to pay careful attention to one's astrology. On this, see Gombrich, *Precept and Practice*, pp. 146–149; and more generally, on the relation between astrology and other Sinhala conceptions, see Steven Kemper, "Sinhalese Astrology, South Asian Caste Systems, and the Notion of Individuality," *Journal of Asian Studies* 38(3)(1979):477–497, and "Time, Person and Gender in Sinhalese Astrology," *American Ethnologist* 7(4)(1980):744–758.

24. In Obeyesekere, *Jewels*, p. 88.

25. See Gombrich, *Precept and Practice*, and Strong, "Merit."

26. Dandris de Silva Gooneratne, "On Demonology and Witchcraft in Ceylon," *Journal of the Royal Asiatic Society, Ceylon Branch* 4(1865/66):19.

27. Gombrich, *Precept and Practice*, p. 166.

28. Ibid., p. 219.

29. Ibid., p. 252, where Gombrich mentions the belief among Sinhala Buddhists "in the strength of mental impulse." For this incident in the story of "The Senior Monk Nāgasēna," see Ranjini Obeyesekere, *Jewels*, p. 55.

30. "Demoness Kālī," in Obeyesekere, *Jewels*, p. 103.

31. For discussions of the inappropriateness of the concept of "evil" to the field of Buddhist moral discourse, see James W. Boyd, "Satan and Māra: Christian and Buddhist Symbols of Evil," *Modern Ceylon Studies* 4(1 & 2)(1973):84–100; Martin Southwold, "Buddhism and Evil," in *The Anthropology of Evil*, ed. David Parkin (Oxford: Basil Blackwell, 1985); and Obeyesekere and Obeyesekere, "Tale."

32. Lowell Bloss, "Nāgas and Yakṣas," in *The Encyclopedia of Religion*, ed. Mircea Eliade (New York: Macmillan, 1987), p. 294.

33. Obeyesekere and Obeyesekere, "Tale," p. 321.

34. Literally, "the island-mountain of *yaksayās*."

35. See Obeyesekere, "The Great Tradition and the Little," pp. 139–153, and "Buddhist Pantheon."

36. For a succinct discussion of the Four Noble Truths (and much else regarding Buddhist doctrine), see Walpola Rahula, *What the Buddha Taught* (New York: Grove Press, 1974).

37. Obeyesekere suggests that this concept of an "immanent Buddha personality or presence" may have its source in an ambiguity in the Canon itself regarding the nature of *nirvāna*. When a disciple asked the Buddha whether an *arhat* (i.e., one who has attained *nirvāna*) is alive or dead or both or neither, the Buddha did not answer. This is one of the "unanswered questions" of the Buddha, unanswered because such questions are unprofitable. Obeyesekere further suggests that it was perhaps never the case that this view or its corollary—that *nirvāna* is a "blowing out" or extinction of the personality—gained popular acceptance in Sri Lanka. For Sinhala Buddhists the Buddha is "alive" (see Obeyesekere, "Buddhist Pantheon," p. 8. See also Gombrich, *Precept and Practice*, p. 106).

38. Obeyesekere, "Buddhist Pantheon," p. 9.

39. Ibid., p. 26 n; and *Pattini*, p. 79.

40. Gombrich and Obeyesekere, *Buddhism Transformed*, p. 20. Obeyesekere has on many occasions emphasized the importance of numerology to Sinhala myths. See, for example, "Popular Religions," in *Modern Sri Lanka: A Society in Transition*, ed. Tissa Fernando and Robert N. Kearney (Syracuse: Maxwell School of Citizenship and Public Affairs, 1979), p. 206.

41. Vallī Ammā, the *kapurāla* of the Vallī Ammā *dēvālē* in Devundara said, is to secure marriages for young unwed women particularly, but men also. For a discussion of the relationship between Kataragama and Vallī Ammā, see Gombrich and Obeyesekere, *Buddhism Transformed*, pp. 165–166.

42. See also Gombrich, *Precept and Practice*, p. 188.

43. For an instructive discussion of Nātha and his relation to the Mahayāna Buddhist figure Avalokiteṣvara, see John Holt, *Buddha in the Crown*.

44. See Obeyesekere, "Buddhist Pantheon," p. 6, and "The Ritual Drama of the *Sanni* Demons: Collective Representations of Disease in Ceylon," *Comparative Studies in Society and History* 11(2)(1969):176.

45. The Three Refuges are as follows: "I go to the Buddha for refuge; I go to the Doctrine for refuge; I go to the Order for refuge." The Five Precepts are undertakings to abstain from (1) taking life, (2) taking what is not given, (3) wrong sexual conduct, (4) telling lies, (5) intoxicating liquors that cause immoral behavior. See Gombrich, *Precept and Practice*, p. 65.

46. Actually, the Ten Precepts—the Five Precepts plus five additional abstinences: (6) from eating solid food after midday, (7) from seeing musical entertainment, dancing, singing, and so on, (8) from wearing finery, (9) from sleeping on high beds, (10) from accepting money—may be taken without entering the Order, and are sometimes taken by the aged. See Gombrich, *Precept and Practice*, pp. 65–66.

47. Discussion of these changes is not immediately pertinent to my concerns here, and I would direct the reader to two recent studies of these developments: Gombrich and Obeyesekere, *Buddhism Transformed*; and George Bond, *Buddhist Revival*.

48. Obeyesekere, "Buddhist Pantheon," p. 10.

49. Obeyesekere, *Pattini*, p. 63.

50. One list of kinds of *prētayō* is as follows: *ganda prētayō* (who are smelly), *pubba prētayō*, *diga lōma prētayō* (who have long knotted hair), *astila prētayō* (who crave wealth), *pipāsika prētayō* (who are thirsty), *yana prētayō* (who desire to travel), *puksika prētayō*, *aksika prētayō* (who desire what they see), *kriṣṇa prētayō* (the *ädurā* had said there were eight but listed

nine). The most important, however—those to whom offerings are made—are said to be: *mala prētayō, ñāti prētayō, gevala prētayō,* and *kāku prētayō.*

51. In one *yaktovil* ceremony in which there was an involvement of *prētayō*, an *ädurā* said that *prētayō* are given to lying and in *tovils* such as this one should not believe everything the *āturayā* says when questioned.

52. For a discussion of this very important figure in contemporary—particularly urban—Sinhala ritual practice, see Obeyesekere, *Pattini,* p. 70; Gombrich and Obeyesekere, *Buddhism Transformed,* pp. 114–132; and Kapferer, *Celebration,* p. 117.

53. Gombrich and Obeyesekere, *Buddhism Transformed,* p. 121, suggest that Sūniyam became a personal guardian, an *iṣṭa dēvatāva,* of ritual specialists by the beginning of the twentieth century.

54. Obeyesekere, *Pattini,* p. 57.

55. *Namaskāraya* is perhaps more correctly understood here as a sign of gratitude (*sälakīma*).

56. See the story of Kālī (Obeyesekere, *Jewels,* p. 101) for an interesting representation of this relation between King Vessamuni and *yakku.*

57. Gooneratne, "On Demonology," p. 14.

58. See Gooneratne, "On Demonology," p. 20; and Obeyesekere, "Ritual Drama," p. 177.

59. As they were told to me they are: Aricci Sanniya, Ericci Sanniya, Kāla Sanniya, Kōla Sanniya, Gulma Sanniya, Vädi Sanniya, Vedi Sanniya, Gini Sanniya (who makes one feverish), Bhūta Sanniya, Abhūta Sanniya, Ävulun Sanniya, Vevulun Sanniya (who makes one tremble), Nāga Sanniya (who makes one see snakes), Kana Sanniya (who makes one blind), Kora Sanniya (who makes one lame), Bihiri Sanniya (who makes one deaf), Ädiri Sanniya, and Dēva Sanniya. See also Paul Wirz, *Exorcism and the Art of Healing in Ceylon* (Leiden: E. J. Brill, 1954), p. 44, and Obeyesekere, "Ritual Drama," p. 189.

60. See especially Obeyesekere, "Ritual Drama," and Kapferer, *Celebration.*

61. See Obeyesekere, "Ritual Drama"; "The Impact of Āyurvedic Ideas on the Culture and the Individual in Sri Lanka," in *Asian Medical Systems: A Comparative Study,* ed. Charles Leslie (Berkeley: University of California Press, 1976); and "The Theory and Practice of Psychological Medicine in the Ayurvedic Tradition," *Culture, Medicine and Psychiatry* 1 (1977):155–181. More generally, see Jean Filliozat, *The Classical Doctrine of Indian Medicine* (Delhi: Munishiram Manoharlal, 1964); and O. P. Jaggi, *Indian System of Medicine.* History of Science and Technology in India, vol. 4 (Delhi: Atma Ram and Sons, 1973).

62. These five elements, moreover, are manifest in the five senses: Ether is the medium of sound, and thus is related to hearing and speaking; Air is related to the sense of touch and thus to the region of the skin and the actions of the hand; Fire manifests itself as light, heat, and color, and thus is related to vision and its organ, the eye; Water is related to the sense of taste and its organ, the tongue; and the element of Earth is related to the sense of smell and its sensory organ, the nose. Sinhalas speak of *pañcakāma,* the perception or enjoyment of the five senses: sound, touch, form and color, flavor, and smell.

63. See Jaggi, *Medicine,* p. 116.

64. Obeyesekere, *Pattini,* p. 44.

65. See Obeyesekere, "Āyurvedic Ideas," p. 203; and *Pattini,* p. 42.

66. See Obeyesekere, "Āyurvedic Ideas," p. 206; and "Ritual Drama," p. 175.

Chapter 2. Malign Glances: *Diṣṭiya* and the Ethics of Composure

1. Traditionally, the Sinhala day consisted of sixty hours (*päya*). This is no longer used, but the concept of the *jāmayas* is still important in ritual practices. See Gananath

Obeyesekere, *The Cult of the Goddess Pattini* (Chicago: University of Chicago Press, 1984), p. 109.

2. Dandris de Silva Gooneratne, "On Demonology and Witchcraft in Ceylon," *Journal of the Royal Asiatic Society, Ceylon Branch* 4(1865/66), p. 44. This is undoubtedly still the most fascinating work on the Sinhala discourse of *yakku*. Indeed, this heterodox work and the other protoethnographic work that preceded it in the magazine *Young Ceylon* between April and June 1850 deserve a study of their own. See, for example, his "Judicial Astrology," *Young Ceylon* 1(3)(1850):63–66, "Charms," *Young Ceylon* 1(4)(1850):82–86, and "Charms (continued)," *Young Ceylon* 1(5)(1850):109–112.

3. I am thinking, of course, of *The Care of the Self*, trans. Robert Hurley (New York: Vintage, 1988).

4. Among useful references for South Asia, see A. M. Hocart, "The Mechanism of the Evil Eye," *Folk-Lore* 49(1938):156–157; Jan Gonda, *Eye and Gaze in the Veda* (Amsterdam, London: North-Holland Publishing Company, 1969); Clarence Mahoney, ed., *The Evil Eye* (New York: Columbia University Press, 1976); Diana L. Eck, *Darṣan: Seeing the Divine Image in India* (Chambersburg: Anima Books, 1981); Lawrence A. Babb, "Glancing: Visual Interaction in Hinduism," *Journal of Anthropological Research* 37(4)(1981):387–401. More generally, see Michel Meslin, "Eye," *The Encyclopedia of Religion*, vol. 5, ed. Mircea Eliade (New York: Macmillan, 1987).

5. For a study of the archaeological ruins of Devinuwara see Senarat Paranavitana, *The Shrine of Upulvan at Devundara*, Memoirs of the Archaeological Survey of Ceylon, vol. 6 (Colombo: Ceylon Government Archaeological Department, 1953). In this invaluable work the author argues that Upulvan and the contemporary deity of Devinuwara, Viṣṇu, are different figures. The latter, he maintains, supplanted the former sometime in the post-Portuguese period. This position appears to be contestable (Gananath Obeyesekere, personal communication). At the least, for the people of Devinuwara there is no difference to be made between them.

6. Visiting this famous Rock Temple at Dambulla myself in early 1987, the *kapurāla* or officiant of the Viṣṇu *dēvālē* showed me the sandalwood image of the god, Uppalavanna/Viṣṇu, repeating the story in all its essential details.

7. See Babb, "Glancing." I am particularly grateful to Preminda Jacobs for bringing this very useful article to my attention.

8. Eck, *Darṣan*, p. 7.

9. Babb, "Glancing," p. 387.

10. Eck, *Darṣan*, p. 9.

11. Gonda, *Eye and Gaze*, pp. 7–8.

12. For some relevant remarks on this subject see Richard Gombrich, *Precept and Practice: Traditional Buddhism in the Rural Highlands of Ceylon* (Oxford: Clarendon Press, 1971), p. 118.

13. Robert Knox, *An Historical Relation of Ceylon* (Dehiwala: Tisara Prakasakayo, 1966).

14. Quoted also in Richard Gombrich, "The Consecration of a Buddhist Image," *Journal of Asian Studies* 26(1)(1966):24.

15. Gombrich, "Consecration," pp. 24–25.

16. For a discussion of *vas dōṣa* see Obeyesekere, *Pattini*, pp. 46–47.

17. As I said in chapter 1, it is typically related to two other malign energies, *kaṭavaha* (literally, "mouth poison"), and *hōvaha*, the malignity of a merely grunted expression.

18. For a survey of the phenomena of the "evil eye" in South Asia, see Clarence Mahoney, "Don't Say 'Pretty Baby' Lest You Zap It with Your Eye," in Clarence Mahoney, ed., *Evil Eye*.

19. "*Mēvavenavā*" is an interesting Sinhala verb. It means something like "to become like

this." It is typically used to indicate something happening where precisely what it is that happened is either assumed to be known (because it is in any case what generally happens in such instances), or is not easily describable, at least in the current context. In this instance, the verb usually used is *kupitavenavā* or *kipenavā*, both of which may be glossed as "to become agitated" or "to become angry."

20. I am alluding, of course, to Richard Rorty's well-known argument, and particularly to his interesting "anthropological" illustration of the Antipodeans. See Rorty, *Philosophy and the Mirror of Nature* (Princeton: Princeton University Press, 1978), Part I.

21. I am grateful to Professor Gananath Obeyesekere for suggesting this.

22. Harischandra Wijayatunga, executive editor, *Prāyōgika Sinhala Ṣabdakōṣaya* (*Practical Sinhala Dictionary*), 2 vols. (Colombo: Ministry of Cultural Affairs, 1982).

23. In its colloquial form, *diṣṭiya,* the word does not appear in any of the major Sinhala-English dictionaries. This in itself is interesting since the two authoritative Sinhala-English dictionaries—Rev. Benjamin Clough's *Sinhala-English Dictionary* (New Delhi: Asian Educational Services, 1982 [originally published in Colombo by the Wesleyan Mission Press in 1830]) and Rev. Charles Carter's *A Sinhalese-English Dictionary* (Colombo: M. D. Gunasena, 1965 [originally published in Colombo by the Baptist Missionary Society in 1924])—were compiled by British missionaries who were much concerned (see chapter 5) to eradicate popular Sinhala beliefs and practices associated with *yakku,* and who were otherwise attentive to its constituent categories and concepts.

24. T. W. Rhys Davids and William Stede, *Pali-English Dictionary* (London: Pali Text Society, 1921).

25. Sir Monier Monier-Williams, *A Sanskrit-English Dictionary* (London: Oxford University Press, 1899).

26. Nevertheless, one of the things that I would like to suggest in the course of this book is that the field of *anthropological* visibility, that is to say, what the anthropologist sees as the important constituents of the object of his or her discourse, is determined by the kind of *problematic* employed—not the other way around. Therefore, this neglect of a fundamental Sinhala concept may not be fortuitous.

27. "Demonology," pp. 46–47.

28. Gananath Obeyesekere, "The Ritual Drama of the *Sanni* Demons: Collective Representations of Disease in Ceylon," *Comparative Studies in Society and History* 11(2)(1969):175–176.

29. The second, briefer reference to *diṣṭiya* appears in Richard Gombrich's *Precept and Practice,* where, in the context of a discussion of notions about the eyes of Buddha images, he writes: "The concept of the dangerous look or gaze (bälma) is common currency among the Sinhalese . . . : for instance illnesses (notably psychological troubles) for which medical diagnosis is not accepted are usually ascribed to the gaze of some evil spirit (yaka)" (p. 139). And later on: "The object of an exorcism is to free the patient from the evil influence (dos or vas) which has fallen on him from the gaze (*bälma* or *dṛṣṭiya,* generally pronounced *bäluma* and *diṣṭiya*) of some evil person or person" (pp. 197–198). A third reference occurs in Kapferer's *Celebration of Demons: Exorcism and the Aesthetics of Healing in Sri Lanka* (Bloomington: Indiana University Press, 1983): "Typically, demons are understood, by exorcists and their clients, to take their victims suddenly and by surprise, and to attack from a world (yaksa loka) outside that of normal human experience. Demons intrude into the experiential world of their victims and are conceptualized as capturing them in their malign eyesight or gaze (yaksa disti). So caught, demonic victims experience emotional, mental, and humoral imbalance" (p. 50). The role of surprise is indeed crucial, and is related to the whole issue of fright and composure discussed later.

30. For an overview of work on "possession" see Vincent Crapanzano, "Spirit Possession," *The Encyclopedia of Religion*, vol. 14, ed. Mircea Eliade (New York: Macmillan Publishing Company, 1987), pp. 12-19.

31. See I. M. Lewis, *Ecstatic Religion: A Study of Shamanism and Spirit Possession*, 2d ed. (New York: Routledge, 1989). Where Sri Lanka is concerned, perhaps the best and best-known work in this vein is Gananath Obeyesekere, "Psychocultural Exegesis of a Case of Spirit Possession in Sri Lanka," in *Case Studies in Possession*, ed. Vincent Crapanzano and Vivian Garrison (New York: John Wiley, 1977), and *Medusa's Hair* (Chicago: University of Chicago Press, 1981).

32. See, for instance, John Blacking, "Towards an Anthropology of the Body," in *The Anthropology of the Body*, ed. John Blacking (London: Academic Press, 1977); and Felicitas Goodman, *How About Demons?: Possession and Exorcism in the Modern World* (Bloomington: Indiana University Press, 1988).

33. Marcel Mauss, "Techniques of the Body," *Economy and Society* 2(1)(1973):70–88; Michel Foucault, *Discipline and Punish: The Birth of the Prison*, trans. Alan Sheridan (New York: Vintage, 1979); and Susan Bordo, "Reading the Slender Body," in *Body/Politics: Women and the Discourses of Science*, ed. Mary Jacobus, Evelyn Fox Keller, and Sally Shuttleworth (New York: Routledge, 1990).

34. One of Gombrich's informants told him that the *yaksayā* shouts "*hū*" and "leaves by the mouth." See *Precept and Practice*, p. 166.

35. The speaker here is S. A. Piyasena. *Vinivida* also has the sense of "perforating," "piercing," or "passing through." It is often used with the verbal noun *penīma* to connote "transparency" (*vinivida penīma*).

36. Steven Collins, *Selfless Persons: Image and Thought in Theravāda Buddhism* (Cambridge: Cambridge University Press, 1982).

37. Gooneratne, "Demonology," p. 47. Wednesday and Saturday are *kemmura davas*, days when it is especially auspicious to ask favours from the *dēvas* or gods.

38. So that when Kapferer, for example (*Celebration*, p. 50), interprets *tanikama* as "a state of isolation, of existential solitude in the world," he is, I think, very much mistaken. He is not only uncritically recasting Gooneratne's conflation in a more updated language, but he is investing it with a very specific kind of modernist psychology. For while *tanikama* does involve a *mental apartness*, so to put it, this does not convey anything of the flavor of that modern Western psychological condition of "loneliness."

39. It is necessary to point out that this idea of the potential "uncleanness" or "impurity" of the blood has little to do with those ideas about the relation between purity and caste that are so familiar in the anthropological literature on South Asian cultural practices.

40. Richard Gombrich and Gananath Obeyesekere, *Buddhism Transformed: Religious Change in Sri Lanka* (Princeton: Princeton University Press, 1988), p. 29.

41. See Kapferer, *Celebration*, p. 50.

Chapter 3. *Tovil Nätīma* (The Dancing of *tovil*)

1. For obvious reasons I have changed the name of the actual *āturayā* whose *yaktovil* forms the basis of the following description. I have, however, kept the names of the performing *ädurās*.

2. I am not describing the offering ceremonies for the *prētayō* and *bahīravayō* here. I should perhaps note, incidentally, that I was not the only ethnographer present and recording this *tovil* occasion. Mr. Noriyuki Ueda of the University of Tokyo, Japan, recorded it on a videocassette recorder.

3. For a description and discussion of the Rata Yäkuma see E. R. Sarachchandra, *The Folk Drama of Ceylon*, 2d ed. (Colombo: Department of Cultural Affairs, 1966).

4. For a discussion of this notion of "stepping" over a *koḍivina*, and on sorcery in general, see Dandris de Silva Gooneratne, "On Demonology and Witchcraft in Ceylon," *Journal of the Royal Asiatic Society, Ceylon Branch* 4(1865/66):68–99. See also Paul Wirz, *Exorcism and the Art of Healing in Ceylon* (Leiden: E. J. Brill, 1954), pp. 194–203.

5. See, for example, Gananath Obeyesekere, "The Ritual Drama of the *Sanni* Demons: Collective Representations of Disease in Ceylon," *Comparative Studies in Society and History* 11(2)(1969):174–216; Lorna AmaraSingham "Laughter as Cure: Joking and Exorcism in a Sinhalese Curing Ritual" (unpublished Ph.D. dissertation, Cornell University, 1973); and Bruce Kapferer, *A Celebration of Demons: Exorcism and the Aesthetics of Healing in Sri Lanka* (Bloomington: Indiana University Press, 1983).

6. A *pandala* generally is a scaffold of sticks over which some vine is grown.

7. See chapter 1 for a discussion of the *hatara varam deviyō*.

8. The word *vīdiya* has presented some difficulty of interpretation. Otaker Pertold, *Ceremonial Dances of the Sinhalese* (Dehiwala: Tisara Prakasakayo, 1930), p. 115n, offers the opinion that it is derived from the Sanskrit *vithi*, or *vithika*, "the original meaning of which is 'road.' " Quoting L. D. Barnett, he continues that "in the Ceylon demon-worship" it is " 'a space of enclosed paths surrounding the site of a ceremony.' " John Halverson, "Dynamics of Exorcism: The Sinhalese Sanniyakuma," *History of Religions* 10(4)(1971):336–337, is in general agreement. Sarachchandra, *Folk Drama*, p. 34 n, on the other hand, suggests that the word is probably derived from the Sanskrit *vedi*, meaning sacrificial altar. Gananath Obeyesekere, *The Cult of the Goddess Pattini* (Chicago: University of Chicago Press, 1984), p. 52, agrees that "street" is most appropriate if we understand "street" to be where the denizens of the periphery of the city reside.

9. The cock is an ever-present feature of all *yaktovil* ceremonies. Cocks are offerings, or rather "sacrifices" (*billa*). See Hugh Nevill, *Sinhala Verse (Kavi)*, vol. 1, ed. P. E. P. Deraniyagala (Colombo: Government Press, 1954), p. 298, for a specimen of verse about the "origin of cocks."

10. As I said in chapter 2, a tray or *taṭṭuva* of offerings (*dola pidēni*) will generally contain small measures of rice (*bat*), vegetables (*elōlu*), *mallun* (a mixture of leaves, coconut, salt, chili peppers, and onions), *roṭi*, sesame seeds (*tala äta*), green grams (*mun äta*), paddy seeds (*vī äta*), dry fish and meat (*goda diya mas*), roasted foods (*pulutu*), flowers (*mal*), and kinds of sweets (*kävili*).

11. See Nevill, *Sinhala Verse*, vol. 1, pp. 306–307, for a specimen of verse on the "origin of limes."

12. The reference to cooking rice here probably has to do with one of the main practices of determining which *yakku* have brought about the affliction of the *āturayā*. In this practice, having marked the side of the pot that faces east, the afflicted person is instructed to pour rice into it. The rice is then cooked and subsequently examined by *ädurās*. By the shapes that appear on the surface of the rice it can be determined which *yakku* are involved.

13. See Nevill, *Sinhala Verse*, vol. 2, p. 10, for a specimen of verses relating to the *īgaha* or arrow.

14. An epithet of the Buddha alluding to his attainment of the status of a Buddha.

15. "*Vatpilivet*" has the sense of religious rites and observances performed in a particular manner by the authorized persons.

16. On *prētayō*, *bhūtayō*, and *bahīravayō*, see chapter 1.

17. The word *kramaya* gives the sense not only of "system" or "method," but of a graduated order of proceedings.

18. Actually, as in much of colloquial Sinhala, there is no pronoun in the surface of the spoken sentence. However, I have used the third person plural nominal pronoun "they" wherever the subject of a verb indicating some action related to *yakku* is implicit.

19. "*Jīvitāntaya dakvā*" is perhaps more closely rendered "until the end of life."

20. This was actually my field assistant, the ever-skeptical A. H. M. Harischandra. He felt that this order (*aṇa*) had something to do with the *ädurā* who had set the sorcery that was responsible for the affliction. Äddin was obviously irritated by his interruption. His response is nevertheless interesting. He seems to suggest that King Vessamuni, the legendary ruler of all *yakku*, authorized the five-year limit.

21. Of this sound Dandris de Silva Gooneratne, "On Demonology," writes: "A *Hoo* shout is one peculiar to the people of this island [i.e., Sri Lanka]. It consists of a loud, single, guttural sound uttered as loud as a man's lungs permit. A quarter of a mile is generally considered to be the distance at which a loud Hoo can be heard" (p. 46 n).

22. The *purahala* or *purālapala* is a *tovil* structure built to support the "corpse" of the *ädurā*. It is erected either in a cemetery or by a stream or other body of water, and to it both the *ädurā* in the bier, or *därahäva*, and the *diṣṭiya* are brought at the end of the Iramudun Samayama.

23. These are usually diagrams with elaborate inscriptions of Sinhala characters drawn on copper sheets. On the subject of "*yantraya*s" see Wirz, *Exorcism*, pp. 123–126.

24. For a sample of *sirasapāda* verses, see Michael J. Egan, "A Configurational Analysis of a Sinhalese Healing Ritual" (unpublished manuscript, 1975), pp. 41–43.

25. See Nevill, *Sinhala Verse*, vol. 1, pp. 101 and 218, for samples of verse dealing with the mat (*pädura*).

26. I could not determine what this pounding signified.

27. This is a gloss of the following Sinhala: "*Sakala Sri Sagara paragataya mana ū Sri Sugata tatāgata apage samma sambuddha rajuttamayanan vahansēgē aṇaguṇa mē sarīra abhyantarē yakun yaksaniyan vāsaya karanna ū tama porondu unā valanguya kiyalā.*"

28. More specifically, "*dakka gannavā*" has the sense of forcing away by goading.

29. This is a gloss of the following Sinhala: "*Mē abhyantarē inna yakun yaksaniyan dolahaṭa tunaṭa nurta gīta āḍiya karalā hū tunak kiyāgena vaturu kalageḍi hatak nāla abhyantarayē at häralā rā tunaṭa yakṣa viman gatavala yanavā kivvā.*"

30. Literally, "This human body will go."

31. The *ädurā* "reading" the letter, Ariyadasa, actually borrowed my glasses at this point, presumably to enhance the comic effect.

32. It was in fact known beforehand that Lila Amma was going to climb up the Flower Shed. This apparently was one of the more sensational demands made by the *yakku*.

33. See Egan, "Configurational Analysis," pp. 145–152; and Kapferer, *Celebration*, pp. 168–175.

34. For minor exceptions, however, see Sarachchandra, *Folk Drama*, p. 32; and Halverson, "Dynamics of Exorcism," p. 338.

35. Sarachchandra, *Folk Drama*; Obeyesekere, "Ritual Drama"; Halverson, "Dynamics of Exorcism"; AmaraSingham, "Laughter"; Kapferer, *Celebration*.

Chapter 4. Exorcisms and Demonic Experience, Anthropology and *Yaktovil*

1. Bruce Kapferer, *A Celebration of Demons: Exorcism and the Aesthetics of Healing in Sri Lanka* (Bloomington: Indiana University Press, 1983). Hereafter, references to this book will be abbreviated *CD* in parentheses in the text. The other texts by Kapferer that I make use of are "Introduction: Ritual Process and the Transformation of Context," *Social Analysis*

1(1979):3–19, hereafter abbreviated *RPTC*; "Entertaining Demons. Comedy, Interaction and Meaning in a Sinhalese Healing Ritual," *Social Analysis* 1(1979):108–152, hereafter abbreviated *ED*; "Emotion and Feeling in Sinhalese Healing Rites," *Social Analysis* 1(1979):153–176; "Mind, Self and Other in Demonic Illness: The Negation and Reconstruction of Self," *American Ethnologist* 6(1979):110–133, hereafter abbreviated *MSO*; "Performance and the Structuring of Meaning and Experience," in *The Anthropology of Experience*, ed. Victor W. Turner and Edward M. Bruner (Urbana: Unversity of Illinois Press, 1986), hereafter abbreviated *PSME*.

2. Talal Asad, "Anthropological Texts and Ideological Problems: An Analysis of Cohen on Arab Villages in Israel," *Economy and Society* 4(3)(1975):251.

3. As opposed, say, to an *institutional* one. My argument here has, I think, much in common with Johannes Fabian's notion of the "cognitive complicity"—as distinct from "political and moral complicity"—between anthropology and colonialism. See Fabian, *Time and the Other: How Anthropology Makes Its Object* (New York: Columbia University Press, 1983), p. 35.

4. See, for example, Nur Yalman, "The Structure of Sinhalese Healing Rituals," *Journal of Asian Studies* 27(1964):115–150; Gananath Obeyesekere, "The Ritual Drama of the *Sanni* Demons: Collective Representations of Disease in Ceylon," *Comparative Studies in Society and History* 11(2)(1969):174–216; and John Halverson, "Dynamics of Exorcism: The Sinhalese Sanniyakuma," *History of Religions* 10(4)(1974):334–359.

5. So wrote Sir James Emerson Tennent, onetime Colonial Secretary, in his *Christianity in Ceylon* (London: John Murray, 1850), p. 229.

6. Prior to the appearance of Kapferer's monograph, Paul Wirz's *Exorcism and the Art of Healing in Ceylon* (Leiden: E. J. Brill, 1954), a compendious, sympathetic, and generally keenly observed description of a large variety of low-country Sinhala healing practices, served as a sort of sourcebook. Dandris de Silva Gooneratne's monograph "On Demonology and Witchcraft in Ceylon," *Journal of the Royal Asiatic Society, Ceylon Branch* 4 (1865/66):1–117, was the seminal work on these practices, one indeed that can be called protoethnographic in its studied attention to the details of local knowledge. See also Gananath Obeyesekere's *Medusa's Hair* (Chicago: University of Chicago Press, 1981).

7. See, for example, Victor Turner, *From Ritual to Theatre* (New York: Performing Arts Journal Publications, 1982), and *The Anthropology of Performance* (New York: Performing Arts Journal Publications, 1987).

8. See, for example, Richard A. Shweder and Robert A. Levine, eds., *Culture Theory: Essays on Mind, Self, and Emotion* (Cambridge: Cambridge University Press, 1986).

9. Talal Asad, "Towards a Genealogy of the Concept of Ritual," in *Vernacular Christianity: Essays in the Social Anthropology of Religion Presented to Godfrey Lienhardt*, ed. W. James and D. M. Johnson (Oxford: JASO, 1988).

10. Edward M. Bruner, "Introduction: Experience and its Expressions," in *The Anthropology of Experience*, ed. Victor W. Turner and Edward M. Bruner (Urbana: University of Illinois Press, 1986). Kapferer's contribution, which appears as chapter 8, is entitled, "Performance and the Structuring of Meaning and Experience."

11. See Richard Rorty, *Philosophy and the Mirror of Nature* (Princeton: Princeton University Press, 1978), and *Consequences of Pragmatism* (Minneapolis: University of Minnesota Press, 1982); and Ian Hacking, *Why Does Language Matter to Philosophy?* (Cambridge: Cambridge University Press, 1975).

12. Readers of V. N. Vološinov, *Marxism and the Philosophy of Language*, trans. Ladislav Matejka and I. R. Titunik (Cambridge, Mass.: Harvard University Press, 1986), will recall his insightful criticism of this kind of appeal to an authentic experience in the work of Wil-

helm Dilthey, and his development of the idea of the psyche as a thoroughly semiotic and *therefore* ideologically constituted domain.

13. Of course, a number of other recent writers on ritual (e.g., Stanley J. Tambiah, "A Performative Approach to Ritual," *Proceedings of the British Academy* 65[1979]:113–169; Edward L. Schieffelin, "Performance and the Cultural Construction of Reality," *American Ethnologist* 12[4][1985]:707–724), influenced by the renewed attention given to language performatives, also argue for a focus on ritual as performance. Here I am referring to anthropological attempts to make use of the famous distinction of J. L. Austin's, *How to Do Things with Words*, 2d ed. (Cambridge, Mass.: Harvard University Press, 1962), between constative statements (i.e., utterances that are strictly declarative, having the property of being true or false), and performative statements (i.e., utterances that neither describe nor express anything but *do* something).

14. One thinks of Maurice Bloch, "Symbols, Song, Dance and Features of Articulation," *European Journal of Sociology* 15(1)(1974):55–81; "The Past and the Present in the Present," *Man* n.s. 12(1977):55–81; and *From Blessing to Violence: History and Ideology in the Circumcision Ritual of the Merina of Madagascar* (Cambridge: Cambridge University Press, 1986).

15. Bloch, "Symbols," p. 76. In a later work, *Blessing,* he puts it this way: "Rituals cannot form a true argument, because they imply no alternative" (p. 182).

16. The collection of articles, "The Power of Ritual," edited by Bruce Kapferer, and which features three programmatic articles of his own, appeared as a special inaugural issue of *Social Analysis* 1(1979). The volume can in many ways be read as a response to, and a rebuttal of, Bloch's controversial Malinowski Lecture (7 December 1976), published as "The Past and the Present in the Present," *Man* n.s. 12(1977):55–81.

17. The classic texts here, of course, are Arnold Van Gennep, *Rites of Passage,* trans. Monika B. Vizedom and Gambrielle L. Caffee (Chicago: University of Chicago Press, 1961), and Victor W. Turner, *The Ritual Process: Structure and Anti-Structure* (Ithaca: Cornell University Press, 1969).

18. See particularly Kapferer, *RPTC,* and Don Handelman and Bruce Kapferer, "Symbolic Types, Mediation and the Transformation of Ritual Context: Sinhalese Demons and Tewa Clowns," *Semiotica* 30(1/2)(1980):41–71.

19. Victor W. Turner, "Dewey, Dilthey, and Drama: An Essay in the Anthropology of Experience," in *The Anthropology of Experience,* ed. Victor W. Turner and Edward M. Bruner (Urbana: University of Illinois Press, 1986), p. 42.

20. Kapferer does not give the source for Eliot's inspiring conception. However, besides his well-known essays in criticism we are reminded that between 1915 and 1916 Eliot himself wrote on the subject of experience and knowledge for his doctoral thesis at Harvard University. Submitted, approved, but never defended, the thesis was published in 1964 under the title *Experience and Knowledge in the Philosophy of F. H. Bradley.*

21. Terence Turner, "Transformation, Hierarchy and Transcendence: A Reformulation of Van Gennep's Model of the Structure of Rites de Passage," in *Secular Ritual,* ed. Sally F. Moore and Barbara G. Myerhoff (Amsterdam: Van Gorcum, 1977).

22. One of the most problematic aspects of this is elaborated in chapter 5, "Exorcisms and the Symbolic Identity of Women."

23. There is in this conception, of course, a long Western tradition. For an excellent discussion, see Rorty, *Philosophy.*

24. Vološinov, *Marxism,* p. 28, his emphasis.

25. This whole conception of subjectivity and identity has been criticized from various points of view. See, for example, Julian Henriques et al., *Changing the Subject: Psychology, Social Regulation and Subjectivity* (New York: Methuen, 1984), and Ian Hacking, "Making Up

People," in *Reconstructing Individualism: Autonomy, Individuality, and the Self in Western Thought*, ed. Thomas C. Heller, Morton Sosna, and David A. Wellbery (Stanford: Stanford University Press, 1986). They all, in some measure, are indebted to the work of Michel Foucault on the question of the subject and power. See, for instance, "The Subject and Power," afterword in *Michel Foucault: Beyond Structuralism and Hermeneutics*, 2d ed., ed. Hubert L. Dreyfus and Paul Rabinow (Chicago: University of Chicago Press, 1983), and "The Ethic of Care for the Self as a Practice of Freedom," *Philosophy and Social Criticism* 12(2–3)(1987):112–131.

26. It might be noted, incidentally, that John Halverson had previously used almost exactly the same terms in his article "Dynamics of Exorcism," an analysis of the *Sanniyakuma*. Kapferer appears unaware of this though he himself sites Halverson elsewhere (see *CD*, 253 n). "The most critical phase of the process of transformation," Halverson had written, "is what Jung calls 'the meeting of the Shadow,' that is, a recognition in oneself of the instinctual, irrational, primitive, violent side of one's own nature" (p. 351).

27. I am referring here, of course, to the insightful notion of Marcel Mauss, "Techniques of the Body," *Economy and Society* 2(1)(1973):70–88, elaborated upon by Pierre Bourdieu, *Outline of a Theory of Practice* (Cambridge: Cambridge University Press, 1973), and "The Genesis of the Concepts of *Habitus* and of *Field*," *Sociocriticism* 2(1985):11–24. The habitus for Mauss consisted of "techniques of the body"—the "ways in which from society to society men know how to use their bodies" (p. 70). This concept, needless to say, foreshadows many of the ideas Michel Foucault was to pursue much later. Bourdieu, "Genesis," while not mentioning Mauss in the lineage of the concept of habitus, offers that it constituted an attempt to break away from "the philosophy of consciousness without doing away with the agent, in its truth of a practical operator of objective constructions" (p. 14).

28. See, for example, Sherry Ortner, *Sherpas Through Their Rituals* (Cambridge: Cambridge University Press, 1978), and Bloch, "Symbols."

29. Bryan Wilson, "A Sociologist's Introduction," in *Rationality*, ed. Bryan Wilson (Oxford: Basil Blackwell, 1969): xi. The debate on rationality and relativism, which has witnessed an interesting dialogue between anthropologists and philosophers, was, of course, in part precipitated by the publication of Peter Winch's *The Idea of a Social Science*. The volume edited by Bryan Wilson, *Rationality*, represented, so to speak, the first round of this debate. Some twelve years later, by which time a number of other theoretical moves had entered the field of argument—largely as a result of Thomas Kuhn's *The Structure of Scientific Revolutions*, the translation of Hans Gadamer's *Truth and Method*, and the publication of Richard Rorty's *Philosophy and the Mirror of Nature*—another collection of articles appeared, *Rationalism and Relativism*, edited by Martin Hollis and Steven Lukes.

30. This is a version of what Talal Asad, "Anthropology and the Analysis of Ideology," *Man* n.s. 14 (1979), has nicely called "the Wizard of Oz theory of ideology" (p. 622).

31. See, for example, Roy A. Rappaport, "The Obvious Aspects of Ritual," *Cambridge Anthropology* 2(1)(1974):3–69; and Tambiah, "Performative Approach to Ritual."

32. In a later work, Kapferer, even remarks, somewhat disparagingly, on what he characterizes as "the grail-like anthropological concern with discovering a unifying definition of ritual" (*PSME* 191). All to the good. But he complains only because, as he sees it, this attempt "often denies or obscures the significance for analysis of the many different forms that are actualized in what we call ritual performance." In other words, attempts at a general definition of ritual are inadequate not because the very conception itself is fundamentally flawed, but because they do not account for all the empirically probable features of what anthropologists are given to calling ritual.

33. See Asad, "Anthropology" and "Towards a Genealogy" for discussions of the impossibility of a universal theory of ritual.

34. Charles Taylor, "Understanding and Ethnocentricity," in *Philosophy and the Human Sciences,* Philosophical Papers, vol. 2 (Cambridge: Cambridge University Press, 1985), articulates an "interpretive" view remarkably similar to Geertz's. In this essay, Taylor argues for a view "marked off" from, on the one hand, "the natural science model" (according to which a culture's self-descriptions are unnecessary for an outsider's understanding, or rather, explanation, of it), and, on the other, the "incorrigibility thesis" (which, "requiring that we explain each culture or society on its own terms, . . . rules out an account that shows them up as wrong, confused or deluded" [p. 123]). This view would require what Taylor calls a "language of perspicuous contrast." "This would be a language," he says, "in which we could formulate both their way of life and ours as alternative possibilities in relation to some human constants at work in both" (p. 125), and as such would involve a constant movement between self and other.

35. Clifford Geertz, " 'From the Native's Point of View': On the Nature of Anthropological Understanding," in *Local Knowledge* (New York: Basic Books, 1983).

36. See Richard J. Bernstein, *Beyond Objectivism and Relativism: Science, Hermeneutics, and Praxis* (Philadelphia: University of Pennsylvania Press, 1983), pp. 8–16, for a discussion of these terms.

37. Bernstein, anyway, seems to think so (*Beyond Objectivism,* pp. 93–96).

Chapter 5. Colonial Christian Discourse, Demonism, and Sinhala Religion

1. It is, of course, true that the British were not the first Christians to colonize Lankā. The Portuguese Catholics and the Dutch Calvinists preceded them. Both involved evangelizing missions. And it is probable that the Catholics, at least, had an impact on indigenous practices in the south of the island. Certainly the attempt to trace this impact would form an important chapter in an overall sketch of the impact of colonial Christian relations with Lankā. However, this is not the task that this chapter has set for itself. The question with which I am concerned has to do with the *conceptual* preconditions of the modern *anthropological conception* of the Sinhala *yaktovil* as "demonism." Neither the Catholic Portuguese nor the Calvinist Dutch were as influential as the British in fashioning *Western knowledges* about Sinhala practices.

2. For a very useful discussion of the importance both of this distinction itself and specifically of the period 1780–1830, see C. A. Bayly, *Imperial Meridian: The British Empire and the World, 1780–1830* (New York: Longman, 1989).

3. The Act was known as "Burke's Act." On the conduct of "colonial business" during this period, see J. C. Beaglehole, "The Colonial Office, 1782–1854," *Historical Studies of Australia and New Zealand* 1(3)(1941):170–189; and D. M. Young, *The Colonial Office in the Early Nineteenth Century* (London: Longmans, 1961).

4. This infelicitous phrase is E. A. Benians's, "The Beginnings of the New Empire, 1783–1793," in *Cambridge History of the British Empire,* vol. 2, *The Growth of the New Empire, 1783–1870* (Cambridge: Cambridge University Press, 1961), p. 2.

5. For a discussion of Portuguese colonial relations with Lankā (1505–1656), see especially P. E. Pieris, *Ceylon and the Portuguese, 1505–1658* (Tellippalai: American Ceylon Mission Press, 1920). For less specialized and more recent treatments, see Colvin R. de Silva, *Ceylon Under the British Occupation, 1795–1833,* vol. 1, *Its Political and Administrative Development* (Colombo: Colombo Apothecaries Co. Ltd., 1953), chapter 1, and E. F. C. Ludowyk, *The Story of Ceylon* (rev. ed.) (New Delhi: Navrang, 1985), chapter 6. A good

source for Dutch colonial relations with Lankā (1656–1796) is K. W. Goonewardena, *The Foundation of Dutch Power in Ceylon, 1638–1658* (Amsterdam: Djambatan, 1958). P. E. Pieris, *Ceylon and the Hollanders, 1658–1796* (Tellippalai: American Ceylon Mission Press, 1918), dated though it is, remains an exemplary work. See also the useful summary in Ludowyk, *Story*, chapter 7.

6. The naval force known as the East Indies Squadron came into being in 1744 to police the Indian waters during the Anglo-French conflict. It first put in at Trincomalee for refitting in July 1746. Trincomalee was valuable to the British because it provided a safe shelter from the northeast monsoon where ships defending the Coromandel Coast could be refitted. For details see the interesting article by H. A. Colgate, "The Royal Navy and Trincomalee: The History of their Connection, c 1750–1958," *The Ceylon Journal of Historical and Social Studies* 7(1)(1964):1–16.

7. See K. M. de Silva, "The Coming of the British to Ceylon, 1762–1802," in *University of Ceylon History of Ceylon*, vol. 3 (Colombo: University of Ceylon Press, 1973), p. 2.

8. There are several important historical works on the British colonial period. I have found most useful the two volumes of Colvin R. de Silva, *Ceylon* (2 vols.); G. C. Mendis's *Ceylon Under the British* (Colombo: Colombo Apothecaries Co. Ltd., 1948); Lennox A. Mill, *Ceylon Under British Rule, 1795–1932* (London: Oxford University Press, 1933); and E. F. C. Ludowyk, *The Modern History of Ceylon* (New York: Praeger, 1966).

9. Klaus E. Knorr, *British Colonial Theories, 1570–1850* (Toronto: University of Toronto Press, 1944), is still perhaps one of the most useful and comprehensive works on the vicissitudes of the ideas that informed British colonial policy between the mid-sixteenth and mid-nineteenth centuries. I have drawn upon it in my characterization of the difference between the Old and the New Empires.

10. Knorr, *British*, p. 129.

11. I have in mind something of the transformation in the strategies of power—from the ritual marking of the body in the spectacle of public torture in the seventeenth and eighteenth centuries to the systems of subjectification in the nineteenth—which Michel Foucault describes in *Discipline and Punish: The Birth of the Clinic*, trans. Alan Sheridan (New York: Vintage Books, 1979). There was articulated, I would argue, a similar kind of transformation between the First and Second British colonial empires. Indeed, some would argue (incorrectly, it seems to me) that it is with the latter phase that colonialism proper—that is, as a "psychological" problematic—begins. For this view see Ashis Nandy's "The Psychology of Colonialism," in *The Intimate Enemy: Loss and Recovery of Self Under Colonialism* (Delhi: Oxford University Press, 1983).

12. Originating in the "methodism" of John Wesley at Oxford in the early eighteenth century, this reforming attitude assumed broader importance when it allied itself with the social forces of the nascent middle classes and their political ideology of economic liberalism. In social and cultural terms, Evangelicalism was a reaction against the rationalism, skepticism, and general worldliness of the eighteenth century. It gave to Victorian society its sense of high moral tone, and facilitated the generation of the regulated and disciplined subjects necessary for the Industrial Revolution.

13. "The most important features of the Evangelical mind were its intense individualism and exaltation of individual conscience, its belief that human character could be suddenly and totally transformed by a direct assault on the mind, and finally, its conviction that this required an educative process" (Eric Stokes, *The English Utilitarians and India* [Oxford: Oxford University Press, 1959], p. 30).

14. Ian Bradley, *The Call to Seriousness: The Evangelical Impact on the Victorians* (New York: Macmillan, 1976), p. 22.

15. See Bradley, *Call*, pp. 74–93.

16. My use of the concept *discourse* here is influenced as much by Michel Foucault as by Hayden White. White, *Tropics of Discourse* (Baltimore: Johns Hopkins University Press, 1978), writes: "Discourse, in a word, is quintessentially a *mediative* enterprise. As such, it is both interpretive and preinterpretive; it is always as much *about* the nature of interpretation itself as it is *about* the subject matter which is the manifest occasion of its own elaboration" (p. 4). And this discourse, White emphasizes, is always (pre)figured *tropically*. That is to say, discourse employs linguistic means of marking out and indeed constituting the field of objects to be considered and the manner in which they are to be considered. Troping, says White, is the "soul of discourse," and as such always involves a certain "intention" or (in Michel Foucault's terms) "will to power." Thus we may speak, in our context, of the "tropics"—and specifically, as we shall see, the *demonological tropics*—of colonial Christian discourse.

17. In work that intersects with the concerns of this chapter, Lata Mani, "Contentious Traditions: The Debate on Sati in Colonial India," *Cultural Critique* 7(1987):119–156, is engaged in an inquiry upon the relation between colonial power and the construction in nineteenth-century India of the practice of *sati* as colonial knowledge.

18. Michael T. Ryan, "Assimilating New Worlds in the Sixteenth and Seventeenth Centuries," *Comparative Studies in Society and History* 23(4)(1981):519–538. See also Bernard McGrane, *Beyond Anthropology: Society and the Other* (New York: Columbia University Press, 1989), for an intersting history of "difference" between the sixteenth and early twentieth centuries.

19. For an elaboration of this point see Talal Asad, "Anthropological Conceptions of Religion: Reflections on Geertz," *Man* n.s. 18(2)(1983):237–259.

20. To reiterate, my principal concern in this paper is not to address the historical sociology of Sinhala Buddhism during the disfiguring period of British colonial rule, though aspects of this history are certainly pertinent to the endeavor I wish to engage. For a historical sociology of Sinhala Buddhism during this period, see Kitsiri Malalgoda's excellent study, *Buddhism in Sinhalese Society, 1750–1900* (Berkeley: University of California Press, 1976).

21. Philip C. Almond, *The British Discovery of Buddhism* (New York: Cambridge University Press, 1988). Almond's scholarship generally deserves considered attention. See especially "The Medieval West and Buddhism," *The Eastern Buddhist* n.s. 19(2)(1986):85–101; "Buddhism in the West: 300 BC-AD 400," *Journal of Religious History* 14(3)(1987):235–245; and *Heretic and Hero: Muhammad and the Victorians* (Wiesbaden: Otto Harrassowitz, 1989).

22. One reason, no doubt, has to do with the curious presupposition among some contemporary scholars of colonial discourse that India provides the exemplary instance of orientalism, indeed sometimes even of colonialism. To be sure, the critical literature on the place of India in the discursive economy of British orientalism is a large and significant one. Instructive as this work is, however, it would be a mistake to assume that a discussion of orientalism in British Ceylon should *necessarily* be worked out *by way of* a discussion of the case of British India—an *ideological* mistake, moreover, in that it repeats the colonial, specifically Indological, assumption regarding the exemplary status of India. This chapter is in part an effort to work against the grain of this assumption.

23. Ananda Wickremeratne, *The Genesis of an Orientalist: Thomas William Rhys Davids and Buddhism in Sri Lanka* (Delhi: Motilal Banarsidass, 1984).

24. As Wickremeratne, *Genesis*, maintains, T. W. Rhys Davids stands alongside Max Muller as one of the great Orientalists of the nineteenth century. He arrived in British Ceylon in 1866 to take up an appointment as Writer in the Ceylon Civil Service. He was twenty-

three years old. In 1873, while serving as Assistant Government Agent in Anuradhapura, he was relieved of his duties and subsequently dismissed from the Colonial Service. He was charged by his superiors with, among other things, having arbitrarily imposed fines on peasants and appropriated the funds for his personal use. In 1874 he left Ceylon to return to England, where he soon established himself as the foremost authority on Buddhist and Pāli studies. In 1881 he founded the Pāli Text Society.

25. Rev. William M. Harvard, *A Narrative of the Establishment and Progress of the Mission to Ceylon and India* (London, 1823), p. lxi. On Hinduism, see P. J. Marshall, ed., *The British Discovery of Hinduism in the Eighteenth Century* (Cambridge: Cambridge University Press, 1970); and on Islam, among many possibilities, see Almond, *Heretic.*

26. David Kopf, *British Orientalism and the Bengal Renaissance* (Berkeley: University of California Press, 1969).

27. David Kopf, "Hermeneutics versus History," *Journal of Asian Studies* 39(3)(1980):497.

28. To be sure, the Orientalists and the Anglicists shared much in common. They shared the idea, for example, of the contemporary degenerateness of "Asiatic" society, and the implicit faith in the superiority of European civilization. Moreover, they both felt keenly that "native society" should be transformed and that European ideas and means would have a beneficial effect in this process. However, they differed in their conception of this process and in their image of the change. Whereas the Orientalists felt it possible to reinvigorate debilitated native institutions and traditions, the Anglicists wished to supplant these with European forms. Perhaps most important for our consideration, they shared a common assumption about the place of "religion" in the social life of the "Asiatic."

29. See Vijaya Samaraweera, "The 'Village Community' and Reform in Colonial Sri Lanka," *Ceylon Journal of Historical and Social Studies* n.s. 8(1)(1980):68–75.

30. See William Jones, "A Discourse on the Institution of a Society," *Asiatick Researches* 1(1806):ix-xvi.

31. In the mid-1770s, for example, Warren Hastings had urged civil servants coming out to India to study Persian and, where possible, Hindustani. And later, at Wellesley's "Oxford of the East," the College of Fort William, Persian, Arabic, Hindustani, and Sanskrit were the chief departments. See Bernard S. Cohn, "The Command of Language and the Language of Command," in *Subaltern Studies IV. Writings on South Asian History and Society*, ed. Ranajit Guha (Delhi: Oxford University Press, 1985), for a fine discussion of the early language policy in British India.

32. If knowledge of the historical Buddha, Gautama, and his doctrines, was lamentably superficial at the end of the eighteenth century, this situation would be slow in changing. In fact, without a knowledge of the Mauryan period of Indian history, that of the Emperor Aṣōka, and of Pāli, the language of the classical Buddhist Canon, it was impossible to arrive at reliable conclusions regarding either the historical personage of, or the doctrines attributed to, Gautama. And both of these took a long time to develop. A breakthrough in the former began with James Prinsep's translation in 1837 of a *Brahmi* inscription, and the (coincidentally) almost simultaneous translation by George Turnour of the Sinhala epic, the *Mahāvamsa*—which enabled a linking of Aṣōka to the Buddhist period. And competence in Pāli, and a corresponding familiarity with the canonical texts, grew slowly through the nineteenth century. Beginning with the seminal work of Turnour, Rev. Benjamin Clough, and Daniel J. Gogerly in the 1830s and 1840s, excellence was achieved in the work of T. W. Rhys Davids only at the end of the nineteenth century. And if Rhys Davids was the Orientalist par excellence of Ceylon, as Ananda Wickremeratne would suggest (and correctly so), a vast ideological distance separates him from Sir William Jones—the distance, in short, of Victorianism, and especially of one of its defining aspects, Evangelicalism. For a general

consideration of European contact with Buddhism, see Guy Richard Welbon, *The Buddhist Nirvana and Its Western Interpreters* (Chicago: University of Chicago Press, 1968); and Almond, *British*.

33. Jones, cited in J. H. Harington, "Introductory Remarks," *Asiatick Researches* 8(1808):529.

34. See S. N. Mukherjee, *Sir William Jones: A Study in Eighteenth-Century British Attitudes to India*, 2d ed. (Hyderabad: Orient Longman, 1987).

35. William Jones, "On the Chronology of the Hindus," *Asiatick Researches* 2(1806):111.

36. The Orientalists, it might be noted, conceived of "India" as spanning a quite broad geographical area (see Jones, "Chronology," pp. 345–346).

37. William Jones, "On the Gods of Greece, Italy, and India," *Asiatick Researches* 1(1806):235–236.

38. Harington, "Introductory Remarks," p. 530.

39. Capt. Colin McKenzie, "Remarks on some Antiquities on the West and South Coasts of Ceylon," *Asiatick Researches* 6(1807):425–454.

40. McKenzie (or Mackenzie, as his name appears elsewhere) arrived in Madras in 1783 at the comparatively late age of twenty-nine during the closing stages of the East India Company's campaign against Tipu Sultan. Apparently a man of great energy, dedication to the Company, and talent with surveys and maps, he was appointed the first Surveyor-General of Madras in 1810, and in 1815, Surveyor-General of India. His association with Ceylon seems to have been a brief if nonetheless significant one. He was Engineer-in-Charge of the expedition against the Dutch in Ceylon in early 1796, but since the campaign was a relatively "tame affair" McKenzie's meticulous preparations went largely unused. Stationed for the most part at Trincomalee in charge of fortifications, he managed to "inspect" and "report" on the forts on the west coast of the island. McKenzie was also a friend of Sir Alexander Johnston, sometime Advocate-General, Chief Justice, and President of the Council in British Ceylon. I am grateful to Professor Nicholas Dirks for telling me about McKenzie's association with Johnston. See his *Hollow Crown: Ethnohistory of an Indian Kingdom* (New York: Cambridge University Press, 1987) for a discussion of some of McKenzie's papers on India. See also W. C. Mackenzie's biography of the colonel (as he later became), *Colonel Colin Mackenzie: First Surveyor-General of India* (Edinburgh and London: W & R Chambers Ltd., 1952), pp. 49–51.

41. Capt. Mahony, "On Singhala, or Ceylon, and the Doctrines of Bhooddha," *Asiatick Researches* 7(1807):32–56.

42. Harington, "Introductory Remarks," p. 529.

43. Joseph Endelin de Joinville, "On the Religion and Manners of the People of Ceylon," *Asiatick Researches* 7(1807):397–444.

44. Quoted in Colvin R. de Silva, *Ceylon*, vol. 1, p. 227.

45. Frederic North was the first Governor of the British possessions in Ceylon. He arrived in October 1798 to replace the East India Company representative, Robert Andrews. (See de Silva, *Ceylon*, vol. 1, p. 57.) North was something of a classicist himself, with a particular love of Greece. He was a patron of the Asiatic Society of Bengal and a friend of the Marquess Wellesley. See Sir Montagu Burrows, "The Conquest of Ceylon, 1795–1815," in *The Cambridge History of the British Empire*, vol. 4, British India 1497–1858, ed. H. H. Dodwell (Cambridge: Cambridge University Press, 1929), p. 403 n. Joinville (or Jonville) was appointed Surveyor-General when, as part of the reforms carried out by North, the first Surveyor-General's Department was formed in August 1800 (de Silva, *Ceylon*, vol. 1, p. 237; and Rt. Rev. Edmund Peiris, "Joinville's Translation of the Kokila Sandesaya," *Ceylon Historical Journal* 3[3/4][1953]:256–267).

46. Frederic North, "Letter to the Secretary of the Society for Asiatic Researches," *Asiatick Researches* 7(1807):396. The reference to Dr. Buchanan's account is to Francis Buchanan, "On the Religion and Literature of the Burmas," *Asiatick Researches* 6(1807):163–308.

47. See K. M. de Silva, "Coming."

48. See Kopf, *British Orientalism*, pp. 127–213.

49. See P. E. Pieris, *Sinhale and the Patriots, 1815–1818* (Colombo: Colombo Apothecaries Co. Ltd., 1950), for an account of the factors leading up to the rebellion; also de Silva, *Ceylon*, chapter 4.

50. See de Silva, *Ceylon*.

51. See G. C. Mendis, ed., *The Colebrooke-Cameron Papers. Documents on British Colonial Policy, 1796–1833*, 2 vols. (London: Oxford University Press, 1956).

52. Charles Grant, *Observations on the State of Society among the Asiatic Subjects of Great Britain, particularly with respects to Morals; and on the Means of Improving It* (London, 1797).

53. For a discussion of the Christian missionary enterprise in general, C. N. V. Fernandez's series of essays are indispensable: "Christianity in Ceylon in the Portuguese and Dutch Periods," *University of Ceylon Review* 6(4)(1948):267–288; "Christianity in Ceylon in the British Period," *University of Ceylon Review* 7(2)(1949):135–141; "Christian Missionary Enterprise in the Early British Period," *University of Ceylon Review* 7(3)(1949):198–207; "Christian Missionary Enterprise in the Early British Period II," *University of Ceylon Review* 7(4)(1949):269–277; "Christian Missionary Enterprise in the Early British Period III," *University of Ceylon Review* 8(2)(1950):110–115; "Christian Missionary Enterprise in the Early British Period IV," *University of Ceylon Review* 8(3)(1950):203–206; "Some Aspects of Christian Missionary Enterprise in the Early British Period (1796–1830) VI," *University of Ceylon Review* 8(4)(1950):264–271; "Christian Missions: IX. Some Aspects of Baptist and Wesleyan Work from 1827–1864," *University of Ceylon Review* 9(2)(1951):106–112; "Christian Missions: X. Some Aspects of the Work of American Missionaries in Jaffna District from 1827–1866," *University of Ceylon Review* 9(3)(1951):191–201.

54. See Fernandez, "Christian Missionary Enterprise in the Early British Period II," pp. 269–277. The missionaries, of course, had much cause to feel apprehensive about the East India Company's attitude toward their work. The first group of missionaries of the London Missionary Society, for example, who in 1804 attempted to set out from England on their way to Ceylon, were delayed because "no vessel of the East India Company was permitted to grant this company of missionaries a passage as they went out in face of the open hostility of the government" (quoted in Fernandez, "Christian Missionary Enterprise in the Early British Period," p. 199).

55. Both the Portuguese and the Dutch had had contingents of missionaries working in the island during their respective periods of rule. See Fernandez, "Christianity in Ceylon in the Portuguese and Dutch Periods," pp. 267–288. The first British missionaries to arrive in British Ceylon were actually members of the London Missionary Society. They arrived in Mannar, in the north of the island, in January 1805. It appears, however, that their activities were confined mainly to Dutch congregations in Jaffna, Colombo, Galle, and Matara. See Fernandez, "Christian Missionary Enterprise in the Early British Period," pp. 198–202.

56. For a fine account of the last phase of the last Sinhala kingdom, see P. E. Pieris, *Tri Sinhala: The Last Phase, 1796–1815* (Colombo: Colombo Apothecaries Co. Ltd., 1939).

57. Pieris, *Sinhale*, p. 591, has argued that the published English translation of the document embodying the articles of the Convention (the original apparently has never been found) "does not adequately reproduce the Sinhalese text by which the Great Chiefs bound themselves." He offers therefore a more accurate one, the fifth clause of which reads as follows: "The Doctrine of Buddha and the Cult of the Devas in which the officials and inhabi-

tants of the aforesaid Rataval have faith must be so maintained that they cannot be broken and their ceremonies, Sangha, Viharastana and Devala maintained and protected" (p. 592).

58. K. M. de Silva, *Social Policy and Missionary Organizations in Ceylon, 1840–1855* (London: Longmans, 1965), p. 67.

59. For twenty-five years after the Kandyan Convention, between 1815 and 1840, there was no substantial change in the colonial Government's relation to Sinhala Buddhism. The missionary agitation against the connection between the British colonial Government and Sinhala Buddhism took shape in the context of the mounting campaign in England against the Government's connection with idolatry in India, and in particular the campaign against the Pilgrim Tax. See Kenneth Ingham, "The English Evangelicals and the Pilgrim Tax in India, 1800–1862," *Journal of Ecclesiastical History* 3(1952):191–200. In British Ceylon, the agitation against the Ceylon Government's connection with Buddhism was launched in 1839 with the publication of a stinging pamphlet by the Wesleyan missionary, the Rev. Robert Spence Hardy, *The British Government and the Idolatry of Ceylon* (London: Crofts and Blenkarn, 1841). The principal argument advanced by Hardy was a comparatively simple one. He maintained that the connection between the British Government and Sinhala Buddhism was in essence a relation between a Christian Government and a system of idolatry. As such, it was in principle a morally inadmissible relation.

60. This was the time of the great coffee boom in Ceylon, which was attracting settlers from England. William Knighton's *Forest Life in Ceylon*, 2 vols. (London: Hurst and Blackett, 1854), gives a vivid account of settler life in Ceylon in a slightly later period. The failure of the new colony to begin to pay its way, and the constant talk of administrative high-handedness and mismanagement, led to the Colebrooke-Cameron Commission of Inquiry of 1829, which ushered in a period of judicial, administrative, and educational reforms in the 1830s. On this see C. G. Mendis's Introduction, in *The Colebrooke-Cameron Papers*. See also Vijaya Samaraweera, "The Colebrooke-Cameron Reforms," in *University of Ceylon History of Ceylon*, vol. 3 (Colombo: University of Ceylon Press, 1973).

61. Homi K. Bhabha, "The Other Question—The Stereotype and Colonial Discourse," *Screen* 24(6)(1983):25.

62. It is the more remarkable for the fact that Upham himself appears never to have witnessed such a performance in the "woods of Ceylon." The full title of Upham's work is *The History and Doctrine of Budhism, Popularly Illustrated, with notices of the Kapooism, or Demon worship, and of the Bali, or Planetary Incantations, of Ceylon* (London: R. Ackermann, 1829).

63. Demonism, of course, was not itself new to Christian discourse. Geoffrey Scarre, *Witchcraft and Magic in 16th and 17th Century Europe* (Atlantic Highlands, N.J.: Humanities Press, 1987), for instance, referring to the European Middle Ages, suggests that it was official church policy to place a "demonological interpretation on beliefs it held to be pagan; in a similar way, all pagan deities were identified with demons" (p. 14). My argument, then, is not that demonism was invented in British Ceylon in the nineteenth century. Rather, what came to be *identified* as Sinhala religion, and how, depended on the specific conditions of the production of knowledge prevailing at the time. Whereas demonism was already part of the conceptual baggage of Christian imagination long before the nineteenth century, it was the transformation in colonial practice that brought it into the vanguard of colonial Christian discourse.

64. Almond, *British*, p. 24.

65. In a dispatch of 26 February 1799, North had written in part that "The Religions professed in our parts of this Island are 1st The Christian, both according to the Presbyterian and Romish Form of Worship, 2ndly the Mohammadan, 3rdly The Doctrine of Boudha and 4thly a wilder and more extravagant system of paganism called by the Dutch the worship

of the Devil, but into the peculiar doctrines of which I have not had the leisure to enquire" (quoted in Tennakoon Vimalananda, *Buddhism in Ceylon under the Christian Powers* [Colombo: M. D. Gunasena, 1963], p. 5); and de Silva, *Ceylon*, p. 241.

66. John Davy, *An Account of the Interior of Ceylon and of its Inhabitants* (London: Hurst, Rees, Orme, and Brown, 1821). Davy was a physiologist and anatomist who served as surgeon and physician to the Governor, Sir Robert Brownrigg, between 1817 and 1819. See M. Y. Gooneratne, *Diverse Inheritance: A Personal Perspective on Commonwealth Literature* (Adelaide: Centre for Research in the New Literatures in English, 1980), pp. 111–119, for a useful discussion of Davy's *Account*.

67. Daniel J. Gogerly, "An Introductory Sketch of Buddhism" (orig. 1847), in *Ceylon Buddhism, Being the Collected Writings of Daniel John Gogerly*, ed. Arthur Stanley Bishop (Colombo: Wesleyan Methodist Book Room, 1908), vol. 1, p. 6.

68. Daniel J. Gogerly, "The Wesleyan Mission Station, Matura," *Friend* 1(4)(1837):101.

69. Sir James Emerson Tennent, *Christianity in Ceylon* (London: John Murray, 1850).

70. Tennent, who in 1859 also published a long history, *Ceylon*, was much admired among the contemporary Ceylonese English-speaking elite for his erudition and his style. He wrote in the progressivist tradition of James Mill and Thomas Macaulay colored by the Victorianism of his day, and evinced a like-minded contempt for anything from the East. Tennent was reliant in his writing on Sinhala religion on the Wesleyan missionary scholars D. J. Gogerly and Robert Spence Hardy. There were also Ceylonese scholars upon whom he relied, particularly on matters concerning Sinhala literature. The most prominent among these were James D'Alwis and Maha Mudaliyar Ernest de Saram. M. Y. Gooneratne, *English Literature in Ceylon, 1815–1878* (Dehiwala: Tisara Prakasakayo, 1968), has suggested that this latter fact gave to Tennent's work a guarded, watchful quality not found in Mill. "Tennent," she writes, "was conscious, as Mill never was, of a literate Ceylonese audience that looked over his shoulder as he wrote their history" (p. 83).

71. Quoted in Harvard, *Narrative*, p. lxi.

72. See Almond, *British*.

Chapter 6. Historicizing Tradition: Buddhism and the Discourse of *Yakku*

1. I am thinking here of James Clifford, "On *Orientalism*," in *The Predicament of Culture* (Cambridge Mass.: Harvard University Press, 1988), p. 260, in particular.

2. This theme has been pursued in relation to medieval Christianity by Talal Asad, "Notes on Body Pain and Truth in Medieval Christian Ritual," *Economy and Society* 12(3)(1983):287–327; "Medieval Heresy: An Anthropological View," *Social History* 11(3)(1986):345–362; "On Ritual and Discipline in Medieval Christian Monasticism," *Economy and Society* 16(2)(1987):159–203.

3. Not the least reason for this must have to do with the way in which the "culture" concept has been construed by nationalists and anthropologists. In this regard, see Jonathan Spencer's notable "Writing Within: Anthropology, Nationalism, and Culture in Sri Lanka," *Current Anthropology* 31(3)(1990):283–300.

4. For Sri Lanka, see Vijaya Samaraweera, "The 'Village Community' and Reform in Colonial Sri Lanka." *Ceylon Journal of Historical and Social Studies* n.s. 8(1)(1980):68–75.

5. Gananath Obeyesekere, "The Great Tradition and the Little in the Perspective of Sinhalese Buddhism," *Journal of Asian Studies* 22(2)(1963):139–153; Obeyesekere, "The Buddhist Pantheon in Ceylon and its Extensions," in *Anthropological Studies in Theravada Buddhism*, ed. Manning Nash (Cultural Report Series no. 13. New Haven: Yale University Press, 1966); Michael Ames, "Magical-Animism and Buddhism: A Structural Analysis of

the Sinhalese Religious System," in *Religion in South Asia*, ed. Edward B. Harper (Seattle: University of Washington Press, 1964); Ames, "Ritual Prestations and the Structure of the Sinhalese Pantheon," in *Anthropological Studies in Theravada Buddhism*, ed. Manning Nash; Nur Yalman, "The Structure of Sinhalese Healing Rituals," *Journal of Asian Studies* 27(1964):115–150; and Yalman, "Dual Organization in Central Ceylon," in *Anthropological Studies in Theravada Buddhism*, ed. Manning Nash.

6. Manning Nash, ed., *Anthropological Studies in Theravada Buddhism*. I am particularly grateful to Professor Nash for reflecting with me on this inaugural moment.

7. This general turn to the study of "peasant" societies in the period after the Second World War gave rise to other notable and related concepts such as "acculturation" and "syncretism."

8. For a survey of this field see, J. W. de Jong, "A Brief History of Buddhist Studies in Europe and America," *The Eastern Buddhist* n.s. 7(1)(1974):55–106; 7(2)(1974):49–82. De Jong perhaps exemplifies the textual scholar's disdain for, and indeed profound misunderstanding of, the field of observed social practice in which missionaries and anthropologists are concerned to work. Speaking of the disappointing amount of reliable knowledge about Buddhism missionaries brought to Europe from the sixteenth to the eighteenth centuries, he writes: "Their knowledge was based upon what they observed, and on discussions with Buddhist priests, but very rarely on the study of the Buddhist literature itself. For these reasons it must have been very difficult to gain a clear notion of the main Buddhist ideas. A religion like Buddhism which is based upon principles which are very different from the guiding principles of Christianity cannot be understood without a thorough study of its scriptures" (7[1][1974]:64). Obviously, for de Jong, what constitutes "Buddhism" is a self-evident matter. Moreover, the question whether there were not good, perhaps ideological reasons why Christian contact with Buddhism before the nineteenth century yielded little reliable knowledge is not perceived by him.

9. A tension (to call it no more than that) of serious conceptual proportions persists between anthropological and Indological conceptions. In this regard, see Stanley J. Tambiah, "At the Confluence of Anthropology, History, and Indology," *Contributions to Indian Sociology* (Special Issue on "Social Anthropology from Sri Lanka") 21(1)(1987):187–216.

10. Copleston's *Buddhism Primitive and Present in Magadha and in Ceylon* (New Delhi: Asian Educational Services, 1984 [orig. 1892]) is important not least because it was written and published at the end of the nineteenth century during the confrontation between Buddhists and Christian missionaries in Lankā.

11. Kitsiri Malalgoda, "Sinhalese Buddhism: Orthodox and Syncretistic, Traditional and Modern," *Ceylon Journal of Historical and Social Studies* n.s. 2(2)(1972):156.

12. There is actually some ambiguity in Malalgoda's critical remark. Since it comes at the beginning of his article on Gombrich's *Precept and Practice*, it is not very clear whether he thinks that this book "adequately discussed and analysed" the question.

13. Bryce Ryan, *Sinhalese Village*, (Coral Gables: University of Miami Press, 1958).

14. Gananath Obeyesekere [Review of Bryce Ryan, *Sinhalese Village*], *Ceylon Journal of Historical and Social Studies* 2(2)(1959):259.

15. Richard Gombrich and Gananath Obeyesekere, *Buddhism Transformed: Religious Change in Sri Lanka* (Princeton: Princeton University Press, 1988).

16. Sherry Ortner, "Anthropology in the Sixties," *Comparative Studies in Society and History* 26(1)(1984):126–166. Obeyesekere's work in the 1970s—beginning, of course, with that other seminal essay in which he coined the phrase "Protestant Buddhism," "Religious Symbolism and Political Change in Ceylon," *Modern Ceylon Studies* 1(1)(1970):43–63, and the sequence on Kataragama and devotional practices, "Social Change and the Deities: The Rise

of the Kataragama Cult in Modern Sri Lanka," *Man* n.s. 12(1977):377–396; and "The Firewalkers of Kataragama: The Rise of Bhakti Religiosity in Buddhist Sri Lanka," *Journal of Asian Studies* 37(3)(1978):457–476 – begins a distinctly social-historical trend in anthropological studies of Buddhism in Lankā.

17. Malalgoda, "Sinhalese Buddhism," p. 164.

18. See John Ross Carter's very fine article, "A History of *Early Buddhism*," *Religious Studies* 13(3)(1977):273.

19. The work of Alasdair MacIntyre is indispensable for the elaboration of the idea that argument and indeed conflict are constitutive of traditions. See, most recently, *Three Rival Versions of Moral Enquiry: Encyclopaedia, Genealogy, and Tradition* (Notre Dame: University of Notre Dame Press, 1990). I will return to what I take to be some of the implications for anthropological discourse of MacIntyre's conception of "narrative traditions" in the conclusion of this book.

20. See Martin Southwold, *Buddhism in Life: The Anthropological Study of Religion and the Sinhalese Practice of Buddhism* (Manchester: Manchester University Press, 1983), p. 115, for a recent statement of this view.

21. See Southwold, *Buddhism*, p. 128. Although I am in obvious disagreement with Southwold, here as elsewhere, I must say that his book has the virtue (lacking in most other treatments of this subject) of at least raising doubts about typical anthropological assumptions regarding the relation between "belief" and "religion."

22. I derive my conception of "discursive tradition" from Talal Asad's useful discussion in "The Idea of an Anthropology of Islam," Occasional Papers Series (Washington, D.C.: Center for Contemporary Arab Studies, 1986), pp. 7 and 14.

23. The *Mahāvaṃsa* is part of a larger tradition of history writing in Sri Lanka. It is preceded by the *Dīpavaṃsa* (Island Chronicle), which covers the same period, though in a less elegant way. Its value, says L. S. Perera, "The Pali Chronicle of Ceylon," in *Historians of India, Pakistan, and Ceylon*, ed. C. H. Philips (London: Oxford University Press, 1961), "is that it stands close to its source and therefore not only gives us a glimpse of the character of that source but hands over the traditions largely as it found them" (p. 31). Both the *Mahāvaṃsa* and *Dīpavaṃsa* are thought to be based on an earlier text, the *Sinhala-atthakathā-mahāvaṃsa*. This tradition of chronicle keeping has continued up to the present. The *Mahāvaṃsa* has been continued in what was called by Wilhelm Geiger the *Cūlavaṃsa*, which takes the record of *sangha* and kingship up to the period of the British occupation of the Kandyan kingdom in 1815. In the late 1970s, then President J. R. Jayewardene undertook to further extend the Chronicle in the *Mahāvaṃsa Nūtana Yugaya*. For a discussion see Steven Kemper, *The Presence of the Past: Chronicles, Politics, and Culture in Sinhala Life* (Ithaca: Cornell University Press, 1992).

24. For a discussion of the place of the chronicles in the construction of the ancient Lankan past see Perera, "The Pali Chronicle"; Walpola Rahula, *History of Buddhism: The Anuradhapura Period* (Colombo: M. D. Gunasena, 1956); and Senarat Paranavitana, "The Introduction of Buddhism," in *University of Ceylon History of Ceylon*, ed. H. C. Ray (Colombo: Ceylon University Press, 1959); and Wilhelm Geiger, *Culture of Ceylon in Medieval Times*, ed. Heinz Bechert (Wiesbaden: Otto Harrassowitz, 1960).

25. Paranavitana, "Introduction of Buddhism," p. 137.

26. For a discussion of the varied historical senses of this important concept in Buddhist tradition in Lankā see John Carter, "History," pp. 266–270. But see also E. F. C. Ludowyk, *The Story of Ceylon* (New Delhi: Navrang, 1985 [rev. ed.]), pp. 46–48.

27. What is important in Ludowyk's *Story* is that he reads the *Mahāvaṃsa* as a literary/historical *text* which employs various tropes and narrative devices to stage a historically

located signifying purpose. In contrast, Rahula's *History*, which, though a work of inestimable value, is more concerned with a straightforward sociohistorical interpretation and recuperation.

28. In the *Dīpavaṃsa*, the theme of "the excellent Lankadīpa" is introduced at (1.17). The actual encounter begins at (1.45) and ends at (1.79). On this earlier Chronicle generally, see Sirima Kiribamune, "The Dīpavamsa in Ancient Sri Lankan Historiography," *Sri Lanka Journal of the Humanities* 5(1 & 2)(1979):89–100.

29. See *Dīpavaṃsa* (1.64–65), where we hear the terrified *yakkhas* think: "Whither shall we go for safety and refuge? How shall we be released from this fearful being? If this powerful Yakkha assumes the form of the fiery element, and burns us, all of us Yakkhas will perish like a handful of chaff, like dust blown away by the wind."

30. See R. A. L. H. Gunawardana, "Kinsmen of the Buddha: Myth as Political Charter in the Ancient and Early Medieval Kingdoms of Sri Lanka," in *Religion and Legitimation of Power in Sri Lanka*, ed. Bardwell L. Smith (Chambersburg: Anima Books, 1978), p. 98.

31. Ibid., p. 98.

32. Kemper's *Presence of the Past* is very instructive in this regard because what he is interested in are precisely the ways in which the "pasts" represented (or "textualized," as he says) in the *Mahāvaṃsa* have been put to political uses.

33. Very curiously, Piyasena paused at one point to indicate that as far as he knew there was still a Great City of Visāla to be found in South Africa. The idea of *yakku* as essentially a cannibalistic species and the powerful, well-traveled image of Africa as a land of cannibalism seemed to come together in his mind.

34. A large jungle area crossing what are today the Central and Uva Provinces. It is the scene of many Sinhala stories involving *yakku*.

35. "*Appō! apiṭa oyo yakku inna tänaṭa yanna bäriya kivvā.*" "*Appō!*" is an expression of alarm or astonishment.

36. Ānanda is the one of two most renowned of the Buddha Gautama's disciples. The other is Sāriputta (Sinhala, Säriyut). A *rahat* is a monk who has attained *nirvāna*, and thus already, though still alive, stands beyond the wheel of *samsāra*.

37. Robes, alms bowl, and umbrella are of course the distinctive accessories of the village monk.

38. "*Tavama mē pava gevaganna bäri-unāṭa mē yaksayā däkkapu gaman denagattā mē kavaruvat novē budurujānam vahanse kenek bava.*" The passage speaks not only to the idea that having done wrong (*pav*), one must inevitably suffer for a commensurate period, often in a degraded form (generally, the idea of *karma*), but also to the idea that the ability to perceive/know things correctly is intimately connected to a moral register of right/wrong actions.

39. In another version of this story the figure of King Vessamuni (*Vessamuni rajuruvō*) occupies the place of this personage. Vessamuni is, of course, the celebrated King of the *yaksayās*.

40. "*Anē yaksayin topaṭa divya lōkayē divya sampattiya sadivya lōkayē sadivya sampattiya manusya lōkayē manusya sampattiya labena pinisa adara apiṭa inna navatänak adaṭa denne.*" A beggar's discourse. "*Anē*" is a plaintive expression, very common in colloquial speech.

41. "*Tō kāgen da mehema navatänak illanne?! Tō dannavay man kavda kiyalā?*" Note that the second person pronoun *tō* carries definite lower-status markings, and is used often in this imperative mood.

42. Power, that is, of discernment. These *yaksayās*, recall, had in previous Buddhist epochs heard the Doctrine. Note also, interestingly, that the storyteller uses the English (or,

more properly, "Singlish") "power" (phonetically, *pavar*), rather than a colloquial Sinhala word such as *balaya*.

43. "*Poḍḍak anaguṇayaṭa valanguvelā giyā.*"

44. "*Onna oya konakin innaya kiyanna ida arala uda ipalin tala tala elavanna.*"

45. "*Dän munṭa magē balaya penvanna ōna.*"

46. An exclamation of distress and surprise.

47. Likewise, an exclamation of distress and surprise.

48. If their lives were ended there would be no time to do good or virtuous works (*pin*).

49. A *yakṣa ädurā, yakṣa väḍakaruvā,* or *yakṣa kaṭṭāḍiya* is a practitioner of the techniques pertaining to *yakku*—that is, *ädurukama* or *gurukama*.

50. These are Sinhala diacriticals. A *rēphaya* is denoted by the Sinhala sign " ර්‍ " placed above a consonant, and gives the "r" sound in the word *dhārma*. A *pāpilla* is the "foot-piece" or vowel sign placed under a consonant in such characters as " කු " ("ku") or " මු " ("mu"). An *älapilla* is the "side-piece" or vowel sign represented by " ා " placed after a consonant, as in the character " බා " ("bā"). An *ispilla* is the "head-piece" or vowel sign denoted by " ි " placed over a consonant, as in the character " මි " ("mi").

51. In another version of this story, one group, the Isivarayō, *wrote* the *mantrayas*, and the other, the Rusivarayō, *performed* the various rites and ceremonies. A tidy division of labor.

52. The practices of indigenous healers known as *vedarālas* or *vedamahattayas*.

53. Piyasena explained, rather matter-of-factly, that since a disciple was still studying (*pādam karanavā*), and the teacher, by contrast, had long ceased to do so, the former must necessarily be more knowledgeable than the latter.

54. A black substance applied to the surface of the inscribed palm leaves so as to make the inscription legible.

55. For a different story about the first practitioners of the arts of *gurukama* see Paul Wirz, *Exorcism and the Art of Healing in Ceylon* (Leiden: E. J. Brill, 1954), pp. 22–23.

56. See K. M. de Silva, *A History of Sri Lanka* (Berkeley: University of California Press, 1981), pp. 92–96.

57. Martin Wickremasinghe, *Landmarks of Sinhalese Literature* (Colombo: M. D. Gunasena, 1948).

58. I am grateful to Charles Hallisey for sharing with me his knowledge of Sri Rāhula Thera and Maitreya Thera.

Chapter 7. The Ends and Strategy of *Yaktovil*

1. The Sinhala term I am translating here, as later, is the common verb *suva karanavā* or the verbal noun *suva kirīma*. They derive from the noun *suva*, meaning "health" but also "happiness," "enjoyment," "pleasure."

2. For a useful collection, see Pierre Bourdieu, *In Other Words: Essays Towards a Reflexive Sociology* (Stanford: Stanford University Press, 1990).

3. Pierre Bourdieu and Pierre Lamaison, "From Rules to Strategies: An Interview with Pierre Bourdieu," *Cultural Anthropology* 1(1)(1986):112.

4. "Strategies," p. 111.

5. Ibid.

6. Talal Asad, "On Ritual and Discipline in Medieval Christian Monasticism," *Economy and Society* 16(2)(1987):197n.

7. Michel Foucault, "The Subject and Power," afterword in *Michel Foucault: Beyond*

Structuralism and Hermeneutics, 2d ed., ed. Hubert L. Dreyfus and Paul Rabinow (Chicago: University of Chicago Press, 1983), pp. 224–225.

8. In the development of my conception of the "strategy" and "technique" of *yaktovil*, I am indebted not only to the work of Asad, Foucault, and Bourdieu, but also to the very thoughtful—and sadly unpublished—work of the late Michael Egan, "A Configurational Analysis of a Sinhalese Healing Ritual" (1975).

9. *Äpa* also has the sense of "bail." It constitutes, in other words, a sort of promise.

10. On this generally, see Paul Wirz, *Exorcism and the Art of Healing in Ceylon* (Leiden: E. J. Brill, 1954); Gananath Obeyesekere, "The Ritual Drama of the *Sanni* Demons: Collective Representations of Disease in Ceylon," *Comparative Studies in Society and History* 11(2)(1969):174–216; and Bruce Kapferer, *A Celebration of Demons: Exorcism and the Aesthetics of Healing in Sri Lanka* (Bloomington: Indiana University Press, 1983).

11. See Wirz, *Exorcism*, pp. 87–89.

12. Gooneratne discusses charms in a number of places. See, especially, "Judicial Astrology," *Young Ceylon* 1(3)(1850):63–66; "Charms," *Young Ceylon* 1(4)(1850):82–86; "Charms (continued)," *Young Ceylon* 1(5)(1850):109–112; and of course, most importantly, "On Demonology and Witchcraft in Ceylon," *Journal of the Royal Asiatic Society, Ceylon Branch* 4 (1865/66):1–117, which in fact draws on the previously published articles.

13. See also Wirz, *Exorcism*, p. 209, for some remarks on kinds of *mantrayas*.

14. This word, *ākarṣana*, is perhaps most often translated as "magnetism." See Gananath Obeyesekere, *The Cult of the Goddess Pattini* (Chicago: University of Chicago Press, 1984), p. 14: "*Ākarṣana* is a 'charge' that 'electrifies' or 'magnetizes' the body."

15. These, again, are Sinhala diacriticals; see chapter 6, note 50. A *kombuva* is a side-piece or vowel sign denoted by " ෙ " and placed before a consonant as in the character "මෙ" (*me*).

16. See Michael J. Egan, "A Configurational Analysis of a Sinhalese Healing Ritual" (unpublished manuscript, 1975), p. 31.

17. Ibid., p. 36.

18. Ibid., pp. 41 and 42.

19. As Obeyesekere, *Pattini*, pp. 48–49, has suggested, this technique rests on the idea of the "power of truth." We have, of course, come across this idea in a variety of areas of Sinhala ritual practice. To recount "truth" will have real effects.

20. Here I should like to record once again my thanks to the energetic staff of the Sinhala Dictionary Department in Colombo, Sri Lanka. I would single out Mr. Somapala, who with great patience and unflagging interest eventually traced this phrase, "*sēman gannavā*" (the verbal noun that sometimes appears in *sēman gänīma*), in the Department's colloquial collection.

21. The word *ōjas* has the sense of the "essence" or "vitality" of the food.

22. For a discussion of Sinhala food practices—which, however, does not mention this intriguing concept—see Nur Yalman, "The Meaning of Food Offerings in Ceylon," in *Forms of Symbolic Action*, ed. Robert F. Spencer (Seattle: University of Washington Press, 1969).

23. There is another sequence—the Dekonavilakku Pidēniya (see chapter 3)—which is perhaps most dramatically about the "deflection" of *diṣṭiya*. In this sequence, recall, the *ädurā*, having deeply inhaled the smoke of the incense called *dummala*, and having begun to shake violently, literally collects the malign energy (*diṣṭiya*) and its ill effects (*dōṣaya*) upon his body and takes them to a structure called a *purālapala* where the malevolent influence is "stopped." As D. A. Ariyadasa, an *ädurā* well practiced in this particular sequence, explained: "I take the *diṣṭiya* that is in the house completely unto my body (*gē ätulē tiyena diṣṭiyat sampūrna mama magē äṅgaṭa gannavā*). Then also I take the *diṣṭiya* of the sick person

completely unto my body (*ledāgē tiyena diṣṭiyat sampūrna mama magē äṅgaṭa gannavā*). All those *diṣṭiyas* fall upon me (*oyo diṣṭi okkōma maṭa vätenavā*). It is that [i.e., the *diṣṭiyas*] that I take to the *purālapala* and commend there (*ēka tamayi mama purālapalaṭa arangihillā bārakaranne*). . . . Having charmed with the *īgaha* and placed it at our head, all the *diṣṭiyas* that are taken by the *īgaha* fall upon our body (*īgahin maturalā, api oluvaṭa tiyalā, īgahin ganna diṣṭi okkōma api äṅgaṭa vätenava*)."

24. "The Demoness Kālī," p. 104, in *Jewels of the Doctrine: Stories of the Saddharma Ratnāvaliya* by Dharmasēna Thera, trans. Ranjini Obeyesekere (Albany: State University of New York, 1991).

25. Ranjini Obeyesekere, *Jewels*, p. 42.

26. "The Apaṇṇaka Jātaka" [no.1], in *Jātaka Stories*, vol. 1, ed. E. B. Cowell (Delhi: Motilal Banarsidass, 1990), p. 3.

27. Lorna Rhodes AmaraSingham, "Laughter as Cure: Joking and Exorcism in a Sinhalese Curing Ritual" (unpublished Ph.D. dissertation, Cornell University, 1973).

28. That is, the Buddha, the Dhamma or Doctrine, and the Sangha or monastic Order in which Buddhists are urged to seek Refuge.

29. And this would not, of course, be inconceivable. For a discussion of the tradition of female mendicants, see Tessa Bartholomeusz, "The Female Mendicant in Buddhist Sri Lanka," in *Buddhism, Sexuality, and Gender*, ed. José Ignacio Cabezón (Albany: State University of New York Press, 1992).

Glossary

ädurā — A practitioner of the arts of controlling the malign figures called *yakku*. Also *yakädurā,* sometimes even *yakädurā mahattayā* (Mr. *yakädurā*). In other areas called, *kaṭṭāḍiya*.

ädurukama — Lit., the "work of the teacher." The practices involved in the controlling of the malign figures, *yakku*. Also, *gurukama*.

aṇaguṇa — The "commands and virtues" of the Buddha. Typically invoked in the effort to secure the obedience of *yakku*.

ārūdhaya — Typically, a condition of being under the influence of a deity.

äsvaha — Lit., "eye poison." The malevolent energy of the eyesight of human beings.

āturayā — A victim of the malign "look" (*bälma*) or *diṣṭiya* of a *yaksayā*.

āturu pandala — The shed where the afflicted person stays during the performance of a *yaktovil* ceremony.

āturuhāmi — Another name for the afflicted person if female. Used in relation to *āturumahatmaya*.

āturumahatmaya — Husband of a female afflicted person, her benefactor.

āvēśaya — Condition of being under the influence of the malign figures called *yakku*. Characterized by trembling and lapses of conscious awareness. In the context of *yaktovil,* a condition that is induced upon the afflicted person by the *yakädurā* in order to elicit a certain kind of speech.

ayila	Offering tray used in *yaktovil* ceremonies. Typically a smaller version of *taṭṭuvas* (which see).
āyūbōvan	Long life. Often exclamatory. Sometimes *āyūbōvēvan*.
baliya	In the context of *yaktovil* ceremonies, a clay representation of the main *yaksayā* who has afflicted the *āturayā*.
bälma	The "look." Most often the "look" of a supernatural figure, whether malevolent or benevolent.
bana	Sermon based on the doctrine of the Buddha.
baṭagaha	Whistle used in *yaktovil* ceremonies.
bera kāraya	Drummer.
bhūtaya	A mean supernatural. Often said to perform the work of deities.
billa	A sacrifice, typically a cock.
brahamana	A Brahmin.
dēva	A benevolent supernatural deity. Also *deviyō*.
dēvālē	The shrine of a *dēva* or *deviyō*. Sometimes *dēvālaya*.
dēvatāva	A godling. A figure intermediate between malevolent and benevolent.
dharmaya	Law, truth, doctrine (Pāli, *dhamma*). Typically of the Buddha.
diṣṭiya	The malign energy of the "look" (*bälma*) of *yakku*. A concept central to the understanding the action of *yakku* and the work performed by *yaktovil*.
dōṣaya	Misfortunes, or troubles, or ill effects. Not necessarily associated with the work of *yakku*, but when it is, it is called *yakṣa dōṣa*, or *tanikam dōṣa* (which latter see).
dummala	A highly pungent incense used in *yaktovil* ceremonies to attract the presence of *yakku*.
hāmuduruvō	Respectful term commonly used to address a Buddhist monk.
īgaha	An instrument of command. A pointer, or rod.
kaḍaturāva	The curtain used to partition off the afflicted person from the practices involved in invoking the presence of *yakku*.
kapurāla	An officiant at the shrine of a *dēva*.
kavi	Verses.
koḍivina	Sorcery.

kumbhāndaya	A class of mean supernaturals.
mal maduva	Lit., "flower shed." Usually the main structure in *yaktovil* ceremonies. Typically decorated with red flowers.
mantraya	Formulaic and magical verses used in both malign and benign practices. Essentially, it is used to "bind" the supernatural figure to the performance of a particular work.
namaskāraya	Gesture of obeisance or profound respect formed by bringing the clasped hands up to the forehead.
nivārnayi	Finished. Marks the removal of *diṣṭiya* or malign eyesight from the body of an afflicted person.
pandam	Torch.
pan̆ḍuru	Coin offering made to a deity.
perahära	Procession, usually in commemoration of a deity.
pidēnna	Offering given to *yakku*. Usually *dola pidēni*.
pin	Merit.
prārthanāva	Fervent rebirth wish, or will to be.
prētayā	The dissatisfied spirit of a deceased person.
purālapala	Platform structure erected in *yaktovil* ceremonies to receive the "body" of an *ädurā* in the elaborate ruse of death played on *yakku*. Also *purahala*.
rahata	One who has all but seen *nirvāna*. He will not be born again to the round of suffering (*samsāra*) which is life. Also *arhat*.
sangha	The Buddhist Order of Monks.
sāntiya	A ceremony of blessing. *Yaktovil* ceremonies invariably involve some conference of blessing unto the afflicted.
sarīra	Body; also *än̆ga*.
sāsana	The teachings of the Buddha as a historical phenomenon. Refers to the periods or epochs when Buddhism prevailed (*buddha sāsanaya*).
sēman gänīma	The act of taking the *sēmanaya* or essence of an offering by imbibing it through the eyes.
sīmāva	Boundary. Often inscribed as part of the sanction (*varama* or *vivaranaya*) issued by the Buddha.

tanikam dōṣa	The ill effects that result from being in a state of vulnerability to the malign eyesight of *yakku*.
tanikama	Condition or state of mental apprehension that makes one vulnerable to the disturbing look of a *yaksayā*.
taṭṭuva	Offering tray used in *yaktovil* ceremonies.
tīnduyi	Finished completely. Marks the removal of the malign influence of *diṣṭiya* from the body of an afflicted person. More emphatic version of *nivārnayi*.
tovil gedara	The house where a *yaktovil* ceremony takes place.
tun dos	Three humors—*vāta, pitta,* and *sema*—which regulate the functioning of the body.
varama	Lit., "warrant." Typically a limited and conditional power issued by the Buddha.
veḍakama	The practices involved in *āyurvedic* healing.
vīdiya	Structure through which the *yakku* enter the performing area of the *yaktovil* ceremony.
vivaranaya	Lit., "permission," or "leave." Like *varama,* a limited and conditional power issued by the Buddha.
yakā	The most feared of the pantheon of malevolent supernatural figures. Also *yaksayā* (pl. *yakku* or *yaksayō*).
yaktovil	Major practice in which an *āturayā* is relieved of the *diṣṭiya* with which he/she has been afflicted. Also simply *tovil*.
yakves	The "costume" or appearance that a *yaksayā* assumes in order to carry out its malign work.
yakvimānaya	The abode of the hosts of *yakku*.

Bibliography

Almond, Philip C. "The Medieval West and Buddhism." *The Eastern Buddhist* n.s. 19(2)(1986):85–101.
——. "Buddhism in the West: 300 BC-AD 400." *Journal of Religious History* 14(3)(1987):235–245.
——. *The British Discovery of Buddhism*. New York: Cambridge University Press, 1988.
——. *Heretic and Hero: Muhammad and the Victorians*. Wiesbaden: Otto Harrassowitz, 1989.
AmaraSingham, Lorna Rhodes. "Laughter as Cure: Joking and Exorcism in a Sinhalese Curing Ritual." Unpublished Ph.D. dissertation, Cornell University, 1973.
——. "Laughter and Suffering: Sinhalese Interpretations of the Use of Ritual Humor." *Social Science and Medicine* 17(14)(1983):979–985.
Ames, Michael M. "Buddha and the Dancing Goblins: A Theory of Magic and Religion." *American Anthropologist* 66(1964):75–82.
——. "Magical-Animism and Buddhism: A Structural Analysis of the Sinhalese Religious System." In *Religion in South Asia*, edited by Edward B. Harper. Seattle: University of Washington Press, 1964.
——. "Ritual Prestations and the Structure of the Sinhalese Pantheon." In *Anthropological Studies in Theravada Buddhism*, edited by Manning Nash. Cultural Report Series no. 13. New Haven: Yale University South East Asian Studies, 1966.
Appadurai, Arjun. "Theory in Anthropology: Center and Periphery." *Comparative Studies in Society and History* 28(2)(1986):356–361.
——. "Introduction: Place and Voice in Anthropological Theory." *Cultural Anthropology* 3(1)(1988):16–20.
Asad, Talal. "Two European Images of Non-European Rule." In *Anthropology and the Colonial Encounter*, edited by Talal Asad. London: Ithaca Press, 1973.
——. "Anthropological Texts and Ideological Problems: An Analysis of Cohen on Arab Villages in Israel." *Economy and Society* 4(3)(1975):251–282.
——. "Anthropology and the Analysis of Ideology." *Man* n.s. 14(1979):607–627.
——. "Anthropological Conceptions of Religion: Reflections on Geertz." *Man* n.s. 18(2)(1983):237–259.
——. "Notes on Body Pain and Truth in Medieval Christian Ritual." *Economy and Society* 12(3)(1983):287–327.
——. "The Concept of Cultural Translation in British Social Anthropology." In *Writing Culture*, edited by James Clifford and George Marcus. Berkeley: University of California Press, 1986.
——. "The Idea of an Anthropology of Islam." Occasional Papers Series. Washington, D.C.: Center for Contemporary Arab Studies, 1986.

——. "Medieval Heresy: An Anthropological View." *Social History* 11(3)(1986):345–362.
——. "On Ritual and Discipline in Medieval Christian Monasticism." *Economy and Society* 16(2)(1987):159–203.
——. "Towards a Genealogy of the Concept of Ritual." In *Vernacular Christianity: Essays in the Social Anthropology of Religion Presented to Godfrey Lienhardt*, edited by W. James and D. M. Johnson. Oxford: JASO, 1988.
Asad, Talal, ed. *Anthropology and the Colonial Encounter*. London: Ithaca Press, 1973.
Austin, J. L. *How to do Things with Words*. 2d ed. Cambridge, Mass.: Harvard University Press, 1962.
Babb, Lawrence A. "Glancing: Visual Interaction in Hinduism." *Journal of Anthropological Research* 37(4)(1981):387–401.
Bartholomeusz, Tessa. "The Female Mendicant in Buddhist Sri Lanka." In *Buddhism, Sexuality, and Gender*, edited by José Ignacio Cabezón. Albany: State University of New York Press, 1992.
Bayly, C. A. *Imperial Meridian: The British Empire and the World, 1780–1830*. New York: Longman, 1989.
Beaglehole, J. C. "The Colonial Office, 1782-1854." *Historical Studies of Australia and New Zealand* 1(3)(1941):170–189.
Benians, E. A. "The Beginnings of the New Empire, 1783–1793." In *Cambridge History of the British Empire*, vol. 2, *The Growth of the New Empire, 1783–1870*. Cambridge: Cambridge University Press, 1961.
Bernstein, Richard J. *Beyond Objectivism and Relativism: Science, Hermeneutics, and Praxis*. Philadelphia: University of Pennsylvania Press, 1983.
Bhabha, Homi K. "The Other Question—The Stereotype and Colonial Discourse." *Screen* 24(6)(1983):18–36.
Blacking, John, "Towards an Anthropology of the Body." In *The Anthropology of the Body*, edited by John Blacking. London: Academic Press, 1977.
Bloch, Maurice. "Symbols, Song, Dance and Features of Articulation." *European Journal of Sociology* 15(1)(1974):55–81.
——. "The Past and the Present in the Present." *Man* n.s. 12(1977):55–81.
——. *From Blessing to Violence: History and Ideology in the Circumcision Ritual of the Merina of Madagascar*. Cambridge: Cambridge University Press, 1986.
Bloss, Lowell. "Nāgas and Yakṣas." In *The Encyclopedia of Religion*, edited by Mircea Eliade. New York: Macmillan, 1987.
Bond, George D. *The Buddhist Revival in Sri Lanka: Religious Tradition, Reinterpretation and Response*. Columbia: University of South Carolina Press, 1988.
Bordo, Susan. "Reading the Slender Body." In *Body/Politics: Women and the Discourses of Science*, edited by Mary Jacobus, Evelyn Fox Keller, and Sally Shuttleworth. New York: Routledge, 1990.
Bourdieu, Pierre. *Outline of a Theory of Practice*. Cambridge: Cambridge University Press, 1973.
——. "The Genesis of the Concepts of *Habitus* and of *Field*." *Sociocriticism* 2(1985):11–24.
——. *In Other Words: Essays Towards a Reflexive Sociology*. Stanford: Stanford University Press, 1990.
Bourdieu, Pierre, and Pierre Lamaison. "From Rules to Strategies: An Interview with Pierre Bourdieu." *Cultural Anthropology* 1(1)(1986):110–120.
Boyd, James W. "Satan and Māra: Christian and Buddhist Symbols of Evil." *Modern Ceylon Studies* 4(1 & 2)(1973):84–100.

Bradley, Ian. *The Call to Seriousness: The Evangelical Impact on the Victorians*. New York: Macmillan, 1976.

Bruner, Edward M. "Introduction: Experience and its Expressions." In *The Anthropology of Experience*, edited by Victor W. Turner and Edward M. Bruner. Urbana: University of Illinois Press, 1986.

Buchanan, Francis. "On the Religion and Literature of the Burmas." *Asiatick Researches* 6(1807):163–308.

Burrows, Sir Montagu. "The Conquest of Ceylon, 1795–1815." In *The Cambridge History of the British Empire*, vol. 4, British India 1497–1858; edited by H. H. Dodwell. Cambridge: Cambridge University Press, 1929.

Calloway, Rev. John. *Yakkun Nattannawa and Kolan Nattannawa*. London, 1829.

Carrithers, Michael. *The Forest Monks of Sri Lanka: An Anthropological and Historical Study*. Delhi: Oxford University Press, 1983.

Carter, Rev. Charles. *A Sinhalese-English Dictionary*. Colombo: M. D. Gunasena, 1965 (orig. 1924).

Carter, John Ross. "A History of *Early Buddhism*." *Religious Studies* 13(3)(1977):263–287.

Carter, John Ross and Mahinda Palihawadana, trans. and eds. *The Dhammapada*. New York: Oxford University Press, 1987.

Clifford, James. "Introduction: Partial Truths." In *Writing Culture: The Poetics and Politics of Ethnography*, edited by James Clifford and George Marcus. Berkeley: University of California Press, 1986.

——. "On *Orientalism*." In *The Predicament of Culture*. Cambridge, Mass.: Harvard University Press, 1988.

Clough, Rev. Benjamin. *A Sinhala-English Dictionary*. New Delhi: Asian Educational Services, 1982 (originally published in Colombo by the Wesleyan Missionary Press in 1830).

Cohn, Bernard S. "The Command of Language and the Language of Command." In *Subaltern Studies IV. Writings on South Asian History and Society*, edited by Ranajit Guha. Delhi: Oxford University Press, 1985.

Colgate, H. A. "The Royal Navy and Trincomalee: The History of their Connection, c 1750–1958." *The Ceylon Journal of Historical and Social Studies* 7(1)(1964):1–16.

Collins, Steven. *Selfless Persons: Imagery and Thought in Theravāda Buddhism*. Cambridge: Cambridge University Press, 1982.

Coomaraswamy, Ananda K. *Yakṣas*. New Dehli: Munshiram Manoharlal, 1971 (orig. 1928).

Coomaraswamy, Sir. M., trans. *Sutta Nipata or, Dialogues and Discourses of Gotama Buddha*. London: Trübner & Co., 1874.

Copleston, Reginald Stephen. *Buddhism Primitive and Present in Magadha and in Ceylon*. New Delhi: Asian Educational Services, 1984 (orig. 1892).

Cowell, E. B. general editor. *Jātaka Stories* (translated from the Pāli). 6 vols. Delhi: Motilal Banarsidas, 1990.

Crapanzano, Vincent. "Spirit Possession," *The Encyclopedia of Religion*, vol. 14, edited by Mircea Eliade. New York: Macmillan Publishing Company, 1987.

Davy, John. *An Account of the Interior of Ceylon and of its Inhabitants*. London: Hurst, Rees, Orme, and Brown, 1821.

de Jong, J. W. "A Brief History of Buddhist Studies in Europe and America." *The Eastern Buddhist* n.s. 7(1)(1974):55–106; 7(2)(1974):49–82.

Derrida, Jacques. *Writing and Difference*. Chicago: University of Chicago Press, 1978.

de Silva, Colvin R. *Ceylon Under the British Occupation, 1795–1833*, vol. 1, *Its Political and Administrative Development*. Colombo: Colombo Apothecaries Co. Ltd., 1953.

——. *Ceylon Under the British Occupation, 1795–1833*, vol. 2, *Its Political, Administrative and Economic Development*. Colombo Apothecaries Co. Ltd., 1962.

de Silva, K. M. *Social Policy and Missionary Organizations in Ceylon, 1840–1855*. London: Longmans, 1965.

——. "The Coming of the British to Ceylon, 1762–1802." In *University of Ceylon History of Ceylon*, vol. 3. Colombo: University of Ceylon Press, 1973.

——. *A History of Sri Lanka*. Berkeley: University of California Press, 1981.

Diamond, Stanley. "Anthropology in Question." In *In Search of the Primitive: A Critique of Civilization*. New Brunswick, N.J.: Transaction Books, 1974.

——. "Theory, Practice, and Poetry." In *Theory and Practice: Essays Presented to Gene Weltish*. Studies in Anthropology 7, edited by Stanley Diamond. The Hague: Mouton, 1980.

Dirks, Nicholas. *The Hollow Crown: Ethnohistory of an Indian Kingdom*. New York: Cambridge University Press, 1987.

Eck, Diana L. *Darṣan: Seeing the Divine Image in India*. 2d ed. Chambersburg: Anima Books, 1981.

Egan, Michael J. "A Configurational Analysis of a Sinhalese Healing Ritual." Unpublished manuscript, 1975.

Fabian, Johannes. *Time and the Other: How Anthropology Makes Its Object*. New York: Columbia University Press, 1983.

Fernandez, C. N. V. "Christianity in Ceylon in the Portuguese and Dutch Periods." *University of Ceylon Review* 6(4)(1948):267–288.

——. "Christianity in Ceylon in the British Period." *University of Ceylon Review* 7(2)(1949):135–141.

——. "Christian Missionary Enterprise in the Early British Period." *University of Ceylon Review* 7(3)(1949):198–207.

——. "Christian Missionary Enterprise in the Early British Period II." *University of Ceylon Review* 7(4)(1949):269–277.

——. "Christian Missionary Enterprise in the Early British Period III." *University of Ceylon Review* 8(2)(1950):110–115.

——. "Christian Missionary Enterprise in the Early British Period IV." *University of Ceylon Review* 8(3)(1950):203–206.

——. "Some Aspects of Christian Missionary Enterprise in the Early British Period (1796–1830) VI." *University of Ceylon Review* 8(4)(1950):264–271.

——. "Christian Missions: IX. Some Aspects of Baptist and Wesleyan Work from 1827–1864." *University of Ceylon Review* 9(2)(1951):106–112.

——. "Christian Missions: X. Some Aspects of the Work of American Missionaries in Jaffna District from 1827–1866." *University of Ceylon Review* 9(3)(1951):191–201.

Filliozat, Jean. *The Classical Doctrine of Indian Medicine*. Delhi: Munishiram Manoharlal, 1964.

Foucault, Michel. *Discipline and Punish: The Birth of the Prison*, translated by Alan Sheridan. New York: Vintage Books, 1979.

——. "The Subject and Power." Afterword in Hubert L. Dreyfus and Paul Rabinow. *Michel Foucault: Beyond Structuralism and Hermeneutics*, 2d ed. Chicago: University of Chicago Press, 1983.

——. "The Ethic of Care for the Self as a Practice of Freedom." *Philosophy and Social Criticism* 12(2–3)(1987):112–131.

——. *The Care of the Self*, translated by Robert Hurley. New York: Vintage, 1988.

Geertz, Clifford. "Thick Description: Toward an Interpretive Theory of Culture." In *The Interpretation of Cultures*. New York: Basic Books, 1973.

——. "Found in Translation: On the Social History of the Moral Imagination." In *Local Knowledge*. New York: Basic Books, 1983.
——. " 'From the Native's Point of View': On the Nature of Anthropological Understanding." In *Local Knowledge*. New York: Basic Books, 1983.
——. "Making Experiences, Authoring Selves." In *The Anthropology of Experience*, edited by Victor W. Turner and Edward M. Bruner. Urbana: University of Illinois Press, 1986.
Geiger, Wilhelm. *The Dīpavamsa and the Mahāvamsa in their Historical Development in Ceylon*, translated by Ethel Coomaraswamy. Colombo: Ceylon Government Printer, 1908.
——, trans. *The Mahāvamsa or The Great Chronicle of Ceylon*. New Delhi: Asian Educational Services, 1986 (orig. 1912).
——. *Culture of Ceylon in Medieval Times*, edited by Heinz Bechert. Wiesbaden: Otto Harrassowitz, 1960.
Godakumbura, Charles. *Sinhalese Literature*. Colombo: Colombo Apothecaries Co. Ltd., 1955.
Gogerly, Daniel J. "The Wesleyan Mission Station, Matura." *Friend* 1(4)(1837):101–107.
——. "An Introductory Sketch of Buddhism." In *Ceylon Buddhism, Being the Collected Writings of Daniel John Gogerly*, edited by Arthur Stanley Bishop. Vol. 1. Colombo: Wesleyan Methodist Book Room, 1908 (orig. 1847).
Gombrich, Richard. "The Consecration of a Buddhist Image." *Journal of Asian Studies* 26(1)(1966):23–36.
——. *Precept and Practice: Traditional Buddhism in the Rural Highlands of Ceylon*. Oxford: Clarendon Press, 1971.
Gombrich, Richard, and Gananath Obeyesekere. *Buddhism Transformed: Religious Change in Sri Lanka*. Princeton: Princeton University Press, 1988.
Gonda, Jan. *Eye and Gaze in the Veda*. Amsterdam, London: North-Holland Publishing Company, 1969.
Goodman, Felicitas. *How About Demons? Possession and Exorcism in the Modern World*. Bloomington: Indiana University Press, 1988.
Gooneratne, Dandris de Silva. "Judicial Astrology." *Young Ceylon* 1(3)(1850):63–66.
——. "Charms." *Young Ceylon* 1(4)(1850):82–86.
——. "Charms (continued)." *Young Ceylon* 1(5)(1850):109–112.
——. "On Demonology and Witchcraft in Ceylon." *Journal of the Royal Asiatic Society, Ceylon Branch* 4(1865/66):1–117.
Gooneratne, M. Y. *English Literature in Ceylon, 1815–1878*. Dehiwala: Tisara Prakasakayo, 1968.
——. *Diverse Inheritance: A Personal Perspective on Commonwealth Literature*. Adelaide: Centre for Research in the New Literatures in English, 1980.
Goonewardena, K. W. *The Foundation of Dutch Power in Ceylon, 1638–1658*. Amsterdam: Djambatan, 1958.
Grant, Charles. *Observations on the State of Society among the Asiatic Subjects of Great Britain, particularly with respects to Morals; and on the Means of Improving It*. London, 1797.
Gunawardana, R. A. L. H. "Kinsmen of the Buddha: Myth as Political Charter in the Ancient and Early Medieval Kingdoms of Sri Lanka." In *Religion and Legitimation of Power in Sri Lanka*, edited by Bardwell L. Smith. Chambersburg: Anima Books, 1978.
Hacking, Ian. *Why Does Language Matter to Philosophy?* Cambridge: Cambridge University Press, 1975.
——. "Language, Truth and Reason." In *Rationality and Relativism*, edited by Martin Hollis and Steven Lukes. Oxford: Basil Blackwell, 1982.
——. "Making Up People." In *Reconstructing Individualism: Autonomy, Individuality, and the*

Self in Western Thought, edited by Thomas C. Heller, Morton Sosna, and David A. Wellbery. Stanford: Stanford University Press, 1986.

Halverson, John. "Dynamics of Exorcism: The Sinhalese Sanniyakuma." *History of Religions* 10(4)(1971):334–359.

Handelman, Don, and Bruce Kapferer. "Symbolic Types, Mediation and the Transformation of Ritual Context: Sinhalese Demons and Tewa Clowns." *Semiotica* 30(1/2)(1980):41–71.

Hardy, Robert Spence. *The British Government and the Idolatry of Ceylon*. London: Crofts and Blenkarn, 1841.

——. *A Manual of Buddhism*. Varanasi: The Chowkhamba Sanskrit Series Office, 1967 (orig. 1853).

Harington, J. H. "Introductory Remarks." *Asiatick Researches* 8(1808):529–534.

Harrison, Peter. *"Religion" and the religions in the English Enlightenment*. New York: Cambridge University Press, 1990.

Harvard, Rev. William M. *A Narrative of the Establishment and Progress of the Mission to Ceylon and India*. London, 1823.

Henriques, Julian, W. Hollway, C. Urwin, C. Venn, V. Walkerdine, eds. *Changing the Subject: Psychology, Social Regulation and Subjectivity*. New York: Methuen, 1984.

Hocart, A. M. "The Mechanism of the Evil Eye," *Folk-Lore* 49(1938):156–157.

——. "Yakshas and Väddas." In *The Life-Giving Myth*. New York: Grove Press, n.d.

Holt, John. *Buddha in the Crown: Avalokiteṣvara in the Buddhist Traditions of Sri Lanka*. New York: Oxford University Press, 1991.

Ingham, Kenneth. "The English Evangelicals and the Pilgrim Tax in India, 1800–1862." *Journal of Ecclesiastical History* 3(1952):191–200.

Jaggi, O. P. *Indian System of Medicine*. History of Science and Technology in India, vol. 4. Delhi: Atma Ram and Sons, 1973.

Joinville, Joseph Endelin de. "On the Religion and Manners of the People of Ceylon." *Asiatick Researches* 7(1807):397–444 (written circa 1801).

Jones, William. "A Discourse on the Institution of a Society." *Asiatick Researches* 1(1806):ix-xvi.

——. "On the Gods of Greece, Italy, and India." *Asiatick Researches* 1(1806):221–275 (written 1784).

——. "Third Anniversary Discourse." *Asiatick Researches* 1(1806):415–431 (delivered February 1786).

——. "On the Chronology of the Hindus." *Asiatick Researches* 2(1806):111–147 (written January 1788).

Kapferer, Bruce. "Emotion and Feeling in Sinhalese Healing Rites." *Social Analysis* 1(1979):153–176.

——. "Entertaining Demons. Comedy, Interaction and Meaning in a Sinhalese Healing Ritual." *Social Analysis* 1(1979):108–152.

——. "Introduction: Ritual Process and the Transformation of Context." *Social Analysis* 1(1979):3–19.

——. "Mind, Self and Other in Demonic Illness: The Negation and Reconstruction of Self." *American Ethnologist* 6(1979):110–133.

——. *A Celebration of Demons: Exorcism and the Aesthetics of Healing in Sri Lanka*. Bloomington: Indiana University Press, 1983.

——. "Performance and the Structuring of Meaning and Experience." In *The Anthropology of Experience*, edited by Victor W. Turner and Edward M. Bruner. Urbana: Unversity of Illinois Press, 1986.

Kemper, Steven. "Sinhalese Astrology, South Asian Caste Systems, and the Notion of Individuality," *Journal of Asian Studies* 38(3)(1979):477–497.

——. "Time, Person and Gender in Sinhalese Astrology," *American Ethnologist* 7(4)(1980):744–758.

——. "The Buddhist Monkhood, the Law, and the State in Colonial Sri Lanka." *Comparative Studies in Society and History* 26(1984):401–427.

——. *The Presence of the Past: Chronicles, Politics, and Culture in Sinhala Life*. Ithaca: Cornell University Press, 1992.

Keyes, Charles, and E. Valentine Daniel, eds. *Karma: An Anthropological Inquiry*. Los Angeles: University of California Press, 1983.

Kiribamune, Sirima. "The Dīpavamsa in Ancient Sri Lankan Historiography." *Sri Lanka Journal of the Humanities* 5(1 & 2)(1979):89–100.

Knighton, William. *Forest Life in Ceylon*, 2 vols. London: Hurst and Blackett, 1854.

Knorr, Klaus E. *British Colonial Theories, 1570–1850*. Toronto: University of Toronto Press, 1944.

Knox, Robert. *An Historical Relation of Ceylon*. Dehiwala: Tisara Prakasakayo, 1966.

Kopf, David. *British Orientalism and the Bengal Renaissance*. Berkeley: University of California Press, 1969.

——. "Hermeneutics versus History." *Journal of Asian Studies* 39(3)(1980):495–506.

Lewis, I. M. *Ecstatic Religion: A Study of Shamanism and Spirit Possession*. (2d edition). New York: Routledge, 1989.

Ling, T. O. *Buddhism and the Mythology of Evil*. London: Allen & Unwin, 1962.

Ludowyk, E. F. C. *The Modern History of Ceylon*. New York: Praeger, 1966.

——. *The Story of Ceylon* (rev. ed.). New Delhi: Navrang, 1985.

MacIntyre, Alasdair. "Epistemological Crises, Dramatic Narrative, and the Philosophy of Science." In *Paradigms and Revolutions: Applications and Appraisals of Thomas Kuhn's Philosophy of Science*, edited by Gary Gutting. Notre Dame: University of Notre Dame Press, 1980.

——. *Three Rival Versions of Moral Enquiry: Encyclopaedia, Genealogy, and Tradition*. Notre Dame: University of Notre Dame Press, 1990.

Mackenzie, W. C. *Colonel Colin Mackenzie: First Surveyor-General of India*. Edinburgh and London: W & R Chambers Ltd., 1952.

Mahoney, Clarence. "Don't Say 'Pretty Baby' Lest You Zap It with Your Eye—The Evil Eye in South Asia." In *The Evil Eye*, edited by Clarence Mahoney. New York: Columbia University Press, 1976.

Mahony, Capt. "On Singhala, or Ceylon, and the Doctrines of Bhooddha." *Asiatick Researches* 7(1807):32–56.

Malalasekara, G. P. *Dictionary of Pāli Proper Names*. London: Routledge and Kegan Paul, 1974.

Malalgoda, Kitsiri. "Sinhalese Buddhism: Orthodox and Syncretistic, Traditional and Modern." *Ceylon Journal of Historical and Social Studies* n.s. 2(2)(1972):156–169.

——. *Buddhism in Sinhalese Society, 1750–1900*. Berkeley: University of California Press, 1976.

Mani, Lata. "Contentious Traditions: The Debate on Sati in Colonial India." *Cultural Critique* 7(1987):119–156.

Marasinghe, M. M. J. *Gods in Early Buddhism*. Kelaniya: University of Sri Lanka (Vidyalankara Campus) Press, 1974.

Marcus, George E., and Michael M. J. Fischer. *Anthropology as Cultural Critique: An Experimental Moment in the Human Sciences*. Chicago: University of Chicago Press, 1986.

Marshall, P. J. "Introduction." In *The British Discovery of Hinduism in the Eighteenth Century*, edited by P. J. Marshall. Cambridge: Cambridge University Press, 1970.
Mauss, Marcel. "Techniques of the Body." *Economy and Society* 2(1)(1973):70–88.
McGrane, Bernard. *Beyond Anthropology: Society and the Other*. New York: Columbia University Press, 1989.
McKenzie, Capt. Colin. "Remarks on some Antiquities on the West and South Coasts of Ceylon." *Asiatick Researches* 6(1807):425–454 (written in 1796).
Mendis, G. C. *Ceylon Under the British*. Colombo: Colombo Apothecaries Co. Ltd., 1948.
——., ed. *The Colebrooke-Cameron Papers. Documents on British Colonial Policy, 1796–1833*, 2 vols. London: Oxford University Press, 1956.
Meslin, Michel. "Eye." *The Encyclopedia of Religion*, vol. 5, edited by Mircea Eliade. New York: Macmillan, 1987.
Mill, Lennox A. *Ceylon Under British Rule, 1795–1932*. London: Oxford University Press, 1933.
Monier-Williams, Sir Monier. *A Sanskrit-English Dictionary*. London: Oxford University Press, 1899.
Mukherjee, S. N. *Sir William Jones: A Study in Eighteenth-Century British Attitudes to India*, 2d ed. Hyderabad: Orient Longman, 1987.
Nandy, Ashis. *The Intimate Enemy: Loss and Recovery of Self Under Colonialism*. Delhi: Oxford University Press, 1983.
Nash, Manning, ed. *Anthropological Studies in Theravada Buddhism*. Cultural Report Series no. 13. New Haven: Yale University South East Asia Studies, 1966.
Nevill, Hugh. *Sinhala Verse (Kavi)*, 2 vols., edited by P. E. P. Deraniyagala. Colombo: Government Press, 1954.
——. *Sinhala Verse (Kavi)*, vol. 3, edited by P. E. P. Deraniyagala. Colombo: Government Press, 1955.
North, Frederic. "Letter to the Secretary of the Society for Asiatic Researches." *Asiatick Researches* 7(1807):396 (written 27 September 1801).
Obeyesekere, Gananath. [Review of Bryce Ryan, *Sinhalese Village*]. *Ceylon Journal of Historical and Social Studies* 2(2)(1959):259.
——. "The Great Tradition and the Little in the Perspective of Sinhalese Buddhism." *Journal of Asian Studies* 22(2)(1963):139–153.
——. "The Buddhist Pantheon in Ceylon and its Extensions." In *Anthropological Studies in Theravada Buddhism*, edited by Manning Nash. Cultural Report Series no. 13. New Haven: Yale University South East Asian Studies, 1966.
——. "The Ritual Drama of the *Sanni* Demons: Collective Representations of Disease in Ceylon." *Comparative Studies in Society and History* 11(2)(1969):174–216.
——. "Religious Symbolism and Political Change in Ceylon." *Modern Ceylon Studies* 1(1)(1970):43–63.
——. "The Impact of Āyurvedic Ideas on the Culture and the Individual in Sri Lanka." In *Asian Medical Systems: A Comparative Study*, edited by Charles Leslie. Berkeley: University of California Press, 1976.
——. "Psychocultural Exegesis of a Case of Spirit Possession in Sri Lanka." In *Case Studies in Possession*, edited by Vincent Crapanzano and Vivian Garrison. New York: John Wiley, 1977.
——. "Social Change and the Deities: The Rise of the Kataragama Cult in Modern Sri Lanka." *Man* n.s. 12(1977):377–396.
——. "The Theory and Practice of Psychological Medicine in the Ayurvedic Tradition." *Culture, Medicine and Psychiatry* 1(1977):155–181.

——. "The Firewalkers of Kataragama: The Rise of Bhakti Religiosity in Buddhist Sri Lanka." *Journal of Asian Studies* 37(3)(1978):457–476.

——. "Popular Religions." In *Modern Sri Lanka: A Society in Transition*, edited by Tissa Fernando and Robert N. Kearney. Syracuse: Maxwell School of Citizenship and Public Affairs, 1979.

——. *Medusa's Hair*. Chicago: University of Chicago Press, 1981.

——. *The Cult of the Goddess Pattini*. Chicago: University of Chicago Press, 1984.

Obeyesekere, Ranjini, trans. *Jewels of the Doctrine: Stories of the Saddharma Ratnāvaliya* by Dharmasēna Thera. Albany: State University of New York Press, 1991.

Obeyesekere, Ranjini, and Gananath Obeyesekere. "The Tale of the Demoness Kālī: A Discourse on Evil." *History of Religions* 24(4)(1990):318–334.

Oldenberg, Herman, trans. *The Dīpavamsa*. New Delhi: Asian Educational Services, 1982 (orig. 1879).

Ortner, Sherry. *Sherpas Through their Rituals*. Cambridge: Cambridge University Press, 1978.

——. "Theory in Anthropology since the Sixties." *Comparative Studies in Society and History* 26(1)(1984):126–166.

Pailin, David. *Attitudes to Other Religions: Comparative Religion in Seventeenth and Eighteenth Century Britain*. Manchester: Manchester University Press, 1984.

Paranavitana, Senarat. "Pre-Buddhist Religious Beliefs in Ceylon." *Journal of the Royal Asiatic Society, Ceylon Branch* 31(82)(1929):302–327.

——. *The Shrine of Upulvan at Devundara*. Memoirs of the Archaeological Survey of Ceylon, vol. 6. Colombo: Ceylon Government Archaeological Department, 1953.

——. "The Introduction of Buddhism." In *University of Ceylon History of Ceylon*, edited by H. C. Ray. Colombo: Ceylon University Press, 1959.

Peiris, The Rt. Rev. Edmund. "Joinville's Translation of the Kokila Sandesaya." *Ceylon Historical Journal* 3(3/4)(1953):256–267.

Perera, L. S. "The Pali Chronicle of Ceylon." In *Historians of India, Pakistan, and Ceylon*, edited by C. H. Philips. London: Oxford University Press, 1961.

Pertold, Otaker. *Ceremonial Dances of the Sinhalese*. Dehiwala: Tisara Prakasakayo, 1930.

Pieris, P. E. *Ceylon and the Hollanders, 1658–1796*. Tellippalai: American Ceylon Mission Press, 1918.

——. *Ceylon and the Portuguese, 1505–1658*. Tellippalai: American Ceylon Mission Press, 1920.

——. *Tri Sinhala: The Last Phase, 1796–1815*. Colombo: Colombo Apothecaries Co. Ltd., 1939.

——. *Sinhale and the Patriots, 1815–1818*. Colombo: Colombo Apothecaries Co. Ltd., 1950.

Rahula, Walpola. *History of Buddhism: The Anuradhapura Period*. Colombo: M. D. Gunasena, 1956.

——. *What the Buddha Taught*. New York: Grove Press, 1974.

Rappaport, Roy A. "The Obvious Aspects of Ritual." *Cambridge Anthropology* 2(1)(1974):3–69.

Rhys Davids, Caroline, trans. *The Book of Kindred Sayings* (a translation of the Samyutta Nikaya), Part I. London: Oxford University Press for the Pali Text Society, 1917–30.

Rhys Davids, T. W., and William Stede. *Pali-English Dictionary*. London: Pali Text Society, 1921.

Ribeiro, João, *History of Ceilão*, translated by P. E. Pieris. Colombo: Colombo Apothecaries Co. Ltd., 1909.

Rorty, Richard. *Philosophy and the Mirror of Nature*. Princeton: Princeton University Press, 1978.

——. *Consequences of Pragmatism*. Minneapolis: University of Minnesota Press, 1982.

Ryan, Bryce. *Sinhalese Village*. Coral Gables: University of Miami Press, 1958.

Ryan, Michael T. "Assimilating New Worlds in the Sixteenth and Seventeenth Centuries." *Comparative Studies in Society and History* 23(4)(1981):519–538.

Said, Edward. *Orientalism*. New York: Vintage, 1978.

——. "Representing the Colonized: Anthropology's Interlocutors." *Critical Inquiry* 15(1988):205–225.

Samaraweera, Vijaya. "The Colebrooke-Cameron Reforms." In *University of Ceylon History of Ceylon*, vol. 3. Colombo: University of Ceylon Press, 1973.

——. "The 'Village Community' and Reform in Colonial Sri Lanka." *Ceylon Journal of Historical and Social Studies* n.s. 8(1)(1980):68–75.

Sarachchandra, E. R. *The Folk Drama of Ceylon*, 2d ed. Colombo: Department of Cultural Affairs, 1966.

Scarre, Geoffrey. *Witchcraft and Magic in 16th and 17th Century Europe*. Atlantic Highlands, N.J.: Humanities Press, 1987.

Schieffelin, Edward L. "Performance and the Cultural Construction of Reality." *American Ethnologist* 12(4)(1985):707–724.

Scott, David. "The Demonology of Nationalism: On the Anthropology of Ethnicity and Violence in Sri Lanka." *Economy and Society* 19(4)(1990):492–510.

——. "Culture and Criticism: Theory and Post-Colonial Claims on Anthropological Disciplinarity." *Critique of Anthropology* 12(4)(1992):371–394.

Shweder, Richard A., and Robert A. Levine, eds. *Culture Theory: Essays on Mind, Self, and Emotion*. Cambridge: Cambridge University Press, 1986.

Southwold, Martin. *Buddhism in Life: The Anthropological Study of Religion and the Sinhalese Practice of Buddhism*. Manchester: Manchester University Press, 1983.

——. "Buddhism and Evil." In *The Anthropology of Evil*, edited by David Parkin. Oxford: Basil Blackwell, 1985.

Spencer, Jonathan. "Writing Within: Anthropology, Nationalism, and Culture in Sri Lanka." *Current Anthropology* 31(3)(1990):283–300.

Stokes, Eric. *The English Utilitarians and India*. Oxford: Oxford University Press, 1959.

Strong, John S. "Merit: Buddhist Concepts." *The Encyclopedia of Religion*, vol. 9, edited by Mircea Eliade. New York: Macmillan, 1987.

Sutherland, Gail Hinich. *The Disguises of the Demon: The Development of the Yakṣa in Hinduism and Buddhism*. Albany: State University of New York Press, 1991.

Tambiah, Stanley J. "A Performative Approach to Ritual." *Proceedings of the British Academy* 65(1979):113–169.

——. "At the Confluence of Anthropology, History, and Indology," *Contributions to Indian Sociology* (Special Issue on "Social Anthropology from Sri Lanka") 21(1)(1987):187–216.

Taylor, Charles. "Understanding and Ethnocentricity." In *Philosophy and the Human Sciences*. Philosophical Papers, vol. 2. Cambridge: Cambridge University Press, 1985.

Tennent, Sir James Emerson. *Christianity in Ceylon*. London: John Murray, 1850.

Turner, Terence. "Transformation, Hierarchy and Transcendence: A Reformulation of Van Gennep's Model of the Structure of Rites de Passage. In *Secular Ritual*, edited by Sally F. Moore and Barbara G. Myerhoff. Amsterdam: Van Gorcum, 1977.

Turner, Victor W. *The Ritual Process: Structure and Anti-Structure*. Ithaca: Cornell University Press, 1969.

——. *From Ritual to Theatre*. New York: Performing Arts Journal Publications, 1982.

——. "Dewey, Dilthey, and Drama: An Essay in the Anthropology of Experience." In *The Anthropology of Experience*, edited by Victor W. Turner and Edward M. Bruner. Urbana: University of Illinois Press, 1986.

——. *The Anthropology of Performance*. New York: Performing Arts Journal Publications, 1987.

Turner, Victor W., and Edward M. Bruner, eds. *The Anthropology of Experience*. Urbana: University of Illinois Press, 1986.

Upham, Edward. *The History and Doctrine of Budhism, Popularly Illustrated, with notices of the Kapooism, or Demon worship, and of the Bali, or Planetary Incantations, of Ceylon*. London: R. Ackermann, 1829.

Van Gennep, Arnold. *Rites of Passage*, translated by Monika B. Vizedom and Gambrielle L. Caffee. Chicago: University of Chicago Press, 1961.

Vimalananda, Tennakoon. *Buddhism in Ceylon under the Christian Powers*. Colombo: M. D. Gunasena, 1963.

Vološinov, V. N. *Marxism and the Philosophy of Language*, translated by Ladislav Matejka and I. R. Titunik. Cambridge, Mass.: Harvard University Press, 1986.

Welbon, Guy Richard. *The Buddhist Nirvana and its Western Interpreters*. Chicago: University of Chicago Press, 1968.

White, Geoffrey M., and John Kirkpatrick, eds. *Person, Self, and Experience: Exploring Pacific Ethnopsychologies*. Berkeley: University of California Press, 1985.

White, Hayden. *Tropics of Discourse*. Baltimore: Johns Hopkins University Press, 1978.

Wickremasinghe, Martin. *Landmarks of Sinhalese Literature*. Colombo: M. D. Gunasena, 1948.

Wickremeratne, Ananda. *The Genesis of an Orientalist: Thomas William Rhys Davids and Buddhism in Sri Lanka*. Delhi: Motilal Banarsidass, 1984.

Wijayatunga, Harischandra, ed. *Prāyōgika Sinhala Ṣabdakōṣaya (Practical Sinhala Dictionary)*, 2 vols. Colombo: Ministry of Cultural Affairs, 1982.

Wijesekera, O. H. de A. "The Philosophical Import of Vedic *Yakṣa* and Pāli *Yakkha*." *University of Ceylon Review* 1(5)(1943):24–33.

Wilson, Bryan. "A Sociologist's Introduction." In *Rationality*, edited by Bryan Wilson. Oxford: Basil Blackwell, 1969.

Wirz, Paul. *Exorcism and the Art of Healing in Ceylon*. Leiden: E. J. Brill, 1954.

Yalman, Nur. "The Structure of Sinhalese Healing Rituals." *Journal of Asian Studies* 27(1964):115–150.

——. "Dual Organization in Central Ceylon." In *Anthropological Studies in Theravada Buddhism*, edited by Manning Nash. Cultural Report Series no. 13. New Haven: Yale University South East Asia Studies, 1966.

——. "The Meaning of Food Offerings in Ceylon." In *Forms of Symbolic Action*, edited by Robert F. Spencer. Seattle: University of Washington Press, 1969.

Young, D. M. *The Colonial Office in the Early Nineteenth Century*. London: Longmans, 1961.

Index

Compiled by Eileen Quam

David Scott teaches in the Department of Anthropology at the University of Chicago.